TIES THAT BIND

EDITED BY

JEAN F. O'BARR   DEBORAH POPE   MARY WYER

TIES THAT BIND

ESSAYS ON MOTHERING AND PATRIARCHY

The University of Chicago Press

Chicago and London

The essays in this volume originally appeared in various issues of SIGNS: JOURNAL OF WOMEN IN CULTURE AND SOCIETY. Acknowledgment of the original publication date can be found on the first page of each essay.

The University of Chicago Press, Chicago 60637
The University of Chicago Press, Ltd., London

94 93 92 91 90 5 4 3 2 1

Library of Congress Cataloging-in-Publication Data

Ties that bind : essays on mothering and patriarchy / edited by Jean F.
   O'Barr, Deborah Pope, and Mary Wyer.
       p.   cm.
   Includes bibliographical references and index.
   ISBN 0-226-61545-6 (alk. paper) : $34.95 (est.). — ISBN
0-226-61546-4 (alk. paper : pbk.) : $15.95 (est.)
   1. Motherhood.   2. Patriarchy.   3. Sex role.   4. Mothers and
daughters.   5. Mothers in literature.   I. O'Barr, Jean F.   II. Pope,
Deborah.   III. Wyer, Mary.
HQ759.T54   1990
306.874'2—dc20   90-11070
                                              CIP

CONTENTS

INTRODUCTION

The geography of mothering is a complex, shifting terrain. On the one hand, there are routes assiduously traveled and surveyed, well marked by popular sentiment and signposted by professional opinion; on the other, there are territories that remain obscured in turns and thickets, unarticulated in their reaches and vistas. Motherhood is arguably the most profound life transit a woman undertakes, the deepest knowledge she can experience. Whether her point of departure is biological or not, mothering is a journey that forever alters and marks a woman's private and cultural condition. It is intensely personal, overwhelmingly private. Yet no woman comes to motherhood in a vacuum. From her earliest years, she has been the recipient of a continuous stream of dictates, determinations, representations, and symbols emanating from her culture, and instructing her in the norms of femininity—a condition exemplified by heterosexual marriage and motherhood. In addition, she will learn that motherhood is constantly mediated by her own, and her culture's, story of daughterhood. Indeed, so intertwined is the experience of being mothered to one's own experience of mothering, that the meanings of either are indecipherable apart.

No landscape is so fundamental to the understanding of our human identity and development, indeed to the very fact, and nature, of our individual and collective survival. Over the past two decades, few have investigated the institution and experience of mothering with more care, urgency, and insight than feminist scholars. Now, as this wealth of scholarship solidifies and extends its base into a new decade, it is the purpose of this collection to capture this intellectual moment. In their individual range and in their overall patterns, these essays evaluate the findings, map the vantage points, and chart the future directions of the study of mothering.

Their dialogue is intense, their insights, challenges and interconnections a testament to the depths of the material to be sounded, no less than to the passion the subjects provoke. Yet one clear consensus is that the culture's guides to mothering, for all the confident input of professional and popular tour leaders, do not read like the Triptik of a trustworthy route with reliable points of interest. Indeed, they are more like medieval maps. Both ancient cartography and modern maternal mythology mark a realm heavily moralized and hortative, with arbitrary boundaries between the civilized and uncivilized, its there-be-dragons warning those who risk departure from the known, and vast expanses of Terra Incognita. Moreover, like maps of old, our models of motherhood have tended to tell more about the fears and fixities, the presumptions and prescriptions of those who produced them, than they have depicted a meaningful territory, or facilitated our understanding of those who inhabit it.

Feminist scholars work toward the complex and nuanced remapping of this literal and psychic geography, seeking to trace not the one high road but the multiplicity of routes; not the level, uniform prospect but a richly varied and variable terrain. Their position is sometimes as pioneers, sometimes surveyors. Often the essays are acts of retrievals, moments less of discovery than recovery, especially of the voice and subjectivity of those who actually mother. This reclaiming of voice is even more necessary where custom and discourse have suppressed it, as with women of color, lesbian mothers, and all whose identities lie outside the white, Western, nuclear model. Thus, while the material and rhetorical enforcement of patriarchal paradigms of motherhood is articulated in these pages, there are important, countering voices asserting their own claims of subjectivity and authority. This assertion proves to be historically deep and invariably culturally resistant; it is the insistent selfhood of those who actually mother: the travelers on this ordinary/extraordinary journey.

Empowering as this act of self-determination proves, what the collection nonetheless underscores is the fact that motherhood as an institution has been named by the authoritative voice not of women but of patriarchal culture. Through the exercise of moral, social, legal, and economic powers, male paradigms of normative gender behavior are continually reinscribed. The presumptive pinnacle of appropriate gender behavior for women is motherhood. Yet the culturally privileged model of mothering, for all the symbolism of sacredness and sway, is disempowered, marginalized, and static, the site of pietistic beliefs that explicitly ritualize a male-defined paragon of Woman in theory, who functions as a social control on women in reality. Indeed, as the essays make clear, the almost fetishized elevation of motherhood as a sentimental ideal, and the norms of femininity to which it is inextricably tied, has historically coexisted with—almost been predicated on—the disempowerment and disregard of individual mothers and children, and the whole constellation of complex physical and emotional labor that marks the privatized work of caring. The disparity between society's official, moral rhetoric on the responsibilities of mothering and its intransigence to economic and legal reforms that would enable women to perform those acts is vast. Moral suasion is invariably invoked to compel the labor and duty of women; it is not a personal or political standard for men. By defining mothering as constitutive of femaleness, individual men are relieved of the obligation to adjust their own advantageously constituted roles to suit it. By defining mothering as essentially biological, moral, and time-less, the patriarchal state is relieved of the necessity to make material, po-litical, and temporal arrangements to assist it.

Mechanisms through which the cultural construction of mothering functions to subordinate the good of women and children to the good of the father/state are primary subjects in the essays and are documented across eras. Essays explore both the means and the rationale of such processes, in the formidably influential aspects of the medical profession, the institutions of colonialism, public policy, the private structures of child care, the various forms of literature, and academic and professional discourse, as all perform the work of ideological reinforcement.

One of the most profound ironies emerging from the feminist critique of motherhood is the extent to which patriarchal ideologies themselves forge the very cultural tensions and private despairs that undermine the healthy functioning of society even as they maintain patriarchy's power. Thus, we exist at the intellectual and personal moment where our understanding of the oppressiveness of the prevailing model of motherhood can begin the demystification necessary to its cultural transformation.

Toward this future, the greatest impact of feminist scholarship on con-cepts of mothering has been to divest them of their biological or moral agency, univocally expressed, outside of time and history, and to demon-strate the importance of understanding mothering within a dynamic, inter-active context of social, political, historical, and sexual factors, multicul-tured, multiracial, and multivoiced. The prevalence of models drawn from white, middle-class experience and shaped by the cultural disposition of male theorists masks the process of gender socialization, the historical con-tingency of family forms, economic shifts in women's roles, and the diver-gent patterns of those not identified with white, Western, nuclear family contexts—in short, the majority of the world's people. Feminists have shown that the dominant models were static in other ways as well, failing to integrate shifts in the meaning of mothering across an individual woman's life course. There is an increasing focus on the actual experience of mother-ing in conjunction with new attention to such factors as age at first mother-hood, number and timing of children, the roles of fathers and other males, and, increasingly pertinent in our own time, the experience of not only mothering adult children but also one's own aging parents.

In sum, all of the essays here originate in an awareness of mothering as a dynamic, interactive process, linking personal and social, biologic and po-litical, variable within an individual context, as well as across cultures and history. In addition, all essays attest to the power of ideological mechanisms to profoundly influence, even determine, a woman's experience as both the provider and the recipient of mothering. The subject of her own reality of mothering, she is simultaneously the object of her culture's scripts. And these are not just the realities of mothers. They exist as an inextricable manifestation of an ideology that fundamentally oppresses all women. Regardless of whether she is ever a mother or not, whether she ever chooses to nurture another or not, no woman remains untouched by the coercive prescriptions for gender behavior. For patriarchy, femininity is not the core of mothering; mothering is the core of femininity. Obligations to perform emotion work, relegation to silence, erasure, loss of subjectivity, complications of separation and autonomy, are not simply mothers' issues; they are women's issues. As such, they are central issues of our culture.

* * *

Situated at the intersection of paradigm shifts and methodological debates, the opening essay, "Mothering: The View from Psychological Research," establishes many of the collection's themes—the weight of white, Western, middle-class norms of the family; the problematic influence of medical models on ideas of gender; the erasure of women's voices, reclaimed in part by new attention to their subjective experience; differing models of race and class; motherhood as an interactive as opposed to a static role; the sentimentality and ignorance that typically mark our culture's expectations of parenting.

Gerson and her co-researchers outline how the field of psychology is in the midst of major transition in its approach to mothering. One of the most significant reformulations has been away from the functional model with its emphasis less on the experience of parenting than on the child-rearing practices by which a mother, as producer, was expected to deliver her healthy, functioning product (offspring) to the marketplace (society). With research attention turning to an understanding of mothering itself as a process of identity formation and intimate experience, Gerson and her colleagues review and critique a wide range of representative studies along a developmental sequence—the decision to become a mother; pregnancy; childbirth and the postpartum period; child rearing in the early years; maternal employment; concluding with work on late parenting. At each stage, they note the importance of demographic trends to a complete understanding, stressing the meaning of the decline in such significant variables as the number of children desired and conceived, decline in the number of unwanted children, the contraction of time spent actively mothering, as well as the rise in the age of first maternity, incidence of maternal employment, increase of one-parent households, and other alternative family structures. Given the importance of these factors, it is clear that the notions of predictable female life stages and the traditional nuclear family that supported earlier psychological frameworks are seriously flawed.

The most recent work moves fruitfully beyond the white, middle-class model that limited earlier inquiries. Gerson argues for the adoption of an "ecological" perspective, one that takes full account of the embeddedness of every facet of mothering within a complex network of cultural, subcultural, and familial relations. Such contextualizing leads to dramatic reinterpretations of such phenomena as postpartum depression. A redirection of causation away from the medical, hormonal model, and toward an analysis of social, marital, and temporal factors, including fatigue and sleep disruption, have produced far more sophisticated, usable findings. Gerson's studies also indicate that the much-publicized concept of the empty nest is, in fact, generally short-lived and overrated, less marked in any case than depressions among young, at-home mothers, and more noticeable in women without professional identities. Further, it masks the reality of the enduring experience of motherhood with its intergenerational contact and relations with grown children.

Failing to see the influence throughout mothering of contextual effects—for example, maternal isolation as well as networks, cultural conflicts as well as supports, the loss or altered expression of professional or sexual identity, the differences along lines of class, race, age, subculture, etc.—produces interpretations that negatively label women to themselves and society; moreover it severely reduces the possibilities of recognizing and encouraging the conditions for confident, successful parenting.

Theoretical models flawed by cultural bias are similarly at the center of "Failures of Volition: Female Agency and Infertility in Historical Perspective," Margarete Sandelowski's critique of the history of the medical profession's treatment of infertility. From the first serious treatises on the condition in the nineteenth century, to contemporary formulations, Sandelowski argues for the determinative influence of beliefs rooted in moralized, pathologized concepts of proper femininity, rather than in scientifically defensible explanations of causation. That is, infertility was seen as incontrovertible evidence of a volitional failure to accept and exhibit desired feminine behaviors. Scientific and popular beliefs about the detrimental effects of higher education, career aspirations, and political rights on the psychology and physiology of women contributed to the moral censure directed toward emancipated women who could not conceive. Though twentieth-century practices replaced the Victorian diagnosis of moral causes, under the impact of psychoanalysis, theoreticians simply substituted unconscious, hostile factors. Where earlier views had blamed women's ambitions for education and work as being the agents of maternal/biologic dysfunction, present medical opinion often finds culprits in delayed child-bearing, career factors, and patterns of sexual activity. Implicitly or explicitly, women's autonomous functioning continues to be seen as perverting biological destiny. The failure to become a mother becomes the failure to be female; the nonmother is, by nature or will, a bad mother. Across time, terminology, and medical advances, women's inner psychology still remains constellated with cultural disturbance, her body with weakness and disease.

Ann Oakley continues the study of the influence of scientific conceptualizations in "A Case of Maternity: Paradigms of Women as Maternity Cases." In their power to shape professional practice and popular advice, these formulations have a corresponding power to frame and determine women's experience. Looking specifically at the two paradigms that govern medical approaches to pregnancy and childbirth, Oakley discusses the mechanistic—mothers as "manipulable reproductive machines"—and the biologically determined—mothers as expressive of a true and proper feminine gender adjustment. As Sandelowski does with infertility models, Oakley also shows how heavily invested these paradigms are in cultural constructions of femininity that lie clearly outside of, and are often directly opposed to, a woman's successful adjustment to motherhood, and her own biology. On the contrary, it becomes all too likely for manifestations of sickness to be attributed to feminine identity problems, while childbirth marks their resolution.

Oakley argues that the rise of obstetrics and gynecology as medical specialties facilitated the subordination of female anatomy to male interpretations, which were themselves inevitably linked to prevailing ideologies of female sexual roles. The enhancement of the doctor's jurisdiction, occasioned by the steady growth in birth technology, had the effect of constituting pregnancy as a disease requiring professional (male) intervention. At the same time, women's own sense of esteem in their role as reproducers and in their shared special knowledge with other women, has been steadily eroded.

Echoing concerns raised by Gerson, Oakley notes that one of the most disturbing effects of the medicalization of pregnancy and childbirth with its attendant paradigms of essentialist biology, on the one hand, and instrumentality on the other, is the separation of reproduction from its social, cultural, even marital context. Oakley's work demonstrates that this separation is itself a significant factor in problems particularly of postpartum adjustment, working to the detriment of mothers and children by obscuring the subjective reality of childbearing. Medical practitioners themselves are similarly blinded to factors that would enable more accurate diagnoses, when they fail to distinguish "the discrete effect of differing institutional components of women's experience of childbearing and motherhood" (75). Oakley concludes with a review of recent research suggesting that the idealization of femininity at the heart of the mother paradigm is not the cure but the cause of adjustment conflicts. She calls for the woman herself to be "restored as the central figure in the biocultural drama" (82).

The beauty of Ann Taylor Allen's essay, "Mothers of the New Generation," lies in its ability to bring the seemingly free-floating ideas and generalizations about mothering and culture to vivid local focus, played out on the tangible, historical stage. Here, in the fascinating microcosm of prewar Germany's Bund fur Muttershaft—at first glance so distant—are represented the very issues and terms that characterize contemporary debates over the moral and political nature of motherhood. Indeed, as Allen explores the evolution in the strategies and positions of these vocal, activist women at the forefront of the battle for mothers' rights, one has an awed sense of their creative, far-sighted vision. Awareness of this historical legacy offers a crucial dimension and inspiration for current debates. Here are the women Oakley would see at the center of the biocultural drama, and drama is the appropriate word for the story of Adele Schreiber and Helene Stöcker, the women who were central to the Bund in its heyday.

Allen fully contextualizes the work of the Bund against the shifting demographics of turn-of-the-century Germany, in terms of its child mortality rates, participation of women in the work force, advances in control of reproduction, and the rising interest of the state in the quantity and quality of its population, which increasingly expressed itself in an unprecedented focus on maternal behavior. The state's response to concerns over infant mortality, population decline, and the changing situation of the family was an even more intensified barrage of moral prescription and mother-blaming—for such sins as their failed "will to motherhood" and their selfish relinquishing of breast-feeding for newer artificial means.

Decrying the absence of material solutions and the hypocrisy of official pronatalist rhetoric, Stöcker and Schreiber situated their response in a fundamental indictment of bourgeois sexual hypocrisy and a political, legal, and economic system that exploited the labor of women, including their work with children. In publications and public appearances, they articulated a sweeping program of reform, working tirelessly for the passage of progressive legislation to ease the burdens of poor, working, and unwed mothers. They endorsed reproductive choice, the separation of motherhood from historically contingent forms of the family, maternal insurance, acceptance of divorce, and full legal and social status for nonmarital sexual relations, especially for children born of such unions.

The struggles of Shreiber and Stöcker with the German state and bourgeois mores over the definition of motherhood, their fight for legal and economic reforms, and the divisions in their own eventual contest for the organization's leadership, resonates with contemporary parallels. As Allen concludes, "the realization of an ideal of motherhood that enhances rather than denies women's individual development—still awaits its fulfillment" (107).

While Allen's essay evokes women's voices raised in the forum of public debates, Sandra Joshel's work is an imaginative, painstaking act of attention to the subtlest of echoes, the all-but-inaudible nuances left by unvoiced women from a remote and multilayered past. Her purpose is to decipher whatever is legible of the true relation of nurses to their nurslings in the early Roman empire. Skeptical of historians' face-value assumptions about intimate, mutually rewarding and unconflicted relationships, Joshel reopens the question of how these women actually felt in her essay "Nurturing the Master's Child: Slavery and the Roman Child-Nurse." While considerable evidence exists about the conditions of these relations, it is in the masters' discourse and control; little is known about the way the women themselves experienced them. Joshel undertakes a delicate, elusive listening for notes of selfhood and constructions of mothering, already muted by the nature of power in their own time. Even her texts are dim—nursling epitaph commemorations. Yet through scrupulous decoding, imaginative reconstruction, and a leap of canny comparison with slave nurses of the American South, Joshel composes a compelling reading of slave women's assertions of their own sensibilities and experiences, and a subversion of the master's terms. Joshel's work restores the subjectivity that power and gender relationships obscure across time and culture. For both Rome and the South Joshel disputes the sentimentalized beliefs of slave loyalty and master-identification, intensified by stereotypes of maternal bonding, arguing persuasively instead for the primary commitment of the nurses' to their own peers and communities, and their efforts to establish their own meanings for their work and conditions of relation. Distinct as Joshel's material is in some ways from other essays, one sees the similar workings of a patriarchal culture's sentimentalized notions of nurturing and maternal behavior, how these work to first mask then deny the realities of political, social, and moral exploitation. Covert as it is, one sees as well the subversion of the official ideology.

The conditions of mothering as surrogate care are further extended and problematized in Margaret Nelson's, "Mothering Others' Children: The Experiences of Family Day-Care Providers." Her study is a troubling documentation of the conflicts inherent between the dominant patriarchal paradigms and discourses of mothering, and the necessity of adjusting subjective experience to a realistic understanding of its physical and emotional labor. Throughout the personal accounts of the care providers she interviews, with few exceptions, their self-descriptions tend to be formulaic, continually intersected by culturally derived images and clichés of "proper" mothering, ones that emphasize selfless giving, intuition, deep attachment, and constant availability. As a group, the caregivers show a pervasive resistance to seeing their work in professional or skilled terms.

There are at least two ironies in this. One is that their labor is constructed in accordance with an ideal that the very need for their service invalidates. Further, the conflicts and demands inherent in the ideal itself are sharply intensified by the conditions of care. As Nelson's analysis reveals, providers constantly work to reconcile their model of mothering with the dilemmas of intensifying attachment, limited authority, the loss of children through age and relocation, financial constraints, physical limitations, and the reality of their status and needs as workers. Though family care providers typically define their worth through their emotional relationships, the nature of their ideal is intrinsically threatening to their affectional boundaries and their needs as workers. Burnout is endemic. Moreover, Nelson argues, the strategy of "detached attachment" providers typically adopt results over time in estrangement from the genuineness of their own feelings and an inability to express them openly. Though Nelson's research is primarily a descriptive, first-person record, it nonetheless raises serious issues for public and private thinking about child care, the conditions and emotional costs to providers, to children, to mothers. At the same time, it implicitly critiques a debilitating model of mothering and the society that requires it.

It would be difficult to find stronger evidence of the centrality to Western ideology of the ideology of mothering than Nancy Hunt's compelling account, "Domesticity and Colonialism in Belgian Africa: Usumbura's *Foyer Social*, 1946–1960." Hunt's subject is the intensive effort mounted by the Belgian colonial government to sever African women from their culture and reeducate them to conform to Western ideals and practices. To do so, the government erased the women's economic identities as farmers and marketers and substituted for their established, extensive kinship networks an artificial, romanticized, nuclear family role of mother/wife. Like Allen's essay on the mother's rights movement in Germany, Hunt's essay takes the workings of family and gender ideology from the abstract realm and gives it intimacy, tangibility, locality.

Established in urban centers, the *foyer sociaux* oversaw the domestic reeducation of African women, teaching them Westernized female duties of sewing, cooking, housekeeping, interior decoration, and hygiene, along with ideological instruction in raising children, and pleasing and submitting to men. Their focus was only to be on domestic matters. Instruction in any skills that could be marketed, even fancy needlework, was strictly forbidden. This would conflict with the women's "evolution" into their new and proper duties as wives and mothers. In the methods and rationale of this energetically pursued course of indoctrination, no less than in its uncertain results, one sees played out the full hypocrisy and patriarchy of Western constructions of gender and power. It is a spectacle where tragedy, triviality, and irrelevance contend.

What is so compelling about the *foyer social* is the way it reveals the essence of Western ideology. In its collision with a profoundly different system of beliefs, it stands divested of the protective cultural camouflage it so often has on its own ground. Hunt's essay exposes the complete collusion between nationalistic ideology and the social construction of gender and race; ultimately, she connects the construction of gender to the very processes of imperialism itself, as it entrenched male dominance over women and whites in their colonial rule. Yet the full history of the movement, as Hunt concludes, qualifies the enduring effects. The outright failures of many of its experiments, the ambiguous outcome of others, as well as the strength of indigenous systems, register the entrenched resistance to the Western constructs.

Like Gerson's, Marianne Hirsch's essay is also a review, focusing on that explosive dyad so central to women's experience. Though all women are not mothers, and all mothers do not have daughters, every woman is herself a daughter, and the stories of this relation remain crucial. Hirsch's point of entry into this charged realm is through an extensive critique of studies that have become classic signposts in the world of mothers and daughters. Her specific interest is in psychological paradigms and in literary analysis. The choice of texts delineates the theoretical approaches currently setting mother/daughter relations in neo-Jungian and French feminist terms. Textual analyses of literary representations of mothers and daughters freely intermix these and other theoretical formulations.

Hirsch describes the conceptual model behind each approach, analyzes its mechanisms, and weighs its strengths and weaknesses. Of the neo-Freudian, object-relations-based work of Chodorow, Dinnerstein, and Flax, Hirsch argues that despite the criticisms such theories are liable to, they claim a fundamental attention through their understanding of mothering—and indeed the private family relations it presupposes—as a social structure which affects all other social structures. Of the Jungian model, Hirsch highlights its recognition and valuing of the continuity of the mother/daughter bond, its dynamic status as an entity that is always in process.

The heart of the essay, though, is Hirsch's appraisal of the degree to which each perspective is able to reconceive or transform those aspects of the mother/daughter relation that have kept its cultural configurations so shadowed by division, baffled passion, and silence. Here, her judgment is qualified. Essentially, she remains skeptical of approaches that are embedded in male-derived theories and discourse, with an ultimately androcentric system at their root. As she begins her essay with Adrienne Rich's *Of Woman Born* as an early turning point in feminist writing about mothers and daughters, she ends with Rich's essay "Compulsory Heterosexuality." In its challenge and vision, Hirsch identifies the agenda that will guide the feminist future: a deconstruction of male paradigms, a displacement of the nuclear family as the presumptive center of inquiry, and an end to the erasure of the mothering experience of lesbians and all those who do not appear in the discourse as it has been spoken.

The last place one might look for a literary account that attempts a narrative experiment in the spirit of Rich's recent critique is in a nineteenth-century, juvenile classic; but, in effect, that is precisely the surprising project Ann Murphy undertakes in "The Borders of Ethical, Erotic, and Artistic Possibilities in *Little Women*." Though Murphy is not expressly in dialogue with Rich, her reading of Alcott's enduring tale is an almost uncanny response. That is, in her subtle and provocative analysis, *Little Women* becomes a subversion of male paradigms, a displacement of the nuclear family, and the site of female erotic currents that dispute, if not finally dislodge, heterosexist presumptions in the construction of mothering.

Murphy's interpretation centers the novel in inward female space and rage, most pointedly rage against the cultural limitations imposed on female development. It is an emotion shared by the daughters and their mother alike, and part of Marmee's driving power. Her central, dominating presence in the all-female household and in her daughters' development conditions the deconstruction of heterosexual desire and encourages in its place a primal, homoerotic desire for the powerful, loving mother.

According to Murphy, the conventionally acknowledged theme of self-sacrifice draws its force, not from incidental domestic strictures or Jo's decisions to abandon her writing but in fact from Jo's choice to abandon the possibility of erotic fulfillment entirely. Jo's crisis is fundamentally a crisis in the object of desire, a quest Murphy argues is problematized by the power and seduction of the mother. Alcott's heroine cannot reconcile her erotic attachments with the compulsory sexual alignments of patriarchal culture. Thus, her thwarted compromise is, in effect, to marry her father in the figure of Professor Bhaer, thereby becoming her mother and reinscribing the mother's ironic power in perpetuating patriarchy by producing daughters schooled in sacrifice and the self-defeating suppression of desire. The pain of Jo's sacrificial redirection is exemplified by her artistic silence and lost power, while Alcott's own struggle to fit her subversive tale of female, community, subjectivity, and desire to the conventions of the patriarchal story is evidenced in the many silences, encodings, and disruptions of the text itself. *Little Women*'s power to counter patriarchy with an alternative vision of adulthood in community and its full recognition of the centrality of the material presence in our lives continues to command a vast, predominately female readership.

The account of the daughter's difficult differentiation from the mother, and the mother's role as the problematic enforcer of patriarchal norms of female sacrifice and denial, told by Alcott, is retold and recomplicated in Anita Clair Fellman's portrayal of the unresolved relationship between Laura Ingalls Wilder, author of the *Little House* series, and her daughter, Rose Wilder Lane. Drawn from extensive research on their lives and personal papers, her study of the passionate knot of dependence and rejection that characterized their lifelong interaction not only gives a living shape to the psychological paradigm she adopts from Chodorow but utterly transforms one's perspective on the *Little House* books as well. Fellman sees in these classic juvenile texts, and in Lane's own journalistic and political writings, the individual struggle to come to terms with a difficult relationship wherein mother and daughter each literally attempted to reclaim her control of their mutual story in order to write the fulfillment of her needs. Especially in Wilder's case, the story was to have considerable political and mythic implications as the popularity of her works helped determine what countless readers came to believe constituted the American pioneer experience.

It is also, predictably, a generational story. In the *Little House* books, Wilder fictionally reconstructed her own past in order to imaginatively redirect a flawed relation with her mother, Caroline, by whom she felt unnurtured. She achieved this by selective memory, sentimentalization, invention, and suppression; but most significant was her ability to reinvent her feelings of maternal deprivation as a moral principle motivating individualism. The unyielding, unnurturant mother is directed onto the character of the frontier itself, an inscrutable mother earth whose favor is always provisional and who gives nothing without struggle. In the wild success that met the books, Wilder's personal terms of reconciliation became elevated to iconic status as American cultural mythology.

The pattern of an emotionally distant mother was continued in Wilder's own relationship with her daughter, Rose Lane, who was herself a well-known expositor of libertarian beliefs. Fellman argues that here, too, Lane's fictional and journalistic writings, including critiques of the welfare state, drew heavily from her own psychological needs to mediate the problematized terms of failed maternal nurturance and incomplete differentiation.

In Shuli Barzilai's study of another children's classic, she literally travels to the other side of the mirror from Fellman's essay on the generational longing of the daughter's for nurturance. In "Reading *Snow White:* The Mother's Story," Barzilai frames the ancient tale as one of a woman who loves too much, a mother who cannot differentiate from her own daughter, through whom she retains continuity with childhood and an all-female world. The story lies in the queen's conflict with patriarchal imperatives decreeing the daughter's separation from the world of the mother and incorporation into the world of father. Barzilai notes that the time-honored stratagems the queen employs to control Snow White—the tight-lacing, poison comb, and poison apple—are variants of the tasks of dressing, combing, and feeding that mothers perform for their children. Her intention in each instance is not so much to kill Snow White, as to infantilize her, return her to her first, helpless state. Such regression would indefinitely extend her unity with her child, while preserving her own youthfulness.

Barzilai rejects conventional interpretations of the tale as a sexual parable with men at the center of female competition. She also revises other feminist readings that portray the queen and Snow White as dissociated parts of one psyche, that is, as representing the angel/monster archetype of patriarchal imagery. Instead, Barzilai locates the fairy tale's center in the issue of separation and autonomy for mothers and daughters, here focused more on the mother's continuing emotional need to mother than on the daughter's need to be independent. The cultural destiny of mothers and daughters is to be parted from each other, rather than continue within a bond of ego extension and mutuality that might form the basis of female community and power. The interest of patriarchy, however, is clearly in the thwarting of potential female alliances and, thus, is served by the perpetuation of mother-daughter conflicts.

Like Murphy, Fellman, and Barzilai, Janet Jacobs's essay is also focused on mothers and daughters, their stories of nurturing and failed nurturing. As such, it is about fathers also, about patriarchy, and sexual and maternal ideology. Its content is the bleakest of all. "Reassessing Mother Blame in Incest" is Jacobs's analysis of the clinical findings that victims of incest characteristically direct greater anger and hostility at their mothers than at their victimizers. Her search for an explanation of this fact leads to a critique of the destructive paradoxes of emotion and withdrawal, power and powerlessness, infant myth and cultural reality that hopelessly compromise the position of the mother in the patriarchal family.

Jacobs argues that the rage of incest victims against their mothers is rooted in perceptions of the mothers' failure to save them, an all-powerful rescue that sentimentalized ideology endows the mother with the means to perform. The cultural pattern of early and exclusive nurturing by the mother confirms in the child perceptions and expectations of omnipotent maternal agency. The reality of the mother's own subordination within a compromising structure of power is a perspective almost always unavailable to the child. The child cannot see that the mother is a dependent, often even a victim herself; thus, the intense focus of blame falls on the mother.

A further factor can exacerbate and complicate this cycle. This happens when the child turns against the mother not only for her perceived collusion or helplessness but also for her failure to present a positive model of femaleness. For the incest victim, the powerless mother betrays more than her daughter; she betrays the entire possibility of empowered, autonomous female identity.

Jacobs believes that the venting of mother blame is a therapeutic stage in the recovery work of incest victims and should not itself be blamed or redirected. She argues for its importance as an externalization of anger, as well as for facilitating the separation and individuation from the mother that must precede the daughter's healing. Once the recovery of autonomy and selfhood has begun, Jacobs suggests that feminist perspectives on gender and psychosexual dynamics of the family can help the victim adjust her perceptions of the mother's role. Moreover, in underscoring her critique of cultural arrangements of mothering, Jacobs points out how those arrangements divert attention from the victimizers themselves.

* * *

The maternal is personal; the maternal is political. Mothering—whether expressed as intimate, private experience, as professional speciality, or service work; whether as academic discourse, governmental policy, or literary form—cannot be understood apart from the forces of ideology and power

whole lifetime, has enriched the study of personality. The second shift is the development of an ecological perspective, particularly in community psychology and family therapy, which requires examination of individual behavior embedded in a network of interlocking systems. For mothering, these systems are the nuclear family, or some variant of it; the extended family; the subculture; and, finally, the dominant culture, including its economic, political, and social spheres. From an ecological perspective, the study of mothering involves generalizing from, rather than ignoring, ethnic and economic differences—in essence, moving beyond the white, middle-class framework that has characterized psychological inquiry.

According to current conceptions of sex-role attitudes, women have viewed themselves and have been viewed by others as traditionally expressive, whereas instrumentality has been the hallmark of masculinity.[2] In fact, women's emotional experience of mothering has not been considered for serious study until the last decade. Instead researchers, from a traditionally masculine point of view, have looked at the instrumental value of mothering to society—the production of adjusted and promising offspring. Feminist research, however, is also concerned with how motherhood is, or is not, instrumental for women in realizing their personal goals.

Before reviewing the empirical literature on motherhood, it is important to note some general United States demographic trends that relate to mothering. Though psychologists would like to believe that demographic changes are secondary to the motivational variables they study, it is frequently the case that they study these variables after noting such changes. Similarly, we are guided in this review by the salience of demographic trends.

Demographic Trends

There is a multitude of relevant and consistently updated demographic statistics published by the U.S. government concerning women's expected and actual fertility, their labor-force participation patterns, divorced and separated women's experiences, marital and family characteristics of various strata of workers, and the situations of day-care and preschool children.[3] These statistics are differentiated by race, class, and

2. Sandra Bem, "The Measurement of Psychological Androgyny," *Journal of Consulting and Clinical Psychology* 42, no. 2 (February 1974): 115–62.

3. U.S. Department of Labor, *Manpower Report of the President* (Washington, D.C.: Government Printing Office, 1973), and *Women Workers Today* (Washington, D.C.: Women's Bureau, 1976); U.S. Bureau of the Census, "Fertility Expectations of American Women: June 1974," in *Current Population Reports*, ser. P-20, no. 277 (Washington, D.C.: Government Printing Office, February 1975).

other factors. In addition, Paul Glick's work reviews changes over the last eighty years in family life-cycle patterns for women. He also considers recent changes, the implications of which can be summarized in two words: massive change.[4]

First, there has been a marked decline in the number of children women plan to have. In 1980, 11 percent of all eighteen- to twenty-four-year-old women expected to have no children, and 17 percent of college-educated women in that age group anticipated never having a child.[5] Women expected to have larger families after World War II, but in the late 1960s the number of children women anticipated dropped precipitously. Whereas 37 percent of women aged eighteen to twenty-four expected to have four or more children in 1955, only 25 percent did in 1967 and 8 percent in 1974. Similarly, whereas 20 percent of married women expected only two children in 1967, as many as 52 percent did in 1974.

Second, there has been a sharp decrease in the number of unwanted births, from one in five in 1966 to one in twelve in 1976. Correspondingly, actual family size has also decreased. In 1965, ever-married women aged thirty to thirty-four had an average of three children while comparable women in 1975 had an average of 2.4 children.[6]

Third, because women are having fewer children, a definite change in the time frame of active mothering has occurred. A woman in the 1970s generally bore children for about seven years (between the ages of twenty-three and thirty), while a woman in the early 1900s gave birth to children for a period of ten years (between twenty-three and thirty-three). Thus, in the 1970s, the typical mother had preschool children for only a little over a decade.[7]

Fourth, women are having children later in life. In 1960, 76 percent of ever-married women aged twenty to twenty-four had children already; in 1977, only 57 percent did. Delayed childbearing is associated with higher educational attainment and labor-force participation; between July 1979 and June 1980, 63 percent of births to college-educated women

4. Paul Glick, "Updating the Life Cycle of the Family," *Journal of Marriage and the Family* 39, no. 1 (February 1977): 5–14, esp. 7.

5. U.S. Bureau of the Census, "Fertility of American Women: June 1980," in *Current Population Reports*, ser. P-20, no. 375 (Washington, D.C.: Government Printing Office, 1982).

6. Department of Labor, *Manpower Report of the President;* U.S. Bureau of the Census, "Population Profile of the United States: 1974," in *Current Population Reports*, ser. P-20, no. 279 (Washington, D.C.: Government Printing Office, March 1975); Planned Parenthood, *Planned Births: The Future of the Family and the Quality of American Life* (New York: Alan Guttmacher Institute, 1977).

7. Paul Glick and Arthur Norton, *1979 Update Population Bulletin* (Washington, D.C.: Population Reference Bureau, 1979), pp. 39–41.

aged eighteen to twenty-nine were first births, compared with only 49 percent for high-school graduates in the same age group.[8]

Fifth, there has been a rise in the incidence of one-parent families, particularly among black women. From 1970 to 1980, the number of one-parent households (with children under eighteen) doubled; those maintained by men increased by 95 percent, by women, 97 percent.[9] While there was a 10 percent rise in the number of white female family heads between 1960 and 1975, there was a corresponding 35 percent increase in the number of black female family heads.[10]

Female employment outside the home has also been on the rise, particularly among mothers with preschool children (57 percent increase between 1960 and 1975). The labor-force participation rate for ever-married mothers with children under six years of age was 18.2 percent in 1955, 25.3 percent in 1965, 38.9 percent in 1975, and 49.9 percent in 1982.[11]

Finally, the last fifteen years have seen an increase in alternative structures for mothering, including households headed by women who never married; cohabitation among unmarried heterosexual couples and among lesbian and gay couples; communal living arrangements; and forms of the postdivorce nuclear family, such as stepfamilies and joint custody arrangements. The experience of mothering in these alternative structures cannot be dealt with here adequately; yet, as Eleanor Macklin indicates, they have been much affected by the feminist movement, and they serve as another reminder of the increased pluralism of the American family today.[12] Another trend not covered in this review is the increase in the absolute numbers, if not in rate per population, of adolescent mothers. Though the rate of nonmarital births among black teenagers is at least five times the rate among white teenagers, Catherine Chilman believes that socioeconomic status rather than race accounts for this difference.[13] Susan Phipps-Yonas has prepared a general review of the psychological aspects of adolescent motherhood.[14]

8. Bureau of the Census, "Population Profile of the United States: 1974"; U.S. National Center for Health Statistics, "Final Natality Statistics: 1978," in *Monthly Vital Statistics Report*, vol. 29, no. 1 (Washington, D.C.: Government Printing Office, 1980).

9. U.S. Bureau of the Census, "Household and Family Characteristics: March, 1981," in *Current Population Reports*, ser. P-20, no. 371 (Washington, D.C.: Government Printing Office, October 1982).

10. Bureau of the Census, "Population Profile of the United States: 1974."

11. Department of Labor, *Women Workers Today;* Bureau of Labor Statistics, *Technical Information* (Washington, D.C.: Government Printing Office, August 1982), pp. 82–276.

12. Eleanor Macklin, "Nontraditional Family Forms: A Decade of Research," *Journal of Marriage and the Family* 42, no. 4 (November 1980): 905–22.

13. Catherine Chilman, "Social and Psychological Research concerning Adolescent Childbearing: 1970–1980," *Journal of Marriage and the Family* 43, no. 4 (November 1981): 793–806.

14. Susan Phipps-Yonas, "Teenage Pregnancy and Motherhood: A Review of the Literature," *American Journal of Orthopsychiatry* 50, no. 3 (July 1980): 403–31.

These trends are the quantifiable manifestation of a complex inter-action of political, historical, economic, and cultural forces. They indicate issues of importance for research and policy formation in the future.

The Family Developmental Framework

In considering the role of motherhood in the lives of women, it is useful to view motherhood as a series of developmental stages. Several ways of conceptualizing the stages exist, as do various reviews of these frameworks and their assumptions.[15] The stages identified by Rhona Rapoport, Robert Rapoport, and Ziona Streilitz are exemplary. According to Rapoport et al., different parental tasks are associated with the fol-lowing stages: (1) decision and preparation for parenting; (2) transition to parenting; (3) early parenting with preschoolers; (4) middle parenting in the school years; (5) parenting with adolescents; and (6) late parenting with adult children and eventual grandparenting.[16]

A weakness of these normative frameworks is their failure to attend to cultural and socioeconomic factors that impinge on the meanings of the stages. Thus, J. Allen Williams and Robert Stockton point to the uniqueness of the black family's life cycle just as James Aldous uses an alternative framework for the divorced woman.[17] Similarly, cohort fac-tors have been ignored. For example, among the cohort of women born in the early 1950s who are delaying motherhood until well into their thirties because of career commitment, Rapoport's stage of late parenting will occur at a different point in the individual life cycle than for women born in the 1930s. In fact Arthur Norton found that cohort membership had a greater effect on the timing of life-course events for women born between 1920 and 1950 than marital history (including divorce patterns), race, and educational level attained.[18]

The cycle of mothering is examined here in relation to the demo-graphic trends cited earlier. Given the decline in number of children desired and conceived, the first stage of motherhood we discuss is de-cision and preparation for parenthood, followed by the transition to mothering. Given the increase in maternal employment, particularly in the early years of mothering, we examine this stage next. The contraction

15. James Aldous, *Family Careers: Developmental Changes in Families* (New York: John Wiley & Sons, 1978).

16. Rhona Rapoport, Robert Rapoport, and Ziona Streilitz, *Fathers, Mothers, and Society* (New York: Basic Books, 1977).

17. J. Allen Williams, Jr., and Robert Stockton, "Black Family Structure and Functions: An Empirical Examination of Some Suggestions Made by Billingsley," *Journal of Marriage and the Family* 35, no. 1 (February 1973): 39–51; Aldous.

18. Arthur Norton, "The Influence of Divorce on Traditional Life-Cycle Measure," *Journal of Marriage and the Family* 42, no. 1 (February 1980): 63–69.

of time spent in active mothering we address in our discussion of late parenting with adult children.

Decision and Preparation for Parenthood

Decision Making

Research in the area of decision making with regard to parenthood has mushroomed in the last decade. Originally an interdisciplinary response by psychologists, economists, and sociologists to concerns about overpopulation and effects of abortion, it also represents an attempt to grapple with changing family patterns and changing role conceptions among young adults.

With population pressures abating in the United States, the relevant task at present is to identify the differences in motivation between women who wish and do not wish to become mothers. From a social psychological perspective, Lois Hoffman and Martin Hoffman stress that any role for women other than motherhood has represented deviance.[19] But Bernice Lott has voiced concern that the most energetic and capable young women today are opting out of motherhood, diminishing the quality of mothering for tomorrow's generation.[20] A few analytically oriented theories have given attention to the question of why women want to have children.[21] This same question can be explored from an intrapsychic angle; from a more normative, attitudinal viewpoint; or from the dyadic perspective of the couple making a decision. What is most challenging is the integration in research design of these various perspectives—a process that reveals how economic factors, social change, couple dynamics, and individual motivation interact with each other.[22]

Recent work emphasizes sex-role attitudes and socialization in relation to the wish for a child. Research indicates that profeminist sym-

19. Lois Hoffman and Martin Hoffman, "The Value of Children to Parents," in *Psychological Perspectives of Population*, ed. James Fawcett (New York: Basic Books, 1973).

20. Bernice Lott, "Who Wants the Children? Some Relationships among Attitudes toward Children, Parents and the Liberation of Women," *American Psychologist* 28, no. 7 (July 1973): 573–82.

21. Sigmund Freud, *New Introductory Lectures on Psychoanalysis* (New York: W. W. Norton & Co., 1965), pp. 112–36; Erik Erikson, "Identity and the Life Cycle," in *Psychological Issues*, monograph 1, ed. George Klein (New York: International Universities Press, 1959).

22. Mark Flapan and Helene Schoenfeld, "Procedures for Exploring Women's Childbearing Motivations, Alleviating Childbearing Conflicts, and Enhancing Maternal Role Development," *American Journal of Orthopsychiatry* 42, no. 2 (April 1972): 389–97; Elizabeth Kirchner and W. Burleigh Seaver, *Developing Measures of Parenthood Motivation*, Final Report, NIH Grant HD-06258-03, NICH and HD (University Park: Pennsylvania State University, Institute for Research on Human Resources, 1977); Linda Beckman, "The Process of Couples' Fertility Decision-Making" (paper delivered at the annual meeting of the American Psychological Association, Toronto, August 1980).

pathies are negatively related to the wish for children, while traditional femininity is positively correlated with such motivation.[23] Career involvement presents a confusing picture, although Lois Hoffman regards career as an attractive alternative to motherhood, particularly for professional women. Linda Beckman finds that career and motherhood are perceived as competing goals.[24]

Another recent focus in the area of motivation for parenting is the assessment of perceived costs and benefits of having children. Researchers have developed several value schema, some theoretically derived and others purely empirical,[25] which they have investigated both nationally and crossnationally.[26] In Hoffman and Hoffman's model, the perceived value of children is pitted against corresponding barriers (such as financial stress) and alternative sources of satisfaction (such as leisure time activities). Elizabeth Kirchner and W. Burleigh Seaver and, more recently, Mary-Joan Gerson have indicated that the perceived value of children is related, respectively, to demographic factors and to crucial personality characteristics such as memory of one's own mother's nurturance.[27] Similarly, the study of childless couples has increased, including the analysis of the unique patterns of childlessness among nonwhite couples.[28]

The decision whether or not to have a child is the first stage in the experience of motherhood. Research in this area has suffered, in particular, because a number of different assessment instruments have been used to study the same variable (such as the perceived value of children) and different levels of motivation identified in the various studies have not been integrated.[29]

23. Inge Broverman et al., *Attitudinal Factors Affecting Family Size*, Final Report, NIH Grant 71-2038 (Worcester, Mass.: Worcester State Hospital, 1975); Mary-Joan Gerson, "Feminism and the Wish for a Child" (paper delivered at the annual meeting of the Eastern Psychological Association, New York City, April 1981).

24. Lois Hoffman, "Effects of Maternal Employment on the Child: A Review of the Research," *Developmental Psychology* 10, no. 2 (March 1974): 204–28; Linda Beckman, *Motivations, Roles and Family Planning of Women*, Final Report, NIH Grant HD-07323 (Los Angeles: University of California, Los Angeles, 1976).

25. Hoffman and Hoffman; Kirchner and Seaver.

26. Lois Hoffman and Jean Manis, "The Value of Children in the United States: A New Approach to the Study of Fertility," *Journal of Marriage and the Family* 41, no. 3 (August 1979): 583–96; James Fawcett, *The Values of Children in Asia and the United States: Comparative Perspectives* (Honolulu: East-West Population Institute, 1974).

27. Hoffman and Hoffman; Kirchner and Seaver; Mary-Joan Gerson, "The Lure of Motherhood," *Psychology of Women Quarterly* 5, no. 2 (Winter 1980): 207–18.

28. Susan Bram, "To Have or Have Not: A Social-Psychological Study of Voluntarily Childless Couples, Parents and To-Be Parents" (Ph.D. diss., University of Michigan, 1974); Sharon Houseknecht, "Timing of the Decision to Remain Voluntarily Childless: Evidence for Continuous Socialization," *Psychology of Women Quarterly* 4, no. 1 (Fall 1979): 81–96; Jean Veevers, "Differential Childlessness by Color: A Further Examination," *Social Biology* 18 (September 1971): 285–91.

29. Mary-Joan Gerson, "A Scale of Motivation for Parenthood: The Index of Parenthood Motivation," *Journal of Psychology* 113 (March 1983): 211–20, esp. 213.

There is a particular need for longitudinal studies in which parental expectations regarding unborn children are related to later conflicts and patterns in child rearing. A related question—that of nonparents' expectations about parent roles—has been examined by Judith Alpert and Mary Sue Richardson using several variations of the Thematic Apperception Test. Results indicate that nonparents perceive the parenting role most positively when it is combined with work roles.[30]

Although a generally positive perception of the parent role is supported by societal expectations and media portrayal,[31] professional literature suggests that parenthood may, for example, negatively affect marital satisfaction, lead to role conflict, and place stress on parents.[32] In general, this parenting literature is not available to preparents. What is available, for the most part, is popular literature that focuses more on how to parent rather than the actual experience of parenting.[33] Although this literature may help to prevent a romanticized perception of parenthood, it is read most frequently by parents after conception. Individuals often have little idea what the role entails when they make a decision to parent.

Two decades ago when Lois Hoffman and Frederick Wyatt analyzed parents' varied and changing reasons for wanting children they found that motherhood facilitated creativity and a reduction in alienation and loneliness.[34] Similarly, contemporary study of both parental motivations and expectations about parenting helps to decipher the meaning of motherhood in our culture and to locate motherhood in the identity structures of today's women.

30. Judith Alpert and Mary Sue Richardson, "Conflict, Outcome, and Perception of Women's Roles," *Educational Gerontology: An International Quarterly* 3, no. 1 (Winter 1978): 79–87. See also Judith Alpert, Mary Sue Richardson, and Fay Shutzer, "Perceptions of Major Roles by College Students," *Psychology of Women Quarterly* 4, no. 4 (Summer 1980): 581–86; Mary Sue Richardson and Judith Alpert, "Role Perceptions of Educated Adult Women: An Exploratory Study," *Educational Gerontology: An International Quarterly* 1, no. 2 (April–June 1976): 171–85, and "Role Perceptions: Variations by Sex and Role," *Sex Roles* 6, no. 6 (December 1980): 783–93.

31. Nancy Russo, "The Motherhood Mandate," *Journal of Social Issues* 32, no. 3 (Summer 1976): 143–54.

32. Boyd Rollins and Richard Galligan, "The Developing Child and Marital Satisfaction of Parents," in *Child Influences on Marital and Family Interaction: A Life-Span Perspective,* ed. Richard Lerner and Graham Spanier (New York: Academic Press, 1978); Carole Holahan and Lucia Gilbert, "Interrole Conflict for Working Women: Careers vs. Jobs," *Journal of Applied Psychology* 64, no. 1 (February 1979): 86–90.

33. Rapoport, Rapoport, and Streilitz (n. 16 above).

34. Lois Hoffman and Frederick Wyatt, "Social Change and Motivations for Having Larger Families: Some Theoretical Considerations," *Merrill-Palmer Quarterly* 6, no. 4 (July 1960): 235–44.

Transition to Parenting

Pregnancy.—Because it is the most biologically linked of all the stages of motherhood, research on pregnancy has been most influenced by the medical model of disease or psychopathological state. Certain psychoanalytic researchers have been particularly prone to such formulations, viewing the process of pregnancy as an ongoing "regression" in the mother-to-be's psychological organization.[35] Considerable biologically based research has focused on the hormonal characteristics of pregnancy. The psychoanalytic and the biological research have been conducted independently for the most part, explaining the same symptomatology one way or the other depending on the orientation of the investigator. An exception is the work of Therese Benedek, who holds that the hormonal changes of pregnancy activate memory traces of the woman's own early experience of being nurtured.[36]

Researchers have viewed the pregnant woman's increased dependency as symptomatic of her regressed state, rather than acknowledging the very real needs that arise due to decreased mobility, increased fatigue, and anxiety about delivery and the health of her child. Naomi Wenner, however, has demonstrated that, even among women considered "immature," when realistic needs were met regression did not occur.[37] Moreover, family systems theory has criticized concentration on one partner's reaction in what is actually an event occurring within a dyadic relationship, which in turn is embedded in a multigenerational and extended family system.[38]

Most of the recent research on pregnancy falls somewhere between the medical model and the family systems or ecological perspective. Focuses include the extent to which pregnancy and motherhood are experienced as stressful; the development of maternal feeling and concurrent changes in feeling toward significant others; the extent to which characteristics measured early in pregnancy are predictive of attitudes and adjustment in later stages of pregnancy and after childbirth; and the variables associated with adaptation to pregnancy.[39] This research, for the most part, is based on small samples and suffers from a lack of

35. Grete Bibring, "A Study of the Psychological Processes in Pregnancy and of the Earliest Mother-Child Relation," in *The Psychoanalytic Study of the Child*, ed. Ruth Eissler and Anna Freud (New York: International Universities Press, 1961), 16:9–72.

36. Therese Benedek, "The Origin of the Reproductive Drive," *International Journal of Psychoanalysis* 41, no. 1 (Winter 1960): 1–15.

37. Naomi Wenner, "Dependency Patterns in Pregnancy," in *Sexuality of Women: Scientific Proceedings of the Tenth Annual Meeting of the American Academy of Psychoanalysis*, ed. James Masserman (New York: Grune & Stratton, 1966), pp. 94–104.

38. Murray Bowen, *Family Therapy in Clinical Practice* (New York: Jason Aronson, 1978).

39. Myra Leifer, "Psychological Changes Accompanying Pregnancy and Motherhood," *Genetic Psychology Monographs* 95, no. 1 (February 1977): 55–96; Judith Ballou, *The Psychology of Pregnancy* (Lexington, Mass.: Lexington Books, 1978); Francis Grossman, Lois

consistency in instrumentation. Nevertheless, there seem to be some cumulative and consistent results indicating that (1) pregnancy is a period of developmental crisis or at least transition; (2) maternal feeling develops over time and feelings toward significant others (mother, husband, self) change over the course of pregnancy;[40] (3) personality variables measured early in pregnancy are related to emotional adjustment to pregnancy;[41] (4) symptomatology is associated with negative attitudes toward pregnancy; and (5) a variety of factors, such as emotional stability, a close relationship with one's mother, and compatibility with one's husband, are associated with a positive attitude toward pregnancy.

The real challenge in the investigation of pregnancy by psychologists is to study the complicated interaction of biological and psychological factors—what Alice Rossi refers to as the biosocial approach[42]—and perhaps, most important, to identify the unique variances accounted for by psychological phenomena. For example, Shirley Feldman and Sharon Nash, in their examination of responsiveness to babies in a waiting-room situation, found that mothers (and not fathers) responded to strangers' babies much more than did pregnant women or their mates, which the authors offer as evidence for experiential rather than hormonal influences on maternal behavior.[43] A cross-cultural perspective is particularly helpful in separating biological and psychological factors.[44]

Childbirth and the postpartum period.—Research on childbirth focuses on the relationship between aspects of delivery and such variables as maternal attitudes, maternal bonding, and childbirth preparation and practices.[45] Much emphasis has been placed on depression during the postpartum period and as such the research is heavily influenced by the medical paradigm. Although depression after childbirth can be related to a variety of psychosocial factors, traditionally it has been attributed

Eichler, and Susan Winickoff, *Pregnancy, Birth and Parenthood* (San Francisco: Jossey-Bass, Inc., 1980); Bibring.

40. S. Albeit, "A Study of Women during Their First Pregnancy" (Ph.D. diss., Yale University, 1975).

41. Flapan and Schoenfeld (n. 22 above).

42. Alice Rossi, "A Biosocial Perspective on Parenting," *Daedalus* 106, no. 2 (Spring 1977): 1–31.

43. Shirley Feldman and Sharon Nash, "The Effect of Family Formation on Sex-Stereotypic Behavior: A Study of Responsiveness to Babies," in *The First Child and Family Formation*, ed. Warren Miller and Lucielle Newman (Chapel Hill: University of North Carolina, Carolina Population Center, 1978), pp. 51–63.

44. Eugene Brody, "The Meaning of the First Pregnancy for Working-Class Jamaican Women," in Miller and Newman, eds., pp. 92–107.

45. Susan Doering and Doris Entwisle, "Preparation during Pregnancy and Ability to Cope with Labor and Delivery," *American Journal of Orthopsychiatry* 45, no. 3 (October 1975): 825–37; Marshall Klaus and John Kennell, *Maternal-Infant Bonding* (St. Louis: C. V. Mosby Co., 1982).

to changes in levels of gonadal hormones and substances that may be associated with the way the central nervous system functions. These biochemical changes may increase susceptibility to affective disorders, as Rhoda Unger's review indicates.[46]

However, in a swing away from biologically oriented research, recent investigations have stressed social changes in the postpartum period. The arrival of the first child can be seen as a crisis for parents, although some investigators view it as a period of transition rather than crisis.[47] Research suggests that it is a more difficult transition for women than for men, particularly for women who had careers outside the home previous to mothering.[48] In an important attempt to investigate racial differences in adjustment to the birth of the first child, Daniel Hobbs and Jane Wimbash have examined the transition to parenthood among black versus white couples.[49]

Emphasizing the psychosocial context in which childbirth occurs has led to a focus on the timing of the first birth. Harriet Presser's work indicates that the timing of young white women's first birth is correlated with their mother's age at first birth, whereas timing for young black women is correlated with their mothers' recent occupations.[50] Phillip Cartright finds that for both black and white women first-birth timing has little effect on the probability of future female family headship, poverty status, or on future fertility rates.[51]

Of related interest is the start of research on the phenomenon of delayed parenthood. In 1978, almost one-third of first births were to women twenty-five or older; in the last decade, first births have increased substantially for women between the ages of thirty and thirty-nine.[52] Susan Bram, in her study of the perceived value of children to young couples in their twenties and thirties, finds similarities between parents and those delaying parenthood; the value perceptions of both groups differ from those of the intentionally childless.[53] In her discussion of delayed motherhood, Jane Wilkie suggests that women who delay motherhood provide a healthier emotional environment for their children

46. Rhoda Unger, *Female and Male* (New York: Harper & Row, 1979).

47. E. LeMasters, "Parenthood as Crisis," *Marriage and Family Living* 19, no. 3 (October 1957): 352–55; Daniel Hobbs, Jr., "Transition to Parenthood: A Decade Replication," *Journal of Marriage and the Family* 38, no. 4 (November 1976): 723–31.

48. Douglass Hall and Francine Gardan, "Career Choices of Married Women: Effects of Conflict, Role Behavior and Satisfaction," *Journal of Applied Psychology* 58, no. 1 (February 1973): 42–48.

49. Daniel Hobbs, Jr., and Jane Wimbash, "Transition to Parenthood by Black Couples," *Journal of Marriage and the Family* 39, no. 4 (November 1977): 677–89.

50. Harriet Presser, "Social Factors Affecting Timing of the First Child," in Miller and Newman, eds., pp. 159–79.

51. Phillip Cartright, "Timing of the First Birth: Does It Matter?" *Journal of Marriage and the Family* 35, no. 4 (November 1973): 585–97.

52. National Center for Health Statistics (n. 8 above).

53. Bram (n. 28 above).

because of their tendency to discourage dependence, encourage verbalization, and invite spouse involvement in child-rearing decisions. At the same time she indicates that mothers who delay may be under greater stress because their own parents are not available to assist with child-rearing functions.[54] Rossi's exploration of the relationship between middle-aged women and their children indicates that older mothers describe their adolescent children as less sociable and more critical than do younger mothers.[55] The most comprehensive general account dealing with the timing of parenthood is Pamela Daniels and Kathy Weingarten's *Sooner or Later.*[56] In an interview-based study, they compare "early timing" and "late timing" mothers, explore special issues such as first births in midlife, and discuss the ways in which different phases of the individual life cycle define the meaning of motherhood in the postpartum period.

As in the study of pregnancy, the optimal model for research on childbirth and the postpartum period is one that considers the interaction of biological, psychological, and social phenomena. Susan Heitler's investigation of postpartum depression provides such a model.[57] Heitler examined several variables and their relation to depression after childbirth: a pregnant woman's unconscious anger toward her mother, later fatigue from delivery, social isolation, and stress. She found each variable except social isolation significantly and uniquely related to postpartum depression.[58] Overall, the transition to parenthood must be viewed as a process involving several interlocking systems. As Carolyn Cowan and Phillip Cowan state in their description of family formation among young couples, "Parental attitudes, then, provide links between individual identity, family practices, and societal norms."[59]

Child Rearing in the Early Years and Maternal Employment

The traditional focus on maternal employment in research on early child rearing is even more to the point today given recent demographic

54. Jane Wilkie, "The Trend toward Delayed Parenthood," *Journal of Marriage and the Family* 43, no. 3 (August 1981): 583–93.

55. Alice Rossi, "Life-Span Theories and Women's Lives," *Signs: Journal of Women in Culture and Society* 6, no. 1 (Autumn 1980): 4–32.

56. Pamela Daniels and Kathy Weingarten, *Sooner or Later: The Timing of Parenthood in Adult Lives* (New York: W. W. Norton & Co., 1980).

57. Susan Heitler, "Postpartum Depression: A Multidimensional Study" (Ph.D. diss., New York University, 1975).

58. See also Judith Alpert, Mary Sue Richardson, and Linda Fodaski, "Onset of Parenting and Stressful Events" (New York University, 1983, photocopied); Mary Sue Richardson and Litlean Kagan, "Social Support and the Transition to Parenthood" (paper delivered at the annual meeting of the American Psychological Association, New York, September 1979).

59. Carolyn Cowan and Phillip Cowan, "Conflicts for Partners Becoming Parents: Implications for the Couple Relationship" (paper delivered at the annual meeting of the American Psychological Association, Los Angeles, 1981).

trends. Approximately 43 percent of all children ages three to thirteen have a mother who works outside the home. In addition, the number of mothers entering the labor force increases every year, and this increase is most striking for mothers with preschool children.

Because of the traditional instrumental view of the function of motherhood, there is a substantial body of research concerning the effect of maternal employment on children. For example, Beckman notes that employment is perceived as limiting the amount of time children can spend with their mothers, but her study does not indicate what this lost time means to the mothers themselves.[60] In this review, the existing literature on effects of maternal employment is presented in order to describe the data base from which parents can make responsible and informed decisions about the timing and nature of their employment.[61]

The major variables studied in research on children's responses to maternal employment include their general mental health, social adjustment, cognitive ability, and achievement motivation. Lois Hoffman summarizes the research on school-age children using five hypotheses: (1) that working mothers provide different role models than nonworking mothers; (2) that employment affects the mother's emotional state; (3) that different situational demands and emotional states of the working mother affect child rearing; (4) that working mothers give less supervision than nonworking mothers; and (5) that the working mother's absence leads to emotional and cognitive deprivation in the child.[62] She finds support for all but the fifth hypothesis. Thus the bulk of available research should be reassuring to working mothers, at least those whose children are of school age.

There are fewer data available about the effects of maternal employment on children younger than school age. Certainly more data on the effects of increased child care by fathers are needed since fathers are assuming more child-care responsibilities as maternal employment increases.[63] As early as 1970, almost 20 percent of children under six were cared for by their fathers during the working hours of their mothers.[64] Very recent research has produced some puzzling results that warrant further investigation. Julia Ericksen, William Yancey, and Eugene Ericksen report that black husbands provide more child care than do white husbands and that both black and white husbands spend more

60. Beckman, *Motivations, Roles and Family Planning of Women* (n. 24 above).

61. For reviews of the literature on the effects of maternal employment, see Bonnie Seegmiller, "Maternal Employment: A Bibliography," *Catalogue of Selected Documents in Psychology* 5, ms. no. 927 (Spring 1975): 233; Claire Etaugh, "Effects of Maternal Employment on Children," *Merrill-Palmer Quarterly* 20, no. 2 (Spring 1974): 71–98; Hoffman (n. 24 above).

62. Lois Hoffman, "The Employment of Women, Education and Fertility," *Merrill-Palmer Quarterly* 20, no. 2 (April 1974): 99–119.

63. James Levine, *New Options for Fathers (and Mothers)* (New York: J. B. Lippincott Co., 1974).

64. Hoffman, "The Employment of Women, Education and Fertility."

time in child care when wives work part-time rather than full-time.[65] In general, surveys indicate that, when mothers work, the preference and practice is for child-care arrangements to be made within the family context. In several national surveys of child-care arrangements Suzanne Woolsey finds that over half of all children of working women are cared for by family members, while 24 percent are cared for by a sitter or friend. Another group of investigators report that 13 percent of children under three years of age spend thirty hours per week or more in non-parental care, although over 35 percent of mothers with children under three are in the labor force. This pattern of familial care is even more characteristic of black and Hispanic families.[66]

Although day-care centers are the least often reported child-care arrangement in the United States,[67] and the least preferred child-care arrangement,[68] most of what we know about the effects of nonparental care in the earliest years of childhood is restricted to formal day-care centers. In general the research on the development of bonding between mother and child indicates no difference between day-care children and children cared for at home by mother or sitter.[69]

There are several important variables to be considered by future researchers investigating the effect of maternal employment on both mothers and children, including class, sex, age of child, mother's attitude toward employment, and nature of work. Distinctions need to be made, for example, between maternal separation and maternal deprivation, between supervised and nonsupervised children, and between consistent and inconsistent child care. Researchers should try to differentiate parenting functions that must be performed by parents from those that can be assumed by others. For better or worse, many parenting functions already are assumed by the mass media, by siblings, by peers, and by "experts."[70]

More specifically, a major focus of research should be variations in self-perception and self-esteem among women who work. The high rate of depression among full-time homemakers suggests that perceived powerlessness and isolation might be offset by some, but not necessarily all,

65. Julia Ericksen, William Yancey, and Eugene Ericksen, "The Division of Family Roles," *Journal of Marriage and the Family* 41, no. 2 (May 1979): 301–13.
66. Suzanne Woolsey, "Pied Piper Politics and the Child Care Debate," *Daedalus* 106, no. 2 (Spring 1977): 127–46.
67. The number of day-care children reported is 326,000 (Bureau of the Census, "Population Profile of the United States: 1974" [n. 6 above]).
68. Woolsey.
69. Urie Bronfenbrenner, *The Ecology of Human Development* (Cambridge, Mass.: Harvard University Press, 1979).
70. Robert Liebert, John Neale, and Emily Davidson, *The Early Window: Effects of Television on Children and Youth* (New York: Pergamon Press, 1973); K. Allison Clarke-Stewart, "Popular Primers for Parents," *American Psychologist* 33, no. 4 (April 1978): 359–69.

work situations. Indeed, more research is needed on demands of different jobs, the various role relationships they entail, and their effects on styles of maternal interaction. Class differences in parenting—for example, the way that white-collar parents stress internal standards while blue-collar parents stress correct behavior—may partially derive from parents' work experiences.[71] Finally, particular attention must be paid to the lives of single parents who attempt to combine work and motherhood.[72]

Most important, we must move, in Urie Bronfenbrenner's terms, from the microsystemic to the exosystemic, from the dyad to the external environment if we wish to understand the full effects of maternal employment.[73] From a dyadic perspective, for example, we must remember that a child influences the type of parenting received.[74] Meanwhile, from an ecosystemic perspective we must recognize that the choice of employment for poor mothers—indeed, the mothers of over one-fourth of the nation's children (and one-half its black children) are impoverished[75]—is quite different from the choice that faces middle-class professional women who have access to round-the-clock child care.

Late Parenting with Adult Children

Research concerned with parenting in its later stages has arbitrarily identified the time when children leave the home as the end of active parenting. This conceptualization is problematic in that late parenting is viewed as an ending rather than a continuing process. Furthermore, it ignores important socioeconomic and racial differences in family structure as well as important cohort factors.

In fact, the emphasis on the end of active parenting derives from the prevailing view that motherhood is a job (albeit unpaid) which ends when the product (offspring) is delivered to the marketplace (society). Research on this stage has been particularly and singularly focused on

71. Victor Gecas and Ivan Nye, "Sexual Class Differences in Parent-Child Interaction: A Test of Kohn's Hypothesis," *Journal of Marriage and the Family* 36, no. 4 (November 1974): 742–49.

72. Sara McLanahan, Nancy Wedemeyer, and Tina Adelbert, "Network Structure, Social Support, and Psychological Well-Being in the Single Parent Family," *Journal of Marriage and the Family* 43, no. 3 (August 1981): 601–12.

73. Bronfenbrenner.

74. Lawrence Harper, "The Scope of Offspring Effects: From Caregiver to Culture," *Psychological Bulletin* 82, no. 5 (September 1975): 784–801; Richard Lerner and Graham Spanier, eds., *Child Influences and Marital and Family Interaction: A Life-Span Perspective* (New York: Academic Press, 1978).

75. Catherine Chilman, "Families in Poverty in the Early 1970's: Rates, Associated Factors, Implications," *Journal of Marriage and the Family* 37, no. 2 (February 1975): 49–63.

the mother, with the exception of one psychoanalytic study.[76] Termination of active mothering has been viewed both negatively and positively. Research on depression in middle-aged women for the most part supports Jesse Bernard's assertion that marriage and children are health hazards for women.[77] Such research validates the notion that when adult children leave home the mother feels bereft in an "empty nest." Marjorie Lowenthal, Majda Thurnher, and David Chiraboga, for example, contend that high school seniors, newlyweds, and preretirement women have better self-concepts, higher life satisfaction levels, and more positive attitudes toward their spouses than do women whose children have just left home.[78]

Newer research, however, views this stage as liberating for mothers. It appears that a change in cultural values and belief systems can result in a change in empirical findings.[79] Recent investigations indicate that the empty nest has a reputation it does not deserve—that the incidence of depression is lower and that of well-being is higher in women whose children have left home than in women living with young children.[80] Elizabeth Harkins notes a depressive reaction to children leaving the home that is a short-lived, transitional phenomenon.[81] One study suggests that women who have developed professional commitments are less likely to experience depression with changes in the mothering role.[82]

Moreover, there are important subcultural differences in late parenting with adult children. A major emphasis of Saundra Murray and Daphne Harrison's article on the mid-life options of black women is the reality of the "full nest"—the necessity black women face, either alone or with husbands, of providing shelter and economic support for their adult children.[83] Harkins found that the failure of children to leave when expected was the one recognizable cause of depression among middle-

76. Nicholas Avery, "Phallic Narcissistic Vulnerability and the Empty Nest Syndrome," *Journal of the American Academy of Psychoanalysis* 9, no. 4 (Fall 1981): 525–37.

77. Jesse Bernard, *The Future of the Family* (New York: World Publishing Co., 1972).

78. Marjorie Lowenthal, Majda Thurnher, David Chiraboga, and associates, *Four Stages of Life: A Comparative Study of Women and Men Facing Transitions* (Los Angeles: Jossey-Bass, Inc., 1975).

79. On this point, see Gregory Bateson, *Steps to an Ecology of Mind* (New York: Ballantine Books, 1972).

80. Lenore Radloff, "Sex Differences in Depression: The Effects of Occupation and Marital Status," *Sex Roles* 1, no. 5 (October 1975): 249–65.

81. Elizabeth Harkins, "Self-Report of Psychological and Physical Well-Being," *Journal of Marriage and the Family* 40, no. 3 (August 1978): 549–56.

82. Judith Birnbaum, "Life Patterns and Self-Esteem in Gifted Family Oriented and Career Committed Women," in *Women and Achievement: Social and Motivational Analyses*, ed. M. Mednick, Sandra Tangri, and Lois Hoffman (New York: Hemisphere Publishing Corp., 1975), pp. 396–419.

83. Saundra Murray and Daphne Harrison, "Black Women and the Future," *Psychology of Women Quarterly* 6, no. 1 (Fall 1981): 113–22, esp. 114.

aged women.[84] Thus black middle-aged women may be at high risk for depression precisely because of the prevalence of the "full nest."

There is a general lack of theoretical work that deals with women at this later stage of life. Then, too, theories concerned with adult development do not take into account the typically interrupted and varied role patterns of mothers.[85] Despite the fact that a high percentage of women work outside the home, researchers have focused primarily on full-time homemakers. It must also be recognized that younger women, who know they will devote only ten years to active mothering, organize their career and motherhood plans differently from older women and experience different psychological disruptions in the stages of motherhood. As Rossi suggests, in the future young women may be affected more by disruptions in their career process than by changes in family patterns.[86]

Rather than restricting ourselves to the empty nest syndrome, psychologists should be concerned with understanding motherhood as an ongoing experience after children have left the home. In the last decade, there has been some research on the relationship between intergenerational contact and a sense of well-being in the elderly.[87] How does a positive versus a negative relationship with a grown child—or no relationship with a child at all—affect the middle-aged mother? How does the presence of young adult children affect the difficult relationship of the middle-aged mother to her own parents? Do Sharon Abu-Laban's findings—that women who have borne three or more children are 15 percent less likely to be institutionalized before the age of seventy-five than are childless women or women with few children—relate only to the structural support that children offer or do large family networks provide emotional sustenance as well?[88] Are offspring in such networks better able to provide support? Certainly as the population ages these issues must be addressed.

Overview

Our reading of the literature reviewed here suggests the need for an ecological perspective toward the role of parenting in adulthood. It

84. Harkins.

85. Rosalind Barnett and Grace Baruch, "Women in the Middle Years: Conceptions and Misconceptions" (paper delivered at the annual meeting of the Eastern Psychological Association, New York, April 1976).

86. Rossi, "Life-Span Theories and Women's Lives" (n. 55 above).

87. Gary Lee and Eugene Ellithorpe, "Intergenerational Exchange and Subjective Well-Being among the Elderly," *Journal of Marriage and the Family* 44, no. 1 (February 1982): 217–24.

88. Sharon Abu-Laban, "Women and Aging: A Futuristic Perspective," *Psychology of Women Quarterly* 6, no. 1 (Fall 1981): 85–98.

is clear that, once the focus is changed from motherhood as instrumental to children's development to motherhood as an identity in a particular set of intimate relationships in a particular subculture and at a particular time in history, then the questions raised in research must necessarily change. Moreover, it is clear that the literature covered here represents both the parent's influence on the child and the child's influence on the parent. The needs of the parent and child cannot be considered in isolation from one another any more than they can be considered in isolation from their social and historical context.

Present public policy as it relates to mothering is clearly entrenched in traditional values. The following statement of policy issues is influenced above all by our belief that mothering or parenting is one of the most important and demanding tasks that an adult undertakes in this society and should be recognized as such. That it has not is probably related to the fact that it is performed primarily by women. Thus any effort to separate parenting responsibilities from gender-specific roles should be encouraged. In particular, these assumptions underlie our policy recommendations: (1) that the well-being of both parents and children is important and that generally an increase in the well-being and self-esteem of one will affect the other; (2) that parents' needs for self-actualization will, however, sometimes conflict with children's needs for care, and any resolution should address the needs of both; and (3) that conflict resolutions will be different for different families, given variation in subcultures, needs, and values, and that therefore governmental intervention should facilitate flexibility.

Policy Issues

First, given the rise in maternal employment coupled with the rise in single-parent families, more child-care facilities should be developed. In a comparative survey of six countries, Sheila Kamerman and Alfred Kahn indicate that the United States lags behind several European countries in the provision of child care and monetary services to protect children and families.[89] Policymakers in this country express concern for children by opposing day care and other alternatives to maternal child care, ignoring research findings and failing to consider the strains such opposition places on families.

What is needed is support for child-care programs from several sources. Governmental support is required in the direct management of programs and in the form of subsidies to ongoing plans. The private sector, instead of developing in-house medical and psychological facilities

89. Sheila Kamerman and Alfred Kahn, *Child Care, Family Benefits and Working Parents* (New York: Columbia University Press, 1981).

to control absenteeism and alcoholism and other stress-related behaviors, should focus its attention on the correlates of these behaviors, such as the strain women experience managing two full-time careers. Day care provided at the work site, for example, would reduce such stress.

We need economic support for innovative programs that allow both parents and nonparents to assume parenting roles with children. There are adults—including nonparents, divorced parents, and parents of adult children—who would like to take on parenting functions. Charles Nakamura et al. recommend high school–based programs in which young people are trained in child care while providing needed services.[90] Such programs would also help prepare young people for the reality of parenthood.

Second, economic support for alternative work structures is necessary. Clearly, as Rosabeth Kanter indicates, the family is embedded in the economy.[91] Our present "nine-to-five work day and overtime when we need you" is not conducive to maternal and paternal involvement in both home and work worlds. When both parents work in our present system, the employed mother experiences role overload in that she generally does more family work, including child and household care. Moreover, innovations that improve the degree of human satisfaction and self-respect at work will likely translate into more vitalized mother-child relationships.[92]

Some of the innovations required include flexible work hours, childcare leaves for both mothers and fathers, expansion of pregnancy leaves, sabbatical programs, four-day work weeks, and alterations in tax structure to enable part-time employment.[93] One such innovative system is "flexitime," under which employees can determine the hours they work on any given day so long as the weekly hours add up to a required total.[94]

Finally, preparent and parent intervention programs must be developed and expanded. Some stages of motherhood are more stressful than others, and preventive programs could increase awareness and help identify coping strategies. For example, intervention programs need to

90. Charles Nakamura et al., "Interdependence of Childcare Resources and the Progress of Women in Society," *Psychology of Women Quarterly* 6, no. 1 (Fall 1981): 26–40.

91. Rosabeth Kanter, *Work and Family in the United States: A Critical Review and Agenda for Research and Policy* (New York: Russell Sage Foundation, 1977).

92. Joseph Pleck, "The Psychology of Sex Roles: Traditional and Non-traditional Views," in *Women and Men: Changing Roles, Relationships, and Perceptions,* ed. Libby Cater and Anne Scott (Palo Alto, Calif.: Aspen Institute for Humanistic Studies, 1976); Jane Flax, "A Materialist Theory of Women's Status," *Psychology of Women Quarterly* 6, no. 1 (Fall 1981): 123–36.

93. Kenneth Kenniston, "The Plight of American Children and Their Families," in *Speaking Out for America's Children,* ed. Milton Senn (New Haven, Conn.: Yale University Press, 1977), pp. 29–35.

94. Halcyne Bohen and Anamarie Viveros-Long, *Balancing Jobs and Family Life: Do Flexible Work Schedules Help?* (Philadelphia: Temple University Press, 1981).

be developed for nonparents who are considering whether and when to parent. Programs of support should be established at a range of sites—hospitals, schools, churches, housing projects—since the social support networks mothers are connected to vary. That mothering is demanding and difficult must be recognized in today's society by policymakers, by feminists, and, most important, by mothers themselves.

Above all, it is the experience of motherhood—its meaning in the lives of women—rather than its usefulness or its psychopathology that should be the focus of future research. In fact, there is yet another pervasive bias present in almost all the work reviewed here that remains as a challenge in future motherhood research. Though twenty years ago Benedek eloquently described the process by which parenthood, as a developmental phase, heals developmental wounds and transforms the childhood traumas of parents,[95] recent feminist-influenced work emphasizes the strains of motherhood to the exclusion of its pleasures. Psychologists who study the experience of mothering must stay attuned to its positive and growth-enhancing aspects. Such truly balanced research could encourage changes in the ecology of motherhood and thus more fully support women in this role.

Department of Psychology
New School for Social Research (Gerson)

Department of Educational Psychology
New York University (Alpert)

Department of Counselor Education
New York University (Richardson)

95. Benedek (n. 36 above).

FAILURES OF VOLITION: FEMALE AGENCY AND INFERTILITY IN HISTORICAL PERSPECTIVE

MARGARETE J. SANDELOWSKI

Rediscovered as a phenomenon of the 1980s, infertility has become the subject of increasing numbers of professional and popular books and articles, autobiographical and fictional accounts, and television news and dramatic features. Although there is no substantive evidence that the overall incidence of infertility in the United States has increased in the past decade,[1] one prominent

Travel for this study was supported by a University of North Carolina at Chapel Hill Foundation Fund award.

[1] *Infertility: Medical and Social Choices*, U.S. Congress, Office of Technology Assessment, OTA-BA-358 (Washington, D.C.: Government Printing Office, May 1988), 49–57. Until 1982, data on the prevalence of infertility were not reliable, and today there is still no conceptual or methodologic consensus concerning how to determine its prevalence. The literature on infertility characteristically refers to the rising incidence of this dysfunction, but there is no hard evidence that the percentage of marital pairs in the United States unable to have the children they desire has, over the past century, been lower than 10 percent or higher than 20 percent. Within any one time period, estimates vary over this range. Although changes in the incidence of infertility in subgroups, such as black women, and in the incidence of certain diseases or conditions associated with infertility, such as venereal diseases and dietary deficiencies, have occurred, the overall prevalence appears to be rather stable. See W. R. Keye, "Psychosexual Responses to Infertility," *Clinics in Obstetrics and Gynecology* 27 (September 1984): 760–66, esp. 760; P. Cutright and E. Shorter, "The Effects of Health on the Completed Fertility of Nonwhite and White U.S. Women Born between 1867 and 1935," *Journal of Social History* 13 (Winter 1979): 191–217; E. Shorter, *A History of Women's Bodies* (New York: Basic, 1982), esp. 266–67, and "Women's Diseases before 1900," in *New*

This essay originally appeared in *Signs*, vol. 15, no. 3, Spring 1990.

infertility specialist has referred to the dysfunction as a growing public health problem of epidemic proportions.[2]

Medical writers and demographers have located the current sense of urgency about infertility in the convergence of several factors, including the growing numbers of upper-income infertile couples seeking infertility services, the increasing numbers of physicians providing those services, the greater availability of and controversy about advancements in conceptive technology, and the evolution of a social milieu conducive to public discussion of infertility.[3] Embedded within this scientific discussion of the new urgency about infertility is also a renewed concern about women's autonomy and the reproductive price of women's expanded freedoms. In this moral dialogue, infertility emerges as the new bedfellow of reproductive freedom, the price liberated women and young, upwardly mobile professional couples pay for prioritizing the establishment of careers, the acquisition of material goods, and the pursuit of sexual pleasure over the having of children.[4] Although typically secondary to strictly scientific discussions of infertility, this dialogue linking women's emancipation with their fertility status has been present in American medical literature since the nineteenth century.

Directions in Psychohistory: The Adelphi Papers, ed. M. Albin (Lexington, Mass.: Heath, 1980), 183–208; and S. E. Tolnay and A. M. Guest, "Childlessness in a Transitional Population: The United States at the Turn of the Century," *Journal of Family History* 7 (Summer 1982): 200–219. Most of the literature cited here contains estimates of prevalence and references to other authors' estimates that generally fall within the 10–20 percent range.

[2] J. H. Bellina with J. Wilson, *You Can Have a Baby: Everything You Need to Know about Fertility* (New York: Crown, 1985), xv.

[3] *Infertility: Medical and Social Choices;* S. O. Aral and W. Cates, Jr., "The Increasing Concern with Infertility: Why Now?" *Journal of the American Medical Association* 250 (1983): 2327–31; S. K. Henshaw and M. T. Orr, "The Need and Unmet Need for Infertility Services in the United States," *Family Planning Perspectives* 19 (July/August 1987): 180–86; M. B. Hirsch and W. D. Mosher, "Characteristics of Infertile Women in the United States and Their Use of Infertility Services," *Fertility and Sterility* 47 (April 1987): 618–25; W. D. Mosher, "Infertility Trends among U.S. Couples: 1965–1976," *Family Planning Perspectives* 14 (January/February 1982): 22–27; and W. D. Mosher and S. O. Aral, "Factors Related to Infertility in the United States, 1965–1976," *Sexually Transmitted Diseases* 12 (July–September 1985): 117–23.

[4] "New Bedfellows: Freedom and Infertility," *Science News* (May 1980): 341–42; C. Kosterman, "When the Stork Doesn't Come," *Leader* (May 1987): 6–7, 14; A. Quindlen, "Baby Craving," *Life* (June 1987), 23–26, esp. 24–25; P. Schroeder, "Infertility and the World Outside," *Fertility and Sterility* 49 (May 1988): 765–67; and K. White, *What to Do When You Think You Can't Have a Baby* (New York: Doubleday, 1981), esp. 138.

Disease, desire, and failures of volition

An important theme in the American dialogue concerning infertility is that it is a biological expression of what Charles Rosenberg described in 1986 as "culpable failures of volition." Rosenberg observed that "the desire to explain sickness and death in terms of volition—of acts done or left undone—is ancient and powerful," especially when there is no consensus about the nature and treatment of a disease.[5] Infertility continues to be an ambiguous condition whose etiology and progress still lack definition. Up to 20 percent of cases remain unexplained, and treatment for infertility is often only tenuously related to the cure of the disorder believed to prevent conception or gestation to term—and to the birth of a baby.[6] Treatments for infertility, such as artificial insemination and in vitro fertilization, may be better conceptualized as services since they circumvent rather than eliminate those factors impeding conception and are also available or potentially available to fertile individuals.[7] Best current estimates of the effectiveness of treatment suggest that only 50 percent of infertile couples undergoing medical therapy will achieve a pregnancy.[8]

Moreover, the philosophical debate continues over whether infertility is a disease in the usual sense and, therefore, whether it wholly belongs in the medical domain of diagnosis and treatment. Infertility has been variously described as a syndrome of multiple origin, a consequence or manifestation of disease rather than a disease entity itself, a biological impairment, a psychosomatic disorder, a condition characterizing a couple rather than an individual, a failure to conform to cultural prescriptions to reproduce, and a failure to fulfill the personal desire to beget a child. There is even the lack of a clear demarcation between infertility and

[5] C. E. Rosenberg, "Disease and the Social Order in America: Perceptions and Expectations," *Milbank Quarterly* 64, suppl. 1 (1986): 34–55, esp. 44, 50. See also S. Sontag, *Illness as Metaphor* (New York: Vintage, 1979).

[6] J. A. Collins, W. Wrixon, L. B. Janes, and E. H. Wilson, "Treatment-Independent Pregnancy among Infertile Couples," *New England Journal of Medicine* 309 (1983): 1201–6; B. E. Kliger, "Evaluation, Therapy, and Outcome in 493 Infertile Couples," *Fertility and Sterility* 41 (January 1984): 40–46; T. J. Mudge, "The Concept of Fecundity," *Clinical Reproduction and Fertility* 1 (1982): 331–32; and B. S. Verkauf, "The Incidence and Outcome of Single-Factor, Multifactorial, and Unexplained Infertility," *American Journal of Obstetrics and Gynecology* 147 (1983): 175–81.

[7] S. Elias and G. J. Annas, "Social Policy Considerations in Noncoital Reproduction," *Journal of the American Medical Association* 255 (January 1986): 62–68, esp. 64.

[8] *Infertility: Medical and Social Choices*, 131.

fertility, the one condition becoming the other as individual reproductive choices and circumstances change over time.[9]

The conventional medical definition of infertility is that it is an
inability or failure to conceive after one year of regular, unprotected
intercourse, the regularity of intercourse and the lack of contraceptive protection documenting the desire to conceive and a deficiency
of the body, not the will. Medical literature has consistently
emphasized the immediate and immediately treatable causes of
reproductive failures, including "female," "male," and "male-
female" factors evident in such clinical phenomena as obstructions
in the reproductive tract, endocrinological irregularities, immuno-
logical incompatibilities, and gonadal dysgenesis.[10]

Yet in the medical literature, these immediate or proximate
causes of the biologic failure to reproduce are recurringly linked to
ultimate causes that suggest that a defect of desire or a failure of
will may also be operating. Physicians and other medical writers
imply that failures of will or desire evident in such individual
choices as delaying childbearing can create the biologic dysfunctions directly responsible for impeding conception and gestation to
term. Biologic dysfunctions in the involuntary domain are the
results of actions in the voluntary domain. The functional ability to
conceive and carry a healthy infant to term and the desire to have a
child accordingly constitute the involuntary/voluntary calculus that
is used to distinguish biological failures from volitional ones as
causes of infertility.

[9] "Infertility" is a label with many denotations and connotations; it is also
descriptive and prescriptive. Medical writers, demographers, epidemiologists, and
social critics have rather consistently noted the conceptual and methodological
difficulties in defining and locating infertility. Included are the problems of
differentiating between fertility and fecundity, permanent and temporary, and
voluntary and involuntary states of fertility in addition to determining the congru-
ence between intentions, behavior, and fertility outcomes. See L. R. Kass, "Babies
by Means of In Vitro Fertilization: Unethical Experiments on the Unborn?" *New
England Journal of Medicine* 285 (1971): 1174–79, and " 'Making Babies' Revis-
ited," *Public Interest* 54 (Winter 1979): 32–60; W. D. Mosher, *Reproductive Impairments among Married Couples, United States* (Hyattsville, Md.: U.S. Department of
Health and Human Services, Public Health Service, National Center for Health
Statistics, 1982); C. Overall, *Ethics and Human Reproduction: A Feminist Analysis*
(Boston: Allen & Unwin, 1987), esp. 137–65; and E. V. Van Hall, "The Infertile
Couple and the Gynecologist: Psychosocial and Emotional Aspects," in *Fertility and
Sterility*, ed. R. F. Harrison, J. Bonnar, and W. Thompson (Lancaster: MTP Press,
1984), 359–68.

[10] S. J. Behrman, R. W. Kistner, and G. W. Patton, *Progress in Infertility*, 3d ed.
(Boston: Little, Brown, 1988); and A. H. DeCherney, ed., *Reproductive Failure*
(New York: Churchill Livingstone, 1986).

Several events within human control have been repeatedly identified as causes of the diminished capacity to reproduce. Delayed childbearing has been implicated in the etiology of infertility through the factor of age, which is inversely related to procreative potential. Delayed childbearing has also been linked to contraceptive use and abortion that have, in turn, been tied to ovulatory irregularities, pelvic infections, and pelvic adhesions impeding conception. In a similar vein, increased sexual activity increases individuals' exposure to contraception, abortion, and sexually transmitted diseases, while certain habits (of eating, sleeping, dressing) and work environments expose individuals to the injuries and toxic agents that create aberrations in the structure and function of the reproductive organs, preventing conception and causing pregnancy loss.[11]

Significantly, the origins of infertility have consistently been linked to individual choices or actions, suggesting that if infertile individuals cannot be blamed for the tubal obstructions and genital infections directly responsible for their not having children, they can be blamed for the past actions that predisposed them to developing these conditions or that initiated the causal chain of infertility.[12] Although infertility has been characterized primarily as a disease, this has failed to remove the burden of volition from infertile couples, particularly infertile women. In a cultural milieu characterized by the expectation that conception can be prevented, terminated, and initiated at will and in which individual habits and life-styles have been persistently implicated in the onset of cancer, heart disease, and other impairments, not having a child—even if by default and not by design—is still viewed partly as a product of individual choice.[13]

---

[11] Aral and Cates; DeCherney, ed.; and *Infertility: Medical and Social Choices*, esp. 61–82.

[12] Blame connotes an intentionality not associated with responsibility. K. G. Shaver, *The Attribution of Blame: Causality, Responsibility, and Blameworthiness* (New York: Springer-Verlag, 1985); and K. G. Shaver and D. Drown, "On Causality, Responsibility, and Self-Blame: A Theoretical Note," *Journal of Personality and Social Psychology* 50 (1986): 697–702.

[13] P. Brickman, V. Rabinowitz, J. Karuza, D. Coates, E. Cohn, and L. Kidder, "Models of Helping and Coping," *American Psychologist* 37 (1982): 368–84; J. H. Knowles, "The Responsibility of the Individual," in *Doing Better and Feeling Worse: Health in the United States*, ed. J. H. Knowles (New York: Norton, 1977), 57–80; R. W. Lidz, "Conflicts between Fertility and Infertility," in *The Woman Patient*, vol. 3, *Aggression, Adaptations, and Psychotherapy*, ed. M. T. Notman and C. C. Nadelson (New York: Plenum, 1982), 131–36, esp. 131; B. G. Rosenkrantz, "Damaged Goods: Dilemmas of Responsibility for Risk," *Milbank Memorial Fund*

Voluntary and involuntary childlessness: A fated inversion

Before 1856, when Augustus Gardner published the first American book devoted exclusively to the subject, there were very few English-language books or papers on sterility.[14] Still, as early as 1797, one medical student observed that sterility was omitted as a diagnostic category in current taxonomies of disease. Suggesting that physicians of the day were not interested in sterility to the extent they should be, because the inability to have children placed no "lives . . . in danger," J. Walker admonished his colleagues to investigate the causes of barrenness with the diligence that the "anxiety of mind" and resulting "evil" associated with "unfruitful marriage" demanded.[15]

Sterility was viewed not so much as a distinctive diagnostic entity but rather as the result of the leukorrhea, cervical and uterine displacements, menstrual irregularities, bowel and bladder problems, and other medical and gynecologic ailments that plagued both women and their physicians. Frequently appearing in nineteenth-century gynecology texts only in passing, in abbreviated discussions, or in an appendix, sterility was conceptualized as a symptom "only to be reached through the malady causing it."[16] If the physician cured this malady, he would also have cured sterility.

Marital sterility became increasingly important to physicians as a separate diagnostic entity and as a social phenomenon in the latter decades of the nineteenth century. Although mechanical explanations for sterility prevailed, the dysfunction provoked continuing disagreements among physicians concerning its cause.[17] In addition, sterility treatments included a variety of cumbersome uterine

---

Quarterly 57 (1979): 1–37; and R. M. Veatch, "The Medical Model: Its Nature and Problems," in *Concepts of Health and Disease: Interdisciplinary Perspectives,* ed. A. L. Caplan, H. T. Engelhardt, and J. J. McCartney (Reading, Mass.: Addison-Wesley, 1981), 523–44.

[14] A. K. Gardner, *The Causes and Curative Treatment of Sterility* (New York: DeWitt & Davenport, 1856); C. M. McLane and M. McLane, "A Half Century of Sterility, 1840–1890," *Fertility and Sterility* 20 (1969): 853–70.

[15] J. Walker, "An Inquiry into the Causes of Sterility in Both Sexes with Its Method of Cure" (Ph.D. diss., University of Pennsylvania, 1797), esp. 7–8, Americana Collection, New York Academy of Medicine, New York.

[16] W. B. Atkinson, ed., *The Therapeutics of Gynecology and Obstetrics* (Philadelphia: D. G. Brinton, 1880), 152; H. J. Garrigues, *A Textbook of the Diseases of Women* (Philadelphia: Saunders, 1894), esp. 654.

[17] J. M. Sims was a prominent proponent of such explanations positing various obstructions as causes of sterility. See J. M. Sims, *Clinical Notes on Uterine Surgery: With Special Reference to the Management of the Sterile Condition* (New York: William Wood, 1866).

supporters and pessaries, slow and rapid mechanical dilatation of the cervix, the application of leeches, cervical incisions and amputations, a variety of local and systemic chemical agents, and electrical therapy, all of which caused considerable and protracted mental and physical discomfort.[18] One Philadelphia physician sarcastically noted that the medical course in the treatment of sterility depended upon the "taste," "inclination," and desire for "gynecological fame" of the physician. He summarized the lack of consensus among physicians about the proper approach to sterility that characterized medical practice, observing in 1878 that "the variety of causes suggested as productive of sterility . . . the versions, the flexions, the strictures, the irritabilities, the inflammations . . . and the number of operations proposed for the relief of these abnormalities . . . the probing, scarifying, stretching, dilating, incising, cauterizing, and amputating . . . are only equalled by the number and variety of instruments . . . pessaries of every imaginable shape and material . . . which have been invented, modified, and improved upon for the performance of these operations."[19]

Physicians' continuing disagreements about what caused sterility and the difficulties they encountered in achieving pregnancies allowed new explanations for sterility to appear, explanations that emphasized human, particularly female, agency. Although knowledge existed of sperm deficiencies and of the male role in producing female sterility through transmission of gonorrhea, physicians were reluctant to accept male responsibility, tending to exonerate the man if only one sperm cell could be shown to be viable.[20]

[18] McLane and McLane; A. H. Curtis, "Progress in the Relief of Sterility," *American Journal of Obstetrics and Gynecology* 8 (1924): 123–29; F. P. Davis, *Impotency, Sterility, and Artificial Impregnation*, 2d ed. (St. Louis: Mosby, 1923); H. D. Fry, "The Relative Merits of Electrolysis and Rapid Dilatation in the Treatment of Sterility and Dysmenorrhea," *American Journal of Obstetrics and Diseases of Women and Children* 21 (1888): 40–48; E. M. Hales, *Diseases of Women, Especially Those Causing Sterility* (New York: Boericke & Tafel, 1878); T. W. Kay, "A Study of Sterility, Its Causes and Treatment," *Journal of the American Medical Association* 16 (1891): 181–84, 222–29, 265–70; M. A. Pallen, "Resume on Incision and Division of the Cervix Uteri for Dysmenorrhea and Sterility," *American Journal of Obstetrics* 10 (1877): 364–89; and F. Townsend, "A Report of Eighty Cases of Rapid Dilatation of the Uterine Canal for the Cure of Dysmenorrhea and Sterility," *American Journal of Obstetrics and Diseases of Women and Children* 22 (1889): 1271–76.

[19] W. R. D. Blackwood, "Who Is to Blame?" *Philadelphia Medical Times* 9 (October 1878): 1–4, esp. 1.

[20] Male sterility was largely equated with impotency. See Gardner; S. W. Gross, *A Practical Treatise on Impotence, Sterility and Allied Disorders of the Male Sexual Organs*, 4th ed. rev. (Philadelphia: Lea Brothers, 1890); A. R. Jackson, "On Some

As a social phenomenon, infertility telescoped physicians' and other social critics' concerns about women's health and their new activism and the relationship of these factors to national growth and prosperity. In fact, women's apparently declining health and its impact on the family and society constituted one of the most important medical, social, and demographic issues of the day.[21] The suggestion of women's as opposed to men's blameworthiness for sterility emerged in the latter decades of the nineteenth century when increasing public attention was directed toward women's new educational and occupational aspirations, their assertions of independence and claim to political rights, and a declining birth rate among what many viewed as the most desirable segments of the population.

The idea of female volition as an explanation for sterility entered the American dialogue at a time when physicians required explanations for sterility and an increasing number of women became noticeably disinterested in having large families or having children at all, willfully preventing conception or impeding the course of pregnancy. Aspiring physicians sought to ground medical practice in science and to separate themselves professionally from their many other competitors providing health care services.[22] In addition, a combination of factors related to the profound socioeconomic changes caused by industrialization, urbanization, and modernization contributed to a beginning emphasis on the quality of life rather than on the quantity of children and to the emergence of a new family role for women that empowered them to make decisions about how many children they would have.[23] Between

---

Points in Connection with the Treatment of Sterility," *Transactions of the American Gynecological Society* 3 (1878): 347–62; E. Noeggerath, "Latent Gonorrhea, Especially with Regard to Its Influence on Fertility in Women," *Transactions of the American Gynecological Society* 1 (1876): 268–300; S. Peters, "Remarks on the Causes of Sterility," *American Journal of Obstetrics and Diseases of Women and Children* 17 (1884): 841–51; and J. M. Sims, "On the Microscope, as an Aid in the Diagnosis and Treatment of Sterility," *New York Medical Journal* 8 (1868–69): 393–413.

[21] J. H. Cassedy, *Medicine and American Growth, 1800–1860* (Madison: University of Wisconsin Press, 1986), esp. 169–87; L. Gordon, *Woman's Body, Woman's Right: A Social History of Birth Control in America* (New York: Penguin, 1977); and J. Reed, *The Birth Control Movement and American Society: From Private Vice to Public Virtue* (Princeton, N.J.: Princeton University Press, 1984), esp. 197–210.

[22] B. Ehrenreich and D. English, *For Her Own Good: 150 Years of the Experts' Advice to Women* (New York: Anchor/Doubleday, 1978), esp. 30–88.

[23] C. Hardyment, *Dream Babies: Three Centuries of Good Advice on Child Care* (New York: Harper & Row, 1983); D. S. Smith, "Family Limitation, Sexual Control,

1800 and 1900, the total white fertility rate decreased 50 percent, at least one half of the decline attributable to a reduction of childbearing within marriage. The years between 1870 and 1915 were especially significant because they were characterized partly by increasingly visible differences in the fertility rates of native white upper-income women and their poorer, black, and immigrant counterparts, native white birth rates lagging far behind those of the other groups.[24] Along with the falling white birth rate, elective abortion had become another public reality by midcentury, increasing among married, native, white, socioeconomically advantaged women who wanted to delay or to stop further childbearing. The heightened visibility of elective abortion among married women, combined with anxieties about the falling birth rate and concerns about professional status as abortion was increasingly commercialized, led physicians to campaign actively to restrict abortion. Moreover, physicians viewed women's ability to abort themselves or to obtain abortions easily as permitting a dangerous departure from women's prescribed family roles.[25]

Physicians specializing in the diseases of women increasingly viewed gynecologic practice in terms of women's procreative capacities. The success of a socially conscious gynecology, a medical and increasingly surgical domain that located women's health in the functioning of their reproductive organs and linked that to the welfare of the family and society, was founded on the principle that women should be fruitful and multiply and that they should restrict themselves to the roles that God and nature prescribed for them, namely, wife and mother. The new veneration of this "true woman,"[26] whose maternal nature was biologically and divinely fixed, made the diagnosis and treatment of sterility integral to the medical care of pubertal females and women of childbearing age. Physicians believed that childbearing preserved the true woman, protected her from the physical and emotional

and Domestic Feminism in Victorian America," in *A Heritage of Her Own: Toward a New Social History of American Women*, ed. N. F. Cott and E. H. Pleck (New York: Touchstone, 1979), 222–45; and V. A. Zelizer, *Pricing the Priceless Child: The Changing Social Value of Children* (New York: Basic, 1981).

[24] Smith, 226; and S. H. Van Horn, *Women, Work, and Fertility, 1900–1986* (New York: New York University Press, 1988), esp. 9–31.

[25] J. C. Mohr, *Abortion in America: The Origins and Evolution of National Policy* (New York: Oxford University Press, 1978), esp. 46–85.

[26] B. Welter, "The Cult of True Womanhood: 1820–1860," in *The American Family in Social-Historical Perspective*, ed. M. Gordon, 2d ed. (New York: St. Martin's, 1978), 313–33.

ravages of her own biological cycles, and protected society from decline and extinction.[27]

Against the backdrop of alarm over falling white birth rates and rising elective abortion rates (miscarriage and stillbirth sometimes also viewed as artificially induced), women's increasingly successful efforts to contracept, women's expansion of their influence in the domestic sphere and increasing forays into the public sphere of higher education, work, and politics, and the continuing vagaries of sterility diagnosis and treatment, volition became an important explanatory variable in the etiology of sterility. The failure to reproduce at all or in sufficient numbers was increasingly viewed as a consequence of the failure to want to reproduce. Although physicians admitted responsibility in many cases for creating female sterility by poor obstetric practice postpartally and by performing sterilizing procedures to control disease and to regulate what they perceived as women's aberrant behavior and sexuality, they also regularly argued among themselves about the abuses of such procedures in terms of the life, health, and fecundity of their patients.[28] Gynecologic practice sought delicately to balance women's overall well-being, located medically in the proper functioning of their reproductive organs, with their procreative potential. Baltimore physician Thomas Ashby reflected on the paradoxical medical practices of curing women's mental and physical dysfunctions by sterilizing them, while at the same time viewing biological maternity as necessary to women's good health, when he warned: "Organs should not be sacrificed to the rule of expediency, but should be preserved in deference to the law of genuine conservatism."[29]

[27] G. J. Barker-Benfield, *The Horrors of the Half-Known Life: Male Attitudes toward Women and Sexuality in Nineteenth-Century America* (New York: Harper Colophon, 1977); H. Green, *The Light of the Home: An Intimate View of the Lives of Women in Victorian America* (New York: Pantheon, 1983); G. H. Napheys, *The Physical Life of Woman: Advice to the Maiden, Wife, and Mother* (Philadelphia: George MacLean, 1869); C. Smith-Rosenberg, "The Female Animal: Medical and Biological Views of Woman and Her Role in Nineteenth-Century America," *Journal of American History* 60 (September 1973): 332–56, and "Puberty to Menopause: The Cycle of Femininity in Nineteenth-Century America," *Feminist Studies* 1 (Winter/Spring 1973): 58–72.

[28] Barker-Benfield, esp. 120–32; and L. D. Longo, "The Rise and Fall of Battey's Operation: A Fashion in Surgery," *Bulletin of the History of Medicine* 53 (1979): 244–67.

[29] T. A. Ashby, "The Influence of Minor Forms of Ovarian and Tubal Disease in the Causation of Sterility," *Transactions of the American Gynecological Society* 19 (1894): 260–71, esp. 271.

It was primarily women who stood accused of delaying child-bearing and of leading lives and developing habits inimical to procreation. In medical literature, marital sterility was increasingly constructed as a social disease, a disorder of civilization and modern living, involving culpable, largely female acts of omission and commission. Washington gynecologist Horatio Bigelow articulated the role of female volition in the etiology of sterility in what he termed the "habit of sterility, self-caused or physical." The moral significance of sterility for him lay in recognizing how men, but especially women, injured themselves and their reproductive functioning by deliberately limiting offspring and engaging in what he considered perverted sexual relations. Bigelow lamented the use of artifices to limit the number of children born, maintaining that even where the desire existed to have children at some future date, the willful induction of temporary sterility often created a "habit," a permanent incapacity that could not be reversed when the desire for children asserted itself. Believing, like most of his medical colleagues, that civilization was harder on women's health than on men's, Bigelow advocated a system of education that taught women the importance of maternity. Deriding the efforts of "advanced female thinkers" of the day to expand women's influence in and beyond the home, Bigelow lamented the "conjugal onanism" that inevitably resulted from the "restless condition" of modern women who aspired to absolute equality with men. He believed that women's failures of volition were clearly antecedent to their increasing sterility. This "restless activity, a dissatisfaction with her duties and calling, and a want of reverence for her special vocation, go hand in hand with sterility." Even inherited sterility was, for Bigelow, ultimately a product of human agency because it was closely linked with willfully contracted, consanguineous marriages.[30]

Bigelow's discussion of the moral or volitional aspects of sterility reflected the very prevalent medical (and other expert males') view that women who reached beyond their appropriate sphere were ultimately to blame for the sterility that constituted such a tragedy to themselves, their families, and to society. A constant theme in medical and other prescriptive literature on women's health and fertility was that expanded education and women's ambitions perverted their biological destiny. Although most women might want eventually to become mothers, their involvement in intellectual pursuits that diverted energy away from the reproduc-

[30] H. R. Bigelow, "The Moral Significance of Sterility," *Obstetric Gazette* 6 (1883): 1–24, esp. 1, 11, 13.

tive organs to the brain would lead to conditions that lowered fertility.[31] Medical and other experts on women's progress particularly focused on intellectual rather than on physical labor as the cause of sterility, since their concern was almost exclusively for the declining birth rates in the classes of women most likely to pursue intellectual careers, namely, white socioeconomically advantaged women. Despite the fact that the incidence of sterility was at least as great in the poorer classes and among those engaged in strenuous physical labor, physicians legitimated their concern about the dysfunction in upper-income white women by theorizing that physical labor and poverty were favorable to fertility, while indolence and wealth were associated with decreased fertility.[32] T. G. Thomas's popular 1891 treatise on women's diseases summarized the "depreciating habits of civilized life" that predisposed the "civilized" woman, in contrast to the "North American squaw" and the "Southern negress," to sterility. These habits, almost wholly in the domain of female agency, included neglect of proper nutrition and outdoor exercise, brain fatigue, improprieties of dress, imprudence during menstruation, and the prevention or termination of pregnancy.[33]

The role of volition in the etiology of sterility continued to be an important feature of physicians' and other social experts' discussions of the dysfunction at the turn of the twentieth century and throughout the Depression era, when fertility rates reached their lowest levels and childlessness rates reached their highest levels. Nativist fears of "race suicide" and of what was viewed as the unchecked fertility of the poorer classes and immigrants and a eugenics movement toward racial improvement prevailed in the opening decades of the new century.[34] In addition, experts continued to emphasize the importance of women's maternal role. Childless women were caught up in the wave of criticism created by the convergence of fears of racial decline and deterioration and women's continuing activism inside and outside of the home, evident in the suffrage movement, increasing divorce rates, and the continu-

[31] J. S. Haller and R. M. Haller, *The Physician and Sexuality in Victorian America* (New York: Norton, 1974), 47–87.

[32] G. S. Bedford, *Clinical Lectures on the Diseases of Women and Children* (New York: Samuel & Wood, 1855); H. F. Campbell, "The Infertility of Women: The Nervous System in Sterility," *Transactions of the American Gynecological Society* 13 (1888): 423–54; and W. C. Taylor, *A Physician's Counsels to Woman, in Health and Disease* (Springfield, Mass.: W. J. Holland, 1871), esp. 325.

[33] T. G. Thomas, *A Practical Treatise on the Diseases of Women*, 6th ed. (Philadelphia: Lea Brothers, 1891), 35.

[34] Gordon (n. 21 above), esp. 95–185; and W. H. Grabill, C. V. Kiser, and P. K. Whelpton, *The Fertility of American Women* (New York: Wiley, 1958), esp. chap. 11.

ing use of birth control. Physician George Engelmann set a moral tone for the new century in a paper read before the obstetric and gynecologic section of the American Medical Association in 1901 when he argued that barrenness was largely and unequivocably independent of physical causes. He offered as evidence the gynecologic progress that had been made over the same period that sterility had increased to 20 percent of married women. Tying sterility to divorce, criminal abortion, and women's "egotism," and noting the ease of conception even in the most adverse of circumstances, Engelmann stated the causes of sterility to be almost wholly "moral" ones.[35]

Although physicians concerned about the relationship between women's health and autonomy allowed for the possibility that sterility was not always a matter of choice—that the will to reproduce could exist along with the inability to reproduce, or that male deficiencies of the body or will played an important role in causation—many directed their enmity at women, who "under the banner of individualism (were) destroying the machinery of society."[36] Using the calculus of ability and desire, socially conscious physicians and other experts warned that if women refused to breed, or succeeded in making breeding a physical impossibility, the end of the race was near. The author of a frequently cited study of one thousand women in the 1926–27 edition of *Who's Who in America* worried that almost one-half of the married women listed there had no children.[37] Physicians continued to warn of the "abuse of self in earlier life"[38] that caused so much sterility, the alarming number of women trying to prevent conception and to destroy fetuses, and the "industrial conditions" and "social customs" that weakened women.[39] One physician lamented that life, for both women and men, was no longer governed by "physiological certainty," but rather by social factors impeding maternity that threatened "the very foundation and stability of our country."[40]

[35] G. J. Engelmann, "The Increasing Sterility of American Women," *Journal of the American Medical Association* 37, no. 14 (1901): 890–97, esp. 894, 897. For corrections, see G. J. Engelmann, "The Increasing Sterility of American Women," *Journal of American Medical Association* 37, no. 23 (1901): 1532–33.

[36] P. Popenoe, *The Conservation of the Family* (Baltimore: Williams & Wilkins, 1926), 136.

[37] P. M. Cope, "The Women of 'Who's Who': A Statistical Study," *Social Forces* 7 (1928): 212–23.

[38] W. W. Hoffman, *Sterility and Choice of Sex in the Human Family* (Pittsburgh, 1916), 24.

[39] Davis (n. 18 above), 112.

[40] R. S. Gregg, "Sterility versus Fecundity, and the Divorce Evil," *Milwaukee Medical Journal* 13 (1905): 60–62, esp. 61–62.

Medical experts pointed to the preventable causes of sterility and the human agency involved in the breaking of hygiene laws.[41] In the 1931 edition of *Sterility and Conception*, the physician author reiterated all of the nineteenth-century professional complaints against modern women who transgressed the laws of nature. In a particularly vitriolic attack against American women, including "fat" women, "academicians," "public women," "detached women," and "social corsairs," C. G. Child declared them "ultimately responsible" for the perceived American population crisis, saying that they ought to play the exacting role in life their reproductive powers demanded of them.[42] Other physicians, well known in the field of sterility, noted the susceptibility of the female reproductive organs to damage, a fact of nature and of civilization that placed a greater burden on women than men to maintain the will and the ability to reproduce.[43] Isidor Rubin, one of the most important and respected clinicians in the area of sterility between the 1920s and the 1950s, commented on the "conspicuous infertility" of women who vied for industrial jobs and executive positions.[44] Some physicians explicitly linked voluntary with involuntary sterility: S. G. Berkow, the author of an influential text on sterility, remarked on the "steady stream of emergence from willful childlessness to involuntary sterility."[45] A 1939 editorial in the *Journal of Contraception* documented the continuing controversy concerning the percentage of truly involuntary sterile marriages.[46]

Interestingly, the early twentieth-century campaign against venereal diseases, sparked by the Progressive impulse toward social reform, temporarily diverted blame from infertile women. This campaign emphasized women's martyrdom at the hands of infected men who did not know any better or who were afraid of making their sexual indiscretions known to their wives. Physician Prince

[41] D. Macomber, "Prevention of Sterility," *Journal of the American Medical Association* 83 (1924): 678–82; S. R. Meaker, "Two Million American Homes Childless," *Hygeia* (November 1927): 546–48.

[42] C. G. Child, *Sterility and Conception* (New York: Appleton, 1931), esp. 12–13.

[43] S. R. Meaker, *Human Sterility: Causation, Diagnosis, and Treatment* (Baltimore: Williams & Wilkins, 1934), esp. 8–10.

[44] I. C. Rubin, "Forty Years' Progress in the Treatment of Female Sterility," *American Journal of Obstetrics and Gynecology* 68 (1954): 324–33, esp. 331. In addition to being a prolific writer, Rubin (1883–1958) left behind six tightly packed file drawers of alphabetized but otherwise uncataloged case files of women he treated for sterility primarily in the 1920s and 1930s. They are housed at the New York Academy of Medicine, New York. I thank John Balkema for facilitating access to these files.

[45] S. G. Berkow, *Childlessness: A Study of Sterility, Its Causes and Treatment* (New York: Lee Furman, 1937), 21.

[46] "Childlessness," *Journal of Contraception* 4 (1939): 58.

Albert Morrow, a key figure in the fight against venereal diseases, was horrified at the incidence of sterile marriages attributable to men's sexual activities outside of marriage. Calling these men honest but ignorant, Morrow chastised them for taking advantage of women's infantile and blind devotion to them, and he chastised physicians for colluding with their male patients by keeping what was referred to as "the medical secret" from women.[47]

Citing key medical figures in the field, such as Emil Noegerrath and Albert Neisser, Morrow located the cause of many miscarriages, ectopic pregnancies, fetal and infant deaths, and sterilizing post-partal infections in the gonorrhea and syphilis wives contracted from husbands. Urging women to interest themselves in the movement for the prophylaxis of social diseases, Morrow reminded them that the burden of shame, suffering, disease, and death lay on their shoulders. He was particularly concerned with the innocent wives who were not safe from prostitutes' "diseases of vice transplanted to the bed of virtue."[48] Sympathetic to prostitutes whom he believed to be products of men's sexual appetites, Morrow held men responsible for the destruction of the health and lives of women and children. Morrow deplored the rampant male egotism, double standard, and the androcentricity of society that faulted only childless wives for sterile marriages and only prostitutes for the spread of diseases.

Morrow was among a contingency of physicians who felt compelled to continue reminding their colleagues and society in general that sterility was largely due to "incapacity and not of choice" and that it was attributable to the male at least as often as it was to the female.[49] These physicians argued that criminal abortion hardly played the role in causing race suicide that venereal diseases did. They noted with concern that in no other branch of medicine were patients subject to such unnecessary treatment as some women suffering from sterility. Even physicians who affirmed women's traditional roles decried the gynecologic practice of blaming women for sterility.[50]

[47] P. A. Morrow, *Social Diseases and Marriage: Social Prophylaxis* (New York: Lea Brothers, 1904), 46.

[48] P. A. Morrow, "Prophylaxis of Social Diseases," *American Journal of Sociology* 13 (1907): 20–33, esp. 22.

[49] P. A. Morrow, "The Relations of Social Diseases to the Family," *American Journal of Sociology* 14 (1909): 622–37, esp. 626.

[50] For literature on venereal disease and male agency in this period, see S. W. Bandler, "The Instincts, the Emotions, and the Endocrines in Sterility," *Medical Record* 97 (1920): 383–91; A. M. Brandt, *No Magic Bullet: A Social History of Venereal Disease in the United States since 1880* (New York: Oxford University Press, 1987), esp. 7–51; A. H. Burr, "The Guarantee of Safety in the Marriage

Although medical ignorance and male pride were cited as continuing problems in the management of marital sterility, seldom were men viewed as deliberately thwarting nature's plan or society's mandate to reproduce, since the power to reproduce and to maintain the integrity of the family had always been vested in women. Physicians tended to depict male volition (their own and husbands') as the reluctant, unwitting, or benevolently misguided aiding and abetting of marital sterility. Men often appeared as the passive accomplices of their birth-controlling wives. The recognition of the male factor in the etiology of sterility may have diverted responsibility for the dysfunction away from women, but it gave them only a temporary respite from blame.

Disguised volition

The idea of female agency in the etiology of sterility assumed a new and more subtle form beginning in the 1940s with the increasing interest in psychosomatic medicine, Freudian concepts of disease causation, and in maintaining women's primary allegiance to the home and family.[51] The dislocations and necessities of the Depression had caused women to choose childlessness or to delay childbearing, and the need for women in the occupations left behind by men fighting in World War II exposed women to life-styles and opportunities that had generally only been available to men. The war itself and a nostalgic desire for tradition and family harmony subsequently created a renewed consensus among all classes about the importance to women, men, and the nation of having children.

Contract," *Journal of the American Medical Association* 47 (1906): 1887–89; C. P. Gilman, "The Crux," in *The Charlotte Perkins Gilman Reader*, ed. A. J. Lane (1910; reprint, New York: Pantheon, 1980), esp. 116–22, for a fictional treatment of the "medical secret"; Gregg (n. 40 above); G. L. Moench, "A Consideration of Some of the Aspects of Sterility," *American Journal of Obstetrics and Gynecology* 13 (1927): 334–45; A. J. Rongy, "Primary Sterility," *American Journal of Obstetrics and Gynecology* 5 (1923): 631–37; R. W. Taylor, *A Practical Treatise on Sexual Disorders of the Male and Female*, 3d ed. (New York and Philadelphia: Lea Brothers, 1905), esp. p. 188.

   [51] F. Dunbar, *Emotions and Bodily Changes: A Survey of Literature on Psychosomatic Interrelationships, 1910–1953* (New York: Columbia University Press, 1954); S. M. Hartmann, *The Home Front and Beyond: American Women in the 1940s* (Boston: Twayne, 1982), esp. 163–86; E. Kaledin, *Mothers and More: American Women in the 1950s* (Boston: Twayne, 1984), esp. 173–89; M. L. Margolis, *Mothers and Such: Views of American Women and Why They Changed* (Berkeley and Los Angeles: University of California Press, 1984); M. Sandelowski, *Pain, Pleasure, and American Childbirth: From the Twilight Sleep to the Read Method, 1914–1960* (Westport, Conn.: Greenwood, 1984), esp. 55–84.

Along with the baby boom, which began in the 1940s and reached its peak in the late 1950s, came a pervasive cultural belief in the value of having many children and the simultaneous belief in the abnormality of having only one or no children. Despite women's apparent adherence to the renewed pronatalist standard, the zeal with which both professional and popular literature on women prescribed marriage and motherhood betrayed the concern that these domestic goals were not the only ones attracting women. Medical and psychological experts were particularly worried about the health and social consequences of women choosing not to fulfill properly the maternal role.[52]

Women's moral failures were recast as psychological aberrations mandating scientific diagnosis and cure; infertility was a symptom of a complex psychic chain of events that were hidden even from the infertile themselves. Although the connection between women's intellectual and professional aspirations and achievements and poor health and lowered fertility continued to be made throughout the 1940s, 1950s, and 1960s with great urgency in both professional and popular literature, infertility now additionally was depicted medically as a maladaptive disguise for and defense against the hostility or fear of reproducing. Psychic factors involving hostility to men and reproduction were included as causes of the structural organic changes, altered reproductive physiology, and aberrant sexual behavior that reduced the chances of conception.[53]

Freudian interpretations of unconscious processes in the causal chain of infertility equated outcome, the failure to reproduce, with unconscious rather than conscious desire or will. Clinicians therefore easily and unerringly proved the presence of unconscious factors by assuming that true desire for children in almost all cases

[52] Hartmann; E. T. May, *Homeward Bound: American Families in the Cold War Era* (New York: Basic, 1988), esp. 135–61; D. L. Poston and E. Gotard, "Trends in Childlessness in the United States, 1910–1975," *Social Biology* 24 (Fall 1977): 212–24; N. B. Ryder, "The Emergence of a Modern Fertility Pattern: United States, 1917–1966," in *Fertility and Family Planning: A World View,* ed. S. J. Behrman, L. Corsa, and R. Freedman (Ann Arbor: University of Michigan Press, 1969); I. B. Taeuber, "Fertility, Diversity and Policy," *Milbank Memorial Fund Quarterly* 49 (October 1971): 208–29; S. Ware, *Holding Their Own: American Women in the 1930s* (Boston: Twayne, 1982), esp. 1–17.

[53] T. Benedek, "Infertility as a Psychosomatic Defense," *Fertility and Sterility* 3 (1952): 527–41; T. Benedek, G. C. Ham, F. P. Robbins, and B. B. Rubenstein, "Some Emotional Factors in Infertility," *Psychosomatic Medicine* 15 (1953): 485–98; C. Bos and R. A. Cleghorn, "Psychogenic Sterility," *Fertility and Sterility* 9 (1958): 84–98; H. Deutsch, *The Psychology of Women,* vol. 2, *Motherhood* (1945; reprint, New York: Bantam, 1973), esp. 113–33; and K. Kelley, "Sterility in the Female with Special Reference to Psychic Factors. I. A Review of the Literature," *Psychosomatic Medicine* 4 (1942): 211–22.

would lead to children, while the true lack of desire would lead to infertility. Freudian interpretations modified the causal chain of infertility by making the desire to reproduce an important determinant of the ability to reproduce and cast doubts on the existence of both accidental pregnancy and involuntary childlessness. Such interpretations, like the overtly moral ones that preceded it, were especially useful in filling the explanatory void created by the persistence of "unexplained" or "idiopathic" infertility, where no organic cause could be found or where conventional medical treatments consistently failed to produce a pregnancy. Such explanations also served to explain phenomena that fascinated clinicians, such as "one-child" sterility; and the occurrence of pregnancy after adoption, before a medical treatment program was begun, and after psychotherapy.[54]

Gynecological literature from the 1940s through the 1960s reflects a concern with what some physicians construed to be the mysteries of the female body and psyche. In fact, gynecology and female psychology were inextricably linked to each other because many believed that female will, informed by the new concepts of hyperfemininity, hypofemininity, and female masculinity, controlled female reproductive capacity.[55] Some even attributed intentional action to pathophysiological phenomena such as repeated miscarriages and unfavorable cervical mucus, evidenced by the clinical terms "habitual" abortion and "hostile" mucus. Virtually no behavior of the infertile woman was free of clinical suspicion. Even douching indicated an ambivalence toward conceiving, since an overemphasis on cleanliness and body integrity was incompatible with sharing the body with husband or fetus.[56] Medical writers

[54] I. C. Fischer, "Psychogenic Aspects of Sterility," *Fertility and Sterility* 4 (1953): 466–71; F. M. Hanson and J. Rock, "The Effect of Adoption on Fertility and Other Reproductive Functions," *American Journal of Obstetrics and Gynecology* 59 (1950): 311–20; M. Heimann, "Psychoanalytic Evaluation of the Problem of 'One-Child Sterility,' " *Fertility and Sterility* 6 (1955): 405–14; E. Jacobson, "A Case of Sterility," *Psychoanalytic Quarterly* 15 (1946): 3300–3350; D. W. Orr, "Pregnancy Following the Decision to Adopt," *Psychosomatic Medicine* 3 (1941): 441–46; L. L. Robbins, "Suggestions for the Psychological Study of Sterility in Women," *Bulletin of the Menninger Clinic* 7 (1943): 41–44; and R. N. Rutherford, A. L. Banks, and H. M. Lamborn, "One Pregnancy Sterility," *American Journal of Obstetrics and Gynecology* 61 (1951): 443–45.

[55] W. S. Kroger and S. C. Freed, *Psychosomatic Gynecology: Including Problems of Obstetrical Care* (Philadelphia: Saunders, 1951).

[56] E. S. Ford, I. Forman, J. R. Willson, W. Char, W. T. Mixson, and C. Scholz, "A Psychodynamic Approach to the Study of Infertility," *Fertility and Sterility* 4 (1953): 456–65; T. E. Mandy, E. Scher, R. Farkas, and A. J. Mandy, "The Psychic Aspects of Sterility and Abortion," *Southern Medical Journal* 44 (1951): 1054–59; and A. Stern, "Ambivalence and Conception," *Fertility and Sterility* 6 (1955): 540–42.

trapped infertile women in a psychological catch-22 situation: both compliance and noncompliance with medical treatments, great desire and equivocal desire for children, and hyperfertility and infertility were all viewed as manifestations of a similar ambivalence toward maternity.[57]

The discovery of the role of unconscious female agency in the etiology of infertility led to the reemergence of the issue of the advisability of treating all infertile individuals. Although there is no evidence that physicians withheld any treatment from any married childless women, even from those women whom physicians had designated as having induced their own sterility by having abortions,[58] there are indications that infertility was not necessarily viewed as a disorder that mandated treatment. In 1916, some physicians had questioned the morality of treating infertile women with pelvic deformities who were certain to face difficult labors or an increased incidence of pregnancy or infant loss.[59] In 1948, eugenicist Paul Popenoe mused that society might do better without the contribution of children by individuals whose inability to reproduce testified to their racial inferiority.[60] In a similar eugenic vein, the editor of the first issue of *Fertility and Sterility* asserted in 1950 that the purpose of the journal and its medical audience was to "improve the quality" rather than merely to increase the numbers of human beings.[61] In 1960, another physician in a popular book on infertility declared that the dysfunction could be defined as a sickness for which care and treatment can be withheld. Stating that money, marital stability, and eugenic fitness ought to determine who receives treatment,

[57] L. Gidro-Frank and T. Gordon, "Reproductive Performance of Women with Pelvic Pain of Long Duration: Some Observations on Associated Psychopathology," *Fertility and Sterility* 7 (1956): 440–47; Mandy et al.; A. H. Marbach, "The Study of Psychosomatic Gynecology and Obstetrics," *Postgraduate Medicine* 30 (1961): 479–88; and R. N. Rutherford, "Emotional Aspects of Infertility," *Clinical Obstetrics and Gynecology* 8 (1965): 100–114.

[58] For example, I. C. Rubin, in "Unintentional Childless Marriage," *Hygeia* 25 (March 1947): 196, observed that physicians wanted to help people who had done "nothing to thwart nature," but never suggested that those couples who had should be denied medical aid. In his paper "Sterility Secondary to Induced Abortion with Special Reference to the Tubal Factor," *New York State Journal of Medicine* 31 (1931): 213–17, he clearly treated infertile women who had elective abortions in their histories.

[59] J. O. Polak, "A Detailed Study of the Pathological Causes of Sterility with the End-Results," *Surgery, Gynecology, and Obstetrics* 23 (1916): 261–68, esp. 266.

[60] P. Popenoe, "Infertility and the Stability of Marriage," *Western Journal of Surgery, Obstetrics, and Gynecology* 56 (1948): 309–10.

[61] P. Tompkins, "Editorial: A New Journal," *Fertility and Sterility* 1 (1950): 1–2, esp. 1.

E. C. Hamblen thanked a "provident nature" that certain dysgenic and poor individuals could not reproduce.[62]

In the 1950s and 1960s, the assumption that unconscious failures of volition existed could justify delaying medical treatment until the patient completed psychological and motivational evaluations and treatment. Finding out why, and even whether, infertile women really wanted to become pregnant assumed great importance. One group of clinicians suggested that infertility might protect vulnerable and even sick women against the psychic hazards of maternity. Citing reports of high infertility in schizophrenics, they noted the frequent association between reproductive failure and emotional distress and the potential dangers of inducing emotionally deprived and impaired women to reproduce through medical treatment.[63]

Other medical and psychological writers observed that assisting the infertile to become parents could be thwarting nature's wishes, given the high incidence of obstetrical and psychological problems in this group of patients. William Kroger, a key figure in the merging of gynecology and psychiatry, warned that aiding the emotionally immature infertile woman to become fertile could "open up the proverbial hornet's nest" and lead to neurotic children, broken homes, and divorce.[64] In a 1952 speech to the American Society for the Study of Sterility, Kroger mused that infertility could be "nature's first line of defense against the union of potentially defective germ plasm" and called the successful treatment of infertility a "hollow triumph" if it led to more emotional pathology.[65]

Despite the methodological problems discovered in the psychological literature on infertility,[66] the location of the origin of infertility in unconscious processes remained appealing through the 1960s. One physician, commenting on a critique of the psychological literature on infertility, advocated improving the methods used to uncover the emotional causes of infertility and emphasized that because the "patient may not be aware that she has any emotional problems," physicians were "at the mercy of [their patients'] unconscious minds [and] willful withholding."[67]

---

[62] E. C. Hamblen, *Facts for Childless Couples*, 2d ed. (Springfield, Ill.: Thomas, 1960), 11.

[63] Mandy et al.

[64] "Emotions Affect Infertility," *Science News Letter* 61 (June 1952): 383.

[65] "Sterility and Neurotics," *Time* (June 1952): 81–82. See also "Infertility May Be Due to Emotional Disturbance," *Science News Letter* 70 (November 1956): 279; and "Infertility in Women," *Science Digest* 35 (June 1954): 50.

[66] R. W. Noyes and E. M. Chapnick, "Literature on Psychology and Infertility," *Fertility and Sterility* 15 (1964): 543–58.

[67] Rutherford (n. 57 above), esp. 105, 114.

For married women trying to have children in the 1940s and 1950s, involuntary childlessness was likely to have been an especially painful and stigmatizing experience. Living in an intensely pronatalist period characterized by a special cultural "aversion"[68] to childlessness, these women constituted a "discarded group of blighted women,"[69] ashamed to reveal their situation and suffer the severe opprobrium that was then attached to childlessness. The author of a 1941 *Ladies Home Journal* article advised her readers that only a small percentage of childless couples did not want children and sympathized with infertile couples whose friends falsely accused them of the selfishness they associated with the deliberately childless.[70] In a 1946 article, the woman author whose own infertility was medically unexplained observed that women had "inadvertently freed themselves from the cradle" by demanding "emancipation from the kitchen." Consistent with physicians' new focus on women's unconscious will in the etiology of infertility, the author found that she was able to conceive only after she stopped striving for a career and started leading the domestic life prescribed for women.[71] By 1958, the idea that the infertile, particularly women, were in some measure to blame for their childless state was pervasive enough to cause more enlightened medical experts to state that the infertile were no more responsible for their infertility than individuals afflicted with other diseases.[72] These physicians underscored that there were childless women who really had done nothing to cause their childless state.

The infertile women who wrote to Dr. John Rock, a well-known specialist in infertility whose research on artificial methods of conception was widely publicized in the 1940s and 1950s, revealed the desperation, shame, and ridicule they endured. Begging him to use their bodies in experiments or to find women willing to bear their husbands' children, these women wrote of the frustration, marital conflict, and isolation they felt because they could not reproduce.[73] One particularly "bruised and battle-scarred" woman

[68] Taeuber (n. 52 above), 217.

[69] B. B. Weinstein, "The Surgical Management of the Tubal Factor in Sterility," *Southern Surgeon* 14 (August 1948): 556–61, esp. 560.

[70] G. Palmer, "Plan for Parenthood," *Ladies Home Journal* 58 (September 1941): 28, 54, 56–58, esp. 28, 58.

[71] "We Wanted a Baby," *Ladies Home Journal* 63 (March 1946): 28–29.

[72] C. L. Buxton and A. L. Southam, *Human Infertility* (New York: Hoeber-Harper, 1958).

[73] Based on an uncataloged collection of over one hundred sets (including replies) of letters, written primarily by infertile women to John Rock and his associate, Dr. Miriam Menkin, at the Free Hospital for Women in Brookline, Mass., between 1943 and 1957. Also included in this correspondence are letters from sterile men, other physicians providing case reports, one would-be grandfather, one woman

remarked that it was hard to keep living and that she was an "outcast with mothers." Raging over the lack of sympathy and help for the infertile when sympathy was so easily aroused by the "armless, legless, blind or deaf," she asked whether "a city of childless people" might be developed "where they can hold their heads as high as anyone." These women wrote to Rock to plead their "very personal case," to mitigate the "stigma" of sterility, and to "explain . . . how it hurts."[74]

Strange bedfellows: Fertility and freedom, infertility and feminism

In 1933, physician Alan Guttmacher noted that fertility and sterility provided "provocative material for the eugenicist, the chauvinist, and the social scientist."[75] More recently Congress-woman Patricia Schroeder observed that infertility has been "a closet problem with a few bursts of sensationalized attention."[76] There has been renewed concern in the 1970s and 1980s about the reproductive price of women's expanded freedoms. Contemporary literature on infertility continues the theme of female volition, a modern convergence of the ideas that infertility is in part a consequence of deliberate efforts to thwart instinct and nature and that it is a manifestation of disguised will. Frequent references to women's new opportunities and sexual freedoms continue the century-old link between women's emancipation, women's repro-ductive capacities, and the public welfare. Women are still reminded of the basic incompatibility of reproductive freedom and reproductive health and of the tragedy they court when they delay having the "multiple pregnancies nature undoubtedly intended."[77] Even fertile women's choice of abortion over adoption as a

---

offering to be a surrogate, and one from a man offering to donate his sperm. The letters, from all over the United States, with six from Canada, France, Australia, and Mexico, were largely responses to articles in newspapers and in journals, including *Your Health, Science Digest, Look, Time, Newsweek, Coronet,* and *Collier's,* that promised "test-tube" and other solutions to childlessness. These letters are part of the John Rock collection at Countway Library, Boston. I thank Richard Wolfe and Anne Needham for access to these letters.

[74] A. M. to John Rock, Chicago, March 26, 1957, and April 6, 1957; F. H. to John Rock, Connecticut, January 24, 1946; T. C. to John Rock, Fort Wayne, Ind., February 8, 1950; John Rock to M.R., Illinois, October 23, 1945.

[75] A. F. Guttmacher, *Life in the Making* (New York: Viking, 1933), 221.

[76] Schroeder (n. 4 above), 765.

[77] T. H. Green, *Gynecology: Essentials of Clinical Practice,* 3d ed. (Boston: Little, Brown, 1977), 331.

solution to unwanted pregnancies has emerged as an act of will that has lowered the supply of available infants and, therefore, increased the demand for technological solutions to infertility.[78] Sterilization "regret" and increasing demands for sterilization reversals are phenomena that have served to affirm the role of volition in creating involuntary childlessness.[79] "Baby craving" and "baby hunger" are the new consequences of the deliberate and unconscious thwarting of the female instinct to reproduce.[80]

The infertile, according to one physician, are still viewed as "traitors to mankind" and "fighting nature," portrayals of the infertile identical to those of a century ago.[81] In a discussion of social policy and infertility, Harriet Simons noted the victim blaming that still influences the way Americans view those affected by the dysfunction.[82] Recent studies of the social milieu of the infertile document the stigmatization and blaming they continue to suffer in the form of advice that reflects the misconceptions that if they only tried harder, or did not try so hard, or had sex the right way, or had the right mental attitude, or really wanted a child, a pregnancy would result.[83] Contemporary psychological literature also continues to conflate voluntary and involuntary infertility and to suggest that infertile women who seek help to achieve motherhood may not really want it, might share with their voluntarily childless counterparts a reluctance to conceive, or might be protected by their infertility from unconscious maternal role conflicts.[84] Some investigators have suggested that where psychological studies fail to uncover emotional problems in the infertile, the problem may lie in the failure of instruments to detect subtle differences or in a

---

[78] *Infertility: Medical and Social Choices* (n. 1 above), esp. 55–56.

[79] G. S. Grubbs, H. B. Peterson, P. M. Layde, and G. L. Rubin, "Regret after Decision to Have a Tubal Sterilization," *Fertility and Sterility* 44 (1985): 248–53.

[80] Quindlen (n. 4 above); L. L. Davitz, *Baby Hunger: Every Woman's Longing for a Baby* (Minneapolis: Winston, 1984).

[81] Bellina and Wilson (n. 2 above), xvi.

[82] H. F. Simons, "Infertility: Implications for Policy Formulation," in *Infertility: Medical, Emotional, and Social Considerations*, ed. M. D. Mazor and H. F. Simons (New York: Human Sciences Press, 1984), esp. 61–70.

[83] C. E. Miall, "The Stigma of Involuntary Childlessness," *Social Problems* 33 (April 1986): 268–82; and M. Sandelowski and L. C. Jones, "Social Exchanges of Infertile Women," *Issues in Mental Health Nursing* 8 (1986): 173–89.

[84] J. R. Allison, "Roles and Role Conflict of Women in Infertile Couples," *Psychology of Women Quarterly* 4 (1979): 97–113; M. E. Pawson, "The Infertile Patient—Does She Always Want a Baby?" in *Research on Fertility and Sterility*, ed. J. Cortes-Trieto, A. Campos da Paz, and M. Neves-e-Castro (Baltimore: University Park Press, 1981), 437–44; D. L. Poston, "Characteristics of Voluntarily and Involuntarily Childless Wives," *Social Biology* 23 (1976): 198–209; Van Hall (n. 9 above), esp. 359–68.

distortion of infertile subjects' scores in the direction of greater social desirability because of their wish to appear normal.[85]

In addition, there is a new kind of failure of volition attributable to infertile women and couples that is most significantly illustrated in some feminist work.[86] Feminists critical of the new conceptive technology and certain surrogacy and adoption arrangements suggest misguided volition on the part of infertile women, a failure of will associated not with causing infertility but with seeking solutions for it deemed hazardous to other women. The infertile woman who cannot choose to have a child at will threatens the idea of free reproductive choice for women. Struggling to ensure the right of women to choose against motherhood, feminists are now increasingly aware of the woman who is not free to opt *for* motherhood. Beyond being politically useful as evidence for women's oppressive socialization to become mothers and their continued subservience to institutionalized medicine, infertile women occupy no more empathic place in many current feminist discussions than in the medical and ethical debates on reproductive technology feminists criticize. Like the mid-twentieth-century medical clinicians who equated reproductive outcome with reproductive desire, some feminist writers equate women's desire for children with their oppression as women, viewing this desire and the anguish women feel when it remains unfulfilled as socially constructed rather than authentically experienced. Like the contemporary infertility specialists feminists describe who exploit infertile women by encouraging their participation in ineffective treatment programs, some feminists exploit these women by implicating them in a patriarchal project aimed at dividing and destroying women. In both cases,

[85] A. M. O'Moore, R. R. O'Moore, R. F. Harrison, G. Murphy, and M. E. Carruthers, "Psychosomatic Aspects in Idiopathic Infertility: Effects of Treatment with Autogenic Training," *Journal of Psychosomatic Research* 27 (1983): 145–51; and P. Slade, "Sexual Attitudes and Social Role Orientations in Infertile Women," *Journal of Psychosomatic Research* 25 (1981): 183–86.

[86] See "Manipulative Reproductive Technologies," in *The Custom-Made Child? Women-Centered Perspectives*, ed. H. B. Holmes, B. B. Hoskins, and M. Gross (Clifton, N.J.: Humana, 1981), 227–300; "Special Issue: Reproductive and Genetic Engineering," *Women's Studies International Forum*, vol. 8, no. 6 (1985); R. Arditti, R. D. Klein, and S. Minden, eds., *Test-Tube Women: What Future for Motherhood?* (London: Pandora, 1984); G. Corea, *The Mother Machine: Reproductive Technologies from Artificial Insemination to Artificial Wombs* (New York: Harper & Row, 1985); A. Donchin, "The Future of Mothering: Reproductive Technology and Feminist Theory," *Hypatia* 1 (1986): 121–37; R. Rowland, "Technology and Motherhood: Reproductive Choice Reconsidered," *Signs: Journal of Women in Culture and Society* 12, no. 3 (Spring 1987): 512–28; and J. M. Stanworth, ed., *Reproductive Technologies: Gender, Motherhood and Medicine* (Minneapolis: University of Minnesota Press, 1987).

women's desires and their agency are distorted and reconstructed to represent neither the wishes nor choices themselves but rather the socialization that feminist probing and consciousness-raising can reveal and change. Accordingly, infertile women and couples often find themselves at a utilitarian-deontological moral impasse, the principle of the greatest good for the greatest number competing with the principle of individual rights and duties. Some feminists suggest that what the infertile perceive as a right to children is no right at all. They suggest that infertile couples consider measuring their anguish against the greater pain and suffering of the relinquishing birth mothers whose children they want to adopt and of the poor and the disabled who will suffer if technological advancements in reproduction and the current adoption and surrogacy process continue to be informed by racist, classist, and eugenic motivations.[87]

Infertility and infertile women themselves challenge ideas of reproductive choice and control by underscoring the biological limits of reproductive freedom for women. They also challenge feminist efforts to at once celebrate women's unique biologic capacities and reject this uniqueness as defining. What the historical dialogue about infertility suggests is the need to avoid grounding positions on the new conceptive technology and alternative parenting arrangements on a foundation of blame and instead to address infertility itself as a source of real (rather than socially constructed) sorrow. By not doing so, even well-intended advocates for women will continue inadvertently to align themselves with those who have over the past century burdened the infertile woman with their concerns about women's gains. In the meantime, the infertile woman remains caught in the crossfire, perceived as both the creator of and martyr to her childlessness.

School of Nursing
University of North Carolina at Chapel Hill

[87] P. Chesler, *Sacred Bond: The Legacy of Baby M* (New York: Time Books, 1988); R. Hubbard, "Test-Tube Babies: Solution or Problem?" in *Elements of Argument: A Text and Reader*, ed. A. T. Rottenberg (New York: St. Martin's, 1985), esp. 365–71; P. Spallone and D. L. Steinberg, eds., *Made to Order: The Myth of Reproductive and Genetic Progress* (New York: Pergamon, 1987). For a more detailed discussion of the problems with some feminist arguments, see M. Sandelowski, "Faultlines: Infertility and Imperiled Sisterhood," *Feminist Studies*, vol. 16, no. 1 (Spring 1990).

A CASE OF MATERNITY: PARADIGMS OF WOMEN AS MATERNITY CASES

ANN OAKLEY

There is no miracle more cruel than this.
I am dragged by the horses, the iron hooves,
I last. I last it out. I accomplish a work.
Dark tunnel, through which hurtle the visitations,
The visitations, the manifestations, the startled faces.
I am the centre of an atrocity.
What pains, what sorrows must I be mothering?[1]

> "Where's my baby? asked Martha anxiously.
> "She's having a nice rest," said the nurse, already on her way out.
> "But I haven't seen her yet," said Martha, real tears behind her lids.
> "You don't want to disturb her, do you?" said the nurse disapprovingly.
> The door shut. The woman, whose long full breast sloped already into the baby's mouth, looked up and said, "You'd better do as they want, dear. It saves trouble. They've got their own ideas."[2]

This essay concerns the ways in which science, whether medical or social, has approached, described, and defined the task of women as childbearers.[3] Drawing on a variety of data—a five-year involvement in a sociological research project on childbirth; observation of medical maternity

---

1. S. Plath, "Three Women," in *Winter Trees* (London: Faber & Faber, 1971), p. 44.

2. D. Lessing, *A Proper Marriage* (London: Granada Publishing, Panther, 1966), p. 167.

3. I have tried to make what I say relevant to North America, but it is inevitably skewed toward British literature and practice.

This essay originally appeared in *Signs*, vol. 4, no. 4, Summer 1979.

work; general, though nonsystematic reading of the relevant psychological/psychiatric and sociological literature—I attempt to unravel some components of the techniques by which women as childbearers have been assigned their place. The result has a certain ambiguity, since what the essay "reviews" is not so much the literature of each discipline, though I have tried to give some pointers, but the manner in which childbearing as a natural activity has been accorded, through scientific translation, a specific cultural status.

Childbirth stands uncomfortably at the junction of the two worlds of nature and culture. A biological event, it is accomplished by social beings—women—who consequently possess a uniquely dual character. In bearing children, women both "accomplish a work" and become "the centre of an atrocity" in Sylvia Plath's words. Childbirth is a constant reminder of the association between women's "nature" and nature "herself"; it must become a social act, since society is threatened by the disorder of what is beyond its jurisdiction. The cultural need to socialize childbirth impinges on the free agency of women who are constrained by definitions of womanhood that give maternity an urgency they may not feel. Thus, just how reproduction has been socially constructed is of prime importance to any consideration of women's position. It may even be in motherhood that we can trace the diagnosis and prognosis of female oppression.[4] Medical science, clinical psychiatry and psychology, and to a lesser extent academic psychology and sociology, are fields in which the function of women as childbearers constitutes legitimate "subject matter." To map out the paradigms of women extant in these areas is to propose a view of science as ideology—as a particular cultural production and representation.[5] Science constructs the culture of childbirth in the industrialized world, as the belief systems of nonindustrialized prescientific societies provoke a plethora of different and (to us) exotic childbirth styles.

As Martha Knowell in Doris Lessing's *A Proper Marriage* becomes aware, the medical managers of childbirth have "their own ideas." Though the organization of hospital maternity work reflects these ideas, they are rarely explicit. One important aspect of medical attitudes toward childbirth is their concealment behind a screen of what purport to be exclusively clinical concerns. Analyzing data from two separate research projects on the medical and social treatment of childbearing women, Hilary Graham and I[6] have outlined the model of reproduction

4. See *Woman, Culture and Society*, ed. M. Z. Rosaldo and L. Lamphere (Stanford, Calif.: Stanford University Press, 1974), especially the papers by N. Chodorow and S. Ortner.

5. See T. S. Kuhn, *The Structure of Scientific Revolutions* (Chicago: University of Chicago Press, 1962).

6. H. Graham and A. Oakley, "Competing Ideologies of Reproduction: Medical and Maternal Perspectives on Pregnancy and Childbirth," in *Women and Health Care*, ed. H. Roberts (London: Routledge & Kegan Paul, 1979), in press.

and its agents—women—that informs medical attitudes to pregnancy and childbirth. Our argument is based on depth interviews with several hundred women having babies in York and London and on detailed observation in maternity hospitals and clinics. Obstetrics is viewed by its practitioners as a specialist subject in which, by virtue of the expertise conferred through specialist medical education, "doctor knows best." The defining characteristic of the corpus of "knowledge" which constitutes obstetrics is its claim to superiority over the expertise possessed by the reproducers themselves. "Obstetrics" originally described a female province. The female control of reproduction is cross-culturally and historically by far the most dominant arrangement. It has, in the industrial world, been transformed into a system of male control.[7] Some medical histories that detail the ascendency of male obstetrics unwittingly evidence this ideological element,[8] but the field in general has been little explored. The Ehrenreich-English pamphlet[9] and Barker-Benfield's[10] analysis of the rise of American gynecology are the best-known accounts of sexual ideology in the reproductive care takeover.

The male obstetricians' claim to monopolize all relevant knowledge developed alongside the control of physical and technical resources (hospital beds, machines for monitoring the progress of pregnancy and labor, the technology of abnormal deliveries—cesarean sections, forceps, ventouse extraction, and so forth) necessary to the care of women during birth within a medical system. The status of reproduction as a medical subject also implies that obstetricians see pregnancy and birth as analogous to other physiological processes as topics of medical knowledge and treatment. Such a view is necessary to fit reproduction into the category of human concerns in which doctors can exercise and enforce their jurisdiction. (In this sense, childbirth is just one more casualty of the "medicalization" of life.)[11] The ideological transformation of the "natural" (having babies) to the cultural (becoming an obstetric patient)

7. See A. Oakley, "Wisewoman and Medicine Man: Changes in the Management of Childbirth," in *The Rights and Wrongs of Women,* ed. J. Mitchell and A. Oakley (Harmondsworth: Penguin Books, 1976). The fact that the medical obstetric care system is controlled by men and by a masculine ideology does not, of course, preclude the incorporation of female obstetricians as a minority group within that system.

8. For example, H. R. Spencer, *The History of British Midwifery from 1650 to 1800* (London: John Bale, Sons & Danielsson, 1927); T. R. Forbes, *The Midwife and the Witch* (New Haven, Conn.: Yale University Press, 1966).

9. B. Ehrenreich and D. English, *Witches, Midwives and Nurses* (New York: Feminist Press, Glass Mountain Pamphlets, 1973).

10. G. J. Barker-Benfield, *The Horrors of the Half-known Life* (New York: Harper & Row, 1976). M. H. Verbrugge provides a general survey of research on medicine and women in "Women and Medicine in Nineteenth-Century America," *Signs: Journal of Women in Culture and Society* 1 (Summer 1976): 957–72.

11. See E. Freidson, *Profession of Medicine* (New York: Dodd, Mead & Co., 1970), p. 251.

is difficult, since obstetricians must deal with the fact that 97 percent[12] of women are able to deliver babies safely and without problems. The process of reconciliation exposes the contradiction. As but one example states: "Difficulties may arise if it is forgotten that, *however natural the processes of pregnancy, delivery and the pueperium should be* in an ideal world, the fact remains that in no aspect of life is the dividing line between the normal and the abnormal narrower than in obstetrics. Seconds of time, an ill-judged decision or lack of facilities, experience or skill, can separate joy from disaster. The safety and efficiency of a maternity service depends largely on recognition of these facts."[13] Other devices for underlining the medical character of reproduction include treating all pregnant women in the same way regardless of the fact that only a few will develop complications; providing institutional, not domiciliary, delivery care; routinizing the frequent use of technological, pharmacological, and clinical procedures; fragmenting reproductive care by separating obstetrics from pediatrics[14] and aligning it with gynecology which treats the diseases of female biology.

In accordance with the emphasis on physiology, the criteria of reproductive success within the medical paradigm are defined in terms of perinatal and maternal mortality rates, and, to a lesser extent, certain indices of maternal and infant morbidity. This restricted interpretation of successful reproductive outcome insists that maternal satisfaction with the childbearing experience should be complete if both mother and baby survive without major impairment to their physical health. Other measures of success, such as the woman's emotional reactions to the experience of childbirth and its management, are not considered relevant. In general, the medical separation of reproduction from its social context ensures a limited status for the reproducer herself. The opening of a chapter on the induction of labor illustrates the dominant medical mode of "conceiving" women as baby-containers:

> The fascination of the uterus to pharmacologists lies in the fact that its behavior varies from day to day and almost from minute to minute, the very reason that it has largely been abandoned in despair by physiologists. It is illogical to consider the problem of the induction of labor in lonely isolation, seeing that the physiochemical changes which then occur in and about the myometrial cells are but an extension and modification of those which occur during each

12. This figure is cited by the Dutch obstetrician G. J. Kloosterman.

13. J. Stallworthy, "Management of the Hospital Confinement," in *Modern Perspectives in Psycho-Obstetrics*, ed. J. G. Howells (London: Oliver & Boyd, 1972), p. 353 (emphasis added).

14. A separation that is reflected in the medical advice literature which divides books about pregnancy/birth from those about child care.

menstrual cycle. The essential problem is not why or how the uterus expels the fetus, but why it tolerates it for so many months.[15]

In this piece, "uterus" or "cervix" is either the subject or object of the sentence forty-six times, almost twice as often as the word "woman" or "women," thus reducing women to their anatomical organs of reproduction.[16] The sole importance of the social context of reproduction to the medical frame of reference is the impact of social factors (marital status, inadequate housing, "neurotic personality," etc.) on reproductive "efficiency."

Two paradigms of women jostle for first place in the medical model and underlie all the characteristics of the medical approach described. The first sees women not only as passive patients but, in a mechanistic way, also as manipulable reproductive machines. The second appeals to notions of the biologically determined "feminine" female. The "reproductive machine" model has informed much of the technological innovation in obstetrics that has taken place in the twentieth century; indeed the mechanical analogy builds directly on the ideological construction of reproduction as abnormal and unnatural that originally facilitated the medical takeover of reproductive care. The most highly developed (in a technological sense) obstetric style in the 1970s, appropriately known as the "active management of labor," embodies a straight physicalist approach to childbirth. "To put the matter rather crudely, obstetrics treats the body like a complex machine and uses a series of interventionist techniques to repair faults that may develop in the machine."[17] The mechanical model is "man-made" and requires regular servicing to function correctly. Thus antenatal care becomes maintenance and malfunction-spotting work, and obstetrical intervention in delivery equals the repair of mechanical faults with mechanical skills. Concretely, as well as ideologically, women appear to become ma-

15. G. W. Theobald, "The Induction of Labour," in *Obstetric Therapeutics,* ed. D. F. Hawkins (London: Baillière Tindall Publishers, 1974), p. 341. See also W. Hern, "Is Pregnancy Really Normal?" *Family Planning Perspectives* 3 (1971): 5–10.

16. It could be argued that these are characteristics of *patienthood* generally. But medical typifications of women do seem to be different from those of men. See, for example, G. V. Stimson, "G.P.'s, 'Trouble,' and Types of Patient," in *The Sociology of the National Health Service,* Sociological Review Monograph no. 22, ed. M. Stacey (Keele, Staffordshire: University of Keele, 1976), and E. Frankfort, *Vaginal Politics* (New York: Quadrangle Books, 1972). Among those who have looked at the effect of perceived status on doctor-patient interaction are D. G. Fish ("An Obstetric Unit in a London Hospital: A Study of Relations between Patients, Doctors and Nurses" [Ph.D. diss., University of London, 1966]), and S. Macintyre ("Who Wants Babies? The Social Construction of Instincts," in *Sexual Divisions and Society: Process and Change,* ed. D. L. Barker and S. Allen [London: Tavistock Publications, 1976]).

17. M. Richards, "Innovation in Medical Practice: Obstetricians and the Induction of Labour in Britain," *Social Science and Medicine* 9 (1975): 598.

chines,[18] as machines are increasingly used to monitor pregnancy and labor and to initiate and terminate labor itself. One machine controls the uterine contractions that are recorded on another machine; regional anesthesia removes the woman's awareness of her contractions so that they must be read off the machine, and patient care comes to mean keeping all the machines going.

But human and mechanical images are discordant. Hence the need to monitor carefully the amount and type of information "fed" to pregnant women. The mechanical metaphor sharpens into an analogy with a computer, for it is only by the careful selection and coding of information that computers can be made to function correctly. The main vehicle for the programming of women as maternity patients is antenatal advice literature. The evolution of this literature in Britain has reflected closely the chronology of expanding medical jurisdiction over birth.[19] Today the emphasis is on the need for women to be informed about the physiology of pregnancy and labor. Yet a clear dividing line is drawn between desirable and undesirable information: the first two sections in Gordon Bourne's widely read *Pregnancy*[20] are entitled "Importance of Information" and "Don't Read Medical Textbooks." Conflict between doctor and patient in the antenatal clinic or the delivery room is interpreted as the doctor's failure effectively to communicate his intentions to the patient (failure to program the computer correctly). A leading article in the *British Medical Journal* put it this way: "The fact that a procedure such as induction of labor, done in good faith for the good of the mother and her baby, had been so misrepresented by the media, was unlikely to be due to some malign purpose, but was more probably disquieting evidence that doctors *were not adequately communicating their intentions to their patients*. . . . The modern woman still wishes to have faith in her doctor—to believe that she can hand over to him, without anxiety, the care of herself, and *more important,* that of her baby."[21]

18. The technical-medical concept of "uterine dysfunction" expresses this idea. Interestingly the first apparatus used in Britain for the automated induction of labor was known as "William"—not "Mary." For a discussion of some of the cross-cultural variations in, and consequences of, interventionist techniques, see I. Chalmers and M. Richards, "Intervention and Causal Inference in Obstetric Practice," in *Benefits and Hazards of the New Obstetrics,* ed. T. Chard and M. Richards (Philadelphia: J. B. Lippincott Co., 1977).

19. A point made by H. Graham ("Images of Pregnancy in Antenatal Literature," in *Health Care and Health Knowledge,* ed. R. Dingwald et al. [London: Croom Helm, Ltd., 1977]). Antenatal advice literature in the United States has had the same character as in Britain, but it seems to have moved more quickly toward a legitimation of the idea that women are people too (see C. A. Bean, *Methods of Childbirth* [New York: Doubleday & Co., 1972], and A. F. Guttmacher, *Pregnancy, Birth and Family Planning* [New York: Viking Press, 1973]). *MS* magazine carried a review of antenatal literature in its December 1973 issue (pp. 101–3).

20. G. Bourne, *Pregnancy* (London: Pan Books, 1975).

21. "Induction of Labour," *British Medical Journal* 27 (March 1976): 729 (emphasis added).

The multiple appearances of the mechanical model in antenatal literature, in medical writing, and in medical practice generally, simultaneously embody a commitment to notions of the feminine woman:

A woman's basic personality will not be changed during her pregnancy, but subtle and minor changes will certainly occur. All women tend to become emotionally unstable at times when their hormone levels are at their highest, such as puberty, pregnancy, the menopause and also immediately before the onset of each menstrual period. It is well known that the majority of impetuous actions and crimes committed by women occur during the week immediately before menstruation.[22]

A woman can never escape her ultimate biologic destiny, reproduction, and a goodly number of psychologic problems encountered in the course of pregnancy are the result of conflicts concerning this biologic destiny.[23]

Doctor: "How many babies have you got?"
Patient: "This is the third pregnancy."
Doctor: "Doing your duty, aren't you?"[24]

The principal import of the feminine model is that a "proper," that is, truly feminine, woman wants to grow and give birth to and care for babies. She regards this, along with marriage, as her main vocation in life. Such women "adapt" or "adjust" well to pregnancy, birth, and motherhood, experience deep "maternal" feelings for their babies and are able to integrate successfully the competing demands of motherhood and wifehood. It follows that the femininity of those women who do not achieve these goals is suspect.[25]

This feminine paradigm of women is presented in parallel with two other ideological tendencies: a hostility to female culture and an identification with masculine interests. The first point is best explained through quotation. "Another hidden anxiety is a fear of the pain of childbirth. All too often the young mother is told of the gruesome imagined experience of older women. . . ."[26] ". . . An effort should be made to

22. Bourne, p. 3.

23. M. Heiman, "A Psychoanalytic View of Pregnancy," in *Medical, Surgical and Gynecological Complications of Pregnancy*, ed. J. J. Rovinsky and A. F. Guttmacher (Baltimore: Williams & Wilkins Co., 1965), p. 473.

24. One cameo from the hospital observations I carried out in 1974–75 as part of a research project on medical and social experiences of motherhood ("Transition to Motherhood: Social and Medical Aspects of First Childbirth," funded by and available from the Social Science Research Council, London).

25. See, for example, L. Chertok, *Motherhood and Personality* (London: Tavistock Publications, 1969).

26. D. Llewellyn-Jones, *Fundamentals of Obstetrics and Gynaecology*, vol. 1, *Obstetrics* (London: Faber & Faber, 1965), p. 65.

restrain or rebuke the parous women who relate their unpleasant experiences to the unsuspecting primigravida."[27] "Why do women have to recount such stories to one another, especially when the majority of them are blatantly untrue? . . . Probably more is done by wicked women with their malicious lying tongues to harm the confidence and happiness of pregnant women than by any other single factor. . . . Perhaps it is some form of sadism. . . ."[28] There is an obvious conflict between the obstetrician's knowledge about reproduction and the received wisdom of women who have actually given birth. The tension between maternal and medical expertise is thematic to modern obstetrics; one medical response is the "husband identification" discerned by Scully and Bart[29] in their survey of women in gynecology textbooks. In one development, that of the "husband-coached childbirth," the husband becomes the doctor's representative and takes over the role of programming the patient for birth.[30]

The prominence of the feminine paradigm in medical attitudes to reproduction has stimulated an enormous amount of research. For example, infertility,[31] habitual abortion, and premature delivery have been analyzed as psychosomatic defenses as a result of a woman's hostile identification with her mother, as a rejection of the feminine role, as a failure to achieve feminine maturity, and as evidence of disturbed sexual relationships with husbands/boyfriends.[32] Much the same hypotheses have been applied to the study of other complications of pregnancy and labor—for example, nausea and vomiting, toxaemia, uterine "dysfunction" in labor—and to the status of the child (its physical condition and behavior) after birth.[33] Grimm[34] has described a great

27. A. E. B. Matthews, "Behaviour Patterns in Labour," *Journal of Obstetrics and Gynaecology of the British Commonwealth* 6 (1961): 874.

28. Bourne, p. 7.

29. D. Scully and P. Bart, "A Funny Thing Happened on the Way to the Orifice: Women in Gynecology Textbooks," *American Journal of Sociology* 78 (January 1973): 1045.

30. R. A. Bradley, *Husband-coached Childbirth* (New York: Harper & Row, 1974).

31. Some such studies are B. B. Rubenstein, "An Emotional Factor in Infertility," *Fertility and Sterility* 2 (1950): 80; E. S. C. Ford et al., "A Psychodynamic Approach to the Study of Infertility," *Fertility and Sterility* 4 (1953): 456; and T. E. Mandy and A. J. Mandy, "The Psychosomatic Aspects of Infertility," *Sinai Hospital Journal* (1959), p. 28.

32. E. C. Mann and E. R. Grimm, "Habitual Abortion," in *Psychosomatic Obstetrics, Gynecology and Endocrinology,* ed. W. S. Kroger (Springfield, Ill.: Charles C. Thomas, 1962); C. Tupper and K. J. Weil, 'The Problem of Spontaneous Abortion," *American Journal of Obstetrics and Gynecology* 83 (1962): 421; A. Blau et al., "The Psychogenic Etiology of Premature Birth, a Preliminary Report," *Psychosomatic Medicine* 25 (1963): 201.

33. For instance, see W. S. Kroger and S. T. DeLee, "The Psychosomatic Treatment of Hyperemesis Gravidarum by Hypnosis," *American Journal of Obstetrics and Gynecology* 51 (1946): 544; W. A. Harvey and M. J. Sherfey, "Vomiting in Pregnancy: A Psychiatric Study," *Psychosomatic Medicine* 16 (1954): 1; A. J. Coppen, "Psychosomatic Aspects of Pre-Eclamptic Toxaemia," *Journal of Psychosomatic Research* 2 (1958): 241; W. A. Crammond, "Psychological Aspects of Uterine Dysfunction," *Lancet* 2 (1954): 1241; D. H. Stott, "Psy-

deal of this research and has pointed out its methodological flaws. Many studies, for example, are retrospective, taking a group of women in whom some pathology of physiology has been identified and then investigating them in isolation from any control group. Prospective research on "normal" women (those without identifiable physiological pathology) itself suffers from a failure to assess personality variables before pregnancy (for example, a woman who is ambivalent about her pregnancy may already be reacting to uncomfortable physical experiences). The psychological variables themselves have a dubious status. How reliable and how valid are the measures employed?

The search for links between femininity and reproduction has also taken psychological "adjustment" to pregnancy, birth, and motherhood as the relevant outcome variable. Indeed, such medical-psychiatric literature is the main repository of psychological research on women. Feminist psychologists have sketched out the place of women in psychology as, in most respects, a mirror image of their ideological, social, and economic location in a male-dominated culture.[35]

Within this context, psychological aspects of reproduction are liable to be treated as epiphenomena of women's physiological status. The cycle of maternity is interpreted as a period of increased vulnerability which may predispose a woman to emotional breakdown. The causal mechanisms that operate are seen in two ways: either as physiological changes that cause psychological problems, or as psychological problems that result from intrapsychic conflict (expressed in terms of a feminine personality structure) due to the stress of reproduction. Postnatal depression may, for example, be attributed to postpartum hormone status,[36] or it may be laid at the door of unresolved conflicts concerning "acceptance of the feminine role."[37] What is left out of the reckoning are

chological and Mental Handicaps in the Child Following a Disturbed Pregnancy," *Lancet* 1 (1957): 1006.

34. E. R. Grimm, "Psychological and Social Factors in Pregnancy, Delivery and Outcome," in *Childbearing—Its Social and Psychological Aspects*, ed. S. A. Richardson and A. F. Guttmacher (Baltimore: Williams & Wilkins, 1967).

35. N. Weisstein, " 'Kinder, Kuche, Kirche' as Scientific Law: Psychology Constructs the Female," in *Sisterhood Is Powerful*, ed. R. Morgan (New York: Vintage Books, 1970); J. A. Sherman, *On the Psychology of Women: A Survey of Empirical Studies* (Springfield, Ill.: Charles C. Thomas, 1971); M. B. Parlee, "Review Essay: Psychology," *Signs: Journal of Women in Culture and Society* 1 (Autumn 1975): 119–38; M. B. Parlee, "Psychological Aspects of Menstruation, Childbirth and Menopause," in *Psychology of Women: Future Directions of Research*, ed. J. A. Sherman and F. L. Denmark (New York: Psychological Dimensions, Inc., forthcoming). I have drawn extensively on Parlee's valuable critique in the latter essay.

36. K. Dalton, "Prospective Study into Puerperal Depression," *British Journal of Psychiatry* 118 (1971): 689–92.

37. O. Ostwald and P. Regan, "Psychiatric Disorders Associated with Childbirth," *Journal of Nervous and Mental Diseases* 125 (1957): 153–65.

the social correlates of postnatal depression. There has, for example, been almost no work on the incidence of postnatal depression in home as opposed to hospital confinements;[38] very few researchers consider the impact of sleep disturbance,[39] exhaustion, social isolation, work overload, etc., on a woman's feelings after the birth of a child. This is all the more surprising in the light of the findings of various studies that mental health symptoms in pregnancy and postpartum do not relate particularly well to one another. Pregnancy symptoms do not predict postpartum symptoms. There appears to be a different etiology to each.[40] Research has tended to focus, once again, on women who have, or have had, postnatal depression, rather than including a control group of women who have not been similarly afflicted.

Markham reports one attempt to remedy this methodological weakness. She followed up a study of eleven patients with postnatal depression by taking a second group of women who had not been classified as suffering from it. She found that they all gave evidence of a depressive reaction also. "The important distinction," she concluded, "between the normal and pathological women was not the fact that both were experiencing depressive reactions but that the normal mothers were able to draw upon a vast arsenal of defenses to ward off or alleviate their depressive feelings."[41] Although Markham concentrates on psychodynamic defenses, one might reasonably ask about the role of social supports in preventing a diagnosis of postnatal depression.[42]

38. Virginia Larsen asked a sample of women for their accounts of pregnancy and postpartum stresses and found that many noted stressful experiences associated with hospitalization (V. L. Larsen, "Stresses of the Childbearing Years," *American Journal of Public Health* 56 [1966]: 32–36). B. A. Cone, in a study of Cardiff women, found that whereas 64 percent of hospital-delivered women classed themselves as depressed after delivery, only 19 percent of the home-delivered women did ("Puerperal Depression" in *Psychosomatic Medicine in Obstetrics and Gynaecology*, ed. N. Morris [Basel: S. Karger, 1972]).

39. I. Karacan and R. L. Williams have studied sleep patterns during pregnancy and the postpartum period and have suggested that sleep disturbance may play a role in the etiology of postnatal depression ("Current Advances in Theory and Practice Relating to Postpartum Syndromes," *Psychiatry in Medicine* 1 [1970]: 307–28).

40. This is reported by A. Nilsson and P. E. Almgren, "Paranatal Emotional Adjustment: A Prospective Investigation of 165 Women," *Acta Psychiatrica Scandinavica. Supplement* 220 (1970): 1–141, and by E. Zajicek, "Development of Women Having Their First Child" (paper delivered at the Annual Conference of the British Psychological Association, York, 1976).

41. S. Markham, "A Comparison of Psychotic and Normal Postpartum Reactions Based on Psychological Tests," in *Premier Congrès international de médecine psychosomatique et maternité*, Société Française de Médecine Psychosomatique (Paris: Gauthier-Villars, 1965).

42. K. B. Nuckolls, J. Cassel, and B. H. Kaplan found that close social relationships with family and friends help to protect against the development of stress symptoms in pregnancy ("Psychosocial Assets, Life Crises, and the Prognosis of Pregnancy," *American Journal of Epidemiology* 95 [1972]: 431–41). The relationship between work and postnatal depression has been largely ignored. E. E. Le Masters ("Parenthood as Crisis," *Marriage and Family Living* 19 [1957]: 352–55) reports that the postpartum reaction of professional women who give up work is exceptionally severe. G. W. Brown and T. Harris (*Social Origins*

Liakos,[43] investigating the four-day "blues" in a sample of Greek women, found that this particular postnatal disturbance was less likely to occur if the mother had either her own mother or her mother-in-law to help after the birth of the child.

In pronouncements about the etiology of postnatal depression and other mental/emotional difficulties which occur during pregnancy and the postpartum period, conceptual formulations of femininity are notably vague, or confused, or both. To take one instance of this, Nilsson, in a survey of paranatal emotional adjustment,[44] reports that women with postpartum adaptational difficulties displayed a tendency toward "denial of their reproductive functions" as measured by the presence of "symptoms from the genital sphere" (for instance, dysmenorrhea) and other relevant symptoms, including late antenatal clinic booking and absence of pregnancy sickness. In other studies,[45] pregnancy sickness is considered a symptom of a rejection of femininity: it seems that the very imprecision of such concepts allows the investigator unlimited license in the interpretation of data. Dysmenorrhea has never been shown to be caused by gender-identity problems and is, as a research concept, itself a victim of the same inadequate conceptualization and loose labeling within a debased psychoanalytic framework.[46] A myopic exclusion of the social and economic context of reproduction allows flexibility in the choice of psychosomatic indices. Thus, for instance, researchers ignore the plausible proposition that late antenatal clinic booking has social causes: a desire to avoid being stigmatized in cases of premarital pregnancy; a dislike of doctors and hospitals; a resentment of the dehumanization of clinic organization (long waiting times, the "assembly line" or "battery hen" feeling); a belief in pregnancy as a "natural," as opposed to medical, process.[47]

In his study Nilsson used a masculinity-femininity scale to assess the orientation of his sample women. This consisted of ten "masculine" and ten "feminine" adjectives from which each woman was invited to choose the five that best, and the five that least, described herself. He found that those women who came out as more masculine than the others reported fewer symptoms during pregnancy and fewer life history symptoms, and

---

of Depression [London: Tavistock Publications, 1978]) report data which show the protective effect of employment on women's mental health.

43. A. Liakos et al., "Depression and Neurotic Symptoms in the Puerperium," in Morris (n. 38 above).

44. A. Nilsson, "Paranatal Emotional Adjustment," in Morris (n. 38 above).

45. For example, that by Kroger and DeLee (n. 33 above).

46. See the review of the relevant literature in M. B. Parlee, "Psychological Aspects of Menstruation, Childbirth and Menopause" (n. 35 above).

47. S. Macintyre, Single and Pregnant (New York: Prodist, 1977); J. B. McKinlay, "Some Aspects of Lower-Class Utilization Behaviour" (Ph.D. diss., University of Aberdeen, 1970); A. Oakley, Becoming a Mother (London: Martin Robertson & Co., 1979).

concluded that masculine women wish to appear healthy and so deny their symptoms. The alternative interpretation is, of course, that cultural femininity is actually (to borrow an analogy) dysfunctional to a problem-free experience of reproduction.[48]

All sorts of signs and symptoms point to failures in femininity development that prognosticate poorly for unproblematic childbirth and adjustment to motherhood in the psychological literature. Chertok,[49] using the concept of a "negativity grid" as an instrument predicting ease or difficulty with childbirth, lists under "womanhood" a profusion of diverse factors: miscarriage, breaking off a love affair, playing boys' games in childhood, and "negative" valuation of sex. Under "abnormal attitudes to motherhood" are included fear of not knowing how to care for the child and problems with sexual intercourse. Why all these factors should be considered to have such an intense relevance to the experience of childbirth, when they clearly can have entirely different origins, associations, and consequences, could be said to constitute a research problem in itself.

Chertok includes "enforced interruption of highly valued employment" as a negative factor. Evidently, though rarely explicitly, rejection of femininity entails, and is entailed by, working or wanting to work outside the home. "In modern western society the rejection of motherhood is in turn reinforced by a demand on the woman to be economically productive. . . . There is no doubt that the emancipation of woman has increased her difficulties."[50] Freud may not have said that anatomy is destiny, but this claim is embedded in much of the psychological research on motherhood. The frequency with which labels such as "adjustment" or "adaptation" stand as synonyms for successful reproductive outcome raises the persistent question: adjustment to what? And the notion that becoming a mother requires such adaptational behavior suggests that what is at issue is a socially coded formula for the production of personalities appropriate to female domesticity. Maternity is reduced, in this category of study, to a mere symbol of the extent to which women are, or are not, enmeshed in a cultural nexus of femininity (which is only one among many meanings of motherhood). That such research conceptually and methodologically parallels the tenets of the existing social order should in itself, as Myrdal[51] and others have noted, raise suspicions about the procedures behind the generation of the data.

48. Alice Rossi has pointed out that, so far as the *physical* dimension of reproduction is concerned, it requires a high level of assertiveness to experience natural childbirth and successful breastfeeding in the United States today ("Maternalism, Sexuality and the New Feminism," in *Contemporary Sexual Behavior: Critical Issues in the 1970s,* ed. J. Zubin and J. Money [Baltimore: Johns Hopkins University Press, 1973]).

49. Chertok (n. 25 above).

50. L. Kaij and A. Nilsson, "Emotional and Psychotic Illness Following Childbirth," in Howells (n. 13 above), p. 381.

51. G. Myrdal, *Objectivity in Social Research* (New York: Pantheon Books, 1969).

The rate at which maladaptation (however measured) to maternity occurs does not necessarily reflect women's problems in becoming mothers. The behavior-producing process and the rate-producing process are, as Kitsuse and Cicourel[52] have pointed out, two differing social facts.

The notion that maladaptation to maternity occurs when women reject their feminine role can be subdivided into the following components: that women dislike menstruation, pregnancy, childbirth, breastfeeding, (hetero)sexual intercourse; their status as wives, husband-servicing work, their husbands; their status as housewives, housework; their status as mothers, childcare work, their children. The use of the word "dislike," as opposed to the emotionally laden "reject" or "deny" exposes the morally condemnatory way in which perfectly reasonable, that is, socially explicable negative attitudes to specific roles/processes/activities, have been interpreted. Approaching these matters with common sense rather than with prejudged normative values about what constitutes feminine womanhood, one might ask, for example, why women should enjoy menstruation or every item of the "femininity rejection" list. Indeed, it is clear that the main reason why women should enjoy or accept these aspects of biological womanhood and cultural femininity is because they are supposed to.

Dana Breen[53] has singled out two alternative perspectives within the psychological literature on motherhood. In the first, reproduction is a hurdle to be overcome: pregnancy is a pathological condition, birth a trial, and a woman's task in becoming a mother is to overcome these obstacles without permanent impairment to her mental health. In the second, which gives a slightly more positive picture, birth represents growth and offers possibilities for personal integration.

The model here is not purely medical but developmental. Yet despite its welcome emphasis on birth as an achievement (a "degree in femininity")[54] rather than a handicap, the framework within which reproduction is analyzed is once again rooted in a psychoanalytic ideology of femininity. For Grete Bibring,[55] one of the most influential proponents of the developmental model, pregnancy is a "normal crisis" (a strangely incongruous notion) in a woman's psychological development. It offers the possibility of growth toward a new goal of feminine maturation. Those women who do not achieve such a goal are, of course, "failures," but to ask what they are failures at is, once more, a political question. Maturational integration of femininity is one response to the

52. J. I. Kitsuse and A. V. Cicourel, "A Note on the Uses of Official Statistics," *Social Problems* 2 (1963): 131–39.

53. D. Breen, *The Birth of a First Child* (London: Tavistock Publications, 1975).

54. A concept referred to by Breen, p. 26.

55. G. Bibring et al., "A Study of the Psychological Processes in Pregnancy and of the Earliest Mother-Child Relationship," *Psychoanalytic Study of the Child* 16 (1961): 22.

stresses of reproduction, but others could include changes in personality structure, in self-concept and relational identities which have the effect of enhancing a perhaps less gender-differentiated sense of individuality.

Two recent psychological studies of the birth of a first child both attempt to revitalize the development model. Breen's study, which makes the essential distinction between the female biological role and the female cultural role (of mother), demonstrates the falsity of the assumed link between traditional femininity and adjustment to motherhood. The most feminine women in her sample were those who encountered problems most often. She concludes: ". . . those women who are most adjusted to childbearing are those who are less enslaved by the experience, have more differentiated, open appraisals of themselves and other people, do not aspire to be the perfect selfless mother . . . and do not experience themselves as passive, the cultural stereotype of femininity."[56] One interpretation of Breen's material is precisely that it is the cultural idealization of motherhood/femininity that poses the greatest dilemma for women in becoming mothers, because their personal experiences of reproduction and motherhood conflict with the cultural paradigm they have been socialized to hold. Breen's attempt to rescue the idea of femininity from the conceptual morass into which many psychological researchers have plunged it is laudable. Yet she ultimately sees no alternative than to ground definitions of femininity and masculinity in the biological substratum of sex differences: femininity equals female nature and adjustment to this nature defines proper femininity.[57]

A similar criticism could be leveled at the other recent psychological study of first childbirth—Shereshefsky and Yarrow's *Psychological Aspects of a First Pregnancy and Early Postnatal Adaptation.*[58] The equation that informs this work is between acceptance of the motherhood role and acceptance of the baby, an equation which begs the unanswered question of what the motherhood role consists of in the minds of the researchers and whether this is in tune with the experiences of the women actually having babies. Nevertheless, many of the conclusions Shereshefsky and Yarrow are able to draw out of their material pose a challenge to the older psychological formulae for maternal success. For example, the role of husbands in taking over some child-care work proved crucial to the women's adaptation, and the women's own previous experience with children proved the only "life history" factor of relevance to outcome. Shereshefsky and Yarrow also observe that the responsibility women are allocated for children's behavior is reflected in that brand of psychological research that studies the correlations between maternal state and

56. Breen, p. 193.
57. Ibid., p. 14.
58. P. Shereshefsky and L. Yarrow, *Psychological Aspects of a First Pregnancy and Early Postnatal Adaptation* (New York: Raven Press, 1973).

infant behavior and then imputes a cause and effect relationship between the two. They find no link between maternal anxiety and infant
colic, though they do report that mothers of colicky infants become
temporarily less confident and less accepting (of the baby) in response to
the infant's behavior. The labeling of maternal personality and behav-
ioral characteristics as causal factors in the provocation of certain infant
conditions is one theme that flows from the use of traditional feminine
paradigms in psychological research. Its longevity can only be accounted
for in terms of its cultural normativeness. It is now beginning to be
diluted by a counterbalancing awareness that in some important ways
infants constitute independent variables. Who they are and how they
behave can affect a woman's experience of the role of mother, her ideas
about herself as a mother and a person.[59]

In brief, psychological constructs of women as maternity cases fail to
separate the biological from the social. They blur the distinction between
what Adrienne Rich[60] has called motherhood as "experience" and
motherhood as "institution." By using a medical paradigm of psychological states as epiphenomena of physiological ones, and by poorly conceptualizing psychoanalytic notions of women, they have been unable to
separate out the discrete effect of differing institutional components of
women's experiences of childbearing and motherhood.

If, in psychology, the psychodynamic structure of the individual is
seen as the main context which interprets the meaning of reproduction,
for sociology the relevant psychodynamic structure is that of the marital
relationship. Marriage replaces femininity as the locus of reproduction.
Thus capturing and intensifying the social reality of female domesticity,
family sociology has promoted (as by far its most influential paradigm of
women) the Parsonian[61] model of their "expressive" (as opposed to the
male's "instrumental") role, a particularly precise reflection of prevailing
cultural values. The focus of the sociological perspective is on the advent
of parenthood, this being assumed to have a greater impact on the
quality of marriage than subsequent childbirths. Most of the literature is
concerned only with first childbirth, relegating others to a position of
minor importance, irrespective of their impact on a woman's identity,
satisfaction, and life-style.[62] Maternity is analyzed as a developmental

59. A. Macfarlane reflects this awareness in his discussion of infant behavior in *The
Psychology of Childbirth* (Cambridge, Mass.: Harvard University Press, 1977).

60. A. Rich, *Of Woman Born* (New York: W. W. Norton & Co., 1976).

61. T. Parsons and R. F. Bales, *Family: Socialization and Interaction Process* (London:
Routledge & Kegan Paul, 1956).

62. H. Graham tested the hypothesis that women's attitudes toward subsequent births
differ from those toward first births and found, instead, significant similarities ("Women's
Attitudes to Conception and Pregnancy," in *Equalities and Inequalities in Family Life*, ed. R.
Chester and J. Peel [New York: Academic Press, 1977]). For a note on other studies, see
Sherman (n. 35 above), p. 207.

stage in the marital relationship. Le Masters's 1957 paper, "Parenthood as Crisis,"[63] was the first to propose the dramatic marital consequences of first childbirth. He delineated the problems urban middle-class couples have with the onset of parenthood as a romantic complex far exceeding that of marriage. But the limits of his research interest were with the impact of childbirth on the husband-wife relationship.

The work of Meyerowitz and Feldman further exemplifies this tradition. According to them, the crisis of a first child's birth is a "significant transitional point in the maturation of the marital relationship—transition from the dyadic state to a more *mature* and *rewarding* triadic system."[64] The outcome variable, which their interviews with 400 primiparous couples was designed to measure, was husbands' and wives' satisfaction with the marital relationship (the emphasis being on sexual satisfaction). More satisfaction was expressed during the pregnancy interview than at five-weeks or five-months postpartum, though there were discrepancies between husbands' and wives' accounts—women, for example, reported sex as more important in the success of a marriage than husbands, a finding which Meyerowitz and Feldman are unable to handle within the prevailing cultural paradigm. They therefore conclude that when women refer to "sex" they mean the entire female-male relationship.

Both these studies, and others of the same genre, are limited through adherence to gender-divisive notions of parenthood, both explicitly in the framework and conclusions of particular studies and implicitly in the instruments of inquiry (methodology, interviewing techniques, interview questions). Transition to parenthood has meant transition to the normative roles of mother-at-home and father-at-work, so that the adaptational tasks of each have been seen as different a priori, rather than contingent on individual circumstances.[65]

Rossi discussed some of these biases in her 1968 paper on "Transition to Parenthood."[66] Her revision of the research problem from "How do married couples adjust to parenthood?" to "What is the effect of parenthood on women?" paved the way for the more radical question: "What does maternity deprive a woman of?" Rossi's demolition of functionalist ideology—her proposition that the instrumentality of maternity is veiled by an ideological appeal to feminine expressivity—

63. Le Masters (n. 42 above).

64. J. H. Meyerowitz and H. Feldman, "Transition to Parenthood," *Psychiatric Research Reports* 20 (1968): 84 (emphasis added). A recent example of this tradition of analysis is R. LaRossa, *Conflict and Power in Marriage: Expecting the First Child* (Beverly Hills, Calif.: Sage Publications, 1977).

65. These consequences of the marital bias are spelled out by R. Rapoport and A. Oakley in "Towards a Review of Parent-Child Relationships in Social Science" (paper delivered at Working Conference, Merrill-Palmer Institute, November 10–12, 1975).

66. A. Rossi, "Transition to Parenthood," *Journal of Marriage and the Family* (February 1968), pp. 26–39.

exposes the sociological paradigm of reproduction as an agent of women's alienation: reproduction does not belong to women if it serves the cause of marriage (and men) first. The general rewards and difficulties of maternity; its contribution to personal growth or to personal disintegration; its capacity to dislocate preexisting social-political identifications and to provide functionally inferior (within a sexist capitalist society) alternatives—all these have been conceptualized as dimensions of wifehood, as contaminating the marital relationship, rather than as influencing the status, identities, and experiences of women. Moreover, the analysis of reproduction as a parameter of marriage reduces the sexual dimension of maternity to the sexual component of wifehood, instigating the same wedge between maternalism and sexuality found in Western industrialized culture generally.[67] The sexual satisfactions of maternity (birth, lactation) itself are muted as a cultural theme—and so, accordingly, is research on these aspects of reproductive behavior.[68] As far as child socialization is concerned, sociological research on parent-child relationships is child centered, not woman focused: as reproduction is attributed a primary meaning within the marital framework, so motherhood becomes the child's, and not the woman's, experience.[69]

Perhaps this is not surprising, because sociology has been one of the most sexist of the social sciences, embodying in its theoretical disposition and conceptual structure the value system of a patriarchal culture.[70] The other sociological area that has included a consideration of reproductive experiences is the fast-growing area of medical sociology. Prior to the expansion of medical-sociological work on reproduction in the 1970s, the main theoretical interest of reproduction to sociologists was the relationship between pregnancy and illness as distinct social roles.[71] Rosengren, the most diligent investigator of this notion, has produced a list of conclusions relating to the sick-role hypothesis: that socially mobile women are more sick-role oriented during pregnancy than others;[72] that

67. A. Rossi, "Maternalism, Sexuality and the New Feminism" (n. 48 above), expands this argument.

68. See N. Newton, "Interrelationships between Sexual Responsiveness, Birth and Breastfeeding," in Zubin and Money (n. 48 above), p. 77.

69. R. Rapoport, R. Rapoport, and Z. Strelitz substantiate and elaborate this bias in their review of the literature (*Fathers, Mothers, and Others* [London: Routledge & Kegan Paul, 1977]).

70. See A. Oakley, "The Invisible Woman: Sexism in Sociology," in *The Sociology of Housework* (New York: Pantheon Books, 1975) for a brief discussion of masculine bias in sociology, and J. Bernard, *Women, Wives, Mothers* (Chicago: Aldine Publishing Co., 1975), for the particular influences of this bias on research on motherhood.

71. See, for example, T. Parsons, *The Social System* (London: Routledge & Kegan Paul, 1951) and *Social Structure and Personality* (Glencoe, Ill.: Free Press, 1965). See also the discussion in J. B. McKinlay, "The Sick Role—Illness and Pregnancy," *Social Science and Medicine* 6 (1972): 569.

72. W. R. Rosengren, "Social Sources of Pregnancy as Illness or Normality," *Social Forces* 39 (1961): 260–67.

sick-role oriented women have longer labors than other women;[73] that middle-class women have higher sick-role expectations in pregnancy than lower-class women;[74] that women who regard pregnancy as an illness tend to express highly "retaliatory" attitudes to child rearing.[75] Such findings are ultimately unimpressive, both because they propose what could equally well be spurious connections and because the exercise of producing the data entails the imposition of certain prejudged values on women's accounts of their reproductive experiences. The general tenor of Rosengren's work imputes an unfortunate moral accountability to women, for they are seen as potentially (if not actually) causing their own (medical and social) reproductive difficulties by maintaining a false image of themselves.

In a thorough survey of the sociology of reproduction and its outcome,[76] Illsley, in 1967, bemoaned the lack of concern shown by sociologists with regard to the influence of social conditions on the course of pregnancy, labor, and delivery and contended that reproductive events can only be understood contextually as components of the woman's life experiences. Illsley deals with (1) the influence of general social factors on reproductive outcome; (2) the effect of biological variables (e.g., maternal health) on social parameters; (3) the relationship between particular factors (e.g., smoking, diet) and reproductive outcome; (4) interaction between social and biological influences; and (5) the relevance of social differences in reproduction to fetal and child health. In this kind of exercise, the sociologist appears as a kind of medical statistician, extrapolating from empirical data a model of social influences on reproductive biology. The sociologist's contribution is not to investigate the women's experiences but to extend the limits of the medical model and propose a more elastic conception of the variables which can be seen to influence the biological outcome of maternity.

Macintyre[77] distinguishes four types of sociological approaches to the management of childbirth. The first is historical/professional, which studies the managers and practitioners of childbirth in a historical context, using a sociology of science, social policy, or sociology of professions framework. The second is the anthropological approach, which focuses on the relation between the management of childbirth and prevailing belief systems in different cultures. Third, patient-oriented studies ar-

73. W. R. Rosengren, "Some Social Psychological Aspects of Delivery Room Difficulties," *Journal of Nervous and Mental Diseases* 132 (1961): 515–21.

74. W. R. Rosengren, "Social Instability and Attitudes toward Pregnancy as a Social Role," *Social Problems* 9 (1962): 371–78.

75. W. R. Rosengren, "Social Status, Attitudes toward Pregnancy and Child-rearing Attitudes," *Social Forces* 41 (1962): 127–34.

76. R. Illsley, "The Sociological Study of Reproduction and Its Outcome," in Richardson and Guttmacher (n. 34 above).

77. S. Macintyre, "The Management of Childbirth: A Review of Sociological Research Issues," *Social Science and Medicine* 11 (1977): 477–84.

ticulate the perspective of the consumers/users of the maternity services. Fourth, studies of patient/services interaction provide a synthesis of the historical/professional and the patient/services approaches by examining the interplay between service providers and service users. In the last five years there has been an expansion of work using all four of these approaches. Renewed efforts to combine historical and sociological perspectives are producing some interesting work on the evolution of obstetrics and its ideological charter of womanhood. For example, Versluysen,[78] tracing the beginnings of the medical colonization of childbirth, has interpreted the eighteenth-century hospital movement as a male device for gaining ascendancy over female health care.

Anthropological accounts of reproduction have provided a very fertile field indeed for expositions of women as maternity cases.

> Whether childbed is seen as a situation in which one risks death, or one out of which one acquires a baby, or social status, or a right to Heaven, is not a matter of the actual statistics of maternal mortality, but of the view that a society takes of childbearing. Any argument about women's instinctively maternal behavior which insists that in this one respect a biological substratum is stronger than every other learning experience that a female child faces, from birth on, must reckon with this great variety in the handling of childbirth.[79]

This statement by Mead is one of the earliest accounts of the differential phrasing of childbirth. Several stimulating accounts of cross-cultural variation in the management of reproduction now exist.[80] Critics of the maternity services recognize the usefulness of the anthropological perspective in demonstrating the "irrationality" of current obstetric practices. The International Childbirth Education Association's document, "The Cultural Warping of Childbirth,"[81] for instance, frequently cited by critics of contemporary maternity care, draws on international data and includes mention of birth practices in some nonindustrialized cultures. Periodically, this anthropological literature gives rise to the sug-

78. M. Versluysen, "Medical Professionalism and Maternity Hospitals in Eighteenth-Century London: A Sociological Interpretation," *Bulletin of the Society for the Social History of Medicine* 21 (December 1977): 34–36.

79. M. Mead, *Male and Female* (Harmondsworth: Penguin Books, 1962), p. 221.

80. These include: M. Mead and N. Newton, "Cultural Patterning of Perinatal Behavior," in Richardson and Guttmacher (n. 34 above); C. S. Ford, *A Comparative Study of Human Reproduction,* Yale University Publications in Anthropology no. 32 (New Haven, Conn.: Yale University Press, 1945). A contribution that draws on these and other studies is A. Oakley, "Cross-cultural Practice," in Chard and Richards (n. 18 above). There was a much earlier interest in cross-cultural differences in childbirth management as evidenced by, for example, G. J. Engelmann, *Labor among Primitive Peoples,* 2d ed. (St. Louis: J. H. Chambers, 1883).

81. D. Haire, *The Cultural Warping of Childbirth* (Seattle: International Childbirth Education Association, 1972).

gestion that a male-supremacist ideology has motivated modern patterns of reproductive care and modern medical paradigms of women as mothers.[82] Niles Newton, the author of various cross-cultural interpretations of reproduction, addressed an audience of male obstetricians some years ago. She invited them to have their pubic hair shaved off every time they gave an important speech. Only thus, she contended, would they begin to appreciate the psychological (not only physical) impact of routine obstetric maneuvers.[83]

But it is in the last two of Macintyre's categories—patient/services interaction and patient-oriented studies—that there has been the greatest growth of work. Although apparently informed by a less paradigmatic approach to the question of what reproduction means to women, studies in these categories range from the clearly programmatic to the straightforwardly descriptive. Accounts of patient/services interaction are less likely than others to be programmatic through their declared concern with both sides of the question. Nevertheless, medical typifications of women as maternity cases may be pervasive in the investigators' account,[84] perhaps reflecting a tendency for sociological researchers to be drawn into an identification with the medical enterprise. N. Stoller Shaw's *Forced Labor,* a study of maternity care in five institutional settings in the United States, is, as far as I know, the only published account based on systematic participant observation of staff-patient interaction in maternity care which does not resort to typifications.[85]

Macintyre's own research on gynecological work, though not concerned with maternity care specifically, has made a valuable contribution in articulating the various presumptions about women and reproduction that lie behind gynecological decisions.[86] Sexuality itself—in the doctor-patient encounter—has contributed another, more esoteric theme. J. Emerson[87] gives an account of how medical definitions of a man's intrusion into a woman's vagina are sustained in the face of counter-themes. Modes of desexualizing the vaginal examination are also taken up by Henslin and Biggs,[88] who rephrase the doctor's dilemma as the need to

82. See, for example, Mead, p. 22; and P. Lomas, "Ritualistic Elements in the Management of Childbirth," *British Journal of Medical Psychology* 39 (1966): 207–13.

83. N. Newton (n. 38 above), p. 17.

84. See Fish (n. 16 above) for an illustration of this tendency.

85. N. Stoller Shaw, *Forced Labor* (New York: Pergamon Press, 1974).

86. Macintyre, "To Have or Have Not—Promotion and Prevention in Gynecological Work," in Stacey (n. 16 above).

87. J. Emerson, "Behavior in Private Places: Sustaining Definitions of Reality in Gynecological Examinations," in *Recent Sociology, No. 2: Patterns of Communicative Behaviour,* ed. H. P. Dreitzel (New York: Macmillan Publishing Co., 1970).

88. J. M. Henslin and M. A. Biggs, "The Sociology of the Vaginal Examination," in *Studies in the Sociology of Sex,* ed. J. M. Henslin (New York: Appleton-Century-Crofts, Inc., 1971).

convert the sacred to the profane—to render the vagina violable, not inviolate.

Individual accounts, legitimated by the blossoming status of ethnomethodological inquiry within sociology, show female sociologists spelling out the nature of their own encounters with reproductive medicine.[89] These offer important insights into the experience of reproductive management and the effect of paradigmatic conflicts between doctor and patient by instituting the subjective experiences of the reproducer as valid data. Yet such accounts have to be based on the fragile equation between sociologist and social-actor roles. A personal predicament can lead to valuable sociological insight, but it says nothing about sociological generalization and is no substitute for the collective predicament, namely the recounting of those experiences which groups of women hold in common.[90]

Patient-oriented studies vary in the extent to which they may propose or support special notions of womanhood. Studies of antenatal care include some (such as those by McKinlay;[91] Collver, Have, and Speare;[92] Donabedian and Rosenfeld)[93] which attempt to elucidate the reason for late antenatal booking, the assumption (usually implicit) being that this "bad" patient behavior is due to the moral irresponsibility of women, who must be remotivated to behave more in accordance with the medical model.[94] On the other hand, some surveys of patient attitudes exhibit no such moral stand, taking as their brief the simple elucidation and measurement of responses to medical maternity care.[95] A few studies have focused in a broader way on the meaning of maternity to women. For

89. N. Hart, "Parenthood and Patienthood: A Dialectical Autobiography," and J. Comaroff, "Conflicting Paradigms of Pregnancy: Managing Ambiguity in Antenatal Encounters," in *Medical Encounters: The Experience of Illness and Treatment,* ed. A. Davis and G. Horobin (London: Croom Helm, Ltd., 1977).

90. For a discussion of the ethnomethodological enterprise, see J. H. Goldthorpe, "A Revolution in Sociology?" *British Journal of Sociology* 7 (1973): 449–62.

91. J. B. McKinlay, "The New Late-Comers for Antenatal Care," *British Journal of Preventive and Social Medicine* 24 (February 1970): 52–57.

92. A. Collver, R. T. Have, and M. C. Speare, "Factors Influencing the Use of Maternal Health Services," *Social Science and Medicine* 1 (1967): 293–308.

93. A. Donabedian and L. S. Rosenfeld, "Some Factors Influencing Prenatal Care," *New England Journal of Medicine* 265 (July 6, 1961): 1–6.

94. This interpretation is made explicit in a recent document issued by the British Department of Health and Social Security ("Reducing the Risk: Safer Pregnancy and Childbirth" [London: H.M.S.O., 1977]), which emphasizes failure in the mother (to attend early for antenatal care; to omit smoking, alcohol, and other "drugs" from the diet) rather than inadequacies in, and dissatisfaction with, the maternity services.

95. For instance, A. Cartwright's survey of attitudes to induction (*The Dignity of Labour* [London: Tavistock Publications, 1979]). The design of such studies may, of course, make it more or less difficult for patients' views to be represented: a yes/no choice does not allow for the inclusion of complex and/or radical responses to the whole cultural phrasing of maternity care.

example, Hubert's[96] study of working-class women in South London illustrates the conflict between the medicial paradigm and the reproducers' attitudes, and demonstrates how the cultural presentation of childbearing and child-rearing acts against a realistic anticipation of these.

Clearly, what the sociology of reproduction has lacked to date is a repertoire of first-hand accounts.[97] Until very recently the reproducers themselves have been represented merely as statistics, and/or they have been manipulated to fit the contours of a largely "ungrounded" theory. The feminine paradigm has been less visible in sociology than in psychology and medicine, for sociological representations of women are more a matter of subtle theoretical distortion or simple omission than dogmatic rhetoric. But in all three fields, it seems that the general cultural idealization of femininity and maternity has been projected wholesale into the scientific representation of reproduction, so that neither this nor the medical/cultural treatment of women as reproducers has been conceptualized as a legitimate subject of study.

Paradigmatic representations of women as mothers are bound to obscure the subjective reality of their reproductive experiences. To uncover this, a nonparadigmatic approach is needed that would enable the reproducer to be restored as the central figure in the biocultural drama of birth. One area which seems to offer at least a partial answer is that of natural childbirth. This notion asserts that within culture women can have babies "naturally." It suggests an opposition to hospitalization, to technology, and to the use of analgesic/anaesthetic drugs. It entails consciousness and control, the active role of the mother as the person having the baby, and the primacy of her needs, rather than the dependent and inactive role of the mother as medical patient. Natural childbirth, however, is usually identified with some regime of breathing exercises as a means of handling the physical sensations of labor by disassociation. The idea is that through concentration on levels and rates of breathing the experience of pain will be concretely as well as ideologically removed from birth. The two "fathers" of natural childbirth were Grantly Dick-Read and Ferdinand Lamaze, both of whom planned to reprogram women so that the same physiological stimuli of labor would produce different responses—less fear and pain. A mechanical analogy

96. J. Hubert, "Belief and Reality: Social Factors in Pregnancy and Childbirth," in *The Integration of a Child into a Social World,* ed. M. P. M. Richards (New York: Cambridge University Press, 1974).

97. A. Oakley, *Becoming a Mother* (n. 47 above), presents such accounts. A second, more analytical, treatment of my research on motherhood is in preparation: "Women Confined: Towards a Sociology of Childbirth." Reproducer-centered research on the sociology of reproduction is growing in Britain. The British Sociological Association's Sociology of Reproduction Study Group has produced a research index which lists these and other studies (available from Annette Scaubler, Department of Sociology, University of Surrey).

prompted the psychoprophylactic model: "Since when have repair shops been more important than the production plant?" asked Dick-Read of "the rising generation of doctors" in his *Childbirth without Fear*. "In the early days of motoring, garages were full of broken-down machines, but production has been improved; the weaknesses that predisposed to unreliability were discovered and in due course rectified. Today it is only the inferior makes that require the attention of mechanics. Such models have been evolved that we almost forget the relative reliability of the modern machine if it is properly cared for. . . . The mother is the factory, and by education and care she can be made more efficient in the art of motherhood."[98]

In its origins and in the model of women it proposes, it could be argued that the ideology of natural childbirth has been no different from that of obstetric medicine in general. Moreover, its ideology—that disassociation of mind from body, of emotions from physical sensations, is the most appropriate remedy for the pain of childbirth—removes the necessity for consciousness from the experience. To point out the value of consciousness is not to endorse the tradition of female masochism but to assign birth a status as an important life event. In this sense, the mechanism of mental detachment is analogous to pharmacological control, since both act to reduce awareness of pain, to distance laboring women from the full experience and personal meaning of birth.[99]

The rejoinder of the medical profession as a whole to the natural childbirth movement has been to legitimize it by including it with the medical brief. Medical advice literature began in the 1960s to propose some form of preparation for childbirth which consisted of relaxation or breathing exercises as an adjunct to medicalized reproduction, employing these techniques "as ameliorative strategies to enhance the mother's experience of hospital-based and pharmacological confinement. Although ostensibly acknowledging the principle of natural childbirth, the concern for psychological and individual control is subsumed by and lost within a system of maternity care which, instead, stresses physiology and medical control."[100] Thus colonized by medicine, natural childbirth all too easily fits the old paradigm. Being "conditioned for childbirth" is like being trained for battle; both birth and war are tests of genderhood: ". . . conditioning a woman for childbirth does very much the same for her that military training does for a young soldier who must face the rigors of battle. No young man wants to die or to suffer the pain of wounds. But with military training he becomes so conditioned that he is able to face death and pain with fortitude, and to come through the

98. G. Dick-Read, *Childbirth without Fear* (London: William Heinemann, Ltd., 1942).

99. See Rich (n. 60 above), chap. 7, "Alienated Labor," for some comments on the ideology of natural childbirth.

100. H. Graham (n. 19 above), p. 24. See also H..Brant and M. Brant, *Pregnancy, Childbirth and Contraception: All You Need to Know* (London: Corgi Books, 1975), p. 194.

experience with a sense of having proved his manhood. . . . "[101] In a gender-differentiated model, natural childbirth becomes, like the other paradigms, a contribution to marital happiness. "The midwife leaves and husband and wife are left alone with their child. . . . They are now a family. They have experienced together something incomprehensibly wonderful—a peak of joy in their married life which will perhaps always be for them a symbol of the deepest sort of love they know. Their marriage has gained something from this. . . . Creative childbirth which is shared by husband and wife thus has significance for a man and a woman which reaches far beyond the act of birth itself and through them has its effects upon society."[102] Less conventional authors translate this to mean "man and woman" rather than "married couple." The message is the same. "If a man makes sure he is with his woman when their child is born, and a woman makes sure that come hell or high water no job, no friend, no enemy, no outside force or institutional rule will keep a father away from his child at birth, then the part a man plays has myriad reflections in time. . . . The father of the newborn is as essential to its present and future life as the mother."[103] Natural childbirth can be, and is, in these ways put to the service of feminine womanhood, dogmatically insisting on the right way to have a baby and the right kind of woman/mother to do so. The meaning of "natural" is confused. But two clear meanings are that birth is (should be) (a) untechnological and (b) animal: "Women can give birth by the action of their own bodies as animals do. Women can enjoy the process of birth and add to their dignity by being educated to follow the example set by instinctive animals."[104] Women are no better than animals, which is, after all, why they pose such a threat to human cultural order.

Organized feminism in its revival since the 1960s has revealed the insidiousness of much feminine propaganda. The movement has shown an overwhelming concern with freeing women from their childbearing and child-rearing roles. Thus, demands have included (in Britain) free abortion on demand, free and better contraception, and more state child care. A major theme has been women's rights to define their own sexuality—whether in a hetero- or homosexual framework.[105] Yet though these notions of liberation are clearly indicated by the pre-

101. C. Tupper, "Conditioning for Childbirth," *American Journal of Obstetrics and Gynecology* (April 1956), p. 740.

102. S. Kitzinger, *The Experience of Childbirth* (London: Gollancz Services, Ltd., 1962), p. 155.

103. D. Brook, *Naturebirth* (Harmondsworth: Penguin Books, 1976), p. 33.

104. Bradley (n. 30 above), p. 12.

105. These concerns are reflected in the early women's movement publications in both Britain and the United States: for example, Morgan, *Sisterhood Is Powerful* (n. 35 above); and M. Wandor, *The Body Politic* (London: Stage 1, 1973). In both these books the meaning of childbirth to women is barely mentioned, apart from, that is, a theoretical-Marxist interpretation of the function of reproduction to the capitalist family.

dominating cultural oppression of women, they also echo the patriarchal view of women as sexual objects condemned by their biology to mother-hood. Relationships between feminism and natural childbirth have been ambiguous, reflecting the feminist ambivalence about the status of wom-en's "suffering" in childbirth. Some feminists[106] have seen technological reproduction, the absolute alienation of childbirth from women through technological mastery[107] of artificial gestation, as offering the only true answer to the dilemma of women's biological destiny. In these ways feminism has not conceptualized reproduction as a female resource, but rather as a handicap, a source or cause of social inferiority. That the two coexist there can be no doubt, and in medical, psychological, and sociological paradigms of women their capacity to reproduce and their secondary social status have certainly been part of the same stereotype. It seems that we have not yet found a way to reconcile the nature of childbirth and the representation of women in culture. By being param-eters of both nature and culture, women as reproducers threaten cul-tural order by interposing nature as a condition of it. The paradigms of women as maternity cases described here can be interpreted as our social response to this essential ambiguity.

Department of Sociology
Bedford College (University of London)

106. S. Firestone, *The Dialectic of Sex* (New York: Bantam Books, 1971), puts forth this viewpoint.

107. The actual character of science and technology under capitalism is patriarchal. See H. Rose and J. Hanmer, "Women's Liberation, Reproduction and the Technological Fix," in Barker and Allen (n. 16 above) for a critique of the technology-will-save-women argument.

MOTHERS OF THE NEW GENERATION: ADELE SCHREIBER, HELENE STÖCKER, AND THE EVOLUTION OF A GERMAN IDEA OF MOTHERHOOD, 1900–1914

ANN TAYLOR ALLEN

"Today the Germans, and not least the German women," remarked British sexologist Havelock Ellis in 1910, "awaking from a long period of quiescence, are inaugurating a new phase of the woman movement . . . based on the demands of woman as mother, and . . . directed to the end of securing for her the right to control and regulate the personal and social relations which spring from her nature as mother or possible mother." Pioneers in this struggle to define and promote a new concept of mothers' rights were two women, Helene Stöcker and Adele Schreiber, both conspicuous members of the left wing of the bourgeois feminist movement and both among the founders of the *Bund für Mutterschutz* (League for the protection of mothers). In 1905, the year when Stöcker assumed leadership of the Bund für Mutterschutz, motherhood—with all its social, political, legal, ethical, and cultural implications—had become the central issue in a debate that continued throughout the prewar period. International in scope, this controversy was particularly vehement in Germany, where feminists emerged not as followers or imitators of the better established British or American movements, but as innovators. Although others have placed the story of the Bund für Mutterschutz in the context of the German women's movement as a whole, they have paid far more

I would like to thank the staff members of the following libraries and archives for their very generous and friendly assistance: the Bundesarchiv Koblenz; the Staatsarchiv Hamburg; the Swarthmore Peace Collection, Swarthmore College; and the Helene-Lange-Stiftung, West Berlin.

This essay originally appeared in *Signs*, vol. 10, no. 3, Spring 1985.

attention to its sensational advocacy of "free love" than to its more central concern—the creation of a concept of motherhood appropriate to the changed cultural, economic, familial, and reproductive patterns of an era hailed by Swedish feminist Ellen Key as "the century of the child." The evolution of this new concept is best understood as a response to the great upsurge of public and official interest in maternal behavior at the turn of the century.[1]

"The sentimental belief in motherhood as an always holy and always reliable natural force must be superseded," wrote Ellen Key in 1911, "and this natural phenomenon must be shaped by culture." In the years between 1900 and 1914, conventional reliance on the infallible maternal instinct had been rudely shaken by widely publicized figures showing a marked decline in the German Empire's crude birth rate. Of course, this trend in itself was hardly novel; crude birth rates in Germany, having reached a peak (39.3 per 1,000 population) in the postwar period 1876–80, had been gradually declining for the following two decades, and large cities such as Berlin had registered a 10 percent decline in the crude birth rate as early as 1881. But many commentators nonetheless warned of a new and unprecedented crisis; they could explain the peak birth rates of the 1870s as an abnormal response to postwar conditions and see the slightly declining figures for the later decades (37.0 for 1881–85 and 36.0 in 1896) as only a return to normal fertility, but they viewed the further decline to 34.3 in the period 1900–1905 as the onset of a new and deplorable pattern. Contributing to their alarm was the also widely publicized decline of the so-called birth surplus. In the period 1880–1900, the rapid decline in the death rate, which had more than offset the slightly diminished birth rate, provided grounds for optimism, even for complacency. But during the period 1900–1905, the surplus of births over deaths declined slightly from 14.8 to 14.4 per 1,000 population, and during the subsequent years from 1906–10 it further decreased to 14.2. The declining surplus was most conspicuous in the cities; in 1903 the Imperial Health Ministry reported that in the 313 urban centers with populations exceeding 15,000, the surplus of births over deaths per 1,000 population had declined in one year from 14.1 to 12.5. More sophisti-

1. The opening quotation is from Havelock Ellis, *The Task of Social Hygiene* (Boston: Houghton Mifflin Co., 1914), p. 95. A narrative history of the Bund für Mutterschutz is in Richard J. Evans, *The Feminist Movement in Germany* (London: Sage Publications, 1976), pp. 115–44. See also Christl Wickert, Brigitte Hamburger, and Marie Lienau, "Helene Stöcker and the *Bund für Mutterschutz*," *Women's Studies International Forum* 5, no. 6 (1982): 611–18; Marie-Luise Janssen-Jurreit, "Nationalbiologie, Sexualreform und Geburtenrückgang: Über die Zusammenhang von Bevölkerungspolitik und Frauenbewegung um die Jahrhundertwende," in *Die Überwindung der Sprachlosigkeit: Texte aus der neuen Frauenbewegung*, ed. Gabriele Dietze (Darmstadt and Neuwied: Luchterhand, 1978).

cated modern analysis has indeed identified 1905 as a key year in the process of demographic transition.[2]

But figures alone are insufficient to explain the sense of impending doom expressed by commentators of all shades of political opinion as the trend continued. "The level of our present-day culture is dependent on the maintenance of our present population density," stated prominent left-wing intellectual and member of the Bund für Mutterschutz Walther Borgius, who went on to warn that population decrease "threatens the future of our culture." Right-wing politicians struck a shriller note. "Is our Fatherland indeed in the declining years of its life?" asked a Catholic Center Party deputy to the Prussian lower house in February 1914. "Where will it end? What will happen to our military strength, now more vital than ever before, what will happen to our labor force, which is desperately needed in the ever more threatening struggle of nations?"[3]

The pessimistic, even catastrophic tone of these comments reflected not only the political but also the intellectual atmosphere of the prewar years. In their preoccupation with struggle for survival and competition for scarce resources, speakers of all political persuasions drew on the stock vocabulary of Social Darwinism that had been popular since the 1880s. But the earlier belief in improvement through natural selection had been modified by the science of eugenics—first popularized in Germany by the periodical *Archiv für Rassen-und-Gesellschaftsbiologie*, founded in 1904—which had shifted the emphasis from the ineluctable laws of nature to the purposeful manipulation of the evolutionary process by human beings. A generation that had lost faith in inevitable and automatic progress saw in the declining birth rate further proof that natural laws alone could not ensure the survival of the German nation or even of Western civilization as a whole. In fact, these figures seemed to confirm a view of civilization itself, or some of its aspects, as a threat to the reproductive process and thus to the continued vigor and strength of the nation. As Elisabeth Badinter has shown, a purely quantitative concern with population growth had been expressed since the eighteenth century by governments that had traditionally exerted moral and legal pressure on women to fulfill their maternal obligations. But at the turn of the century the eugenicists emphasized not simply the quantity of offspring but their quality, which could be ensured only by responsible parental behavior. Moreover, the increasing ability of women to avoid childbearing chal-

2. Ellen Kay, "Mütterlichkeit," in *Die Mutterschaft: Ein Sammelwerk für die Probleme des Weibes als Mutter*, ed. Adele Schreiber (Munich: Albert Langen Verlag, 1911), p. 600. On the demographic transition, see John E. Knodel, *The Decline of Fertility in Germany, 1871–1939* (Princeton, N.J.: Princeton University Press, 1974), esp. pp. 5, 56–58.

3. Walter Borgius, "Bevölkerungsstatistik und Mutterschutzbewegung," *Mutterschutz* 3, no. 11 (1907): 440–47, esp. 445; Prussia, Haus der Abgeordneten (House of Representatives), 34 sess., *Stenographischer Bericht*, February 23, 1914.

lenged traditional views of maternity as inevitable destiny or as moral and religious imperative. Increasingly, Germans came to think that the survival of the nation depended not on passive and animal maternal "instinct" but on what was widely termed the "will to motherhood."[4]

Among both health ministry officials and private citizens, a heightened concern with maternal behavior was first triggered not so much by the birth rate as by the more easily controllable death rate. In a nation justifiably proud of its reputation for medical progress, the figures on infant mortality (i.e., death in the first year of life), first published separately in 1901, caused widespread concern. The increasingly detailed analysis of the infant death rate published by the Imperial Health Ministry in the years 1901–14 themselves attest to the changing attitudes of a society that had accepted frequent infant death in the nineteenth century with indifference or fatalism. "We believed that the high mortality rate of children in their first year was the result of natural selection which eliminated the weaker constitutions," wrote a Berlin physician and infant-welfare advocate in 1911. "Now we know that it is a great national misfortune." Despite the steady decline from 24 per 100 live births in 1872–75 to 21.3 in 1896–1900, the infant mortality rate of the empire surpassed that of many other countries; the German figure of 20.4 in 1903 was considerably higher than the figures published by Finland (12.7), France (13.7), and England (13.2), and was surpassed only by the figures for such notoriously backward countries as Russia (27.2) and Austria (21.5). Infant mortality rates varied widely according to locality; for the same ten-year period (1893–1903) Bremen published an average rate of 16 per 100 live births; Aachen, 40; and Stettin, 45. Still more striking were seasonal variations; in 1903, the number of infant deaths from digestive diseases in cities with populations over 15,000 ranged from a low of 1,271 in February to a high of 10,643 in August, and in the unusually hot summer of 1911, the August death rate rose 47.7 percent over that of the previous year.[5]

Of the many possible interpretations for these statistics, both government and the medical establishment chose those that placed responsibility

4. A general account of the eugenics movement in Germany is Hans-Günther Zmarzlik, "Social Darwinism in Germany Seen as a Historical Problem," in *From Republic to Reich: The Making of the Nazi Revolution*, ed. Hajo Holborn, trans. R. Mannheim (New York: Pantheon Books, 1972); cf. Mark H. Haller, *Eugenics: Hereditarian Attitudes in American Thought* (New Brunswick, N.J.: Rutgers University Press, 1963), pp. 8–20. Elisabeth Badinter, *Motherhood, Myth and Reality: Motherhood in Modern History*, English ed. (Paris: Flammarion, 1980; New York: Macmillan Publishing Co., 1981).

5. Kaiserin Auguste-Victoria Haus, *Säuglingsschutz in Gross-Berlin: III internationaler Kongress für Säuglingsschutz, 1911* (Berlin: J. Stilke, 1911), p. 6; *Reichsanzeiger* (April 22, 1903). Tables and other government documents concerning the campaign against infant mortality are in the archive of the Kaiserliches Gesundheitsamt (Imperial Health Ministry, hereinafter KGA), Bundesarchiv Koblenz, R/86, v. 931.

for infant mortality chiefly on mothers. Explanations stressing such social causes as poor housing and sanitation were superseded at the turn of the century by a nearly exclusive emphasis on the new preference for artificial as opposed to breast-feeding. The development of sterilization techniques, warned medical authorities, had led to overconfidence in bottle feeding, the dangers of which were clearly shown by the summer peak in infant deaths due to spoilage of milk. Indeed, statistics did show higher mortality among artificially fed infants; one study carried out in Berlin from 1900 to 1903 showed that 19.75 percent of bottle-fed infants, compared with only 6.98 percent of breast-fed babies, had died in their first year. From this simple analysis proceeded an equally simple and traditional solution—women must be persuaded on both hygienic and ethical grounds to breast-feed. This was the theme of a flood of circulars published during these years by both federal and state governments and by charitable organizations concerned with infant protection. "Attention, all mothers, if you value the lives of your children," proclaimed one such leaflet published by the Society for the Prevention of Infant Mortality, "every mother should try to nurse her child herself!" A statement published by the Imperial Health Ministry in 1906 blamed the decline of breast-feeding on women's "love of comfort or their fear of damaging their own bodies." Many state governments initiated educational programs; the Health Ministry of Bavaria, for example, set up counseling centers for mothers with the primary purpose of "giving the most widespread possible encouragement to the breast-feeding of infants." For mothers who were not able to nurse, local governments and charitable organizations attempted to make available supplies of uncontaminated cow's milk, at the same time instructing mothers in its storage and preparation. Evidence of the "gratifying increase of activity in the prevention of infant mortality" hailed by the Prussian Health Ministry was the founding of the government-subsidized Kaiserin Auguste-Viktoria Haus in 1909, which became a center both of philanthropic activity and of infant welfare research.[6]

Although accurately identifying artificial feeding as a major cause of infant death, these programs relied chiefly on the same moral pressures that governments had exerted on mothers for more than a century. To be sure, modest advances in protective legislation for women workers took some account of the economic pressures that prevented women from

6. Arthur Keller and C. J. Klumker, *Säuglingsschutz und Kinderfürsorge in den europäischen Staaten* (Berlin: J. Springer, 1912), pp. 1212–14; "Mütter, beachtet!" (June 6, 1904), "Bayern: Entschliessung des Kgl. Staatsministeriums" (September 12, 1907), and "Preussen: Ministerialerlass" (June 16, 1908), all in KGA, R/86, v. 2376. On the history of sterilization techniques, see Kaiserin Auguste-Victoria Haus, p. 6. For England, see Carol Dyhouse, "Working-Class Mothers and Infant Mortality in England, 1895–1914," *Journal of Social History* 11, no. 2 (Winter 1978): 248–62.

breast-feeding in a period when the percentage of married women in the full-time work force was rising from 12.04 percent in 1895 to 26 percent in 1908. In 1903, legislation extended women industrial workers' eligibility for maternity insurance benefits from four to six weeks; in 1908, laws prohibited the employment of women in industry for two weeks before and six weeks after childbirth. But the insurance coverage, paid only at the level of sick pay (from 50 percent to 75 percent of an often inadequate daily wage) was available only to workers in certain industrial jobs, while larger occupational groups such as domestic and agricultural workers were left completely unprotected. Bourgeois feminists and socialists criticized the well-meaning efforts of local authorities—such as the free medical care and welfare payments granted to a few of the neediest mothers by the Berlin city council in 1905—as pitifully inadequate. "Social reform is being prescribed to us in homeopathic doses," objected a socialist member of the Berlin city council. "But at least the ice is now broken. . . . We hope that great results will follow these limited ones."[7]

It was the Bund für Mutterschutz, first founded in 1904, that took the lead in denouncing such token remedies and demanding radical and creative solutions. The Bund (which despite its philanthropic sounding name was devoted more to the rights than merely to the protection of mothers) was first founded by Ruth Bré as a utopian venture but was soon taken over in 1905 by a varied group of left-wing intellectuals, male and female, liberal and socialist. Under the leadership of Helene Stöcker, the group included such well-known male politicians as Friedrich Naumann and Anton Erkelenz, such eminent professors as Max Weber and Werner Sombart, and such prominent feminists as Lily Braun and Marie Stritt. By 1908 the Bund had ten affiliated local branches in cities all over the empire and was engaged in practical philanthropy, political activism, and theoretical debate, carried on chiefly through the periodicals *Mutterschutz* and *Die neue Generation* and through well-attended public lectures.[8]

Within this organization Helene Stöcker and Adele Schreiber played conspicuous and contrasting roles. Approximately the same age (Stöcker was born in 1869 into a pastor's family in Elberfeld, Schreiber into a physician's household in Vienna in 1872), both had aspired in youth to higher education. But while Stöcker, who was one of the first women to enter the University of Berlin in 1896, fulfilled her ambition by earning her doctorate from the University of Bern in 1902, Schreiber received only unsystematic instruction in secondary school subjects. Having qualified as a secondary school teacher, Stöcker was also active as a scholar and

7. On maternity benefits, see Alfons Fischer, "Staatliche Mutterschaftsversicherung," in Schreiber, ed. (n. 2 above), pp. 302–5. Discussion of charitable measures is in Berlin, Stadtverordneten-Versammlung (city council), *Stenographischer Bericht*, March 2, 1905.

8. See Evans (n. 1 above), pp. 127–30. According to Evans, the organization's total membership in 1908 was 3,726.

a lecturer on the Romantic movement and on Nietzsche, whom, despite his antifeminist remarks, she admired for his courageous advocacy of a higher code of ethics to replace a conventional morality grown corrupt and archaic. Nietzsche's own interpretation of evolution, which emphasized not blind and irresistible natural forces but the heroic will, stimulated his disciple's interest in the science of eugenics. A gifted theoretician and trenchant writer, Stöcker was the intellectual leader of the movement. "Her personality," wrote a sympathetic colleague, Grete Meisel-Hess, "expresses a calm self-confidence; no attack can intimidate her or deter her from her chosen course of action." The more practically inclined Schreiber mentioned socialism—to which she was introduced by August Bebel's *Die Frau und der Sozialismus*—as the major formative influence on her intellectual development, although she did not actually join the Social Democratic Party until after the war. Extensive travel, especially to London where she observed the settlement house movement, gave her a perspective on social policies in other countries. Schreiber, wrote Meisel-Hess, "is a speaker *par excellence*. Her arguments are strictly logical. . . . The rhythm of her speeches expresses a passionate temperament which she controls with visible effort, but with outstanding success."[9]

The interests of these two women represent the confluence of intellectual currents that produced the Bund's view of motherhood. At its base was the progressive German liberalism of the late nineteenth century, which protested against the narrow self-interest into which traditional ideals of laissez-faire had degenerated and sought a compromise between individualism and social commitment. Such a program required an increasing openness to certain goals advocated in the past chiefly by socialists. An organization with many socialist members, the Bund often joined the Social Democratic Party in advocating welfare legislation and in denouncing the abuses of capitalism. The incorporation of such social goals reinforced the traditional emphasis of German liberalism on the positive role of the state, to which feminist reformers assigned an increasing responsibility for the welfare of the individual and of society as a whole. But liberal individualism remained the most important principle of the Bund. Opposing the collective approach to child care advocated by socialist theorists such as Bebel and Charlotte Perkins Gilman, whom they otherwise admired, they hailed motherhood as the highest individual fulfillment and the mother-child bond as the most sacred of ties. An

9. On Stöcker, see, e.g., Ingeborg Richarz-Simons, "Helene Stöcker: Sozialreformerin und Pazifistin," Helene Stöcker Papers, Swarthmore Peace Collection, Swarthmore College (typescript); and her own unpublished autobiography, "Lebensabriss," also in the Swarthmore Peace Collection. On Schreiber, see vol. 1 in her "Nachlass," a collection of personal papers held in the Bundesarchiv Koblenz. The quotation from Meisel-Hess is in *Hamburger Fremdenblatt* (August 16, 1908).

important influence on this exalted view of motherhood was the Swedish author Ellen Key, who called for a "new sexual morality . . . where the light will radiate from the child." Another heritage was that of radical feminism, as represented by forerunners such as Annie Besant and by contemporaries such as Margaret Sanger and Emma Goldman. But there was an important difference of emphasis between these feminists and those of the Bund. Although Besant, Sanger, and Goldman extolled the value of motherhood, they devoted their most energetic and highly publicized efforts to the cause of birth control—that is, to the assertion of the right to refuse motherhood. The German feminists reversed these priorities: though many were strong advocates of reproductive freedom, they placed major emphasis on the right to become a mother with the full respect and support of society.[10]

The first step in forming a new concept of mothers' rights was to expose the real disregard, even contempt, for mothers that underlay official pronatalist rhetoric. To support their case, the feminists eagerly publicized selected statistics—the mortality rates for illegitimate children—which had been noted but not emphasized by the health ministry. The overall infant mortality rate was alarming, but the figures for illegitimate infants were even more shocking; in 1901, 33.9 illegitimate and 19.4 legitimate infants per hundred died in the first year of life, and in 1905 these figures had hardly changed (19.4 for legitimate, 32.6 for illegitimate children). The mothers' rights advocates were quick to debunk conventional Darwinian views of this death rate as the result of inevitable and beneficial natural selection and to attribute it instead to the prejudice and callousness of a society that praised motherhood only within the rules of conventional morality. "The unmarried mother is abandoned and without rights, subject to every kind of ostracization and contempt," charged Schreiber in 1904. The fate of these children showed the ineffectiveness of governmental breast-feeding propaganda. "The exceptional circumstances in which the unmarried mother finds herself," explained Schreiber, "dictate that she can seldom nurse her children, but is almost always forced to entrust the child shortly after its birth to strange people, in order not to be disgraced by the open acknowledgement of her motherhood." Existing laws provided that illegitimate children had "no relationship" to their biological fathers and were thus entitled to no inheritance from them and to support only at the mother's usually lower standard of living—an obligation that fathers often easily evaded. Schreiber eloquently cited a widely publicized case of infanticide by a homeless and destitute unmarried mother to prove her case against such "man-

10. Ellen Key, *Love and Marriage*, trans. Arthur Chater (1911; reprint, New York: Source Book, 1970), p. 191. On the differences between German and Anglo-Saxon ideas of liberalism, see Leonard Krieger, *The German Idea of Freedom: History of a Political Tradition* (Boston: Beacon Press, 1957).

made" laws. Thus depicted, the situation of the illegitimate child revealed the futility of government-sponsored "educational" programs that placed the responsibility for infant mortality on mothers themselves without regard for the social, economic, and legal disadvantages they suffered. The solution to this problem was not, as conservative moralists claimed, the prevention of "immorality" but rather the recognition of motherhood itself as a vital contribution to society, deserving of support rather than scorn. "It is a disgrace to our culture . . . that women are forced to conceal the maternity of which they should be proud. . . . No woman can 'fall from virtue' through motherhood."[11]

Stöcker and Schreiber soon moved beyond the denunciations of bourgeois sexual hypocrisy and the double standard that had become traditional in the feminist movement to a far more radical critique of accepted family and reproductive patterns. Earlier generations of German feminists had followed kindergarten founder Friedrich Froebel in assigning to woman a nurturing and philanthropic social mission based on her role within the nuclear household. Even the frank and fearless crusaders against prostitution had implicitly supported conventional morality by urging it on men as well as women. But the *Mutterschutz* activists at first proposed not to enforce or to reform conventional morality but to supersede it with what they termed a "new ethic." To Stöcker the plight of the unmarried mother was just one symptom of the sickness of a patriarchal sexual order in which marriage and prostitution were parallel and complementary institutions. Within a system that catered to every male need, women were condemned to sexual exploitation as wives or prostitutes, or to the unhealthy asceticism of the "respectable" spinster. Thus only a new morality based on "the affirmation of life and all its healthy instincts" could ensure women's right to the enjoyment of sexuality and of motherhood, its natural consequence. In an essay published in Stöcker's periodical *Mutterschutz*, Henriette Fürth subjected to scholarly scrutiny defenses of convention based on history and tradition. "Nature knows only motherhood, not marriage," she declared, quoting Johann Jakob Bachofen's monumental work *Das Mütterrecht* (1861) to support her assertion that the "eternal, life-giving principle" of maternity was more basic to civilization than the shifting and transitory forms of marriage and patriliny. Mothers' rights advocates increasingly expanded their arguments to include women's rights to define new economic, familial, and cultural institutions that supported motherhood.[12]

11. *Hamburger Fremdenblatt* (October 23, 1906); *Hamburger Generalanzeiger* (November 18, 1906). Mortality rates for infants are in H. C. Behr-Pinnow, *Erhaltung und Mehrung des Nachwuchses* (pamphlet), KGA, R/86, v. 2375.

12. Helene Stöcker, "Zur Reform der sexuellen Ethik," *Mutterschutz* 1, no. 1 (1905): 1–12; Henriette Fürth, "Ehe und Mutterschaft," *Mutterschutz* 1, no. 7 (1905): 265–79, esp. 268.

Implicit in their historical analyses of primitive culture was an interest in matriarchal family structures, of which the unmarried mother's family was taken as a modern example. To create a matriarchal utopia was, in fact, the aim of the original founder of the Bund für Mutterschutz, Ruth Bré. Bré, the author of a book entitled *Das Recht auf Mutterschaft* (The right to motherhood), proposed in 1904 that unmarried mothers and their children be settled in rural communes. "The mothers of the new generation should make a new home for themselves on the soil," she proclaimed. The members of the commune, she stipulated, would be supported partly by their own agriculture and handicrafts but primarily by a tax-supported "maternity income," available to all married and unmarried mothers, which, by subsidizing a "simple life" for both mothers and children, would enable them to live independently of paternal support and domination. Echoing the principles of the eugenics movement, Bré insisted that no mother could be admitted without a satisfactory health certificate "because we should attempt to protect whatever is strong and healthy and thus encourage motherhood as a social contribution." Eccentric and impractical, Bré's proposal is significant chiefly as a contribution to feminist utopian literature, bearing a marked resemblance to another contemporary example of the genre, Charlotte Perkins Gilman's *Herland*. Other members of the Bund rejected Bré's explicit advocacy of the matriarchal family. Both Stöcker and Schreiber argued along with Bachofen that the matriarchal family was a primitive social form, superseded first by its antithesis, the patriarchal family, and then (or so the feminists hoped) by the higher synthesis of marriage as "a bond between equals." Likewise Bré's proposed exclusion of sick and handicapped mothers from her utopia provoked both practical and theoretical opposition, leading her to protest that her opponents "completely ignored racial hygiene and proposed to raise the sick at the expense of the healthy, thus squandering our national wealth and strength." Although the Bund was taken over in 1905 by a group based in Berlin and headed by Stöcker (Bré soon resigned in protest), the issues of matriarchy and "racial hygiene" remained central to the organization's subsequent theoretical speculation and political activities.[13]

Having rejected the female separatism advocated by Bré, the members of the Bund now set about creating a new basis for the heterosexual family with, as Stöcker declared, "all the seriousness which such an undertaking requires." True acceptance of the unmarried mother, Stöcker reasoned, required the legal and social recognition of her nonmarital sexual relationship. This simple premise, once accepted, provided a basis

13. Ruth Bré's real name was Elisabeth Bonness. For an account of Bré's plans and Stöcker's response, see *Berliner Tageblatt* (February 27, 1905); and a statement by Bré herself, quoted in Schreiber, "Nachlass" (n. 9 above), vol. 17; see also Evans (n. 1 above), pp. 120–22.

for the spirited exploration of an immense variety of nonmarital relationships and their social implications. As editor of the periodical *Mutterschutz* and its successor, *Die neue Generation*, Stöcker published articles by
such internationally known authors as Havelock Ellis, Sigmund Freud,
Alfred Moll, and Magnus Hirschfeld on topics ranging from the sexual
customs of antiquity to the legal status of homosexuals. But the heterosexual relationship remained the center of concern; resolutions passed at the
general meeting of 1907 demanded equal status for husband and wife
within marriage and "the legal recognition of free relationships, provided
that 1) there is no legal hindrance to these relationships and 2) that the
children produced by them are given equal status to those produced by
legal marriage." This advocacy of what was popularly termed "free love"
provoked a mixture of fascination and horror, not only in conservative
and clerical circles but also within the feminist movement itself. Condemning these proposals as invitations to "sexual anarchy," prominent
feminist Helene Lange defended the institution of the family as the
necessary protective environment for the "coming generation."[14]

Stöcker and Schreiber responded to such criticism by denying that
laws set up for the advantage of men truly protected women and children.
Far from discouraging parental care, they claimed, the new morality
sought to provide it for the many illegitimate children who had been
neglected through law and custom. Schreiber went on to defend the right
to divorce—a central principle of the "new ethic"—as in the best interests
of both parents and children. "Inner disharmony and not the dissolution
of the tie, is what hurts the child," she stated. "Children suffer nowhere so
much as in an unhappy household." An energetic advocate of child-abuse
legislation, Schreiber also challenged traditional ideas of paternal authority, which protected not the child but the abusive or irresponsible father.
Against the legalistic code of marriage, she defended the more humane
morality of motherhood. "A healthy woman who denies her child the
breast," she declared, "is behaving immorally—but an unmarried mother
who defies all pressures and takes her child to the breast is heroic, not
immoral." Protesting that monogamous and lifelong unions remained
the highest ideal, Stöcker defended the "new ethic" as a summons, not to
license, but to a higher level of responsibility. "They say that we want to
encourage free relationships. That's not so. Rather, these free relationships obviously already exist, and we want to purify them and, by
social recognition, raise them to a higher level."[15]

14. Stöcker's statement appeared in *Mutterschutz* 1, no. 1 (1905): 1–2. Resolution of the
general convention in 1907 is quoted in *Mutterschutz* 3, no. 2 (1907): 76–80, esp. 78. Lange's
opinion is in "Feministische Gedankenanarchie," in *Frauenbewegung und Sexualethik*, ed.
Gertrud Bäumer et al. (Heilbronn: Verlag von Eugen Salzer, 1909), p. 50.

15. Schreiber's ideas on marriage and the family were expressed chiefly through
public lectures, which were extensively reported in the press. For the passages quoted, see

In the struggle against crippling prejudice, the Bund called on the state for aid. A petition directed to the Reichstag in 1906 declared that, since the "degeneration of sexual life" in modern society—manifested by such problems as prostitution, venereal disease, and pornography— could not be remedied by police repression but only by public enlighten- ment, sex education should be included in school curricula. Anticipating one obvious objection, the petition argued that parents themselves often lacked the scientific qualifications to present such education in a "method- ical and organized fashion." Schreiber's advocacy of sex education aroused widespread interest; when the police of Hamburg forbade her lecture on this topic in 1908, she delivered it to an enthusiastic crowd in the neighboring city of Altona. "The room was not only full to the last seat," reported a local newspaper, "but was overflowing with an attentive audience which gave the speaker enthusiastic applause."[16]

Another attempt to enlist government support for the exercise of responsible motherhood was the campaign for expansion and improve- ment of state-supported maternity insurance coverage. Originally a socialist campaign, it was supported in the period 1905–11 by the Social Democratic Party and the mainstream *Bund deutscher Frauenvereine* (League of German women's organizations) as well as by the Bund für Mutterschutz. The petition submitted to the Reichstag by the Bund in 1907 appealed to the growing public concern not only for infant mortality but for the effects of inadequate care on children who survived—effects manifested by the unsatisfactory health of military recruits in industrial areas. The damage to the younger generation, often caused by economic pressures that forced women to return to work and prevented them from breast-feeding, could not be solved, the petition implied, by pious plati- tudes condemning the employment of mothers. The text of the petition, which termed the mothers' employment "a necessary result of our eco- nomic development," refutes the conclusion drawn by historian Richard Evans that by urging women to "give birth to large families of children" the mothers' rights advocates devalued "all the efforts of the feminist movement to open up careers to women." In fact, the sponsors of the petition constantly affirmed their conviction that the modern woman should achieve the admittedly difficult goal of balancing motherhood and economic self-sufficiency. In a series of essays in *Mutterschutz*, the socialist feminist Henriette Fürth looked forward to a future when human beings would be valued "according to their achievements as workers, and not

---

the summary of her lecture "Sittlichkeit und Kindesrecht," in *Kleine Presse* (Frankfurt) (September 28, 1907). The quotation from Stöcker is from *Mutterschutz* 3, no. 2 (1907): 183.

16. For the petition, entitled "Einfügung der geschlechtlichen Belehrung in den Schulunterricht," see Schreiber, "Nachlass" (n. 9 above), vol. 29. For Schreiber's lecture, see *Hamburger Fremdenblatt* (March 14, 1908).

according to their sex." Schreiber campaigned tirelessly for the repeal of rules that required the dismissal of certain women professionals, such as teachers, when they married or became pregnant. The improvement of maternity insurance, the 1907 petition stated, would be but one step in the creation of "new social forms in which the mother's work can proceed without damage to the new generation."[17]

The maternity insurance petition called for financial support at the level of the mother's full daily wage (whether she was married or not) for six weeks before and six weeks after delivery, free medical care from a midwife or physician plus household help if necessary, and supplementary "nursing premiums" to mothers who continued to breast-feed after three months. Such benefits, supported by contributions from employers and from all male and female workers, were recommended for women in all occupations and for the female dependents of male workers. The revision of the Imperial Insurance Code that was passed by the Reichstag in 1911 did include some limited improvements in maternity coverage; while maintaining the previous time period and level of support (six weeks of sick pay), the new code provided coverage for previously unprotected occupational groups and gave local insurance authorities the option of providing medical care and "nursing premiums." Some hailed these limited reforms as a sign of increased concern for mothers, but Schreiber, along with left-wing male colleagues, drew an ironic contrast between the generous attitude of the right-wing parties toward the military and their callous neglect of the needs of women and children. The current Reichstag's disregard of women's demands, she stated in 1911, was just one more proof of the need for woman suffrage. Only through the attainment of equality in the male sphere could the rights of women in the female sphere be ensured.[18]

The Bund's practical work, in which Schreiber played a leading role, consisted chiefly of establishing homes for unmarried pregnant women. The policy of many existing homes—limiting admission to married women or those "who had fallen for the first time"—made this a necessary task. Petitions directed by local branches of the Bund to state and muni-

---

17. For the petition, see Schreiber, "Nachlass" (n. 9 above), vol. 29. For a scholarly treatise on this issue, see Henriette Fürth, *Die Mutterschaftsversicherung* (Jena: G. Fischer, 1911). Evans's statement is in Evans (n. 1 above), p. 168. Fürth's article, entitled "Mutterschaft und Ehe: Die Frau als Arbeitsgenossin des Mannes," appeared in *Mutterschutz* 1, no. 11 (1905): 427–48, esp. 429. Schreiber's stand on marriage restrictions was reported by the *Leipziger neueste Nachrichten* (January 15, 1908). Cf. Mary Lynn McDougall, "Protecting Infants: The French Campaign for Maternity Leaves, 1890–1913," *French Historical Studies* 8, no. 1 (Spring 1983): 79–105.

18. For new insurance regulations, see Germany, *Reichsversicherungsordnung, Juli 1911* (Imperial Insurance Regulations, July 1911) (Munich, 1914), 19:195–200. For Schreiber's speech, see *Volkszeitung* (Berlin) (April 21, 1911).

cipal authorities (only a few of which received a response) graphically depicted the situation of the unwed mother in labor, rejected by her family, destitute and homeless. The founding of maternity homes received far more support from the local branches than the more controversial proposals for sexual reform. But Stöcker and Bré (now no longer a member of the Bund) flamboyantly publicized this more "respectable" cause as well. In 1911 the city council of Charlottenburg sued them for libel for asserting that a woman in labor had been turned away from several local hospitals because she had no money and had finally given birth in a police station. Schreiber, who was actively involved in the founding of a model maternity home in the Berlin district of Schöneberg in 1904, insisted that such institutions must do everything possible to strengthen the mother-child bond. Thus she encouraged breast-feeding not only for its hygienic but also for its emotional value. "A flood of warm life engulfed her," wrote Schreiber of a neglectful mother who was finally persuaded to breast-feed her baby, "and a flower of precious love unfolded. Now she would work, beg, starve—face the scorn of society—all for her child!" This typically sentimental passage suggests that for Schreiber, as for many of her colleagues, nurturing children remained a specifically, indeed supremely female activity, bound up with female physical and psychological characteristics. Despite their rejection of Bré's separatist utopia, residual matriarchal feeling was evident in their failure to integrate the father, whose role was limited to procreation and financial support, into the intimate world of mother and child. Badinter notes the tendency of early twentieth-century reformers to limit the authority of the once all-powerful father, assigning his disciplinary responsibilities to the state and his educational and nurturing role to the now self-confident mother.[19]

In a period of growing concern for population growth, control over the birth and rearing of the younger generation could be a source of power. As the crude birth rate continued to decline (from 34.3 per 1,000 in 1901–5 to 31.7 in 1906–10), official attention shifted from death rates to birth rates. Socialists attributed parents' decisions to produce fewer children to poverty and the rising cost of living caused by protective tariff policies, but right-wing politicians blamed prosperity, which had, in the words of the Prussian minister of the interior, "encouraged self-indulgence and disinclination to put up with the inconvenience of raising children." "The vulture of depopulation spreads its wings over the German Empire!" warned an inflammatory right-wing pamphlet, which went on to prophesy that Germany would soon have "more coffins than cra-

19. On the libel suit against Stöcker and Bré, see *Berliner Tageblatt* (May 24, 1911). The quotation from Schreiber is in "Pflanzstätten der Mutterliebe," in "Nachlass" (n. 9 above), vol. 31. Exclusion of the father is discussed in Badinter (n. 4 above), pp. 285–92.

dles!" Governmental pronatalist policies relied increasingly on coercion rather than persuasion; not only did the number of prosecutions under Section 218 of the criminal code, which forbade abortion, rise from 411 in 1902 to 1,678 in 1914, but early in 1914 new laws were proposed forbidding the sale of contraceptive devices and the spread of birth-control information.[20]

The issue of reproductive freedom caused bitter conflict within the feminist movement itself. At the 1908 general meeting of the central German feminist organization, the Bund deutscher Frauenvereine, a legal commission headed by Marie Stritt (then both president of the organization and a member of the Bund für Mutterschutz) brought forward a draft proposal demanding the repeal of Section 218 and thus the legalization of abortion. Stritt saw reproductive freedom as not just a personal but also a political right that could be used purposefully in the struggle for social reform. "The right of women freely to refuse motherhood," she declared in 1908, "will lead to a better, more healthy and more moral world." In an impassioned discussion of Stritt's proposal, another member of the Bund für Mutterschutz, Maria Lichnewska, argued against the repeal. "The future of our state," she proclaimed, "lies in the will of the woman to motherhood"—a will that must be reinforced by coercive pressure. But both Stöcker and Schreiber maintained their long-standing support for freedom of choice. When the numerical strength of conservative and religious women's organizations in the Bund deutscher Frauenvereine resulted in the defeat of Stritt's proposal, Stöcker continued in her vocal opposition to Section 218 and to other laws limiting reproductive self-determination. "Motherhood," she declared in 1909, "which is one of the highest achievements of women, should not be compelled by the threat of imprisonment, but must be responsibly chosen. Considering the awesome responsibility of parents for their children, it is vitally important that this most serious of commitments not be left to blind chance."[21]

In 1910 a bitter conflict between Stöcker and Schreiber, involving both personal and political issues, caused the latter to resign from the

20. On the continuing decline in crude birth rates, see Knodel (n. 2 above). On the debate over the significance of the decline, see Haus der Abgeordneten (n. 3 above). The pamphlet is *Die Furcht vor dem Kinde: Ein Mahnruf an das deutsche Volk* (Düsseldorf, 1914), held in KGA, R/86, 237, v. 12. On prosecutions for violation of Section 218, see Luc Jochimsen, ed., *218: Dokumente eines Hundert-Jahren-Elends* (Hamburg: Konkret Buchverlag, 1971), p. 16.

21. Stritt was quoted in *Vorwärts* (November 2, 1908). A short account of the 1918 meeting is in *Die Frauenbewegung* 12 (September 1908): 154–55. A more complete account of the debate, including the quote from Lichnewska, is given by Evans (n. 1 above), pp. 132–35. Evans bases his account on the archive of the Bund deutscher Frauenvereine, which was closed and inaccessible when I did this research. Stöcker's opinion is from her lecture "Mutterschutz und Abtreibungsstrafe," in Schreiber, "Nachlass" (n. 9 above), vol. 28.

Bund along with many of her colleagues, including Fürth, Lily Braun, and Frieda Radel. Retreating from some of Stöcker's more radical positions, Schreiber set up her own organization, the *Verein für Mutter-und-Kindesrecht* (The society for mothers' and childrens' rights), devoted chiefly to the counseling and practical welfare work that had always been her chief interest. But she continued to advocate a new reproductive ethic based on freedom rather than compulsion, responsibility rather than ignorance. The state that demanded population growth, she insisted, must use positive rather than negative incentives. Using sociological evidence that the rate of infant mortality in working-class families rose along with the number of births, she denied that a mere increase in the crude birth rate ensured a growing and healthy population. "The women's movement has always emphasized quality over quantity," she explained. While explicitly rejecting the "birth strike" advocated in 1913 by two socialist physicians as a means of dramatizing women's grievances, she castigated a government that "demands ever more children but cares little how many of them die, or if the quality of those who survive is so low that they can only do harm to society."[22]

In their concern for the "quality" of the new generation, feminists such as Stöcker and Schreiber insisted that the "right to motherhood" could never be absolute. Indeed, despite their rejection of Bré's proposal to require a health certificate of all mothers as a qualification for aid, the mothers' rights advocates had always agreed that some individuals—especially those afflicted with venereal diseases or hereditary ailments—should not reproduce. Their discussion of the means to this end, however, showed awareness of possible conflicts between the rights of the individual and those of the "new generation." While sharing Bré's concern for eugenic selection, the leadership of the Bund had raised practical objections—that little was known about which diseases were hereditary, that the health of the father was as important as that of the mother, and that the child's hereditary traits could often be modified by the environment. Their refusal to turn away sick or handicapped mothers exposed the mothers' rights advocates to criticism within the eugenics movement; their activities, argued an editorial in the *Archiv für Rassen-und-Gesellschaftsbiologie* in 1905, were "worthless from the point of view of racial hygiene." At a convention held in 1907, the Bund passed a resolution that a health certificate be required of all candidates for marriage. But they rejected a proposal advocating the prohibition of marriage to

22. The dispute is described by Stöcker in a pamphlet, *Krisenmache: Eine Abfertigung* (Berlin, 1910), Helene Stöcker Papers (n. 9 above); and from Schreiber's point of view by her colleague Henriette Fürth, "Die Lage der Mutter und die Entwicklung des Mutterschutzes in Deutschland," in Schreiber, ed. (n. 2 above). Material on Verein für Mutter-und-Kindesrecht is in Schreiber, "Nachlass" (n. 9 above), vol. 39. The quotation from Schreiber is in *Die Zeitung* (Düsseldorf) (February 11, 1911).

those with unsatisfactory health certificates because, in the words of Dr. Max Marcuse, "legal prohibitions on marriage . . . could not prevent illicit sexual intercourse and illegitimate births." In the debate on Section 218, Stöcker argued for the legalization of abortion on eugenic grounds "as an important method of improving the race. Children of parents afflicted by contagious diseases, heart disease, or insanity should not be born."[23]

In most of their proposals for implementing eugenic theory, the German feminists emphasized education to reproductive responsibility rather than coercion. "In the place of the old commandment, 'be fruitful and multiply,'" stated Schreiber, "we now have a new one, 'Be cautious in your reproduction and improve the race.'" Far from rejecting liberal ideas of individual freedom, Schreiber often argued for them on eugenic grounds; sexual freedom for young people would reduce the prevalence of prostitution and venereal disease, she speculated, and economic self-sufficiency for women would enable them to choose young, healthy fathers for their children without regard to conventional economic and social considerations. Against the crude Social Darwinism invoked in official pronatalist rhetoric, contributors to Stöcker's *Die neue Generation* advanced the more sophisticated principles of eugenics. The improvement of the human race, argued prominent Dutch physician and birth-control advocate Johannes Rutgers, must be achieved not through passive submission to natural laws but by an ever more purposeful and conscious control of reproduction. "Natural selection," he argued, "must be superseded by human selection, and involuntary by voluntary reproduction." Women's increasing control over their own reproductive potential, he continued, was an important step toward this goal; healthy mothers might decide to produce many children, while women who were weak or afflicted with hereditary ailments might choose to abstain.[24]

These humane and progressive eugenicists tended to avoid the issue of coercive measures as they might be used on the "unfit" mother who, despite all persuasion to the contrary, insisted on reproducing. Allusions to involuntary eugenic sterilization in Stöcker's *Mutterschutz* were infrequent and tentative; Fürth, in a 1905 series strongly supporting measures

23. Walther Borgius, "Mutterschutz und Rassehygiene," *Mutterschutz* 1, no. 6 (1905): 207–12, esp. 210. A. Ploetz, "Bund für Mutterschutz," *Archiv für Rassen-und-Gesellschaftsbiologie*, vol. 2 (1905), reprinted in Schreiber, "Nachlass" (n. 9 above), vol. 31. The resolutions of the Bund and Marcuse's comments are in *Mutterschutz* 3, no. 2 (1907): 76–80, esp. 78; Stöcker, "Mutterschutz und Abtreibungsstrafe" (n. 21 above). On the eugenics movement and American thought on birth control, see Linda Gordon, *Woman's Body, Woman's Right: A Social History of Birth Control* (New York: Grossmann Publishers, 1976), pp. 116–58.

24. See reports of Schreiber's public addresses in *Die Zeitung* (Düsseldorf) (February 11, 1912), and *Frankfurter Zeitung* (March 27, 1903). Johannes Rutgers, "Rassenverbesserung," *Die neue Generation* 1, no. 1 (1908): 24–28, esp. 28.

to encourage healthy motherhood, suggested that "we should also not exclude the possibility that we could, through humane and painless means, follow the example of Lycurgus and encourage the reproduction only of healthy and sound elements of the population. Of course, not just in the sense of bodily strength. . . . Clearly each individual who is born should be kept alive, and preventive efforts could work only toward the prevention of reproduction among the degenerate. But this is only a minor issue," she added, almost anxiously. In the United States, several states soon passed laws providing for the sterilization of the "unfit" (Indiana passed such a law in 1907, and by 1914 eight more states had followed suit). These laws brought the issue to the attention of the European public. By 1911 references to eugenic sterilization among the German radical feminists had become more explicit. In a contribution to the volume of essays edited by Schreiber entitled *Die Mutterschaft*, Maria von Stach argued that, because the social legislation of the modern state had mitigated the effect of the original "barbaric forms of selection through poverty and sickness," a more humane and purposeful form of selection could now ensure "that the biologically inferior elements of the population [would] not reproduce." Stach alluded favorably to the use of humane sterilization techniques in Oregon and Connecticut but advocated compulsion only in "extreme cases." Schreiber was even more definite in her support of the American precedent. At the conclusion of an essay recommending both reproductive freedom of choice and support for mothers, she added, "And it will also be desirable—as we are told by both the neo-Malthusians and the eugenicists—to prevent the reproduction of alcoholics, feeble-minded persons and other abnormal individuals who could never be persuaded to use birth control, through laws such as those which have been passed in parts of the United States."[25]

While justified in pointing out the authoritarian implications of such ideas, Evans exaggerates when he describes them as symptomatic of a catastrophic "decline of liberalism" in the Bund or in the movement as a whole. In their discussion of eugenic sterilization, the German feminists took their inspiration not from the conservative or racist ideologies then current in Germany but from American legislation that in its own time was generally considered humane and progressive. Indeed, in 1927 a Virginia statute providing for the sterilization of the mentally retarded was upheld by a Supreme Court Justice famous for his enlightened

---

25. Fürth, "Mutterschaft und Ehe" (n. 17 above), pp. 430–36, esp. p. 435; Maria von Stach, "Mutterschaft und Bevölkerungspolitik," in Schreiber, ed. (n. 2 above), p. 197; and Adele Schreiber, "Missbrauchte Mutterschaft," in Schreiber, ed., p. 215. On the American sterilization laws, see Harry H. Laughlin, *Eugenical Sterilization in the United States: A Report of the Psychopathic Laboratory of the Municipal Court of Chicago* (Chicago: Psychopathic Laboratory of the Municipal Court, 1922); and Haller (n. 4 above), pp. 124–43.

opinions: "Three generations of imbeciles is enough!" stated Justice Oliver Wendell Holmes in the case of *Buck* v. *Bell*. During this period, therefore, the idea of involuntary sterilization of the "unfit" was not so repugnant to the liberal conscience as it later became, especially because progressive eugenicists defined unfitness without reference to such clearly discriminatory criteria as race or class. Moreover, German liberals, who tended to view human rights as realized through rather than asserted against the state, might be expected to show even less apprehension than their American counterparts about potential abuses of state power.

The low priority assigned by Stöcker, Schreiber, and their associates to sterilization, voluntary or involuntary, as a eugenic measure may be inferred from the infrequency of their references to it. Sterilization was not mentioned in the numerous programs of the Bund or of the Verein für Mutter-und-Kindesrecht, and was discussed only twice in Schreiber's massive volume, *Die Mutterschaft*. Methods of "negative eugenics" such as sterilization, wrote Havelock Ellis, a frequent contributor to *Die neue Generation*, were not "the whole of eugenics, or indeed . . . in any way essential to a eugenic scheme. . . . There remains the field of positive eugenics, which is concerned not with the elimination of inferior stocks, but with ascertaining which are the superior stocks and with furthering their procreative power."[26]

Although the immediate, practical results of the work of Stöcker, Schreiber, and their colleagues were limited, its effect on public opinion was considerable. Certain of their more controversial positions were rejected not only by their opponents but also by their feminist associates and even by many members of the Bund für Mutterschutz. Indeed, the status and image of Stöcker and Schreiber as pioneers were enhanced by their isolation within the feminist movement; bourgeois feminists regarded issues concerning sexuality, reproduction, and the restructuring of the family as threatening to conventional morality, and socialist feminists saw the same issues as tainted with bourgeois individualism. But the public greeted these controversial ideas, if not with unqualified support, at least with enormous interest. "This lecture, distinguished for its intellectual richness and beautiful delivery," read a newspaper report of one of Schreiber's speeches, "was well received even by those who did not agree with the speaker." Some of the more practical proposals made by the two feminists were at least partially carried out during World War I and the interwar period. The wartime and Weimar years saw maternity

26. Evans (n. 1 above), p. 169; Oliver Wendell Holmes, Buck v. Bell (1926), reprinted in *Eugenics Then and Now*, ed. Carl Jay Bajema (Stroudsburg: Dowden, Hutchinson & Ross, 1976), pp. 156–64; Havelock Ellis, *Studies in the Psychology of Sex* (Philadelphia: F. A. Davis, 1920), 6:217. On the American legislation, see Rudolph Vecoli, "Sterilization: A Progressive Measure?" *Wisconsin Magazine of History* 43, no. 3 (1960): 190–202.

insurance coverage considerably extended, although time limits and benefits still fell below the demands of the 1907 petition. The Weimar constitution provided that "legislation shall provide opportunities for physical, spiritual, and social development to illegitimate children equal to those provided for legitimate children," and feminists such as Schreiber, Marie-Elisabeth Lüders, and Marie Munk worked energetically if unsuccessfully to fulfill this constitutional principle through concrete legislative reforms. The rate of infant mortality continued to decline despite the hardship and malnutrition of the wartime and immediate postwar years. Although this decline was chiefly the result of such long-term trends as improved medical care and sanitation and the decline in fertility itself, health ministry officials also credited an increase in breast-feeding, due in part to wartime shortages of cow's milk but also to improved maternity insurance coverage and the counseling centers set up by such organizations as the Bund and the Verein für Mutter-und-Kindesrecht. The National Socialist government likewise carried out some of the measures recommended by the Bund by passing legislation that improved the legal status of (Aryan) illegitimate children, by granting various financial benefits to (Aryan) parents, and by enforcing certain forms of eugenic selection—albeit forms antithetical to the progressive ideals of most Bund activists. Indeed, the National Socialists violated the most fundamental tenets of the mothers' rights movement in their utter contempt for the political, economic, and reproductive rights of women and countless other peoples. Because of their political views and activities, both Stöcker and Schreiber (who was also endangered by her Jewish ancestry) were forced into exile when the National Socialists took power.[27]

A reappraisal of the contribution of mothers' rights advocates to the feminist movement and to the evolution of Western ideas of the maternal role is essential. Historians have often taken a predominantly negative view both of the maternal ideology itself and of its interpretation by these German feminists. French historian Badinter, who traces the genesis of the modern concept of motherhood to eighteenth-century ideals of feminine domesticity and self-effacement, perceives at the beginning of the

27. On Schreiber's lecture, see *Münchener neueste Nachrichten* (February 24, 1905). On the attitude of socialist feminists toward family and reproductive issues, see Karen Honeycutt, "Socialism and Feminism in Imperial Germany," *Signs: Journal of Women in Culture and Society* 5, no. 1 (Autumn 1979): 30–41. Material documenting the extension of maternity insurance, 1914–29, is in the archive of the Reichsversicherungsamt, R/89, v. 2122, Bundesarchiv Koblenz. On maternity benefits during the Weimar period, see Renate Bridenthal, "Something Old, Something New: Women between the Two World Wars," in *Becoming Visible: Women in European History*, ed. Renate Bridenthal and Claudia Koonz (Boston: Houghton Mifflin Co., 1977), p. 443. On Nazi population policy, see Gisela Bock, "Racism and Sexism in Nazi Germany: Motherhood, Compulsory Sterilization, and the State," *Signs* 8, no. 3 (Spring 1983): 401–21.

twentieth century only a reinforcement of such maternal "masochism" by such new intellectual trends as Freudian psychoanalysis. Commenting more specifically on the work of the German activists, both Richard Evans and German feminist Marie-Luise Janssen-Jurreit express concern about the authoritarian, even totalitarian implications of their program. Janssen-Jurreit, in fact, goes so far as to include it in her sweeping indictment of the wide array of ideas that, "publicized through Utopian-sounding reform programs," anticipated "the measures of the Nazi state." But without ignoring the problematic aspects of their thought, historians must view Stöcker and Schreiber in the context of their own period and avoid oversimplified comparisons with or causal linkages between their ideas and those of National Socialism, of which they were both opponents and victims. Authority and coercion played an exceedingly minor role in their vision of a new generation of mothers. On the contrary, they emphasized freedom both from restrictive laws and from the traditional ethic of maternal self-effacement.

Sexual freedom rather than subordination, economic self-sufficiency rather than dependence, a conscious preference for quality over quantity of offspring, and responsibility rather than blind submission to instinct—all these became the central principles of an evolving concept of motherhood that, though always controversial, has been profoundly influential in the twentieth century. Many of the problems raised by the German mothers' rights advocates—the balance between parental and economic responsibilities, the role of the father, the authority of the state over the family—are still discussed today. Their goal—the realization of an ideal of motherhood that enhances rather than denies women's individual development—still awaits its fulfillment.[28]

Department of History
University of Louisville

28. Badinter (n. 4 above), pp. 260–91; Evans (n. 1 above); Janssen-Jurreit (n. 1 above), p. 169.

NURTURING THE MASTER'S CHILD:
SLAVERY AND THE ROMAN CHILD-NURSE

SANDRA R. JOSHEL

Slavewomen accepted the challenge of the tasks they had been set, and created a spiritual bond between themselves and their charges that often lasted for the rest of their lives. [JOSEPH VOGT, *Ancient Slavery and the Ideal of Man*]

What you want from me? say Sofia. I feel something for you because out of all the people in your daddy's house you showed me some human kindness. But on the other hand, out of all the people in your daddy's house, I showed you some. Kind feeling is all I have to offer you. [ALICE WALKER, *The Color Purple*]

Classicist Joseph Vogt and novelist Alice Walker offer divergent views of the feelings of a child-nurse for her privileged nursling, perhaps because the former looks through the eyes of the nursling and the latter through the eyes of the nurse. In Rome, as in the antebellum American south, the child was often a slaveholder and the nurse a slave or, in Rome, an ex-slave, freeborn foreigner, or lower-class citizen. The social distance and power relations between nurse and nursling give the intimate relations at the

I am indebted to Stephen Pfohl, Amy Richlin, Peter Weiler, Janet James, and the readers for *Signs* for their substantive criticisms and comments.

This essay originally appeared in *Signs*, vol. 12, no. 1, Autumn 1986.

center of nursing a contradictory quality. At least, we would expect that the feelings of nurse and nursling might differ and that their views would involve contradiction and ambivalence.

Yet when modern historians discuss the evidence for the perspectives of nurse and nursling, they generally envision an intimate relationship, assuming the equal and mutual attachment of caretaker and charge.[1] For Vogt, nurses reveal how master-slave "relationships could result in intimacy, trust and friendship." Vogt invokes the image of the black mammy of the antebellum American south, but a mammy unambiguously accommodating of her enslavement and respected by a master who saw her as the happily devoted servant.[2]

M. I. Finley has criticized these characterizations and pointed out the difficulty of ascertaining the views of any slave. In *Ancient Slavery and Modern Ideology*, he argues that Vogt simply selects from a body of anecdotal evidence those pieces that conform with his desire to reveal a humanitarian attitude in Roman society. Drawing "a sharp distinction between more or less humane treatment of individual slaves by individual masters and the inhumanity of slavery as an institution," Finley examines such master-slave relations as examples of "the ambiguity inherent . . . in the reduction of human beings to the category of property." Analysis of the slave's feelings is problematic primarily because the pertinent statements in ancient literature reflect only the views of the slaveholder. However, Finley does not distinguish between the literature addressed to the upper-classes and epitaphs authored, not by the nursling, but by the nurse or her peers.[3]

This paper examines the relationship between nurse and nursling through nursling epitaph commemorations and the literature of the early Empire and discusses what they said (and did not say) about their relationships. While the voice of the upper-class nursling, expressed in the literature of the early Empire, makes explicit statements about feelings, loyalty, and duty, the child-nurse does not reciprocate in kind. The nurse's voice can be heard only in epitaphs dedicated by her or her peers, where lived experience lies masked in the rituals of death and circumstances of commemoration.[4] I draw on the testimony of masters and slaves from the

---

[1] In a positive, negative, or neutral way: Joseph Vogt, *Ancient Slavery and the Ideal of Man*, trans. Thomas Wiedmann (Cambridge, Mass.: Harvard University Press, 1975), 105 ff.; R. H. Barrow, *Slavery in the Roman Empire* (London: Methuen, 1928), 37–38; Susan Treggiari, "Jobs for Women," *AJAH* 1 (1976): 76–104, esp. 89. Abbreviations used throughout are found in *L'année philologique*.

[2] Vogt, 104–9, esp. 105.

[3] M. I. Finley, *Ancient Slavery and Modern Ideology* (New York: Viking Press, 1980), 107, 122, 99–119.

[4] Citations of epitaphs, unless indicated otherwise, are to the *Corpus Inscriptionum Latinarum* (CIL), vol. 6. The nurses discussed here include all women entitled *nutrix* (cf.

American south to indicate how the nursling's view might distort the nurse and her lived reality. Although the explicit statements of mammies cannot prove what the Roman nurse felt, their divergence from their nurslings' views suggests the need for caution in reading nurses' epitaphs solely in terms of upper-class views and underscores the value of exploring other lines of interpretation.

The work of nursing

The Roman nurse took care of young children, and her duties, both physical care and what we might label socialization, brought her into intimate contact with her nursling. She was a wet-nurse and, after weaning, fed the child and was its primary caretaker.[5] Some nurses, too, remained with their adult charges as personal servants.

Controlling women's biology was an important element of the coercion that surrounded the nurse's service. The child-nurses of the upper classes, often slaves, did not choose their work; they were chosen, used by their owners because of their physical condition—the wet-nurse was simply a slave who was lactating. Although manumission appears to have been common for slave nurses, the ex-master, usually the nursling or his/her parent, maintained a claim to the ex-slave's labor and deference.[6] Even in the case of free women who hired out their services and, unlike slaves, could be said to have chosen their work, compulsion, albeit of a different sort, remained a factor, for economic necessity was the motivation for

---

educatrix, 9792, and *mamma*, 2210) in *CIL* 6, the largest collection of inscriptions from the city of Rome, and in *Notizie degli Scavi* (*NS*), excepting those whose epitaphs clearly postdate A.D. 193, and the slaves and freedwomen of the imperial family (4352, 5201, 8943, 8941, 10909, 20042). Tatia Baucyl—— (8942), nurse of Domitilla's children, was not an imperial freedwoman and is included.

[5] The job titles of nurses in epitaphs reflect these duties: *nutrix lactaria* (wet-nurse, 27262), *nutrix et mammula* (nurse and foster-mother, literally, "little breast," 16450), *nutrix assa* (dry nurse, 29497), *cunaria* (cradle rocker, infant attendant, 27134). Soranus, *Gynecology*, trans. Owsei Temkin (Baltimore: Johns Hopkins University Press, 1956), 2.93–126; cf. *Digest*, 50.13.1.14. See Treggiari, 87–89; Natalie Kampen, *Image and Status: Roman Working Women in Ostia* (Berlin: Gebr. Mann Verlag, 1981), 109–10 (for images of nurses, 33 ff., 82 ff., 96, 146–49); Keith Bradley, "Wet-Nursing at Rome: A Study in Social Relations," in *The Family in Ancient Rome*, ed. Beryl Rawson (Ithaca, N.Y.: Cornell University Press, 1986), 201–29, which appeared too late to be considered here.

[6] Legal restrictions on the manumission of nurses were eased (*Digest* 40.2.13; cf. Gaius, *Institutes*, 1.19); the epitaphs testify to what appears to be the frequent manumission of nurses (see n. 38 below). On *obsequium* (proper respect), *officicum* (duty), and *operae* (work days), see Georges Fabre, *Libertus: Recherches sur les rapports patron-affranchi à la fin de la république romaine*, Coll. Ecole Française de Rome (Paris: De Boccard, 1981), 148–50, 225–26, 318 ff.; Susan Treggiari, *Roman Freedmen during the Late Republic* (Oxford: Oxford University Press, 1969), 69 ff. (with analysis of other scholars).

taking up this occupation.[7] Lacking the money, skills, and connections to enter other trades, the poor woman simply used or rather permitted someone else to use her body, the Roman hierarchies of gender and class sanctioning such use.

The opinions of elite nurslings

The literature in which nurses are discussed is biased by both gender and class; its authors, all male, focus on the relationship of upper-class nurslings and their slave or foreign nurses, although the nursing of slave children was common. Whether negative or positive, their opinions have fixed certain "truths" about nurses, in effect displacing and disguising the power relations of gender, class, and slavery that define the social position of the male author or his audience. These dynamics lie at the origin of nursing and explain the coercion surrounding the nurse's labor.

These authors focus not on the child-nurse herself but on the person produced by the use of a child-nurse. The Greek physician Soranus who discusses nurses in a work on female biology and health care is concerned primarily with the physical well-being of the child. The philosopher Favorinus is anxious about the character and moral fiber of a child whose noble mother does not intend to nurse him herself. Tacitus, senator and historian, and Quintilian, famous as a teacher of oratory, comment on the child's early socialization as an important component in the training of an orator.[8]

Generally, these authors see the use of child-nurses as a less than ideal practice and often an undesirable one. Any nurse other than the mother robs children of their natural sustenance[9] or the means by which they grow in likeness to their parents, especially the father.[10] The "bad" nurse, characterized by Favorinus as "a slave or of servile origin . . . , of a foreign and barbarous nation, . . . dishonest, ugly, unchaste and a wine-bibber," presents a dual threat: she endangers both her charge's physical well-being and his or her moral and intellectual development.[11] In Soranus's opinion, the nurse's sexual activity and drinking spoil her milk and make her less attentive to her charge's needs. Moreover, an ill-tempered nurse will raise

---

[7] See Dio of Prusa, *Discourse*, 7.114; Epictetus, 3.26.7; Plutarch, *De vitando aere alieno*, 6, discussed by Susan Treggiari, "Urban Labour in Rome: *Mercennarii* and *Tabernarii*," in *Non-Slave Labour in Graeco-Roman Antiquity*, ed. Peter Garnsey, *PCPS* suppl. vol. 6 (Cambridge: Cambridge Philological Society, 1980), 48–64, esp. 49.

[8] Soranus, cf. 2.87; all quotations of Favorinus are from Aulus Gellius, *The Attic Nights of Aulus Gellius*, trans. John C. Rolfe, Loeb Classical Library (Cambridge, Mass.: Harvard University Press, 1982); Tacitus, *Dialogue on Oratory*, 28–29; Quintilian, *Oratorial Training*, 1.4.4–11.

[9] Soranus, 2.87.

[10] Favorinus, 12.1.8, 11–15, 20.

[11] Ibid., 12.1.17.

a child of similar character because children take on the disposition of their nurses. According to Tacitus and Quintilian, the speech, stories, and beliefs of ignorant caretakers corrupt children's minds and spirits.[12]

However, the practice of nursing is not bad simply because of bad nurses; handing children over to slave attendants is itself part of the decadence of an imperial society that has abandoned the virtues of ancestors who reared their own children or delegated responsibility to some upright elder female relation.[13] These upper-class authors associate corrupt or foreign nurses and the very use of child-nurses with other signs of moral decay, arguing that parents' abdication of responsibility results in weak and degenerate offspring and the passing of antique excellence.[14] Just as the high price paid for a cook signals a turn away from the simplicity of the early Republic, the foreign nurse marks a turn away from traditional family relations.[15]

Like the cook, the nurse becomes a means of talking about a society altered by an empire that brought wealth in the form of taxes, booty, and conquered peoples—slaves.[16] For Tacitus, Quintilian, and Favorinus, the conquest of empire was, of course, an event long past, but wealth and its use continued to be a primary concern. Thus, by focusing on nurses they discussed an aspect of empire, the relations of conqueror to conquered, and an aspect of property holding, the relations of master to slave.

In effect, in the literature the concern with decadence displaces acknowledgment of the power of the conqueror, slaveholder, or upper classes. The nurse's reported lack of chastity, drinking, ill-temper, vulgar speech, alien manners, and superstitions becomes more important than the basic facts of her service—her own lack of power, or her slave status, or her status as a foreigner, or her poverty. The nurse symbolizes decadence, yet in reality she was a manifestation of imperial power—Rome's dominance over foreigners—and of the master's power over the slave.

The dangers of the "bad" nurse are mitigated in the depictions of the "good" nurse, a woman who tends her charges without damage to their bodies and minds, loves them, and remains loyal. Instructions on the correct way to use child-nurses suggest that a woman can be *made* a good

[12] Soranus, 2.88; Tacitus, 29.1; Quintilian, 1.1.4–5, cf. 1.1.8–9.

[13] Tacitus, 28.4–5; Plutarch, *Life of Cato the Elder*, 20.2–3.

[14] See Donald Earl, *The Political Thought of Sallust* (Cambridge: Cambridge University Press, 1961), 41 ff., and *The Moral and Political Traditions of Rome* (Ithaca, N.Y.: Cornell University Press, 1967), 17 ff. for discussion and sources on Roman laments of degeneracy.

[15] Livy, *Histories*, 39.6; and Pliny, *Natural History*, 9.67.

[16] Roman authors frequently criticize the use of domestic servants and rarely address the social and economic effects of large-scale slavery. On domestic slaves as a sign of decadence, see Cicero, *In Defence of Sextus Roscius Amerinus*, 133–34 (cf. *Against Piso*, 67); Seneca, *On the Tranquility of the Mind*, 8.6, and *Moral Letters*, 27.5–8, 47, 110.17, 122.15–16; Petronius, *Satyricon*, passim. On slavery and conquest, see Keith Hopkins, *Conquerors and Slaves* (Cambridge: Cambridge University Press, 1978), 99 ff.

nurse by diligent supervision; alternatively, in anecdotes, a nurse simply *is* loving or loyal. In these accounts, the good nurse is so because she is either firmly under the control of her employer or she has a disposition that makes control of her unnecessary. In effect, in the vision of male authors, the nurse's deleterious influence on the child can be limited, and even curtailed, by regulating her as a technical object or by imaging her as completely invested in her nursling. The good nurse is an ambiguous figure. Either she is to be acted upon, to be treated as if she were a tool under the control of its owner, or she becomes a subjective being who acts, feels, and thinks.

Technical regulation characterizes Soranus's advice on child-nurses. The selection of a nurse necessitates a meticulous physical examination and consideration of the woman's age, health, build, color, breast size and shape, as well as attention to the characteristics that ease the employer's task of regulation—self-control, sympathy, good temper, tidiness. Not only her child-care duties but her own activities and physical routine must be carefully controlled and monitored: she must "abstain from coitus, drinking, lewdness, and any other such pleasure and incontinence."[17] Thus regulated, the nurse will produce good milk and devote herself to her charge. Although Soranus does not specify a slave nurse, his instructions for selection and treatment resemble the judicious purchase and use of property—of an object for one's control.

Yet, to regard the nurse as a technical object in need of calibration cannot be really satisfying because of the issue of the nursling's feelings. Implicitly, the charge's affection would be received by a nurse who was controlled and compelled by her employer to give the child attention. The motivations of slave nurses would pose a special problem. Even a kind and humane master like Pliny believed that slaves were moved by fear; not even a kind and considerate master could feel safe, much less loved, by his slaves.[18]

It is in this context that we should view the anecdotes that describe the good nurse as freely loving and devoted. Fronto claims the nurse's love for her charge makes her hostile to the adolescence that removes the beloved child from her care. Suetonius reports that nurses buried the abandoned Nero and the murdered Domitian—at the moment when they could have easily and even legitimately ignored their tie to their former charges. The anecdotes feature nurses as unambivalently committed and devoted to their charges, portraying women who spontaneously take up the duty imposed on them.[19]

[17] Soranus, 2.88 (cf. Quintilian 1.1.4), 2.99 ff., 2.93–98.
[18] Pliny, *Letters*, 1.4, 3.14.5.
[19] Fronto, *Letters*, 2.124 (Loeb Classical Library); and Suetonius, *Life of Nero*, 50, and *Life of Domitian*, 17.3. Compare stories of the "faithful slave": Seneca, *On Benefits*, 3.23.2–3,

The ideological construction of these portrayals of the good nurse's subjectivity is evident in their uniformity: she feels loving loyalty to master-nurslings, undisturbed by any of the fear, resentment, or resistance attested for other slaves. Such feelings would be disruptive and disturbing, for they point to the origins of her situation and to the reality of the power relations between nurse and nursling, between nurse and the nursling's parents. The literature attends to the loyal, loving nurse and thus obscures the existence of such feelings. The nurse as subject is a single-minded person; when she thinks and feels, she thinks and feels exclusively out of love and duty to her charge.

The good nurse, especially when her subjectivity is displayed, appears to be connected to the "bad" mother who then bears the blame for the failures of contemporary parenting. According to Tacitus, women used to find their glory in devoting themselves to home and children. The mother who refuses to nurse her own child is only concerned about her beauty in Favorinus's opinion. Her abdication of traditional responsibilities means the child must be handed over to others, and the parents thereby "sever, or at any rate loosen and relax, that bond and cementing of mind and of affection with which nature attaches parents to their children."[20] In effect, the mother's self-concern disrupts the parent-child relationship and opens the way for the intrusion of the foreigner, the slave nurse. The Roman child, in this scenario, will be either corrupted by the bad nurse or rescued by the mother surrogate, the good nurse. In both cases, there is danger—the first poses a threat to the child's mind and body, and the other weakens parental control and filial piety (*pietas*).

An emphasis on the failure of upper-class women as mothers draws attention away from the power relations of gender and the practical reality of slavery. The issue is not simply the master's power over the slave, but the slaveholder's power to command the female slave to fulfill the nurturing functions of women of the slaveholding class, who either do not or have refused to fulfill these functions. In effect, the idea that the use of child-nurses signals decadence, then, defines decadence as in part a condition that results from the failure of men to force women into fufilling their traditional (and male-defined) child-care duties. Failure to control upper-class women necessitates control of those who do tend the children, a

25.1; Appian, *Civil Wars*, 4.43 ff.; Valerius Maximus, *Memorable Deeds and Savings*, 6.8. Stories of wives often follow a similar pattern (Appian 4.39–40; Valerius Maximus 6.7). Compare Vogt (n. 1 above), 133 ff.

[20] Tacitus, 28–29. Favorinus, 12.1.8–9; 12.1.21. Favorinus compares such women to those who abort a child to preserve their appearance. Compare Juvenal, *Satires*, 6.592–600; Ovid, *Amores*, 2.14. On abortion, see Enzo Nardi, *Procurato aborto nel mondo greco romano* (Milan: Guiffrè, 1971); the review of Sheila Dickison, "Abortion in Antiquity," *Arethusa* 6, no. 1 (Spring 1973): 159–66; W. J. Watts, "Ovid, the Law and Roman Society on Abortion," *Acta Classica* 16 (1973): 89–101.

control facilitated by status and class-conscious ideologies and practices. Since the nurse substitutes for the upper-class woman, the literature images her, strikingly, as culpable for the most serious flaws of the *matrona*—unchastity and wine drinking.[21]

Male views of the nurse who attends and serves female charges grown to adulthood also portray the nurse as a substitute: here, she stands in for the woman who acts contrary to men's expectations and desires.[22] In this literature, nurses share the characteristics of old women in parallel roles who, as Amy Richlin points out, "constitute a sort of uncanny other." In tragedy and epic, the nurse as advisor abets action that has destructive impact on men; in elegy, transformed into the figure of *lena* (female procurer), companion, witch, or elderly female counselor, she serves "to remove the attractive young woman from the poet's exclusive control and to pervert the sexual behavior of the mistress."[23]

The devoted mother-surrogate, who is normally seen as a good nurse, here is seen to have perverted the role of the mother who properly accommodates her daughter to male control. As a sort of conspiratorial agent of unrest among women in general, she is portrayed as someone who encourages the tendencies of free women to resist traditional gender relations in which woman is subordinate and accessible. The poet or husband/author images that it is the nurse's intrusion, not the independent action of the woman, which thwarts his desire. Thus, in literature upper-class women who benefit from the privileges of their class, any woman whose "wayward" desires we now might perceive as instances of differentiated gender power, and women who counsel one another all appear in male ideology as stories of the bad *matrona* or the bad nurse. Like slavery itself, the power relations of gender that circumscribe child-nursing, on the one hand, and the author's own privileged position, on the other, do not receive comment.

The use of nurses, slave or freed, also created contradictions in master-slave and patron-freedmen relations or, rather, in the master's/author's vision of these. The nurse regulated essential elements in her nursling's life; the elite child relied on her or his nurse for food, physical care, and emotional support. In the master's writings (and in reality), however, proper and legal control belonged to master and patron, and the paternalis-

---

[21] On unchastity and wine drinking in early law, see Alan Watson, *Rome of the XII Tables* (Princeton, N.J.: Princeton University Press, 1975), 31–38; Geoffrey MacCormack, "Wine-Drinking and the Romulan Law of Divorce," *Irish Jurist* 10 (1975): 170–74.

[22] Juvenal, *Satires*, 6.354; Apuleius, *Metamorphoses*, 8.10; Martial, 11.78.7–8.

[23] Amy Richlin, "Invective against Women in Roman Satire," *Arethusa* 17, no. 1 (Spring 1984): 67–80, esp. 71–72, and *The Garden of Priapus* (New Haven, Conn.: Yale University Press, 1983), 113–14. Compare the nurse of Myrrha, Ovid, *Metamorphoses*, 10.382–464. For the nurse, *lena*, advisor, see Ovid, *Amores*, 1.8; Propertius 4.5; Tibullus, 1.5; cf. Martial, 11.78.7–8.

tic view saw the slave as dependent on the master for food, clothing, and care.[24] As Orlando Patterson has pointed out, paternalism provided a sort of camouflage for the master's own dependence.[25] Yet, this camouflage could not effectively obscure relations between the slave nurse and the child, for there was no question about who took care of and fed whom. Dedications to a *nutrix lactaria* or *nutrix et mammula* implicitly acknowledged this.

Perhaps it was the nursling's difficulty with acknowledging his childhood dependence that enhanced his satisfaction in taking care of his former nurse. Certainly Pliny's gift of a farm to his nurse and the arrangements for its management suggest more than an example of a former nursling's affection for his nurse. In a letter delegating the management of the farm, Pliny takes obvious pleasure in taking care of his nurse, and his concern for the farm's success and her welfare is self-conscious and studied. The published letter demonstrates Pliny's solicitude for his former nurse, but it also displays a reversal of the original relationship of his dependence and her control, featuring a charge who now controls his nurse's material existence and a nurse who is dependent on her nursling. In adulthood, the charge has reestablished the proper relations of subordination, much to his satisfaction.[26]

The testimony of black mammies

The factor of race as well as differences in economic structure and patterns of slaveholding and manumission prohibit direct comparisons between Rome and the antebellum American south, but a juxtaposition of the black mammy's views and her master-nursling's assumptions suggests the degree to which Roman authors may have omitted the nurse's sensibilities and experience. Surviving testimony shows us that the southern slaveholder's vision of the nurse does not describe her understanding of herself and her relationship with her elite charges. Because she occupied a different position in that relationship and in the wider society, the black nurse saw differently, rephrased the slaveholder's terms, and had concerns other than those the slaveholder ascribed to her.

Although the black mammy often occupied a more central and authoritative position in the household, she, like the Roman nurse, raised her

---

[24] Seneca, *On the Tranquility of the Mind*, 8.8; Pliny, *Letters*, 8.16. Pliny likes to see himself as an indulgent father to his slaves (*Letters*, 1.4, 5.19.1, cf. Seneca, *Moral Letters*, 47.10). On the vision of southern slaveholders, see Eugene Genovese, *Roll, Jordan, Roll* (New York: Random House, 1976), 75–87; Leon Litwack, *Been in the Storm So Long* (New York: Random House, 1980), 189–93, 359–63.

[25] Orlando Patterson, *Slavery and Social Death* (Cambridge, Mass.: Harvard University Press, 1982), 337. Compare Genovese 89–91, on mutual dependency, 344.

[26] Pliny, *Letters*, 6.3.

master's children; an intimate relationship was established out of her physical care and socialization of the child. Mammies per se were found on large plantations where there might also be other nurses, but on most plantations and sizable farms a black woman raised the white children. Often, too, these women took care of both white and black children, including orphans or young slaves removed from the care of their parents.[27]

In contrast to the Roman authors discussed above, southern planters did not view the use of slave nurses as a decadent practice. They comment on their own dependency and readily admit the nurse's importance. If the testimony of Annie Laurie Broidrick of Mississippi is typical, whites both loved and feared the slave women who raised them. "We had the greatest love for her, but it was tempered with fear, for she never overlooked a fault."[28] Like the Romans, however, southern whites believed in the nurse's love and loyalty. In fact, no others from the antebellum south are so idealized for their devotion.

The nurse's affection and loyalty were there, but not in the way understood by masters who had difficulty seeing beyond their own feelings and their need for the nurse's love and trust.[29] With the advance of the Union army and eventually emancipation, mammies, especially, did not behave as their masters expected. Their actions (and in some cases departure) bewildered and disappointed their former masters. Grace Elmore was incensed when Old Mary, the family nurse, left without warning: "One cannot expect total sacrifice of self, but certainly there should be some consideration of others. Old Mary is off my books for any kindness or consideration I may be able to show her in after years. I would not turn on my heel to help her, a more pampered indulged old woman one could find no where."[30]

When such behavior could not be explained by Yankee instigation, it was attributed to a lack of discipline, and too much familiarity and indulgence. Blame was placed on the slave, her actions seen as a betrayal of mutual duties and affections. Intimacy, as Eugene Genovese observes, "turned every act of impudence and insubordination—every act of unsanctioned self-assertion—into an act of treason and disloyalty, for by repudiating the principle of submission it struck at the heart of the master's moral self-justification and therefore at his self-esteem."[31] In fact, slaveholders'

[27] Genovese (n. 24 above), 353–65. For nurses of slave children, see James Curry, *Liberator* (January 10, 1840), in *Slave Testimony*, ed. John W. Blassingame (Baton Rouge: Louisiana State University Press, 1977), 133; Frederick Douglass, *Life and Times of Frederick Douglass* (1892; reprint, New York: Macmillan Co., 1962), 27–36.

[28] Genovese (n. 24 above), 354.

[29] For the slaveholder's need for his servants' love and trust, see Genovese, 344, cf. 91; on the misapprehension and assumptions of slaveowners, see Litwack, 152–63, 293–96; Genovese, 97–112.

[30] Litwack, 302, cf. 301.

[31] Genovese, 91.

original assumptions about their slaves' feelings inhibited any understanding that these women might have had their own sense of freedom and that love and devotion had come from an individual whose participation in the intimate relationship was, at least in origin, coerced.

The nurse's demonstrated affection for the white family could have been a response to coercive elements in her situation; in any case, it did serve to alleviate or transpose her condition as a slave. In the first place, loyalty and affection could secure protection. "Of course," a Virginia planter stated in 1865, "if a servant has the charge of one of my little ones, and I see the child grow fond of her, and that she loves the child, I cannot but feel kindly towards her." Such kind feeling often protected the mammy from whippings and sale, and this immunity might extend, though less fully, to her husband and children.[32] Moreover, affection and devotion were critical to the maintenance of mammy's authority. Her position and power depended on her relationship with the white family. Without their attachment and her demonstration of devotion, she had no authority. She was not "some pathetic appendage to the powerful whites of the Big House," but her place required her active participation in a paternalistic "system of reciprocal obligations defined from above."[33]

Yet the dependency of whites and their need for mammy's love and approval empowered the nurse; at least, within the system, these were the means of rephrasing the relations of domination in intimate interactions. The dependency of whites, well known to their servants, and whites' need for their servants' love gave the slave an advantage; servants used it, pushing their owners into a reversal of roles when possible.[34] The testimony of slaveholders recounts mammy's assumption of authority and her continued regulation of the affairs of a former nursling.[35] Adulthood brought the child the total power of the slaveholder, but it did not erase the nurse's experience of the child's helplessness and vulnerability nor the nursling's experience of loving and fearing mammy.

The nurse, however, had other feelings and concerns than the white family and her white charges. James Curry reports that his mother, a slave on a North Carolina farm, was much occupied with the slave orphans committed to her care and that they and her own children defined her sense of responsibility. "Their master will not clothe them, and I cannot see them go naked; *I* have children and I do not know where their lot may be cast; I may die and leave them, and I desire to do by these little orphans, as I should wish mine to be done by."[36] In one contemporary account,

[32] Ibid., 357–58. See Curry (on the beating of his mother by her former nursling and the girl's father), 132–33, and Litwack (n. 24 above), 54.

[33] Genovese (n. 24 above), 360–61.

[34] Ibid., 344–47; Litwack, 387 ff.; Douglass (n. 27 above), 99, 146–47, 185 ff.

[35] Genovese, 355.

[36] Curry, 133–34.

Louisa, a just liberated slave on a Georgia plantation, carefully tended the children left with her, but she did not object when the Union soldiers threatened to set fire to her master's home. Surprised at the apparent incongruities of her behavior, the officer asked for an explanation. "Cause there has been so much devilment here," Louisa responded, "whipping niggers most to death to make 'em work to pay for it."[37] Louisa acted responsibly in terms of her charges, but her loyalties and feelings also were grounded in the slave community of which she was a member.

The discussion of mammies in the antebellum south suggests the need for an examination of the statements made by the Roman nurse in her own terms and in a perspective that acknowledges that she might have had feelings and concerns different from those ascribed to her by her social betters. While we cannot simply assign the views of black nurses to Roman nurses, we can cautiously use their explicit statements and the divergence from their masters' vision to open areas of investigation and speculation about the Roman nurses appearing in epitaphs.

Nurse's epitaphs

For information on nurses' views, we must turn to stone epitaphs dedicated to and by nurses (N = 57).[38] In Rome, individuals who have no voice in the literary sources could be inscribed in history, as it were, by themselves and their social peers through the practice of commemoration in sepulchral inscriptions. The use of large chamber tombs (*columbaria*) and the popularity of burial societies (*collegia*, composed of the slaves and freedmen of one family, or of those with the same occupation, or of men and women whose shared interest was named burial) insured individual commemoration for those undistinguished by wealth or social rank. In general, commemorators included the deceased, the deceased's family

[37] Litwack, 163.

[38] Of the nurses, 7 percent (N = 4) were slaves; 15.8 percent (N = 9), uncertain slaves; 52.6 percent (N = 30), freedwomen; and 24.6 percent (N = 14), uncertain freeborn. Slaves and freedwomen have formal status indication, or their legal status is suggested by other information in the epitaph. The terms "uncertain slave" and "uncertain freeborn" are not Roman legal categories; they reflect our uncertainty. Nurses in these two categories have the name forms appropriate for a slave (a single name) or a freeborn citizen (the nomen, also borne by freed slaves) without formal status indication, and nothing in the epitaph points to their precise legal status. The notation of work itself in the presentation of nurses places these women in a select group within the conventions of the sepulchral inscriptions of imperial Rome: those for whom work had a special significance. Occupational title appears in only about 10 percent of the city's epitaphs: see Pertti Huttunen, *The Social Strata of the Imperial City of Rome*, Acta Universitatis Ouluensis, ser. B (Oulu: University of Oulu, 1974), 48. Of the 1,328 individuals with job titles, over 60 percent of both men and women were slaves or freed slaves.

who had the primary responsibility for commemoration, and often colleagues and social peers, including fellow slaves and ex-slaves. In effect,
then, the practice of self-commemoration and the dedication of epitaphs by
family and peers make the epitaph a document written by the person it
describes or by someone close to her/him. Nurses or their peers in most
cases were responsible for their own presentations.[39]

An epitaph is a record of identity, both of the deceased and the
dedicator (where named), and it is clear that presentations of identity were
self-conscious and directed toward an audience. Public festivals and private ceremonies took place at the tomb, so the epitaph served to keep the
name and identity of the deceased and the commemorator before the eyes
of the living, especially the deceased's family and peers who shared the
tomb and participated in the rituals. Epitaphs also provide insight into the
social context of those involved; since commemoration depended on social
relations as well as on financial resources (and for those with few resources
the former will have been critical), an epitaph reflects the social experience
of dedicator and deceased.[40]

Unfortunately, compared with the dramatic testimony of Louisa or
James Curry, the voice of the Roman nurse is faint, for her presentation
consists not of thoughts and sentiments, but of the bare record of a name,
with or without proper indication of legal status, occasionally an age at
death, the social relations evidenced in the circumstances of burial, and an
occupational title. Yet three observations can be made that do throw some
light on the views of child-nurses: first, that the nurse is usually located
among her peers; second, that in this context, the epitaphs reveal the
multiple source of parenting available to the children of slaves and freed
slaves and the special role of the nurse; and third, that the nurse showed a
preference for a "status-free" title as opposed to a name-form declaring her
a slave or freed slave.

The title "child-nurse" seems to have identified the nurse to her peers,
and, even when her nursling belonged to the upper classes, she appeared
not simply as the caretaker of some elite child (as in the views of male
authors), but as a person with family ties and other social relations.

> To the Spirits of the Dead.
> To Volussia Felicla [sic],
> nurse of Torquata.

---

[39] For good general descriptions of death and burial in Rome, see Keith Hopkins, *Death
and Renewal* (Cambridge: Cambridge University Press, 1983), 201–56; and J. M. C. Toyn-
bee, *Death and Burial in the Roman World* (Ithaca, N.Y.: Cornell University Press, 1971).

[40] For sepulchral and burial costs, see Richard Duncan-Jones, *The Economy of the Roman
Empire: Quantitative Studies* (Cambridge: Cambridge University Press, 1974), for Africa,
79–80, 99–101, and for Italy, 127–31, 166–71.

Verecundus, son, set this
up for a well-deserving
mother.

[*CIL* 6.29550]

Arruntia Cleopatra, freedwoman
of Lucius, nurse.
Lucius Arruntius Dicaeus, freedman
of Lucius, foster-brother.[41]

[*CIL* 6.5939]

Cornelia Prima,
nurse of Scipio.

[*CIL* 6.16128]

The nurse was usually commemorated by an unnamed dedicator (see table 1) or by a family member (Felicla). Of the unnamed dedicators, four women shared their epitaph with a family member or social peer (Cleopatra), and twelve appeared alone (Prima). The location of some of these epitaphs, and the usual pattern in similar cases, point to dedication by the nurse herself, a family member, a fellow slave or ex-slave, or some other peer.[42] Even when she is a dedicator and commemorates a nursling (see table 2), relations with peers define her; the nursling's family often was of

TABLE I **EPITAPHS DEDICATED TO CHILD-NURSES**

Dedicator	Unclear[a]	Family of Child-Nurse	Charge or Charge's Family	No Named Dedicator	Total
Legal status of child-nurse:					
Slave.	. . .	. . .	. . .	3	3
Uncertain slave	. . .	1	1	1	3
Freed slave.	. . .	5	10	10	25
Uncertain freeborn	1	. . .	2	2	5
Total	1	6	13	16	36
	(2.8)	(16.7)	(36.1)	(44.4)	(100)

SOURCES.—All the epitaphs come from the *Corpus Inscriptionum Latinarum*, vol. 6, and *Notizie degli Scavi*.
NOTE.—Numbers in parentheses are percentages.
[a]Dedicator's name and epitaph obscured by breakage (21710).

[41] In light of Cleopatra's job title, it would seem that Dicaeus was her son and the foster-brother (i.e., nursed by the same woman) of her charge (rather than her foster-brother); see n. 52 below.

[42] Five (7393, 6323, 5939, 7618, 4457), perhaps seven (9245, 9901b), were buried in chamber tombs (*columbaria*) set aside for the staff of one family. For patterns of commemoration among slaves and freedmen in a household, see Marlene Boudreau Flory, "Family in *Familia*," *AJAH* 3, no. 1 (1978): 78–95, esp. 80–87; and Susan Treggiari, "Jobs in the Household of Livia," *PBSR* 43 (1975): 48–77, esp. 48–49, 59.

TABLE 2 **EPITAPHS DEDICATED BY CHILD-NURSES**

Deceased	Member of Nurse's Family	Charge (Commemorated by Nurse Alone)	Charge (Commemorated by Nurse and Others)	Freed Slaves of Nurse	Self	Total
Legal status of child-nurse:						
Uncertain slave..	1	. . .	5	. . .	. . .	6
Freed slave.....	1	1	2	. . .	1	5
Uncertain freeborn......	. . .	5	3	1	. . .	9
Total........	2	6	10	1	1	20
	(10)	(30)	(50)	(5)	(5)	(100)

SOURCE.—All epitaphs come from the *Corpus Inscriptionum Latinarum*, vol. 6, and *Notizie degli Scavi*.
NOTE.—Numbers in parentheses are percentages.

slave origin or included slaves or freedmen who in some cases belonged to the same household (see 7355, 12600, 12366). Although conclusions on the status of nurslings and their families can only be suggestive because the pattern of names in the epitaphs is the primary means of ascertaining the legal status of individuals in these inscriptions as in 12366, the repetition of patterns that point to slave and freed families suggests that the nurse and nursling in these epitaphs often came from the same social group.[43]

> To Volusia Ru[fa?].
> Volusia Philete, nurse,
> to one well-deserving.
> [*CIL* 6.7355]

> To the Spirits of the Dead.
> To Athenais, well-deserving.
> She lived one year, two months, nine days.

[43] The nursing of slave children is indicated in 7355 (see Treggiari, "Jobs for Women" [n. 1 above], 88). On the family ties among fellow slaves and freedmen, see Boudreau Flory (n. 42 above), 82 ff. Only one nursling can be identified as a member of the equestrian or senatorial order (16587, *PIR*² C. 1590): the pattern of names indicates that the nurse was not a freedwoman of her charge or his father. The lack of dedications to elite charges is not surprising, for we would expect that members of the elite would put up epitaphs for their own. Dedications to very young children are uncommon: see A. R. Burn, "*Hic breve Vivitur*, a Study of the Expectation of Life in the Roman Empire," *Past and Present* 4 (1953): 2–31, esp. 5; W. F. Wilcox, "The Length of Life in the Early Roman Empire," *Actes du Congrès international de population*, vol. 25, *Démographie historique* (Paris, 1937), 14–22, esp. 18–19; Huttunen (n. 38 above), 46; cf. Keith Hopkins, "On the Probable Age Structure of the Roman Population," *Population Studies* 19 (1966): 245–64, who points out that the underrepresentation of children aged one through nine is exaggerated.

Hilara, nurse, and Thesmus and
Eutychus, father, set this up.

[*CIL* 6.12600]

To the Spirits of the Dead
To Gnaeus Arrius Agapetus.
Arria Agapete, mother, and
Bostrychus, father, and
Helpis, *mamma*, and Fieie [*sic*],
nurse, set this up for a very
dutiful, well-deserving son.
He lived three years, forty-five days.[44]

[*CIL* 6.12366]

Epitaphs in which the nurse was either a primary or secondary dedicator to a charge, indicate the multiple sources of parenting available to the
children of slaves and freedmen, especially those from the same household:
parents, other relatives, the nurse assigned to care for the household's
children, and other members of the parents' social circle (see 7355, 12600,
12366).[45] These epitaphs suggest a special role for the nurse involved with
families that could be disrupted by the sale as well as the death of one of its
members. The children (like Athenais and Agapetus) tended to die very
young: ten of the thirteen for whom an age is given (12299, 12366, 12600,
16587, 17157, 20938, 25301, 34383, 35123, *NS* 1925, 230) were younger
than six years old at death, and two others (7741, 18073) were younger than
fourteen. Many of them had lost one or both parents. The absence of the
natural mother is particularly significant, especially in the cases of young
children like Athenais. In thirteen of the sixteen epitaphs dedicated to

---

[44] In 6.7355, neither nurse nor charge has status indication, but the location of the stone in
the tomb set aside for the domestic staff of the Volusii in light of Philete's job title suggests that
Philete was a freedwoman of the Volusii and her charge Ru[fa?] either a freedwoman or the
daughter of freed slaves from this household. See n. 42 above. In 6.12600, the child, her
nurse, her father, and Thesmus, whose relationship is not identified, all have the name form
appropriate for slaves (personal name without nomen, the Roman family name). See nn. 38,
above, 45 and 46 below. In 6.12366, no one has status indication: Agapetus and his mother
have the name forms of freeborn citizens or freedmen; his father, *mamma*, and nurse, have the
name forms of slaves. Since the son takes both his mother's nomen and the feminine form of
her cognomen, his father, with a servile name form, was most likely a slave. See n. 38 above.

[45] In five epitaphs (12366, 12600, 18073, 25301, 35123), the responsibility of commemoration was shared by another individual who was not identified as nurse or family, although one
woman and one man were entitled *mamma* (12366) and *tata* (25301), nursery terms for parent
or grandparent. Here, the individual simply appears to have been a member of the parents'
social circle and, like the nurse, associated in the deceased's upbringing (each child has the
appropriate parent). On the term *mamma*, see Suzanne Dixon, "Roman Nurses and Foster
Mothers: Some Problems of Terminology" (paper delivered at the classical section of
A.U.L.L.A. XXII, Canberra, August–September 1983).

nurslings (seven of the ten whose commemorators include family members), the mother is missing, leaving the nurse as the primary maternal figure (seven children are less than six years old; one, less than fourteen).[46]

Connected to their charges by ties beyond those of caretaker, these nurses call to mind Louisa or the mother of James Curry, rather than the nurse of upper-class, male-authored literary accounts. Like Louisa or Curry's mother, Philete, Hilara, or Fieie expressed their attachment to a community of peers, and the epitaphs depict them as members of that community, but they also show them acting on behalf of its members. The contrast with the literary sources is striking. Elite authors, preoccupied with the relationship between upper-class nurslings and their slave (or foreign) nurses, did not consider the nurse who cared for the children of the household's slaves and freedmen. The epitaphs suggest, however, that when the nurse described her own experience, such relations were central to her.

The exception to this general picture is found in the epitaphs in which nurses are commemorated by former charges ($N = 11$) or their parents ($N = 2$).[47] Whatever feelings, ties, or sense of duty lie behind these dedications, they belong to the nursling, not to the nurse.

---

[46] In the six epitaphs where the nurse is the sole dedicator (7355, 12299, 15952, 16587, 15157, 34383) and in one case where the nurse is associated with her charge's freedman (6686, included among epitaphs of nurslings where the nurse is a codedicator), parents or other family members, those normally responsible for burial, are missing. Only two (7741, 12366) of the other nine joint dedications include both parents. Five others (12600, 18073, 25301, 35123, NS 1925, 230) include the father but not the mother; another epitaph (20938), a grandmother but neither father nor mother. In two cases where the dedicators include the child's father, the deceased include a woman identified as his wife: in one (35123), another epitaph (35122) suggests she may not have been the child's mother; in the other (25301), the wife died at age fourteen and the child at age four. Unless the wife's age is a mistake, she would not have been the child's mother. A high death rate from childbirth and associated complications would augment the maternal role of the nurse. The inscriptional evidence would seem to suggest a higher death rate for women in their reproductive years (see Burn, 12); however, according to Hopkins (contra Burn, see n. 43 above), the customs of commemoration may exaggerate the death rate of women in childbirth. Acknowledging that "relatively more women died during the reproductive period," Hopkins argues that the increased commemoration of women between fifteen and twenty-nine years old may not result solely from increased mortality "but because the younger they died the more chance there was of having husbands still surviving to commemorate them" and possibly because of "their heightened social estimation, for at this age (15–29) they would be wives as well as daughters" (Hopkins, 246, 261). For comparison with the tax census data from Egypt, which show high death rates for women between fourteen and forty years old, see M. Hombert and C. Préaux, "Recherches sur le recensement dans l'Egypte romaine," *Papyrologica Lugduno-Batava* 5 (Leiden, 1952), 40–159. On comparisons with other pretransitional societies, see Donald Engels, "The Use of Historical Demography in Ancient History," *Classical Quarterly* 34, no. 2 (1984): 386–93, esp. n. 7.

[47] One of these inscriptions (7290) does locate the nurse among her peers. For this example, see Treggiari, "Jobs for Women" (n. 1 above), 88–89.

To the Spirits of the Dead.
To Servia Cornelia Sabina,
     freedwoman of Servius.
Servius Cornelius Dolabella
     Metillianus
set this up for his well-deserving
nurse and foster-mother.
[*CIL* 6.16450; *ILS* 8532]

Strikingly, the epitaph evidence for the elite's attachment to its child-nurse is more limited than modern commentators like Vogt imply. Only three of the nursling-commemorators (1354, 16440, and 16450) can be identified as members of the senatorial or equestrian order.

Regardless of their charge's social position, nurses used a name form that did not explicitly indicate their status as slaves, freedwomen, or freeborn citizens. Proper status indication, part of the formal name of every individual, would have indicated the nurse's relationship to a particular authority: the slave nurse should name her master; the freedwoman, her patron (ex-master); the freeborn citizen, her father. However, formal notation of legal position is found for only eleven nurses (19.3 percent). In the sepulchral inscriptions as a whole, this proportion is not unusual, but because men and women with an occupational title often included status indication in their name-form, the absence of status indication in the name-form of nurses is noteworthy.[48] Even if we eliminate epitaphs dedicated to and by charges, where the relations conveyed by proper status indication may have been replaced by or irrelevant to the social relationship featured in the epitaphs, the pattern persists. When these are not counted, 71.4 percent ($N = 20$) of the nurses in epitaphs lack formal status indication: three were probably slaves, and seventeen probably freed-women.

Among the eighteen nurses who worked for the upper classes, as in the epitaphs of Volussia Felicla and Cornelia Prima, there is an absence of formal status indication (72.2 percent, $N = 13$) and a job title that includes the name of the nursling (88.9 percent, $N = 16$).[49] The charge's name is not necessarily evidence for the "spiritual bond" between the nurse and her elite charge; nor is the job title necessarily an attempt by the nurse to bask

[48] See Lily Ross Taylor, "Freedmen and Freeborn in the Epitaphs of Imperial Rome," *AJPH* 82 (1961): 113–32; Huttunen (n. 38 above), 137, 139, 140–42, 187–88.

[49] In addition, two of the slave nurses included among those with status indication (6324, 7618) identify themselves in a way that emphasizes the charge; technically, they do not have proper status indication: e.g., "Stactes *nutricis* Sisennae *f(ilii)*," 6324. Properly, the genitive of the master's name should follow the slave's name; here, it follows the occupational title, focusing attention on the person cared for, not the master. Compare the emphasis on the name of the "employer" (Treggiari, "Jobs for Women" [n. 1 above], 76–77).

in the borrowed glory of her ex-master's social standing, or a manifestation of her pride in serving an eminent person. Such translation of the nurse's terms assumes the perspective of the nursling and the master, and over-looks the possibility that the nurse had a different understanding of her position within the relationship.

This is not to argue that Felicla and Prima had no positive feelings toward their upper-class nurslings, but only to acknowledge that nursing was a job which in most cases they had no choice about performing. Indeed, Favorinus's observation that children were handed over to who-ever was lactating suggests the degree to which even the biology of the female slave was subject to her master's or mistress's needs.[50] Her lack of choice was implicitly acknowledged by the slaveholder in his concern about the nurse's affection and sympathy for his child and in the regulations designed to control both her behavior and her treatment of the child. The environment in which the job of nursing and the relationship of nurse and her upper-class charge existed was thus a coercive one. When Servius Cornelius Dolabella Metillianus, consul of A.D. 113, called Sabina "well-deserving nurse and foster-mother" (literally, "little breast": "nutrix et mammul[a] bene merens"), the feelings were his, not hers. Fronto's claims about the nurse's affection for her nursling represent what he believed, or wanted to believe, not necessarily what the nurse felt. When we try to understand Felicla or Prima, we must be careful that we have not substi-tuted the nursling's perspective for the nurse's; that is, assigned the patron's feelings to the ex-slave and/or shaped the nurse to fit her ex-master's image.

There is another possible reading of the job title "child-nurse" with the charge's name and without the nurse's status indication. The identity "slave" or "freed slave" would have signaled Felicla's or Prima's subordi-nation to authority; the identity "nurse" emphasized her own authority, albeit over a child. In effect, the nurse, her family, or peers focused attention on her parental role and responsibility rather than on her submis-sion to the authority of master or patron. Since nurslings like Torquata and Scipio were members of the social elite, the emphasis on the cared-for may have announced that a socially prominent and powerful person once relied on a Felicla or Prima. Implicitly, this form records the dependence of a master or patron who in reality had authority over slaves and freedwomen.

Yet, these terms embody a certain ambivalence. The nurse does not identify herself as a slave or ex-slave and admit her subordination, but in presenting herself as the child-nurse who cared for a particular individual her terms implicitly admit to the control of her body as a woman and/or a slave. The ambivalence of her terms, it seems to me, reflects her position. In parenting and in interacting with the child, Felicla and Prima had

[50] Favorinus (n. 8 above), 12.1.17.

experienced their control over the master-nursling and the dependence of the slaveholder. They could see the lie of the slaveholder's paternalism that saw the slave as needy and the slaveholder as caretaker—but as former slaves, they had experienced directly the power of master over slave.

The nurse's terms, like the views of male authors, focused on the relationship of nurse and nursling and set at a distance the relations of domination. These are only implied in the pattern of names that show her to be the ex-slave of the nursling she herself names in her occupational title. Nurses like Felicla and Prima would appear to fit the slaveholder's vision of the nurse. As Eugene Genovese has observed of domestic slaves in the antebellum south, however, it would have been difficult for them to speak of their own lives without reference to those they served.[51]

The history of black mammies in the American south suggests that the Roman nurse's reference to those she served might have had a different significance from that assumed by male authors who represented the vision of the slaveholder. While these authors' views of nurses did not attend to the power relations of gender and slavery, they did assume them in what they chose to discuss. The epitaph records of freed nurses, however, omitted the relations of slavery, preferring to emphasize work that depended on gender, for only in the relationship at the center of that work could a child-nurse in some sense transform the terms that she and the slaveholder shared. Her resource for power, or perhaps a feeling of control, and a basis on which to claim privileges for her own children lay in her relationship with her nursling and the nursling's family, a relationship in which by wider social terms she was unempowered.[52] For her own and her family's protection, she could not eschew that relationship nor throw resistance in her master's face.[53] Her master could read her terms as devotion, pride in serving a socially prominent person, or borrowed status; but she (and we) might read a message to other slaves and freedwomen about her own control and her master's dependence.

Department of Liberal Arts
New England Conservatory

[51] Genovese (n. 24 above), 351.

[52] Treggiari, "Jobs for Women" (n. 1 above), 89, has emphasized the favored position of the nurse's child as foster-brother (*conlactaneus, conlacteus,* named in 5939, 6324, 7393, 9901a) to a member of the social and political elite, pointing to Gaius Caecina Tuscus, the foster-brother of Nero who governed Egypt. It should be added that the nurse's child was not favored in his own family relations: he had to share his mother with another and shared his mother's attention with a usurper. Moreover, despite a shared childhood and nourisher, the nurse's child could never rise to the rank of his foster-brother. The nurse's child, therefore, could observe from intimate experience the privilege conveyed by the accident of birth.

[53] Compare Genovese, 584, 598, on forms of resistance.

MOTHERING OTHERS' CHILDREN:
THE EXPERIENCES OF FAMILY DAY-CARE PROVIDERS

MARGARET K. NELSON

In her early writing on the sociology of emotions, Arlie Russell Hochschild introduced the concept of the "sentient actor" as a reminder that humans are neither simply "bloodless calculators" nor "blind expressers of uncontrolled emotions" but that in everyday life humans constantly bridge the gap between pure reason and pure emotion: "Human beings, as sentient actors, are aware of their experiences and consciously respond to their feelings and the cultural expectations concerning them."[1] Hochschild's notion of "emotion management" refers to this conscious effort of bringing feelings into line with what is deemed appropriate in a given situation. Thus, for example, enacting the social roles of friend, lover, or bride requires knowing the appropriate "feeling rule" (what others expect one to feel) and making efforts to bring emotions into line with it. This private act of emotion management is "transmuted" into emotional labor when it is put to commercial

I would like to thank Emily K. Abel, Joanne Jacobson, Bill Nelson, Burke Rochford, and Joan Smith for their help and support on earlier drafts of this paper. I also appreciate the comments and advice I received from the editors and readers of *Signs*.

[1] Arlie Russell Hochschild, "The Sociology of Feelings and Emotion: Selected Possibilities," in *Another Voice: Feminist Perspectives on Social Life and Social Science*, ed. Marcia Millman and Rosabeth Moss Kanter (Garden City, N.Y.: Anchor/Doubleday, 1975), 283.

This essay originally appeared in *Signs*, vol. 15, no. 3, Spring 1990.

uses.[2] In such cases as the airline stewardesses Hochschild so vividly describes, company manuals detail the appropriate professional response to various scenarios, thus requiring their employees to supply emotional labor (now directed by supervisors) along with physical labor.

These concepts are a useful starting point for an analysis of the relationships between family day-care providers and the children in their care. Family day-care providers must distinguish between the feelings they have toward their own children and the nonresident children for whom they provide paid care, and they must expend the emotional labor necessary to sustain the appropriate attitude.[3] Yet the particular context in which they work, and the particular task in which they are engaged, implies a special relationship to these issues.

Because family day-care providers work alone and within the home rather than leaving it for an institutional setting as most service workers do and because within the home they charge money for labor that women are supposed to supply without financial compensation, their feeling rules are ambiguous. In both the private realm and the public world, feeling rules are relatively clear: in private life feeling rules are set by cultural expectations; in commercial life they are dictated by supervisors. Family day-care providers who enlarge the private sphere to include paid work must create their own feeling rules as well as the rules governing display of feelings. Providers must decide, for example, how close they should become to these children, how much physical affection they should express, what is acceptable and unacceptable behavior from a child, what kind of discipline should be used, and how to respond to a child's questions about sex or religion. In sum, the provider must determine how to act, as all parties agree she must, like a mother toward children who are not her own.

This is difficult. The context in which family day-care providers work, and their ongoing involvement in the care of very young children, engenders emotions and calls for the exercise of skills that

[2] Arlie Russell Hochschild, *The Managed Heart: Commercialization of Human Feeling* (Berkeley and Los Angeles: University of California Press, 1983), 19–20.

[3] I use the term "emotional labor" rather than "emotion management" because family day-care providers are engaged in a commercialized transaction even though, as Hochschild notes, family day-care providers do not completely fit her definition of jobs which require emotional labor. The missing component is the absence of an emotional supervisor. While parents act as emotional supervisors in the sense that they are constantly assessing the providers, they neither train the providers nor have access to complete information about what happens during the day; and in contrast to customers, children are unlikely to lodge complaints. Hochschild, *The Managed Heart*, 147.

are structurally inappropriate. Family day-care providers become enormously attached to the children in their care and, in some respects, giving them good care means treating them like their own. Yet these feelings cannot be allowed to flourish because they lack the privileges of motherhood and because they must commodify caregiving. Their emotional labor involves dismantling, or reducing the intensity of, these same feelings. They thus differ radically from the airline stewardesses whose emotional labor entails the manufacture and pretense of warm sentiments in a context where neither feelings nor display come easily.

Methods

In the summer of 1986 I mailed a questionnaire to each of the 463 registered day-care providers in the state of Vermont; responses were received from 225 providers (a response rate of 49 percent). The following summer I distributed questionnaires to 105 unregistered family day-care providers located through snowball sampling techniques.[4] The questionnaires covered a range of issues, including the number of years the women had been providing child care, reasons for opening a day-care home, characteristics of the children in care, working conditions, income from and expenses of child care, attitudes toward child care, future plans, problems, and background information.[5]

[4] In the course of distributing questionnaires to unregistered providers, I picked up an additional ten registered providers, bringing the total for that group to 235. The organization of family day-care in Vermont offers three legal alternatives. Licensing is required of providers with more than six full-time nonresident children. Because almost all licensed day-care occurs in formal centers rather than private homes, no licensed providers are included in this analysis. Registration is required of those who offer care to children from more than two different families and may legally include six full-time children of preschool age and four part-time school-age children. Women caring for (any number of) children from no more than two different families may remain unregistered. Those who care for more than this number and fail to register constitute the "illegal" population of family day-care providers. See Vermont, Department of Social and Rehabilitation Services, *Journal for Family Day Care Homes* (Waterbury, Vt.: Division of Licensing and Registration, 1985). A recent study of child care in Vermont estimated that approximately 75 percent of all children under the age of six with parents in the labor force were in (legal or illegal) unregulated care (see Amy Davenport, *The Economics of Child Care* [Montpelier, Vt.: Governor's Commission on the Status of Women's Childcare Task Force, 1985]).

[5] In this essay, unless otherwise indicated, all numerical descriptions derive from these data. For the issues under investigation in this paper, the distinction between registered and unregistered family day-care providers is not significant.

Over a two-year period, I conducted lengthy semi-structured interviews with thirty registered day-care providers (twenty-one of whom had also completed questionnaires) and forty unregistered day-care providers (ten of whom had also completed questionnaires). Questions in the interviews dealt with a wide range of issues, including relations with children and parents, the impact of the work on members of the provider's family, and sources of stress and satisfaction. I also conducted interviews in 1989 with sixteen women who had ceased providing family day-care. Each interview lasted at least one hour; many ran for several hours.[6]

Because I was particularly interested in allowing the description of family day-care to emerge from the point of view of the providers themselves, the questions in the interviews were open-ended. For example, the issues in this paper emerged from such questions as, "Could you tell me how you feel about the children in your care?" or "What do you want to be offering to the children in your care?" Areas of concern raised by women in the beginning of the study were pursued in subsequent interviews, and questions were designed to encourage a full discussion of issues.

The family day-care providers in this study were almost uniformly married women (86 percent) with children of their own (96 percent). Over half (56 percent) of the women had at least one child of preschool age and therefore cared full-time for both their own and nonresident children. The women in the study ranged in age from twenty-one to seventy-one with a mean of 34.5. The number of years of involvement in the occupation ranged from recent initiates who had been working for less than a year to one woman who had been offering care for twenty-three years; the median number of years as a family day-care provider was three. Most (94 percent) of the women had completed a high school education, and half of the women had some education beyond high school. With one exception, all of the women who were interviewed were white.

Alignment with mothering

The twentieth-century American cultural ideal of mothering assumes intense, exclusive bonds between the mother and her child, and it assumes a mother's willingness to respond to her child's emotional and physical needs even when to do so is at the cost of

[6] In what follows, unless otherwise indicated, all quotations are taken from these interviews.

her own well-being.[7] Yet a mother's obligations are balanced by her prerogatives; mothers have enormous leeway in defining the morality and discipline appropriate to their children's care.

In the public world of paid care giving, teachers, nurses, and institutional child-care workers engage in many of the same activities as mothers but with different prerogatives, and they must accomplish their tasks without becoming overly attached to, or identified with, their clients.[8] Drawing on Parsonian terminology, Sara Lawrence Lightfoot distinguishes between the appropriate attitudes of parents and teachers: "Parents have emotionally charged relationships with their children that rarely reflect interpersonal status or functional considerations. Children in the family are treated as special persons, but pupils in schools are necessarily treated as members of categories. From these different perspectives develop the particularistic expectations that parents have for their children, and the universalistic expectations of teachers."[9] Similarly, Sandra Scarr suggests that professional care givers should maintain an emotional distance from their charges: "A teacher is not fulfilling her role of impartial instructor about the world outside of the parent-child bond if she spends her time on affection and comfort for individual children."[10] While some observers proclaim this distinction a functional necessity for accomplishing educational goals, others emphasize that the distinction may be implemented primarily as a step toward claiming a professional status for care giving. As Chiara Saraceno notes: "In order to maintain a professional image and to avoid the 'feminine vocation trap' evoked by working with young children and promulgated by employment policies, [some workers] stress their expertise and professional

---

[7] In spite of much recent talk about "parenting," the burden for a child's well-being still rests on mothers. See Susan Rae Peterson, "Against 'Parenting,' " in *Mothering: Essays in Feminist Theory*, ed. Joyce Trebilcot (Totowa, N.J.: Rowman & Allanheld, 1984), 62–69; and Janet Farrell Smith, "Parenting and Property," in Trebilcot, ed., 199–212.

[8] Sara Freedman, "To Love and to Work: The Ghettoization of Women's Labor in the Home and the School" (Boston, Mass., 1987, typescript); Jeff Hearn, "Patriarchy, Professionalisation, and the Semi-Professions," in *Women and Social Policy: A Reader*, ed. Clare Ungerson (London: Macmillan, 1985), 190–206; Carole Joffe, *Friendly Intruders: Childcare Professionals and Family Life* (Berkeley: University of California Press, 1977); Magali Sarfatti Larson, *The Rise of Professionalism: A Sociological Analysis* (Berkeley: University of California Press, 1977); Sarah Lawrence Lightfoot, *Worlds Apart: Relationships between Families and Schools* (New York: Basic, 1978); Sandra Scarr, *Mother Care/Other Care* (New York: Basic, 1984).

[9] Lightfoot, 22.

[10] Scarr, 192.

handling of children, focusing on the more formally educational aspects of their work."[11]

The day-care providers in my study dismissed the professional model of care giving: they found it irrelevant. Only 24 percent of the questionnaire respondents said that it was "very important" to offer children a structured or planned day; only 39 percent of the respondents indicated that they thought it was "very important" to include educational activities in the daily round of events. When women were asked questions about the concrete differences they perceived between the care they gave and that offered to children in a day-care center, they were quite articulate and insistent: they responded that day-care centers do not encourage the "warmth, love and intimacy" that can be found in a family setting; centers do not offer the "one-on-one" care of a home. Some providers suggested that because day-care centers, like schools, follow a schedule of activities, they do not allow for a free-flowing responsiveness to the individual child's needs and interests. Almost all of the women interviewed believed that a home is the preferable location for the daily care of young children.

The family day-care providers in my study did not dismiss mothering as a model for their involvement with children. The women viewed the development of personal and intimate relationships as an essential component of family day-care: 75 percent of the questionnaire respondents agreed with the statement, "A family day-care provider should be like a mother to the children in her care." In discussing their feelings about the children the women used familial analogies: "They are my part-time kids"; "I'm like a second mom"; "I think of them as members of my extended family"; "These [children] are like my own kids"; "I'm offering closeness and security—my motherhood." Moreover, most family day-care providers wanted to create for the children in their care the same environment they assume prevails in a home with a mother present. Eighty-one percent of the questionnaire respondents felt it was "very important" to provide "a homelike atmosphere." Interviews confirmed this approach. "What are you trying to provide for the children in your care?" I asked. The responses were surprisingly consistent: "I'm trying to give the children a sense of family"; "I try to make the child comfortable here"; "I try to give them the experiences I gave to my own children"; "I want

[11] Chiara Saraceno, "Shifts in Public and Private Boundaries: Women as Mothers and Service Workers in Italian Daycare," *Feminist Studies* 10, no. 1 (Spring 1984): 20–21.

this to be a nurturing place"; "They should be at home here"; "I like this being just like a home." When I asked, "What do you do with the children," the analogy to a mother's care emerged again: "I don't schedule the day. They do their thing and I do mine around whatever they are doing. . . . If the ironing's got to be done, the ironing gets done. If the laundry's got to be done—I don't do all of these things after they leave at night. I don't do a thing any different than I did when I was home with my own two. What's got to be done gets done." Although most women do not find time to attend to much housework, some can, and they see their actions as beneficial to the children: "They see you doing these things and it's just like mom."

This merging of paid and unpaid care for the majority of providers in my study is rooted in a desire to care for their own children while earning a living. The women defined themselves as mothers who are committed to mothering as their primary role.[12] Even those women who had worked previously as paid care givers in an institutional setting did not offer this experience (or an interest in building on the knowledge they had gained there) as an explanation for why they began to provide care at home. They said simply that they wanted to be home while their children were growing up.

Vermont family day-care providers seem to accept the role of substitute mother for their paid care giving, and they experience that care giving much as mothers do. As they give the children the security of a home, five days a week, for eight or nine hours each day, sometimes over a period of several years, family day-care providers "learn to love" the children. Seventy-seven percent of the questionnaire respondents agreed with the statement, "I get emotionally involved with the children in my care." These day-care providers spoke about the rewards and satisfactions of their work in terms similar to those of mothers. From her interviews with fifty-eight middle- and fifty-six working-class mothers, Mary Georgina Boulton noted that, though their children's dependence could be a burden, mothers derived enormous satisfaction from being

[12] A good characterization of this kind of woman can be found in Kristin Luker, *Abortion and the Politics of Motherhood* (Berkeley and Los Angeles: University of California Press, 1984). Family day-care as an extension of mothering is presented differently, though equally concretely, for a substantial minority of the women who see in the provision of child care a way to further satisfy a thwarted maternal impulse. Women who could not afford a larger family, women who could not (physically) bear more children, women who longed for a daughter and had only sons (or vice versa), and women whose grown children have left them pining over an empty nest, all located their motivation in an as-yet unfulfilled need to mother.

needed.[13] The family day-care providers I interviewed also spoke about being relied on and loved by the children in their care, and they see this as a positive feature of their work: "Cassie left the other day and told me she loved me. Things like that are the reward. What can you have more than a child that loves you?" Boulton discovered that mothers found child care a rewarding way to improve upon their own childhood experiences, "to relive experiences from the past altered to be as she would have liked them to have been."[14] Many of the day-care providers I interviewed have a similar motivation: "Well, my child care style is very different than when I grew up. I wasn't getting . . . the things that I'm giving these kids I babysit for. . . . My mother was not loving, she wouldn't cuddle or hold me or much communicate at all . . . . I guess I just realized if I can help the next kid not to get into the kind of situations I did, more power to me. I want to show some of these kids there's somebody out there who cares because there wasn't anybody for me and I don't want that to happen to other kids." Like the mothers in Boulton's study, these family day-care providers spoke of the pleasures derived from observing the children "doing all the cute things children do." Some women gave a less-than-specific answer when asked, "What are the rewards of care giving?" and said, "the same rewards a mother gets," as if without elaboration anyone could understand what was meant.

These family day-care providers also see the same kinds of problem with their work that mothers see.[15] The contemporary organization of child care relies on a single individual with full responsibility for that care. Family day-care providers find not only that this responsibility is burdensome but also that it is isolating and interferes with their attempts to engage in other pursuits.[16]

---

[13] Mary Georgina Boulton, *On Being a Mother: A Study of Women with Pre-School Children* (London: Tavistock, 1983), 104–9.

[14] Ibid., 110.

[15] For research on mothers' attitudes toward their role, see ibid.; L. Comer, *Wedlocked Women* (Leeds: Feminist Books, 1974); Betty Friedan, *The Feminist Mystique* (New York: Norton, 1963); H. Graham and L. McKee, *The First Months of Motherhood* (London: Health and Education Council, 1980); Sheila Kitzinger, *Women as Mothers* (New York: Random, 1978); Helen Z. Lopata, *Occupation: Housewife* (New York: Oxford University Press, 1971); Ann Oakley, *Housewife* (New York: Viking, 1979); Adrienne Rich, *Of Woman Born: Motherhood as Experience and Institution* (New York: Norton, 1976).

[16] In fact, for family day-care providers, the conflict between child care and other activities may be more intense than it is for mothers. The demands of child care are greater, the larger number of children creates more housework, and the care givers' quasi-professional status may mean they must meet higher standards for that work.

Similarly, Boulton found that mothers felt isolated when they stayed home to take care of their children: few people came to visit, and the mothers found it hard to pack up their children to go out. The more middle-class respondents in Boulton's sample of mothers felt that as the children monopolized their attention, they lost a sense of individuality.[17] Again, this is much like the family day-care providers in my study who say that because they are constantly dealing with children's concerns, they feel their own integrity and awareness of a larger world to be threatened.

The similarities between providers and mothers are in part a result of the structural compatibility of the two roles, but it is also a cultivated similarity. Vermont family day-care providers talk about the skills they draw on in ways that depend upon their experiences caring for their own children. As one woman said, "I've been told—and I feel—that [my own children] are great kids. . . . The way I raised them is what I do with the kids I babysit for . . . and [my children] are doing fine so far." Indeed, because they see the work as an extension of mothering, they believe they are prepared to handle the job without receiving formal training.[18] One woman laughed at a question about her qualifications: "A woman came the other day and she was asking, 'What special training do you have in dealing with children?' And I said, 'I'm the mother of six children, that's all the special training that I feel like I need.' As far as taking a book that tells me how to deal with children . . . I don't want that. I don't believe in book-raising children." Yet for many women, locating the source of skills in the experience of mothering is tantamount to saying they have no skills at all. "I don't have any skills," said one woman; "anyone who has been a mother can do this," added another. In further discussions, however, it became clear that the women have refined the skill Sara Ruddick defines as "maternal thinking."[19] For example, when asked how they had changed over time, many women said they had become more patient. The definition of patience that one respondent (a provider for twenty-three years) gave me suggests that this aspect of the care giver's experience is particularly complex: "Patience is understanding the individuality of all of these children. . . . I could have another 181 [day-care children] and each one of them would be different again. There's no two that need the same amount of loving or need the same amount of reprimanding. Each one needs a little

[17] Boulton, 95.

[18] Even those who had undergone extensive training to become nurses or teachers, when asked what skills they drew on, mentioned motherhood before their occupation.

[19] Sara Ruddick, "Maternal Thinking," in Trebilcot, ed. (n. 7 above), 213–30.

extra something of some sort which is fun finding with that individual."

The conflation of the mother role with the provider role was so complete that when I asked, "Do you feel differently about your own children and the other children in your care?" the answer I almost uniformly received was, "I treat them all the same. If my child gets a treat they all get a treat. If my child does something wrong, she is punished, if another child does something wrong, she is punished in just the same way."

Tellingly, in emphasizing external behavior (the way the children are treated) the providers avoided answering the question about the way they felt about the children. It is a form of denying that their feelings for their own children differed from their feelings for their clients.[20] Having dismissed professional care giving, the provider embraces mothering. Having done so, she cannot easily speak about the manner in which she deviates from this ideal.

Deviating from the mothering ideal

A contradiction is present. Mothering is the most desirable style for a family day-care provider, but it is a style she must adopt incompletely. Motherhood confers the privileges of claiming, molding, and keeping; other people's children cannot be claimed, molded, and kept. To think that one can do so with other people's children creates a situation where one can only be disappointed. Motherhood denies a financial calculus and limits, yet a day-care provider who refuses reimbursement or fails to establish limits to the care she gives invites exploitation. The family day-care provider cannot answer a question about feeling directly because there is no direct way to describe how one maintains an ideal by deviating from it.

The limits of responsibility

One of the most painful aspects of mothering is the realization that the capacity to protect one's child is limited. A mother cannot watch every move or inoculate her child against every hurt. A mother has

[20] Alternatively, this answer might be taken as an indication of the difficulty of separating treatment and feeling. Care giving involves instrumental tasks and emotions. We care for someone because we care about them; when we care about someone we take care of their needs. Yet if it were just this difficulty, we might find that mothers could not separate the tasks and the emotions. However, most mothers can separate the two easily: I love my child but I hate changing diapers, getting up in the middle of the night, and losing contact with the adult world.

to rely on the hope that she has equipped her children to deal with life's vagaries. For day-care providers the limits of protection are narrowed. The day-care provider can ensure a loving and safe environment for specified hours; she cannot ensure that the child is being adequately clothed, fed, and nurtured during the hours that the child is with her or his parents. Children go home at the end of the day, and the parents may or may not attend to the cough or diarrhea properly. Children leave for good after a couple of years, and the parents may or may not complete the job of teaching a child to share or to have good manners.

Limited authority

Competent and successful caring for children relies on certain skills. Because the family day-care provider is dealing with many children at once, discipline and the imposition of routines are not just matters of individual style but practical necessities. All children have to nap at the same time, eat the same food, and follow the same rules.[21]

The Vermont day-care providers in my study indicate that they feel enormous satisfaction from exercising their managerial abilities, but that they are often thwarted in their attempts to do so.[22] Parents give explicit instructions pertaining to the care of their own children. These instructions can undermine a provider's confidence; they can also serve to remind the provider that her authority is limited: "[I don't like it when] they're saying, well, I'm still in charge even though I'm not here, therefore I'm going to tell her like I would tell a teenage babysitter the rules." In addition, state regulations constrain their ability to operate as a small business and create a climate of distrust about possible mistreatment of children in their care.[23] As one woman said, "You don't yell out the back door to the children because someone might hear you."

[21] Providers and parents both speak about the ease with which children adapt to this group life. What they fail to note is that group living disempowers children by discouraging them from making the kinds of demands for attention and immediate need fulfillment that might lock the provider into an intense, personal struggle. For a useful discussion of this point, see Elaine Enarson, "Toward a Theory of Waged Mothering: The Case of Family Day Care" (University of Nevada, Reno, 1987, typescript).

[22] Feminist analysis has uncovered the many ways in which the development of "maternal thinking" is undermined by the authority of male experts. Barbara Ehrenreich and Deidre English, *For Her Own Good* (Garden City, N.J.: Doubleday, 1978); Alison Jaggar, *Feminist Politics and Human Nature* (Totowa, N.J.: Rowman & Allanheld, 1983).

[23] The rules for registration of Vermont's Department of Social and Rehabilitation Services determine the number of children that can be cared for within the home by

The awareness that one's authority is limited shows up most clearly in discussions about discipline. Most providers in my study feel that it is wrong—and even cruel—to spank someone else's child, even though many of them find it an appropriate disciplinary technique for their own children. The concern also shows up at the other end of the spectrum. Some providers worry about showing too much physical affection. Thus, although providers say that they do with others what they did with their own children, probing suggests that their commonsense response is challenged by the consciousness that the child is not their own.

Loss

Though some children stay with the same day-care provider for years, it is invariably the case that the relationships are temporary. Mothers go in and out of the work force, parents change jobs, and families move; ultimately children outgrow the need for this kind of daily care. The relationships are also contingent: a parent can withdraw a child at any moment the parent decides that a different situation is preferable. For whatever reason, the children will leave, and the provider may never see them again.

In some ways the most painful losses are those initiated by a parent out of dissatisfaction. These losses threaten the provider's self-confidence as well as her relationship to a child: "One day [the mother] called me up and said she wasn't going to bring her child back because she didn't think he was happy here. . . . I was upset because I thought I did something wrong. I thought I had let his crying bother me too much. . . . I even started to wonder whether I should be taking care of other people's kids." The more expected losses are anguishing as well; tears came to one provider's eyes when she described to me how loss interrupts intense relationships: "I lost one to kindergarten and some going [to a sitter] closer to home. It's very hard. You feel like you're losing a part of you." (When these losses are anticipated, a provider can do some of the preparatory work of grieving in advance. This might help them deal with the actual moment of parting; it cannot alleviate the pain altogether.) The link between loss and affection is demonstrated in the frequency with which the providers in my study, when asked to discuss their feelings about children, spontaneously spoke about

---

a family day-care worker and the kind of discipline that can be used. The registration process opens the provider to public scrutiny and limits her ability to take in and care for children as she sees fit. See Vermont, Department of Social and Rehabilitation Services (n. 4 above).

losing them: "I love these children. I feel terrible when I lose one." The inevitability of loss makes becoming too attached to the children an emotionally risky proposition.

Financial realities

Family day-care providers do this work because they need the money. If they become too attached to the children in their care, that is, if they identify too strongly with the model of mothering, they impair their ability to have a businesslike relationship with parents; they cannot require that they be paid at the end of the week, nor can they impose restrictions on the hours of care they provide.

The feeling rule: Detached attachment

The providers did not explicitly acknowledge that the care they offer is different from mothering. Yet the emotional component of that care, what I call the feeling rule of "detached attachment," is characterized by the limits drawn around the care givers' emotional engagement with the children.

The providers in my study frequently referred to this detachment they have created and the emotional labor in maintaining it: "I reserve something, knowing that they're not mine"; "I hold back a little"; "I don't want to get too attached." Some developed this approach because of what they termed an earlier "mistake." Almost every provider could talk about one child to whom she had become overly attached; almost every provider spoke about not letting this happen again: "I won't take one on from six months and watch it grow up like that again if I've got any feeling that they're going to be taken away from me. . . . I felt that I was doing a good job and I enjoyed [the child] just as much as [the parents] did, watching it grow up and being a part of its life. Maybe I did get too attached."

It was clear that many providers believe that attachment to the children draws them into making decisions which, though grounded in ideals about mothering, are not in their interests:

The latest [child] leaves close to six. It's too long for me. But what happened with one of them is—I had her before when her mother worked [close by] and she was getting picked up [at] 4, 4:30. And then her mother changed jobs and was working [farther away]. And because I had already had her and there was so much going on anyway with the family, . . .

I decided to keep her. She'd been through enough changes
and I didn't want her to go through another change.

I had one parent that owed me money when she left. . . .
It was as much my fault as it was hers because I just let it go
on and on for six months. But she was in the process of a
divorce. It was really affecting the child that I had. I just
could not put that child through one more trauma of having to
go to a new sitter on top of everything else he was going
through. He was three years old and I could just see what this
divorce was doing to this little boy. . . . It was really my fault.
I should have given him up. I just couldn't because I
wouldn't put him through not knowing where he was going
to go.

It is also clear that even though detached attachment is a stance
developed out of necessity, it is difficult to sustain emotionally.

I don't think I want that emotional attachment—again. And
the worrying and thinking about the baby like it's your own
and then suddenly realizing you have no say. And when the
baby's gone from your door you have no say in what happens
to it. That's kind of hard to deal with because I invest a lot of
emotional time with the kids to try to keep them happy and
secure and everything. And then you wonder. They leave.
. . . I think with the baby I'm trying to not get attached
because I don't want to have to think about it or worry about
it . . . but I know it's not going to work. . . . And I know after
a matter of time it will be the same thing all over again. I'll
be attached and thinking why's that mother doing that. And
then thinking, you have nothing to say about it. It's not your
kid. But in a way when you have them for so many hours it's
hard to find that balance.

The providers in my study admitted that they had a different sort
of relationship with their clients' children than their own, but
rather than articulate this in terms of their learned skills and
abilities as professionals, they saw the provider/child relationship
in terms of the absence of the conditions of mothering. A provider
in another study put it this way: "All the developmental hurdles—
moving from bottle to cup, giving up the pacifier, becoming
toilet-trained, eating a variety of foods, learning to cooperate,
accepting discipline—are relatively easy to accomplish in day-care,
because these are not my own children. We are not engaged in a
life-or-death power struggle, which I believe mothering entails.

Because I'm not their mother, they don't have to relinquish any power to me in the process of toilet-training, nor do I 'win' anything. It is just my job."[24]

The mother is someone the day-care provider can draw on to remind the child that day-care is only day-care—that it does not supplant but rather supplements the family. In the process the provider deflects the child's attachment to her. Vermont family day-care providers feel strongly that to do otherwise would be wrong, that it is an integral part of their job to sustain the mother/child bond: "I know Sarah really likes me. I know she does, I can tell. And I like Sarah. She's a nice little girl. . . . I can't give what Sarah needs. I can give her the attention, I can care for her, I can make her feel good about herself, but I'm not her mother. . . . You want to give the child what he [*sic*] needs without giving so much that you are interfering with the way he or she feels about his own parents." Incorporating the preservation of the mother/child bond into their responsibilities also is a reminder that the provider's attachment to the child needs to stay within limits:

> With my nieces, I'd have to stop and say to myself, "you're not their mother." For an example, the older one . . . had long hair and she wanted her hair cut. She wanted me to cut her hair. And I said, "Are you sure you want your hair cut?" And she said, "Oh, I'm sure I want it cut." And I said, "All right, after your bath tonight I'll cut your hair." And I did it and I never thought about it. And I put the kid to bed and I was upset all night. I said, I don't believe I cut her hair without asking her mother. . . . All night I just tossed and turned. . . . I just agonized all night long about how I could do that *without even thinking of the mother*. Those girls were becoming more and more my own.

Yet the manner in which providers talk about the emotional labor involved in maintaining a detached attachment makes it clear that the process is a difficult and continuous one:

> Q: Can you talk about your feelings toward the children?
> A: I get very attached and yet I try to keep myself somewhat removed. The first year was hard because I got frustrated . . . because I cared for them so much. I wished I could go home and tuck them in. You know, you see a little

---

[24] Selma Dendy, "Mothering Others, Mothering My Own," in *The Mother's Book*, ed. Ronnie Friedland and Carol Kort (Boston: Houghton Mifflin, 1981), 78.

guy come in at 7 in the morning and you know he's not going
to bed until 10 o'clock, it breaks your heart. Or to wake him
up (at the end of nap time) when he's the first one to go to
sleep. That's the caring I feel for them. I do. I like to hold
them if they cry. They need that.

Q: You said you hold yourself back a little from loving the
children, can you talk more about that?

A: I'm afraid to get too emotionally involved with them
because it hurts if I see things happening in their private
lives. I try not to look at them as my own kids because if I do,
it's hard to explain. I want to love them and treat them with
lots of care but I want to hold back a bit and not mother them
too much because if I do the mothers resent that to some
degree.

Q: So how do you hold back?

A: It is hard to describe. Maybe I don't hold them as much
as when I had my own kids because there are six of them. I
guess I don't hold back as much as I think I hold back. To me
what happens here is just like when my three were at home.
. . . But I can't put them in the car and take them into the
grocery. It's as much as a family setting as I can give but it's
still not a family setting. . . . They have responsibilities just
like my own girls do upstairs. And I'm doing with the kids
what I did with mine. So maybe I'm not holding back as
much as I think.

The provider has to find a balance between attachment and
distance, between her needs and those of the children. The balance
must be recreated daily because the provider doubts her ability to
be detached, to remain detached, even while it is a perspective she
seeks to adopt.

Refusing a client

Family day-care providers, unlike mothers, can choose whether or
not to care for a child. Yet the ideal of the good mother fundamentally rejects the notion that a woman should refuse to care for any of
her children. The providers in my study refused to care for children
if they thought the relationship would require too great an emotional commitment, or if they felt too little commitment to the child.

The most difficult choices involved children who were neglected or abused by their parents. In these cases the day-care
providers felt that they would have to assume the full burden of

ensuring that the child had a loving and safe adult/child relationship. This meant abandoning a commitment to detached attachment as well as abandoning a commitment to sustaining the child's
bond with her/his own parents. In most of these situations providers would not keep the child. They sometimes offered justifications
that concealed the real reasons for their decisions. They said that it
was not good for a child to be with others who have so much more,
or that the child was disruptive to the group, that they could not be
fair to everyone in a situation where one child needs constant
attention. Although there is guilt involved in making these choices
("I could have done him some good"), fundamentally the providers
felt they had no option but to rescue themselves from a situation
that would have been too costly in emotional terms:

> I had a child I took care of for a couple of years . . . and once
> she came and she had a mark on her bottom . . . and she went
> down for her nap and she woke up and she still had the mark
> and that really just blew my mind. Instant tears and the
> whole thing because I had become very attached to the little
> girl at that point. I had to remove myself from the situation
> because I couldn't deal with it any more. . . . I was scared of
> being *too* attached to the child. . . . There would be days
> when . . . she would say, "Please, I don't want to go home,"
> and she would start to cry and my kids would start to cry
> because they didn't want her to go home. It was causing too
> many problems.
>
> It just pulled at my heart. . . . When the little girl came
> she just reeked and I bathed her. You know, I had fixed her
> up so cute. But I can't do that everyday. I just don't have the
> time. And the next day she said to me, "Would you bathe me
> again?" I just cried over her but . . . I thought, I really can't do
> this.

Because the family day-care providers defined their worth
through their emotional relationships rather than through the
exercise of a distinct set of skills, and because they drew on the
satisfactions of their relationships as part of their compensation,
they saw no advantage to providing care for children whom they
could not learn to love.[25] "I had a little boy once. He was about

---

[25] Family day-care providers also claimed other compensations besides the
satisfactions of their relationships. Money is an obvious one. Others included the
savings from not having to go out to work (e.g., not having to pay for clothes,
transportation, and child care), the benefits of being able to stay at home with their
own children, and tax advantages (from unreported incomes or from deductions).

three years old. And he was a totally obnoxious little kid. He was really smart but he was . . . I don't even know what it was but we definitely had a personality clash and I kept him about three days and I told his mother that I had too many I couldn't handle another. . . . But he was just a little boy that I didn't feel comfortable with . . . I wouldn't take care of a child I didn't like. It wouldn't be fair to the child or to me."

The providers thus saw their emotional relationships with their clients' children as an essential and functional, rather than burdensome, aspect of their work. If the relationship was not a good one, they could not do their job properly.

Burning-out on mothering

The work of family day-care providers aligns them with mothering, but the model of mothering is particularly threatening to them. The ideal of deep emotional involvement and selfless giving draws them into a denial of their own needs as workers.

The turnover among family day-care providers is high; 37 percent of the registered providers in Vermont in 1986 were no longer involved in this kind of care in 1987;[26] 63 percent of the questionnaire respondents said they thought of the work as temporary. The women in my study gave a variety of reasons for believing they would soon move on, the most common of which was growth of their own children and the consequent erosion of the original motivation for becoming involved in the occupation. However, when the sixteen women who were no longer working as family day-care providers talked about their feelings, they explicitly named "burnout" as a factor in their decisions.[27] They were tired of struggling to keep a distance from the children, of separating from children to whom they had become attached and of maintaining a

[26] This figure derives from a comparison of the state lists of registered family day-care providers for two consecutive years, 1986 and 1987. A recent analysis of child care in Vermont gave a somewhat lower figure; see Davenport (n. 4 above).

[27] Hochschild's discussion of the human costs of jobs requiring emotional labor focuses on the worker's estrangement from her own feelings. Providing family day-care poses a different kind of threat. Mere display or pretense ("seeming to love the job") is a less central concern. Alienation from the self is less likely to be an issue because the women genuinely become attached to the children and can acknowledge openly the feelings generated through their daily activities. Thus while Hochschild sees burnout in service work as having roots in a worker's too wholehearted identification with the job and an inability to see that the job requires acting, burnout among family day-care providers has a different source (Hochschild, *The Managed Heart* [n. 2 above], 187).

balance between their mother-like tasks and their responsibilities as workers.[28] One woman said, "I think that's part of what was making me burned out. I really felt that was where some of it was, from letting myself become too attached to the children. You have to keep a little bit of distance. Because, I think the fact that I had them here all the time they became . . . so much a part of my family—that made it kind of crazy. . . . [During the time they were with me] I was their sole person for support, authority, love or whatever."

Family day-care providers are not alone in facing these kinds of dilemmas. As others have shown, many paid care givers are drawn to their jobs by the desire to provide a service.[29] They derive meaning from their emotional attachments to clients.[30] They also often find that the contexts in which they work impede the full expression of their affection and concern.[31] Yet, the study of family day-care providers has particular relevance for feminist theorizing about the work of mothers, about women as workers, and about the forces that distort care giving precisely because their work both embraces and rejects the traditional mothering model. The stance of "detached attachment" requires a genuine, caring relationship with a child first and foremost; but still this investment must attend to the needs of the worker/mother. That detached attachment is difficult to sustain and renew is evidence for the confrontation between a traditional ideology of mothering as "not work" and the reality not only that mothering is work (for all women) but also that for family day-care providers mothering has also become an occupational role. If the broad parameters for this confrontation are set by patriarchal capitalism, women who leave their children with family day-care providers, albeit unwittingly, exacerbate it. They

---

[28] The emotional issues are not the only ones that contribute to burnout. Some women tire of struggling with parents about the obligations of each party to the relationships; others find that they can no longer mediate between the demands of their jobs and those of their family members.

[29] Michael Lipsky, *Street-Level Bureaucracy: Dilemmas of the Individual in Public Services* (New York: Russell Sage, 1980); Patricia Cayo Sexton, *The New Nightingales: Hospital Workers, Unions, and New Women's Issues* (New York: Enquiry Press, 1982); Ann Withorn, *Serving the People: Social Services and Social Change* (New York: Columbia University Press, 1984).

[30] Rebecka Inga Lundergren and Carole H. Browner, "Caring for the Institutionalized Mentally Retarded: Work Culture and Work-based Social Support," in *Circles of Care*, ed. Emily K. Abel and Margaret K. Nelson (Albany: State University of New York Press, in press); Kari Warness, "Caring as Women's Work in the Welfare State," in *Patriarchy in a Welfare Society*, ed. Harriet Holter (Oslo: Universitetsforlaget, 1984), 67–87.

[31] Timothy Diamond, "Nursing Homes as 'Trouble,'" and Karen Sacks, "Does It Pay to Care?" both in Abel and Nelson, eds.

assume that providers will act "like mothers" during their own daily absence. In so doing, they redefine mothering for themselves "to incorporate some kind of working experience" outside the home.[32] Yet they are unwilling to accept the broader implications of this redefinition, that if they want family day-care providers to assume some of the burdens of mothering, they might also have to grant them some of the privileges.[33]

The generation of children who were raised in this kind of care might better understand the bind in which family day-care providers are placed; they might both accept nonexclusive bonds with their own children and acknowledge the emotional and practical needs of others who care. Meanwhile, the experiences of family day-care providers highlight the struggles accompanying the changing meaning of mothering.

Department of Sociology
Middlebury College

[32] Saraceno, 24.

[33] Barbara Katz Rothman argues, "Someone who has given prolonged personal care to a child should have continued legal visitation rights to that child, and should not be subject to 'firing' without cause by the parents" (Barbara Katz Rothman, *Recreating Motherhood: Ideology and Technology in a Patriarchal Society* [New York: Norton, 1989], 258).

DOMESTICITY AND COLONIALISM IN BELGIAN AFRICA: USUMBURA'S *FOYER SOCIAL*, 1946–1960

NANCY ROSE HUNT

By 1957, 15 percent of the African women living in the colonial city of Usumbura, Ruanda-Urundi (present-day Bujumbura, Burundi), were participating in a government-sponsored educational and social welfare program.[1] *Foyers sociaux*, or social homes, were Belgian domestic training institutions for African women, founded for married women living in colonial urban centers. Some women were learning to cook, mend, iron, and wash clothes, and how to wean their infants and decorate their homes, and a select few were being trained to work (for pay) as auxiliary aids or monitors in the classroom. European women circulated in the African quarters, visiting and inspecting the students' homes and helping women prepare for annual most-beautiful-house contests. Graduation ceremonies, holiday celebrations, and displays of students' projects were other annual events sponsored by a *foyer social* that marked

I am grateful for a Fulbright fellowship to Burundi in 1984–85. My thanks also go to Nina Adams, Kenneth Curtis, Steven Feierman, Jonathon Glassman, Paul Landau, Elizabeth Schmidt, Ann Stoler, Jan Vansina, and the anonymous *Signs* readers for their comments on earlier drafts of this article.

[1] Usumbura, Foyer Social, Rapport annuel, 1957, 1, 4, 9, Bureau de la Mairie, Bujumbura. The total female population figure includes 11,642 women and 2,500 single women. The number enrolled includes 1,885 enrolled at the central *foyer* as well as 156 newly enrolled and 146 re-enrolled women attending the branch *foyer* at Ngagara. Figures from the military camp and the Faubourg rural were not used to derive the percentage.

This essay originally appeared in *Signs*, vol. 15, no, 3, Spring 1990.

in a public, ritualized way the continuity of the program and the progress of its students. A colonial centerpiece, Usumbura's *foyer* was proudly celebrated in Belgium's annual reports to the United Nations and served to legitimize Belgian administration of this trust territory.[2]

Despite the many historical studies that have appeared since the 1970s about the impact of colonialism on African women, surprisingly little attention has been paid to colonial efforts to domesticize women.[3] Since the 1970s, and especially since Ester Boserup pointed out that colonial notions of development for women meant "training for the home,"[4] historians have been refining interpretations of changes in African women's economic lives. Yet, the study of the relations between ideology and the construction of gender under colonialism has been slighted.[5] In refusing to equate women with domesticity, historians have acknowledged this equation as a colonial legacy without exploring its historical content and implications.[6]

The operations and curricular structure of Usumbura's *foyer social* point to important connections between Western family

[2] Reporting the activities and growth of *foyers sociaux* in Ruanda-Urundi was the principal Belgian response to annual queries by the United Nations about progress in ameliorating the condition of African women. See, e.g., R/RU (139) no. 4, 1951, pt. 3, question 132, Archives Africaines, Brussels (hereafter cited as AA). (*Foyers sociaux* is the plural of *foyer social*.)

[3] There are exceptions. Recent work on related issues includes Deborah Gaitskell, "Housewives, Maids or Mothers: Some Contradictions of Domesticity for Christian Women in Johannesburg, 1903–39," *Journal of African History* 24, no. 2 (1983): 241–56, and " 'Christian Compounds for Girls': Church Hostels for African Women in Johannesburg, 1907–1970," *Journal of Southern African Studies* 6, no. 1 (October 1979): 44–69; Kristin Mann, "The Dangers of Dependence: Christian Marriage among Elite Women in Lagos Colony, 1880–1915," *Journal of African History* 24, no. 1 (1983): 36–56; and Audrey Wipper, "The Maendeleo ya Wanawake Movement in the Colonial Period: The Canadian Connection, Mau Mau, Embroidery and Agriculture," *Rural Africana* 29 (Winter 1975–76): 195–214. For a general review of literature on African women, see Margaret Strobel, "African Women: A Review," *Signs: Journal of Women in Culture and Society* 8, no. 1 (Autumn 1982): 109–31.

[4] Ester Boserup, *Women's Role in Economic Development* (New York: St. Martin's Press, 1970), esp. 122.

[5] Claire Robertson makes a similar argument in "Developing Economic Awareness: Changing Perspectives in Studies of African Women, 1976–1985," *Feminist Studies* 13, no. 1 (Spring 1987): 97–135.

[6] In 1975, 50 percent of all nonformal education offered to African women was in domestic science. Home economics development programs remain "solidly housework-based, a result of the success of women as domestics," despite international development agencies' claims that they are moving away from knitting, cookery, and child care to income generation and appropriate technology projects. See Barbara Rogers, *The Domestication of Women, Discrimination in Developing Countries* (London and New York: Tavistock, 1981), esp. 86, 88.

ideology, the colonial construction of womanhood and domesticity, and the emergence of a colonized African urban elite. Why was reaching and communicating with African women through the *foyer social* a prized colonial agenda? What were the implications of African women's participation? Some African women did rebel against colonial power in Usumbura, but their resistance was not sparked by the seemingly beneficent *foyer social*.[7] Because neither colonial coercion nor African resistance were explicitly expressed, the *foyer* permits us to refine our understanding of what Georges Balandier has called "the colonial situation": "a force acting in terms of its own [sociological] totality."[8] Colonialism has too often been imagined as an "abstract force, as a *structure* imposed on local *practice*,"[9] but it was not anonymous, indivisible, or all-imposing. The colonizing process encompassed a disparate array of actors in metropolitan and colonial contexts, including women. In local settings, colonial encounters entailed mutual processes of cultural incorporation and transformation, rather than complete cultural annihilation.

The *foyer social* was a colonial project to revise and refashion gender roles, family life, and domestic space enacted by European nuns and social workers and African women within classrooms, households, and an African urban community. A "peculiar intimacy between dominators and dominated" intentionally fostered by the homelike atmosphere of the *foyer* belied the tension about authority and deference that pervaded the institution.[10] Inscribed in this tension is the fact that although the *foyer* was designed to instill Western family ideology into urban African life, limits were set on the degree of emulation that was possible. For elite Africans, measures designed to seduce their participation and cooperation were as salient as forms of distancing from the colonizer.[11] Although

[7] Nancy Hunt, "Colonial Sexual Insults and Female Indignation: Swahili Women's Resistance to the Single Women's Tax in Usumbura" (Madison, Wis., 1988, typescript).

[8] Georges Balandier, "The Colonial Situation: A Theoretical Approach (1951)," in *Social Change: The Colonial Situation*, ed. Immanuel Wallerstein (New York: Wiley, 1966), 34–61, esp. 35.

[9] Ann Laura Stoler, "Rethinking Colonial Categories: European Communities in Sumatra and the Boundaries of Rule," *Comparative Studies in Society and History* 31, no. 1 (January 1989): 134–61.

[10] Gerald Sider, "When Parrots Learn to Talk, and Why They Can't: Domination, Deception and Self-Deception in Indian-White Relations," *Comparative Studies in Society and History* 29, no. 1 (January 1987): 3–23, esp. 11.

[11] On hegemony as a "process of incorporation," see Raymond Williams, *Marxism and Literature* (Oxford: Oxford University Press, 1977), 108–41. On colonial processes of incorporation and distancing, see James Boutilier, "Papua New Guinea's Colonial Century: Reflections on Imperialism, Accommodation, and Historical

targeted for special attention and inducements by the *foyer*, their distinct place in the racist colonial hierarchy was ultimately reinforced, even as their elite position among Africans was simultaneously delineated.

The colonial context

The Union des Femmes Coloniales established the first lay-operated housekeeping and social welfare centers for young girls in two Congolese cities in 1926. Directors of Catholic missions and private social service agencies, with the agreement of the Belgian administration, sent the first social workers to Leopoldville in 1933, Elisabethville in 1934, and Coquilhatville in 1938. *Foyers sociaux* were opened to teach home economics and maternal hygiene, in response to what was considered an urgent problem: women living in urban centers. After the war, Belgian colonial authorities decided to create a specialized service for the *foyers*.[12] This decision reflected a larger shift in colonial urban policy, away from discouraging rural-urban migration and toward fostering the long-term urban residence of certain workers and their families.[13] Although private social-service agencies usually continued to operate the institutions, they received full governmental funding, and the European staff were no longer nuns but social workers.

A large colonial literature that both addressed the social problems facing women in the city and explained why the *foyers* would remedy this social and moral crisis emerged after World War II.[14] The phenomena of adultery, prostitution, alcoholism, divorce, and

Consciousness," in *History and Ethnohistory in Papua, New Guinea*, ed. Deborah Gewertz and Edward Schieffelin (Sydney: University of Sydney, 1985), 7–25.

[12] See Union des Femmes Coloniales, undated statement received by Première Direction, Justice et Affaires Indigènes, ca. 1927, Fond A. I. 1394, dossier no. 2, "Protection de la femme noire," Archives Africaines (AA). J. Van Hove, "Situation actuelle du Service Social—ses prochaines réalisations," *Révue coloniale belge*, no. 114 (July 1, 1950), 463–64. The first social workers were sent to Stanleyville during World War II.

[13] Carol Dickerman, "City Women and the Colonial Regime: Usumbura, 1939–1962," *African Urban Studies*, no. 18 (Spring 1984), 33–48, esp. 34–35.

[14] For examples of this literature, see Sister Julienne de Cornillon, "Service social à Usumbura," *Grands Lacs* 64 (February 1, 1949): 93–95; S. Dobriski-Gabszewicz, "Les centres sociaux du Congo Belge et du Ruanda-Urundi," *Revue colonial belge* 8, no. 176 (1953): 90–92, and "Développement et évolution des services sociaux d'Afrique Belge," *Problèmes sociaux congolais*, no. 43 (December 1958), 7–21. For a more detailed review of this literature, see Nancy Hunt, " 'We Refused to Be Insulted': African Women's Resistance to Belgian Colonization in Usumbura, Ruanda-Urundi, 1941–1962" (M.A. thesis, Sangamon State University, 1985).

a demographic pattern of men outnumbering women were of long-standing concern to Belgian authorities and missionaries. Colonial commentators thought women in the cities were floundering, disoriented, vulnerable, and corruptible due to idleness, excessive leisure, and a void of custom. The notion that the moral authority of customary culture did not extend to urban centers was ubiquitous in Belgian colonial discourse. To cure these ills, colonial social workers, officials, missionaries, and sociologists hoped to create a new tradition, culture, and source of authority over women, and a new locus of socialization—the nuclear family. This process of inventing a colonized urban tradition would begin through women and in *foyers sociaux*. Whereas men would be useful to the colony as producers, as a labor force, women would be important as reproducers, as mothers and wives ensuring the vitality and perpetuation of this labor force and the proper rearing of children. According to this colonial vision, a woman was not to have any cash-generating activities; this would have conflicted with her central role as the "base of evolution." She was to represent and radiate moral standards and behavior for men and children, through the "civilized" institution of the nuclear family.[15] This logic was encapsulated in the aphorism: "To instruct a boy is . . . to form a man; to instruct a girl is to form a family."[16] This new kind of family would be monogamous, authority would be vested in the husband, and its generating force would be a Western "notion of the spouses which must be the base and without which the family cannot play its role of social cell and cement of 'evolved' society."[17]

Colonial domestic education for women was not unique to the Belgian Congo and Ruanda-Urundi,[18] nor was it new to Belgian colonialism.[19] What made the *foyer* novel in Belgian Africa was its

[15] See, e.g., "La femme indigène, base d'évolution," *La chronique congolaise* (September 3, 1949), 3.

[16] *L'action sociale au Congo Belge et au Ruanda-Urundi* (Brussels: Centre d'Information du Congo Belge et du Ruanda-Urundi, n.d. [ca. 1953]), 101.

[17] A. Sohier, "Le rôle de la femme dans la famille indigène congolaise," *Zaire*, no. 4 (1947), 443–45.

[18] Homecraft classes for girls and adult women were common under other colonial regimes; in addition to the works cited in n. 3 above, Perlman and Moal's annotated bibliography is a useful beginning for sensing the range of domestic schools for girls and adult women in colonial Africa. Homecraft and/or maternal hygiene were being taught to adult women in French Equatorial Africa and in colonial Ghana, Zimbabwe, Zambia, Sudan, and Kenya. It is unclear if some of these programs were directed at urban elite women. See M. Perlman and M. P. Moal, "Analytical Bibliography," in *Women of Tropical Africa*, ed. Denise Paulme (Berkeley and Los Angeles: University of California Press, 1963), 288–93.

[19] Domestic education for girls was introduced in Belgian Africa in the Leopoldian period (1885–1908); Barbara Yates, "The Missions and Educational Develop-

attention to the urban elite or *évolués*. The Belgian term *évolué* was loosely applied to those who had been educated by and/or were salaried workers of Europeans. Jean-Marie Domont's prescriptive manual of proper behavior for *évolués* explained that to be an *évolué* one had to do more than speak French and wear Western dress. One had to fulfill moral, familial, professional, and civic duties, while serving as a model for less privileged Africans.[20] During the post–World War II period, anxieties about *évolués* dominated colonial attention. Roger Anstey has shown that it was a period of "bitter *évolué* feeling" because inadequate measures had been taken to permit elite men to assimilate and distinguish themselves from the mass of Africans.[21] Hence, associations of *évolué* men received official encouragement, *cartes de mérite civique* (cards of civic merit) were invented to legally and symbolically reward worthy *évolués*,[22] and *foyers sociaux* were promoted to provide *évolué* men with *évolué* wives.

Usumbura was the principal administrative and commercial center of the Belgian-administered territory of Ruanda-Urundi.[23]

---

ment in Belgian Africa, 1876–1908" (Ph.D. diss., Columbia University, 1967). Virtually all educational opportunities for African women and girls in the Belgian Congo and Ruanda-Urundi were oriented toward domestic training and more rigidly so than in other African colonial regimes; Helen Kitchen, ed., *The Educated African: A Country-by-Country Survey of Educational Development in Africa* (New York: Praeger, 1962). See also Barbara Yates, "Colonialism, Education and Work: Sex Differentiation in Colonial Zaire," in *Women and Work in Africa*, ed. Edna G. Bay (Boulder, Colo.: Westview, 1982), 127–51.

[20] See Jean-Marie Domont, *Elite Noire*, with a preface by M. Gustave Sand (Léopoldville: Imprimerie du Courrier d'Afrique, 1948). Merlier situates the *évolués* in class terms as *"petit bourgeois"* in character, occupying "subaltern" positions in the colonial system; Michel Merlier, *Le Congo de la colonisation à l'indépendance* (Paris: François Maspero, 1962), 186, 196. (The plural of the male noun *évolué* is *évolués;* when used as an adjective in this paper *évolué* will be used regardless of gender and number.)

[21] See Roger Anstey, "Belgian Rule in the Congo and the Aspirations of the 'Evolue' Class," in *The History and Politics of Colonialism, 1914–1960*, ed. L. H. Gann and Peter Duignan (Cambridge: Cambridge University Press, 1970), 2:194–225, esp. 202.

[22] As of 1948, eligible *évolués* could apply for *cartes du mérite civique* and, beginning in 1952, card holders could apply for the ambiguously higher status of *immatriculation*. See Anstey, esp. 194–96; and Crawford Young, *Politics in the Congo* (Princeton, N.J.: Princeton University Press, 1965), 196–97.

[23] When Belgian administration began in 1921, Usumbura's total population was only 2,656. Twenty years later, the population was 6,660. In 1947, there were 12,346 Africans in the city, and ten years later they numbered 44,685. Carol Dickerman, "Economic and Social Change in an African City: Bujumbura, Burundi, 1900–1962" (Ph.D. diss., University of Wisconsin—Madison, 1984), 20–21.

The city's two main African urban quarters, Belge and Buyenzi, were distinguished from each other by religion. Buyenzi was Usumbura's core community of fishermen, traders, and farmers, who shared a common religion (Islam), spoke a common language (Swahili), and whose urban residence and culture predated colonialism. Most women of Buyenzi were, and are, farmers and petty traders. Swahili was the lingua franca of the other urban quarter, Belge, as well, but the men of this predominantly Roman Catholic quarter held more of the European-created, salaried, auxiliary positions than Buyenzi men. The men and women of both quarters represented a diverse range of residential and ethnic origins: Rwandans, Burundians, and Congolese were found in each. Yet those of Belge were more affected by the new opportunities of the colonial city. While many in Buyenzi had watched the colonial city grow up around their African community, most of those in Belge had migrated to the city where the men sought jobs with European employers. Many Belge women engaged in forms of commerce and artisanal work that could be done in the home, especially beer brewing.[24]

Until the mid-twenties, African Christians and African Muslims lived together alongside Arab and Asian traders. In 1927, African residents were separated into two urban locations. This forced relocation and segregation was based not on ethnicity but on notions of fulfilling a civilizing mission and what should constitute an African elite to fill the city's labor requirements. Fearful of the influence of Islam, Belgian authorities and missionaries wanted to circumscribe the influence of the Muslim, polygynous Swahili and civilize the Catholic *évolué* (evolved) or *évoluant* (evolving) population as much as possible.[25] Belge was supposed to be the *évolué* quarter of Usumbura,[26] but its occupants were thought by missionaries and colonial officials to suffer from "an unbelievable weakness of character." Family life was "if not nonexistent . . . at least very deficient," and Africans had little sense of the wife's role and duties. One colonial response to this apparently immoral situation of "drinking, dance and misconduct,"[27] idle women, and vulnerable

[24] Hunt, " 'We Refused to Be Insulted' " (n. 14 above), 11, 23–30.

[25] On this policy of segregation, see Dickerman, "Economic and Social Change in an African City," 178–79, 192–94.

[26] Eighty to 85 percent of Belge's residents were Catholic in 1957, and many of them had received some education; Usumbura, Centres extra-coutumiers, Rapport annuel, 1957, p. 34 (hereafter cited as CecRa), Bureau de la Mairie, Bujumbura. Fifty-three percent of the men and 22 percent of the women could read and write in 1959; CecRa, 1959, 22.

[27] de Cornillon (n. 14 above), 93–94.

young girls was to teach the wives of *évolués* their proper roles and duties. In 1946, the White Father and White Sister missionaries of Usumbura's Catholic mission created the city's original *foyer social* as a complement to their work with male *évolués*.

Colonial constructions of wifehood and motherhood

According to the mission guidelines for a program of social assistance for women, workshops and house visits would be organized to teach the wives of *évolués* domestic skills.[28] Although only African women would receive the training, the entire family would benefit: "The purpose pursued in the centers . . . [is to] organize a normal social life in basing it on religious and moral principles and particularly to give an important role to the family such as it is conceived in our milieu of ancient Christian civilization. . . . The indigenous peoples of the centers are too mixed together for traditional custom to still have a sufficient influence as moral rule and sanction. The only means of lifting up this new society is to solidly establish the family: father, mother and children."[29] The missionaries agreed that only women of monogamous marriages in "regular households," that is, those deemed socially acceptable, and fiancées living "regularly" before a monogamous marriage, regardless of religion, would be eligible since "to act otherwise would risk perverting the entire plan."[30]

Pleasing husbands was one of the reproductive labor skills advanced by the program. The church generally advised *évolués* to look for wives of an equal level of "evolution,"[31] and the program for women was intended to reduce existing incongruities between elite men's level of "evolution" and that of their wives.[32] Teaching women domestic tasks would give wives educations "parallel" to their husbands': men and women needed different educations, such "according to the psychological requirements which are appropriate."[33] It was assumed that women had a natural feminine

[28] Vicariat apostolique de l'Urundi, Rapport annuel, 1946–47, typescript, 4–5, Archives de la Société des Missionnaires d'Afrique (Pères Blancs), Rome (hereafter cited as PBA).

[29] de Cornillon, 94.

[30] Ibid.

[31] See, e.g., R. P. Langouche, "Notes sur le mariage des catholiques dans l'Urundi," n.d. [ca. 1949], dossier no. 862E, 6, PBA.

[32] Vicariat apostolique de l'Urundi, Rapport annuel, 1946–47, typescript, 5, PBA.

[33] de Cornillon, 94.

psychological propensity for motherhood and domesticity, and the lessons were expected to draw on and shape this tendency, to instill in a wife "devotion, unselfishness and discreet and intelligent collaboration in the profession of the husband."[34]

On April 15, 1946, two White Sister nuns began giving lessons to Barundi and Congolese women of Belge. They were assisted by colonial women—usually the wives of European officials and other residents. By the end of July, fifty-four women had enrolled and thirty-four attended regularly; by March 1947, 104 had enrolled and seventy-five attended regularly.[35] Ninety percent of these women were said to be wives of the "Catholic elite."[36] Sister Nolly, a White Sister who helped organize this first *foyer,* recalled that most of the students tended already to be somewhat "evolved," having "a bedroom for two for the couple, for example."[37] It was hoped that this elite would in turn "radiate in the indigenous milieu and prolong our action."[38] Sister Nolly also recalled that some Buyenzi women came to the nuns and asked to join because they had heard what the Belge students were doing.[39] Thus, in June 1947, the nuns founded a new section for Buyenzi women.[40] The rules requiring that members be "monogamist from a regular situation" did not apply to these Muslim women from a polygynous culture.[41] Rather the nuns hoped that once they gained the trust of the Swahili woman, the moral issues of polygamy could be addressed. By the end of November 1947, 241 women were enrolled, 142 from Belge and 99 from Buyenzi.[42]

In 1948, the work of the White Sisters was assumed by three professional social workers from the private Catholic social service organization, Assistance Sociale au Congo, and the workshop

[34] Ibid.

[35] de Cornillon, 93; Fond R/RU no. 1 (139) 1948, Territoire d'Usumbura, Rapport annuel, 1948, pt. 3, 83/7bis, AA.

[36] Vicariat apostolique de l'Urundi, Rapport annuel, 1946–47, typescript, 5, PBA.

[37] Sister Nolly, untaped interview with Nancy Hunt, December 11, 1984, Bujumbura. Sister Nolly (formerly Sister Rosalie) and Sister Gabrielle de Marneffe (formerly Sister Julienne de Cornillon) interviewed on November 13, 1984, also untaped, were present in Usumbura when the workshop began. They attributed its founding to the influence of Monseigneur Martin who thought something must be done to "evolve" women. Hereafter all interviews will be indicated by interviewee name and the interview date; all interviews were conducted by the author in Bujumbura and were taped unless otherwise indicated.

[38] de Cornillon, 95.

[39] Sister Nolly, December 13, 1984.

[40] de Cornillon, 93.

[41] Ibid., 94–95.

[42] Fond R/RU no. 1 (139), 1948, pt. 3, 83/7bis, AA; de Cornillon, 95.

became a state-sponsored *foyer social*.[43] Its location was moved outside of mission property to a government building located just next to the governmental *évolué* center for men, the Cercle du Progrès on Route de Cyangugu. Some students moved with the institution and later received certificates from the new *foyer*.[44] The greater resources, staffing, and physical space of the new institution allowed more women to attend. Programs expanded, and women of all races and religions were encouraged to enroll.[45] A large new building, still standing and in use today, was opened in 1953.[46] Located on the central avenue bisecting Belge and Buyenzi, it was easily accessible to women of both communities.

Like the mission program, the government-sponsored program was welcomed by colonial commentators as a promising counter-balance to the problems of single women and prostitution in the African urban neighborhoods.[47] "The purpose is to withdraw them from a hardly favorable atmosphere, that is the demoralizing cabarets and dancings, and to form them to the discipline and spirit of body and devotion. It is hoped that the effort leads to the formation of a feminine elite in the largest social sense."[48] The state-sponsored *foyer* was specifically directed at married women. Like the mission-organized program, the intention was to teach them to be better wives and mothers, not to give them employable skills: "The *Foyer Social* is not . . . a school where indigenous women learn to become professional seamstresses or cooks by trade, but rather a '*foyer*,' that is a house where all the women are at home and feel they are at home, and where the social assistants help them to become prudent ladies of the house, model wives and mothers of the family. The *Foyers Sociaux* will have filled their mission if the houses of the indigenous centers that they serve become cleaner and more orderly, if the families are better fed, the husbands and children better clothed."[49]

In 1953, the number of women seeking to enroll at the *foyer* exceeded that which could be accepted.[50] European women con-

[43] P. Jean Perraudin, *Naissance d'une église: Histoire du Burundi chrétien* (Ngozi, Burundi: n. p., 1963), 190.

[44] Catherine Mirerekano, February 20, 1985; Judith Curinyana, February 19, 1985.

[45] Belgium, Ministère des Colonies, *Rapport soumis par le gouvernment belge à l'Assemblée générale des Nations Unies au sujet de l'administration du Ruanda-Urundi* (Brussels, 1921–60), 1951, 112 (hereafter, cited as *Rapport*).

[46] Ibid., 1954, 231. The Centre Socio-Educatif is now located in this building. It is the institutional successor to the colonial Foyer Social; hereafter cited as CSE.

[47] Fond R/RU no. 1 (139), 1948, pt. 3, 83/7–83/7bis, AA.

[48] Ibid., 83/7bis.

[49] *Rapport*, 1951, 112.

[50] Fond R/RU no. 3 (140), Territoire d'Usumbura, Affaires indigènes et main d'œuvre, Rapport annuel, 1953, 6bis, AA.

tinued to encourage particular women to enroll. Thérèse Namugisha, a Rwandan beer brewer whose husband worked as a domestic servant for Europeans, recalled that the wife of her husband's boss taught at the *foyer* and encouraged her to attend.[51] Catherine Mirerekano, the daughter of a Burundian chief, educated by African nuns and married to an agricultural assistant who had attended the most exclusive school in Ruanda-Urundi, lived in the *évolué* housing for clerks in Belge. Because of her husband's social standing, it was assumed she would attend. "At this time my husband was in charge of the petty functionaries. It was indispensable that I go there . . . even the *bazungu* [white people] came to explain to us."[52]

Rather than focusing on *évolué* women, as did the White Sisters, the government-organized program instituted a curricular hierarchy through which the "better elements" might advance. All women began with the *cours de masse* (basic course), general lessons in sewing and knitting for the "mass" of women, intended "not to teach them to make embroidered dresses, artistically made, but simple clothes easy to finish and thanks to which the members of the family will always be clean and well-groomed."[53] Occasionally teachers provided impromptu instruction in domestic and maternal hygiene.[54] Moral messages about proper wifehood and motherhood accompanied these lessons, which were held twice a week and lasted from six months to a year, "following the capacities of the women and the regularity of their presence."[55] The provision of free sewing and knitting materials for preliminary exercises may have encouraged higher enrollment.[56]

The basic course was used to identify a tiny minority of best students who would continue in the housekeeping classes.[57] These classes were designed "to form true ladies of the house, capable of maintaining the house, making their house interior pleasant and offering to their husband, when he returns home from work, a clean table, an appetizing dinner, and washed, ironed, and mended laundry. Each week at the *Foyer*, they wash their laundry, do ironing and mending, and receive as well a few practical notions in

[51] Thérèse Namugisha, February 25, 1985.

[52] Catherine Mirerekano, February 20, 1985.

[53] *Rapport*, 1954, 230.

[54] Ministère des Colonies, Deuxième Direction Générale, "Programme d'activités d'un Foyer Social," n.d., 5, CSE.

[55] *Rapport*, 1954, 230.

[56] Ministère des Colonies, Deuxième Direction Générale, "Programme d'activités d'un Foyer Social," 4.

[57] *Rapport*, 1954, 230–31.

gardening. Another morning is reserved for a cooking lesson: they prepare a complete meal that they consume together at the *Foyer*."[58] Félicita Zamukwereza of Belge received a certificate in 1955 for completing the housekeeping course. She had regularly attended and passed "tests in knitting, sewing, washing, ironing, mending, cooking and cleaning with Distinction."[59] Lessons in gardening, domestic economy and thrift, familial hygiene, child rearing, and familial education were also included.[60] Forty-eight women were admitted to these housekeeping classes in 1950 and 1951, seventy-two in 1952, ninety in 1953, and sixty in 1954.[61]

In 1953, after the *foyer* moved to its present location, a "model house" was built for housekeeping lessons. This house, comprising a dining room, kitchen, and bedroom, was the size of an *évolué* family home of the time. The dining room included a buffet with meat platters, small platters, deep platters with covers, salad, gravy, and sugar bowls, soup and dinner plates, saucers, cups, glasses, salt shakers, and dessert plates with blue flowers. Forks, knives, coffee spoons, and sugar spoons were kept in a covered rack. A crucifix hung on the wall.[62] These domestic objects—hardly those of a family of modest means—show the *foyer*'s curricular emphasis on Western cuisine, dining etiquette, and Christian morality. Although all women who enrolled at the *foyer* were learning some Western skills, those in the more advanced housekeeping classes were trained in model behavior in a model home, with material accoutrements presupposing a bourgeois standard of living.

A higher, third level in the curricular hierarchy was for the most gifted women, who were trained to be *foyer social* monitors, that is, assistants of the European social workers. A formal two-year course of training was instituted in 1953, and twenty-nine women from Belge and six from Buyenzi were selected to participate. Eligibility standards were reminiscent of those used by the White Sisters in their original *foyer*: each candidate, regardless of religion, had to be from a "regular matrimonial situation," exhibit "irreproachable conduct in order to be able to exercise a favorable influence," and

---

[58] Ibid., 231.

[59] Certificate of Félicita Zamukwereza, November 26, 1955, miscellaneous files, CSE.

[60] CecRa, 1951, 14; Usumbura, Foyer Social, Rapport annuel, 1954, CSE; CecRa, 1956, 94.

[61] *Rapport*, 1954, 233. In 1951 and 1952, these courses were held six half-days a week, and the entire course was to last six months. By 1953, as enrollment increased, each group of twenty to twenty-five women had classes three times a week; *Rapport*, 1951, 114; CecRa, 1952, VI; Fond R/RU no. 3 (140), 1953, 6bis.

[62] Inventory attached to letter, Gilberte De Clerq to Monsieur d'Attaché aux Affaires Sociales du Burundi, October 20, 1961, "Remise-Reprise" file, CSE.

have the consent of her husband.[63] These students received special training in sewing (including buttonholes, slits, collars, tapered necklines),[64] smocking, home economics, professional ethics, hygiene, child care, first aid, etiquette, and enough elementary reading and writing to "decipher sewing patterns and note attendance in classes."[65] Students also received religious and moral lessons regarding the mutual duties of the spouses and the education of children. After receiving their diplomas, these monitors were eligible, following their *évolué* husbands, to apply for a *carte du mérite civique*.[66] Although monitors were trained to perform semiprofessional work as teachers in *foyers,* breaking with the colonial notion that women should not work outside the home, their high rank served to create a hierarchy among African women in which those with senior *évolué* rank were examples for and teachers of their juniors.

Just as housekeeping classes were designed to redefine the meaning of wife for an emerging female elite, the *foyer* was also concerned with revising the meaning of African mother. An extensive sociomedical program concerned with prenatal care, maternal hygiene, and child rearing reached *évolué* and non-*évolué* women. Layette classes, organized for pregnant women who wished to prepare their infants' trousseau before giving birth, were first offered in 1951. Students also received advice on child rearing and infant and maternal hygiene at these sessions.[67] The staff was intent on "destroying all superstitions concerning pregnancy and birth."[68] In 1957, they were pleased to present statistics indicating the "evolution of the psychology of pregnant women" who formerly "refused to prepare the layette of the future baby, claiming that that would bring misfortune to the baby."[69] Increasingly, women attended during the earlier months of pregnancy, apparently because of incentives in the curriculum. In 1951, each woman made six swaddling clothes and four short-sleeved shirts. In 1957, each woman was first obliged to make four swaddling clothes, four pairs of shorts, one linen infant's vest, one small shirt, one baby's dress, and assorted bonnets, and then, if she had completed this program

[63] Ibid.

[64] Usumbura, Foyer Social, Rapport annuel, 1954.

[65] CecRa, 1951, 14; CecRa, 1952, sec. 6; *Rapport,* 1954 (n. 45 above), 233.

[66] "Carte du mérite civique," *Aequatoria* 11, no. 3 (1948): 103–5.

[67] CecRa, 1951, 14; Usumbura, Rapport annuel, Foyer Social, 1954; and CecRa, 1960, 37.

[68] Ministère des Colonies, Deuxième Direction Generale, "Programme d'activités d'un Foyer Social," 7.

[69] Usumbura, Foyer Social, Rapport annuel, 1957, 6–7, Bureau de la Mairie, Bujumbura.

in time, she could purchase a small bed sold at the *foyer* and prepare sheets and a pillow case for it.[70] The *foyer*'s nurse also held meetings with mothers, taught familial and infant hygiene courses, visited women who were sick or had just given birth, and until 1954, assisted with the prenatal, gynecological, and infant consultations at the dispensary operated by the colonial health service in Buyenzi. In 1954, the *foyer* opened a branch in the new, outlying urban quarter of Ngagara, where it operated its own independent program of infant consultations. By 1956, the sociomedical program included infant consultations at Ngagara four times a week; preschool consultations at the central *foyer* twice a month; and a service once a week for sickly and malnourished children, where children were weighed and received milk and other foods, and mothers learned how to raise and nourish their children. In addition, twice a week open *petits soins* sessions were held, in which women could receive advice on minor health matters and watch demonstrations in proper child rearing. In these open sessions, which had begun in 1954 as a formal infant-rearing course, women were also taught how to bathe babies, when to wean them, and how to prepare infant pap. The focus was on weaning, "how to proceed, the ideal period, [and] unfortunate consequences if it is realized too late," since African women were thought to be "strongly ignorant of its importance."[71] These open sessions and preschool children consultations were open to all women attending *foyer* classes, and the other layette and hygiene courses were open to any woman. Thus motherhood training was more accessible than housewifery lessons.

Enrollment at the *foyer* expanded over the years. Those in the monitor and housekeeping classes attended much more consistently than those in the basic course. Measured in terms of numbers of women participating, the sociomedical and mothering classes and programs were the most popular *foyer* activities.[72]

[70] CecRa, 1951, 14; and Usumbura, Foyer Social, Rapport annuel, 1957, 5, 7.

[71] *Rapport*, 1954, 230. Congrès Colonial National, *La promotion de la femme au Congo et au Ruanda-Urundi* (Brussels, 1956), 273. In the classes for monitors, how to use baby bottles was a part of the curriculum; Usumbura, Foyer Social, Rapport annuel, 1954.

[72] The basic course was not exactly well attended: in 1954, average attendance was 27 percent for the women of Belge and 30 percent for the women of Buyenzi. Attendance at the housekeeping classes was 75 percent in the same year, although these women were selected in terms of their attendance record in previous basic classes, a reflection itself of their ability to allocate time for the *foyer* endeavor (*Rapport*, 1954, 232; Usumbura, Centres extra-coutumiers, Rapport annuel, 1952, sec. VI, unpaged). Layette classes were also relatively popular; average attendance in 1954 was 36 percent; *Rapport*, 1954, 232; CecRa. 1952, sec. 6. Least popular were the child care classes in which the average attendance in 1954 was only 21 percent. This lack of popularity might have reflected the fact that participants were subject to home visits after having given birth; *Rapport*, 1954, 232.

The provision of diverse entry points into this colonial social order was a way of dividing women into categories. First, women were classified according to colonial notions of morality, based on religious criteria. The Christian women of Belge were treated differently from the Muslim women of Buyenzi. Although both Catholic women of Belge and Muslim women of Buyenzi were selected to attend house-keeping classes, the two groups were taught separately, and the women of Belge were given more attention. In 1954, the sixty women were divided into three groups, two of fifteen Belge women each, and one of thirty Buyenzi women.[73] Of the thirty-five women selected to participate in monitor classes in 1953, twenty-nine were from Belge and six from Buyenzi. Classes begun in 1956 to prepare young girls for marriage and to keep them from loitering in the streets were divided into Muslim and non-Muslim groups.[74]

Cross-cutting the division of women by moral criteria, the curricular structure further differentiated between elite house-wives and ordinary, non-évolué mothers. The higher up a student went in the domestic curricular hierarchy, the greater the emphasis on her representing a "true lady of the house" and the more concrete was the model projected for emulation. The blocks of évolué houses in Belge were an obvious manifestation of a group of people who had greater access to colonial privileges, with rela-tively superior jobs, working conditions, and incomes.[75] The struc-ture of the foyer's curriculum—with all women taking the basic course, only a select few taking the housekeeping classes, and yet a smaller number being trained as monitors—also suggested levels of "evolution." Privileging a select few who deferred to colonial values and adopted colonial ways and giving them the aura but not the reality of power may have enhanced an incipient consciousness of class divisions forming among Africans in the city.[76]

House visits and husbands

A continual tension over how to achieve discipline, deference, and emulation without direct coercion marked the administration of the

[73] Usumbura, Foyer Social, Rapport annuel, 1954; CecRa, 1954, ch. 7.

[74] CecRa, 1956, 94; CecRa, 1959, 57–58; and CecRa, 1960, 37.

[75] Dickerman, "Economic and Social Change in an African City" (n. 23 above), 182; and Côme Surumwe, "Histoire de Camp Belge de Bujumbura" (Mémoire, Ecole Normale Supérieure du Burundi, 1970–71), 21, 25.

[76] Although Belge was to be the évolué quarter, there were levels of "evolution" within its confines. Salaried, educated workers were the upper echelon in this class structure still in the process of formation. They lived in free housing in durable structures, given to them by their employers (the government as well as private firms), and located in special subquarters; Dickerman, "Economic and Social Change," 102; Surumwe, 21, 25.

foyer. As the *foyer* nurse explained at a colonial congress in Brussels, the Usumbura staff wanted to foster simultaneously discipline and trust. The curriculum was designed to accept rather than penalize women for their irregular attendance and to be like a "home": "These classes shouldn't give the impression of a school, it is necessary that little by little the women consider the *Foyer Social* as being an integral part of their lives. It is necessary that they should always be welcome, that they laugh and sing there, that they feel free there, that they can come between the hours of the classes."[77] Yet as part of the *foyer*'s "methodology" of "moral order,"[78] rules were established, which women were expected to follow. Women were to arrive for lessons on time. They were to wash their hands beforehand. They were to show respect toward their teacher. They had a ticket that they were to bring with them whenever they came to study. They were supposed to inform the director whenever they moved, married, or gave birth so that she could add this to the records. These regulations were printed in Swahili and Kirundi, and students were supposed to take them home to their husbands.[79] Women who were not well behaved were asked to leave.[80]

An emphasis on willing submissiveness and acquiescent emulation especially marked house visits. All women who were enrolled at the *foyer* were susceptible to home visits.[81] Physical access to women's homes gave European social workers, and before them the White Sisters, the opportunity to enter into women's private worlds and inspect for cleanliness, propriety, and display of material goods, and generally to evaluate women's achievement in emulating what was taught in the classroom. Dorothéa Shabani remembered the early house visits of the White Sisters at the time her mother was attending the mission *foyer:*

> The white nuns used to come and check and see how people lived, how they stayed at home, how the Christians displayed their Christianity at home. To see how the Christians were at home. *Or else!!* . . . At home, they always found

[77] Ministère des Colonies, Deuxième Direction, "Programme d'activités d'un Foyer Social," 6.

[78] Congrès colonial national, *La promotion de la femme au Congo et au Ruanda-Urundi* (Brussels, 1956), 271–72.

[79] "Impanuro zimwe zimwe zerekeye abagore biga muli foyer social A.S.A.C.," n.d., mimeographed typescript from miscellaneous files, CSE.

[80] Angèle Makala was expelled for disciplinary reasons in 1959, and her polite letter written to the *foyer* director did not gain her readmittance (Angèle Makala to director of the *Foyer social,* June 5, 1959, miscellaneous files, CSE).

[81] Fond R/RU no. 3 (140), 1953, 6bis, AA.

crosses displayed. They found things like . . . my mother . . .
she always displayed crosses with photographs of Blessed
Mary. She used to teach us in the morning, asked us in the
evening how we played with friends. Father and mother, we
all sat in the evening and prayed together. Always before
sleeping. . . . When they came, we were always very happy
because for children that meant some medals, or some holy
pictures. They always gave us some small gifts. This always
made us happy.[82]

Catherine Mirerekano fondly remembered being visited by *foyer*
social workers and monitors.

They came, passed the whole day at the house. They taught
us cleanliness at the house, especially the bed, the children's
bed, how to make it, how to cover the bed with bedspreads
and checkered sheets. This day was truly joy, a holiday. . . .
They visited the whole house. . . . The leader came to see
and make the patrol . . . a Rwandan . . . She had a *carte du
mérite civique*. . . . The French woman who taught us and
examined us was a better friend. It was she who helped us do
all the house. . . . They told you in advance in order to obtain
good results. If they appreciated the work, they gave you
good advice. They helped us a tiny bit. They returned to see
if you had put everything in place, there where it should be,
if you had cooked. Once the patrol was finished, they went
off.[83]

Dorothéa and Catherine's recollections of house visits are
cheerful yet not without a shade of ambivalence. Dorothéa's
memory of gifts of medals and holy pictures as well as *"Or else!!"*
warnings discloses the seductive yet threatening meaning of these
visits for a young girl. Catherine recognized a visit's purpose was
"patrol," to verify the following of lessons, "to avoid," as she
explained, "all cheating."[84] Dorothéa's memory evokes an image of
being rewarded for family togetherness and piety, whereas Catherine's "holiday" conjures an image of approval for domestic cleanliness and bourgeois taste in interior decoration. For the nuns,
Christian medals and crosses were displayed; for the European
social workers, bedspreads and checkered sheets. House visits

---

[82] Dorothéa Shabani, February 26, 1985.
[83] Catherine Mirerekano, February 20, 1985.
[84] Ibid.

advanced colonial knowledge of colonized society because they permitted entry into African households, where colonial representatives evaluated and attempted to alter family behavior and domestic space. In Usumbura, the historical shift from nun visitations to social worker visitations entailed differences in how domesticity and housewifely activity was evaluated and shaped, and signified that "the relationship between family and state was subtly changing."[85]

House visits were considered the "best point of contact" with the *foyer*'s students, and social workers in Usumbura wished they had more time for such visits.[86] They were carefully advised on how to handle them delicately.

At first she [the social worker] won't make any remarks, she will strive especially to be of service and to be interested in all that is told to her. Once confidence is established, after one or two visits, it's then only that the Social Auxiliary will be able to assert her demands; at each visit she will call attention to only one point, she will enter it on the card and will verify at the next visit if this point is observed. For example: lack of ventilation, unwashed dishes, an unmade bed, disorder, etc. These visits will be numerous, systematic and repeated; they naturally mustn't assume the character of meddling or of a police raid; all the trust of the native would be lost.[87]

The house visits were also a means of gathering intimate details about African households. Besides a record for each woman with notes on class progress, household condition, and "information received from third parties, visits to her family, her evolution, etc.,"

[85] Anna Davin, "Imperialism and Motherhood," *History Workshop*, no. 5 (Spring 1978), 9–66, esp. 13. House visits were not invented on colonial terrain, nor were they always welcome. "Lady health visitors" had been inspecting the hygienic and familial conditions of working-class homes in metropolitan contexts since the turn of the century as part of larger campaigns to transform European working-class life by "teaching the ideology as well as the skills of domesticity" (Davin, 38). For the British case, see also Celia Davis, "The Health Visitor as Mother's Friend: A Woman's Place in Public Health, 1900–14," *Social History of Medicine* 1, no. 1 (April 1988): 39–59. On the work of visiting nurses in Belgium and extracts of their reports on visits to working-class homes, see *L'assistance sociale et l'Oeuvre Nationale de l'Enfance* (Brussels: Oeuvre Nationale de l'Enfance, n.d. [ca. 1927]).

[86] Usumbura, Foyer Social, Rapport annuel, 1957, 11.

[87] Ministère des Colonies, Deuxième Direction Sociale, "Programme d'activités d'un Foyer Social."

each student of the *foyer* had a social card. The social cards itemized each woman's ethnic background, religion, type of marriage, bridewealth payments, sources of revenue (including money received from her husband), husband's job and salary, the size and condition of housing, and types of kitchen utensils and bedding. "These elements will be gathered only bit by bit," the *foyer* staff was informed, "because a first contact will not permit asking all this information, the one concerned will be mistrustful, she isn't confident yet."[88]

Although the colonial administration in Brussels expected these visits to be made to all women connected to the *foyer*,[89] the students of the housekeeping and monitor classes in Usumbura were visited most frequently. In 1951, the staff made 565 house visits.[90] In 1954, the number increased to 1,182: the nurse made 292 visits; forty visits were made to those enrolled in the most-beautiful-house contest; 250 of 1,129 students in the basic course were visited; and a total of 600 visits were made to the homes of the sixty housekeeping-class students.[91] House visits also varied in duration and tone. Thérèse Namugisha, a housekeeping student, remembered a visit as a special, joyful occasion when her home was turned into the *foyer* and all the students and instructors came. "During the year of completion, if it was a question of preparing food, they cooked at your house. . . . Everybody, with the students, came to prepare the meal at your house. They swept the house, mended your clothes and went home, leaving all [the food] behind. The day after they went elsewhere and did the same thing. . . . They helped me. We cooked together. . . . They knew Swahili. . . . We talked of our works and they looked at how the house was. . . . It was good."[92] Yvonne Mawazo, a poorer woman who attended the basic course, recalled the house visit as a perfunctory inspection of the tidiness of her home and colonial entry into her private space. "They came one time [to my house]. . . . They found it swept. They found me outside. They entered and went even into the bedroom and found that my bed was well made."[93]

The Usumbura *foyer* staff considered the visits the "most beautiful part" of their work because of the "moral influence" the

[88] Ibid.
[89] Ibid.
[90] *Rapport*, 1951, 114.
[91] Usumbura, Foyer Social, Rapport annuel, 1954. The reports calculate the total as 1,082 rather than 1,182.
[92] Thérèse Namugisha, February 25, 1985.
[93] Yvonne Mawazo, February 15, 1985.

visits had on the families.[94] The results of this social work tended to be "encouraging" yet mixed: "Many of the houses of graduates can be visited spontaneously: their cleanliness, their appearance are impeccable. Other elements are more rebellious towards the housekeeping training."[95] The colonial administration in Brussels advised that house visits would be more "effective" if they were made after 4:30 because the husband would have returned from work: "It is necessary to interest him also in these initiatives, in order that he help his wife and attach himself to his home."[96] The list of rules and guidelines that were handed out to the students closed with a message to their husbands, asking them to send their wives to the *foyer* regularly and to help their wives to follow the advice received at the *foyer*.[97] Before a woman could begin the monitor classes, she had to have the permission of her husband.

In seeking the cooperation and consent of husbands, the *foyer* attempted to shape marital relations and bolster men's marital authority by delegating the privilege of colonial power to them. For instance, in 1955, the director of the *foyer*, Mlle Frankard, spoke at the local *évolué* center for men, Cercle du Progrès, on "The *Foyer Social* and Husbands." "We have noticed that many women start the course . . . but by negligence or lack of perseverance abandon coming after a few tries. A little more severe and regular surveillance on the part of the husband could only lead to excellent results."[98] She reiterated the outlines of the model *évolué* couple's family life. "I am certain that each of you . . . wishes to find a pleasing interior when you return home from work. Isn't there a way, from time to time, to lend a hand in helping your wives create this attractive atmosphere? . . . The wife musn't be considered only as the property of the husband but also as his collaborator. To cite only a few examples: meals eaten in common, common meetings and receptions, outings and trips as a family."[99] A savings bank at the *foyer* where women could save money was another effort to encourage family thrift and reshape spending patterns, perhaps even giving some wives greater monetary control.[100] Mlle Frankard told the members of the local *évolué* society that establishing a family budget was a good example of collaboration between spouses because a study had just been conducted by the mission

[94] CecRa, 1954, ch. 7.

[95] *Rapport* (n. 45 above), 1951, 114.

[96] Ministère des Colonies, Deuxième Direction Générale, "Programme d'activités d'un Foyer Social," 3.

[97] "Impanuro zimwe zimwe" (n. 79 above).

[98] "Le Foyer Social et les Epoux," *Temps Nouveaux d'Afrique* (July 17, 1955), 3.

[99] Ibid.

[100] CecRa, 1949, 18–19.

showing that most husbands spent a good part of their salaries on themselves.[101] Later in the year, the director thanked the husbands for their assistance and said the *foyer* personnel noticed a marked improvement during house visits: "Here we must especially thank the husbands of our women who have favored by their support the execution of advice given as to the improvement of hygienic conditions, upkeep of the house, etc."[102]

African monitors were used increasingly to make house visits.[103] Godelieva Murekeyisoni, a Rwandan monitor, recalled how she "helped the people to change."

> We organized ourselves in groups to see the cleanliness in the house. . . . They learned to wash their children, dress them, make the bed, clean their husband's clothes and perform bodily hygiene. They learned to clean cooking utensils, plates. Everything. A pregnant woman would be able to know what to eat the moment of giving birth, how to make the baby's clothes before giving birth. . . . They changed a lot and in the end it was good. We made sure of that. . . . We went slowly since many didn't comprehend well, but all the same, they managed to be able to do it.[104]

Visits conducted by African monitors made their African students uneasy, according to the *foyer*'s annual report. "It is rather difficult to visit at home with the monitors. In effect, if the indigenous women very easily welcome the European staff to their homes, they are much more reticent vis-à-vis the monitors and the husbands do not like having other women intrude into the privacy of their household (we have had several remarks on this subject)."[105] The blame for this reticence was directed at the monitors, and more time was spent teaching the technique of the home visit to them. Yet this passage also indicates that the colonial women themselves were not always welcome and encountered reluctance and objections, especially from husbands. It suggests that not all African women and their husbands were interested in colonial approval, and some resented colonial intrusion into their homes.

---

[101] "Au Foyer Social d'Usumbura: Distribution des prix," *Temps Nouveaux d'Afrique* (December 4, 1955), 5.

[102] Ibid.

[103] In 1951, the monitors were helping with house visits, whereas in 1960 they were doing most of this activity (*Rapport*, 1951, 114; and CecRa, 1960, 38).

[104] Godelieva Murekeyisoni, March 8, 1985.

[105] Usumbura, Foyer Social, Rapport annuel, 1957, 11. The same uneasiness is evident in Mirerekano's recollection of house visits (n. 83 above).

The institutionalization of domesticity

Although the *foyer* sanctioned separate spheres for women and men as well as women's confinement in the private sphere, house visitations by *foyer* representatives of colonial rule brought the public eye into the private sphere. The *foyer*'s festive occasions and special events were recurring public rituals that similarly institutionalized a colonial vision of private life by offering urban Africans "new traditions of subordination" celebrating domesticity.[106]

Christmas, New Year's, and other holiday teas and parties were organized, and all the women of the *foyer* and their families were encouraged to attend. Women who completed the housekeeping and monitor classes received certificates at graduation ceremonies. Europeans and *évolués* attended, colonial officials made speeches, the graduating women sang songs composed for the occasion, and prizes were awarded.[107] Exhibits of student work were displayed for the African and European publics.[108] "We are satisfied in general with the good mentality and cordial understanding reigning among the women of the *foyer*. At the moment of the celebrations and reunions, the European population is always agreeably surprised by this fine ambience which makes one think that the women find themselves at the *foyer* a bit like at their homes."[109]

In attending these rituals, the women came into contact with the larger colonial world beyond the *foyer* in their capacity as wives. These repetitive ceremonies were part of the colonial invention of a new tradition of family activity, marital togetherness, and mutual deference to colonial rule. This was most clearly demonstrated by the most-beautiful-house contests: not women but married couples entered these contests, which were funded by the colonial urban authorities as part of a general effort to encourage residents of the African urban quarters to decorate their homes according to European tastes. Mirerekano remembered joining the contest with her husband, the holder of a *carte du mérite civique*.[110] "We made demonstrations in front of our house, the most original as could be. . . . Our husbands helped us with the decorations and ornaments on the outside. On the inside of the house we did it ourselves. . . . The

[106] For a discussion of the invention of tradition generally, see Eric Hobsbawm and Terence Ranger, eds., *The Invention of Tradition* (Cambridge: Cambridge University Press, 1983); the quotation is from 227.

[107] In 1951, women received gifts "proportioned" according to their attendance and the grades they received on class projects (*Rapport*, 1951, 114).

[108] Ibid., 114; CecRa, 1951, 15; Usumbura, Foyer Social, Rapport annuel, 1954; CecRa, 1958, 60.

[109] Usumbura, Foyer Social, Rapport annuel, 1954.

[110] Catherine Mirerekano, February 20, 1985.

white who was in charge passed to see . . . if the preparation was good, the right place to put the flowers, etc., how you put this, how it was necessary to put this and that."[111] The director of the *foyer social* was proud that first prize usually went to a house in which the wife had faithfully attended the *foyer*.[112]

Although in 1954, only twenty-eight families enrolled (this was attributed to the population having been notified late), "Nevertheless, we noticed that these families made real efforts to present truly coquettish interiors which amazed the jury which was composed of 12 people this year. . . . The delivery of the prizes will take place at the end of January and a small celebration will be organized in order to encourage a large number to enroll for the next contest. . . . A contest of house grounds (*parcelles*) will take place at the same time."[113] The contest was used to help publicize the *foyer social* and was intended to let the better students set an example for the residents of the quarter; it also rewarded them and their husbands materially and socially for their emulation of European ways. These contests were thought to have a "stimulating educational capacity," and the colonial office in Brussels recommended that other contests—for the most beautiful garden and the cleanest baby—be tried as well.[114]

Family ideology and colonized domesticity

House visits, contests and ceremonies, sewing, housekeeping, motherhood classes, and meetings to solicit the cooperation of husbands in disciplining wives were interlocking elements in the Belgian colonial project to refashion gender roles and instill a Western family ideology into African urban life. The *foyer* was a prized agenda because it enabled colonial knowledge of African urban households, their redefinition and bounding as the domestic, private sphere, and their differentiation according to new colonial representations of social class.

The *foyer* was formalized as an institution within a colonial context of racism. The *foyer* was not about assimilation or about Westernization. It was about "colonial mimicry."[115] The word *évolué*

---

[111] Ibid.

[112] "Le Foyer Social et les Epoux" (n. 98 above).

[113] Usumbura, Foyer social, Rapport annuel, 1954.

[114] Ministère des Colonies, Deuxième Direction, "Programme d'activités d'un Foyer Social," 5.

[115] Homi Bhabha, "Of Mimicry and Man: The Ambivalence of Colonial Discourse," *October* 28 (Spring 1984): 125–33.

was always a misnomer in Belgian colonial discourse, for civilization could never be reached by nonwhites. Civilization was exclusively white.[116] Complete duplication of the trappings of European life was not only structurally impossible, but also strategically not permitted by the curriculum and activities of the *foyer*. As early as 1896, colonial wisdom contained the notion that girls receiving domestic education should not be shown "civilization . . . in a glass of frothy wine or a beautiful gown nor in unknown or refined food."[117] The aspirations of ordinary women attending *foyer* mass classes were similarly restrained: they could make simple clothes but not embroidered dresses. Tension over the incorporation and distancing of Western products was most pronounced with the elite. Directions from Brussels encouraged the staff to use local items as much as possible to encourage thrift in family spending patterns. Yet the staff was advised that among *évolués*, "it is already too late, the European products are employed by preference, and the women have the impression that it would be returning to a savage state."[118] Catherine Mirerekano recalled learning to prepare cauliflower with cream sauce and rare meat as well as many Burundian dishes "in an improved way *a l'européenne.*"[119] Likewise, the contents of the *foyer*'s model home were hardly those of an African family of modest means; yet they were equally not those of a European colonial family. Instead, a new "not quite/not white" colonized culture of *évolué* domesticity was being fashioned in Usumbura.[120]

Though many of the city's women learned to make cauliflower with cream sauce, enjoyed the home visits of European critics, and generally deferred to European domestic values and practices, African women were not "simple-hearted victims of colonialism."[121] To reduce the participation of African women in the *foyer* to an

---

[116] "In the minds of the colonizers . . . [civilization] was conceptualized not as Western civilization, but 'civilization' unqualifed and sole. The bearers of the 'civilization' identified themselves by the symbol of colour. A 'civilized man' was a 'white man' " (Hilda Kuper, "Colour, Categories and Colonialism: The Swazi Case," in *Colonialism in Africa, 1870–1960*, ed. Victor Turner [Cambridge: Cambridge University Press, 1971], 3:286–309, esp. 290).

[117] Yates, "Colonialism, Education and Work" (n. 19 above), 131.

[118] Ministère des Colonies, Deuxième Direction Generale, "Programme d'activités d'un Foyer Social," 5.

[119] "You see they insisted a lot on the preparation of dishes coming from products taken from tinned cans. The preparation consisted of a mixture with beans in a way that would be conservable and transportable" (Catherine Mirerekano, February 20, 1985).

[120] Bhabha, 132.

[121] Ashis Nandy, *The Intimate Enemy: Loss and Recovery of Self under Colonialism* (Delhi: Oxford University Press, 1983), xiv.

interiorization of colonial ideology as it was formally articulated would oversimplify what was a contradictory and individualized process of women making choices within a complex colonial situation of varying cultural and economic constraints and opportunities. Moreover, many women chose not to go.[122] Mirerekano explained, "Whoever could enter the *foyer*, rich or poor. Admission was open to all . . . but the poorest did not like to go there."[123] A woman had to have leisure time to attend the *foyer*, which despite the impression of colonial observers, was not the case for the majority of women who, married or not, were farming, trading, or engaging in other forms of informal labor to get by, feed their children, or supplement their husbands' wages.[124] As Dorothéa Mwayuma of Belge recalled, "I was not going there. . . . I did not want to, I knew the hoe, to farm only."[125] Yohali binti Mtoka of Buyenzi echoed: "My *foyer* was to farm only."[126] Among those who did go, the *foyer* vision that women should confine themselves to the domestic sphere and let their husbands be the breadwinners was not easily or fully accepted. Judith Curinyana abandoned her commercial sewing after having participated in the *foyer*, yet she turned to other forms of petty trade to support herself after being widowed. Her daughter became a professional seamstress. Thérèse Namugisha continued with her beer brewing and make-shift home bar; and Catherine Mirerekano went on to be an independent and successful businesswoman, supporting her family and buying a house, while her husband pursued a political career in pre- and postindependence politics.[127] Finally, in picturing why African women verbalized such ardent memories of their *foyer* experiences and why so many muted others went, we need to be careful not to assume that their motives and experiences corresponded to colonial intentions, even if their actions met colonial desires. Many Usum-

[122] Evidence from the mid-fifties indicates that Burundian women were less inclined to go to the *foyer* than were Congolese. Within some elements of Burundian culture, high female status was associated with domestic assistance, confinement to the home, and freedom from domestic chores. Attending a *foyer* where one was learning to wash and iron clothes might have been perceived as demeaning, and in the city Burundian women apparently had domestic servants to do these types of domestic tasks more often than did Congolese women (Foyer Social, Rapport annuel, 1957). Unfortunately, there is not other evidence by which to build this line of analysis. Attendance statistics do not exist in terms of ethnic background or urban quarter.

[123] Catherine Mirerekano, February 20, 1985.

[124] See Hunt, " 'We Refused to Be Insulted' " (n. 14 above), 51–66.

[125] Dorothéa Mwayuma, February 16, 1985.

[126] Yohali binti Mtoka, February 5, 1985.

[127] Judith Curinyana, February 19, 1985; Thérèse Namugisha, February 25, 1985; and Dorothéa Shabani, February 26, 1985. On Paul Mirerekano's life and career as a Hutu politician, see René Lemarchand, *Rwanda and Burundi* (New York: Praeger, 1970).

bura women may not have valued an alien, colonial, and imposed domesticity "filtered uncritically through European categories of thought."[128] Nor would they have equated domesticity with "denigration."[129] The African women of Usumbura came from cultures where women were esteemed for skill in creating domestic objects by hand—Barundikazi and Banyarwandakazi for basket making, and Swahili women for prayer mat making. Some *foyer* opportunities may have resonated with and been interpreted as enriching African domesticities.[130]

Though we cannot know, finally, why African women chose to participate or whether their participation signified a real acceptance of the family ideology promoted by the *foyer*, the institution and its projected aura of intimacy and homelikeness seems to have been most appreciated by those who reached the higher levels of the curricular hierarchy. Reverse communication across the color line (from colonized to colonizer) was planned and expected to occur in intimate colonial encounters between European and African women. Judith Curinyana and Thérèse Namugisha, for example, recalled a mutual sharing of information among European and African women about food.[131] "They taught us to use condiments there . . . European cuisine . . . but they asked us to show them Burundian cuisine and we taught them how to prepare beans . . . how the Barundi and Banyarwanda prepare beans, how to add oil, and then they accepted."[132]

The negative image of colonial women as more racist than colonial men has inspired recent scholarship on colonial women's

[128] Eleanor Leacock and June Nash, "Ideologies of Sex: Archetypes and Stereotypes," in *Myths of Male Dominance: Collected Articles on Women Cross-Culturally*, ed. Eleanor Burke Leacock (New York and London: Monthly Review Press, 1981), 243.

[129] See Marilyn Strathern, "Domesticity and the Denigration of Women," in *Rethinking Women's Roles: Perspectives from the Pacific*, ed. Denise O'Brien and Sharon W. Tiffany (Berkeley and Los Angeles: University of California Press, 1984), 13–31. Domesticity may have been embedded as if a natural, unitary category for the African women of Usumbura, although differently embedded than it is within European cultural thought. See also Olivia Harris, "Households as Natural Units," in *Of Marriage and the Market: Women's Subordination in International Perspective*, ed. Kate Young, Carol Wolkowitz, and Roslyn McCullagh (London: CSE Books, 1981), 49–68; and Olivia Harris and Kate Young, "Engendered Structures: Some Problems in the Analysis of Reproduction," in *The Anthropology of Pre-Capitalist Societies*, ed. Joel S. Kahn and Josep R. Llobera (London: Macmillan, 1981), 109–47.

[130] On such cultural resonance in a related South African context, "where domesticity has never been unambiguously confining," see Gaitskell, "Housewives, Maids or Mothers" (n. 3 above), esp. 251.

[131] Judith Curinyana, February 19, 1985; Thérèse Namugisha, February 25, 1985.

[132] Judith Curinyana, February 19, 1985.

"positive" contributions to "mutual understanding" among the races.[133] The danger is in romanticizing the experiences and accomplishments of European women in colonial contexts, as if they were an exception to colonial racism. The incorporation of European women into positions as professional social workers did not "feminize" Belgian colonialism.[134] Rather, embedded within Belgian colonial paternalism was a maternalism which was used among women.[135] Such colonial intimacy did not preclude power relations or antagonism. Maternal tone was selective: the female adult sometimes disciplined and sometimes nurtured the female child.

Not all African women would have cared to teach European women to cook beans. Likewise, the *foyer* was not identically preoccupied with all women. Colonial domesticity was not a unitary category.[136] Historically, mission nuns and their social worker successors projected it differently. Within the governmental *foyer*, domesticity was promoted differently to Africans as the institution served to create divisions among them. The state-sponsored program accentuated housewifely and companionate conjugal behavior as students' socioeconomic and curricular status rose. Elite families received more and different attention—in the classroom, during house visits, and in the new colonial urban traditions of ceremonies and house contests. The *foyer* was elaborated as an important colonial institution in the post–World War II period when the stabilizing of urban households as nuclear families and representing African elite distinctiveness were significant concerns to colonial authorities. The public rituals of colonized domesticity marked *évolué* wives and homes as distinct and superior, promoting

[133] Helen Callaway, *Gender, Culture and Empire: European Women in Colonial Nigeria* (Urbana and Chicago: University of Illinois Press, 1987), 240. For an example of such a negative stereotype, see Michael Banton, "Urbanization and the Colour Line in Africa," *Profiles of Change: African Society and Colonial Rule*, ed. Victor Turner in *Colonialism in Africa, 1870–1960*, 5 vols., ed. L. H. Gann and Peter Duignan (London: Cambridge University Press, 1969), 3:256–85, esp. 280.

[134] Callaway has argued that in Nigeria the official colonial worldview was "feminized" as European women were incorporated in greater numbers into professional positions and as wives were allowed to be mothers in the colony (Callaway, 47).

[135] Belgian colonial policy is commonly characterized as paternalist; see Thomas Hodgkin, *Nationalism in Colonial Africa* (London: Frederick Muller, 1956), esp. 51–52. Belgian policy was also paternalist *toward* European women—at home and even more so in the colony; see C. Debroux, "La situation juridique de la femme europeenne au Congo Belge de 1945 a 1960," *Enquêtes et documents d'histoire Africaine* 7 (1987): 14–23.

[136] Olivia Harris and Kate Young warn that "we need to investigate the degree to which different social systems . . . affect the unity of this category" (n. 129 above), 112.

an emerging class of Africans who "lived in beautiful houses."[137] The *foyer social* thus became a key part of colonial efforts to solidify the class structure of Usumbura's African residents and inscribe within this class structure colonial standards of prestige and status. In so doing, the *foyer* worked to establish, maintain, and enhance hierarchies among women, among Africans, between men and women, and between white colonials and Africans.

Department of History
University of Wisconsin—Madison

[137] Yvonne Mawazo, February 15, 1985.

MOTHERS AND DAUGHTERS

MARIANNE HIRSCH

In 1976 Adrienne Rich alerted us to the silence that has surrounded the most formative relationship in the life of every woman, the relationship between daughter and mother: "The cathexis between mother and daughter—essential, distorted, misused—is the great unwritten story. Probably there is nothing in human nature more resonant with charges than the flow of energy between two biologically alike bodies, one of which has lain in amniotic bliss inside the other, one of which has labored

---

EDITORS' NOTE: *Marianne Hirsch's central question challenges the ideas expressed on mothering in several other pieces in this issue. She asks whether all our theories about women's sexuality and mothering are not still so enmeshed in the language of male thinkers that our very experiences as we describe them become a shadowing forth of some man's theory. Even if we deny that this does describe our experience, we continue to use the theorist's phrasing in our denials.*

I am grateful to the Wellesley Center for Research on Women whose grant enabled me to do a great deal of research for this essay and for the comments of other Mellon Seminar members to whom I presented some of these ideas. I wish to thank the members of the Dartmouth University Seminar on Feminist Inquiry and of the Newberry Library feminist criticism group for their reactions, especially Elizabeth Abel and Brenda Silver for their detailed suggestions.

This essay originally appeared in *Signs*, vol. 7, no. 1, Autumn 1981.

to give birth to the other."[1] Since Rich demonstrated the absence of the mother-daughter relationship from theology, art, sociology, and psychoanalysis, and its centrality in women's lives, many voices have come to fill this gap, to create speech and meaning where there has been silence and absence. In fact, the five years since the publication of Rich's book have seen a proliferation of writings that have both documented the relationship from its most personal resonances to its most abstract implications and uncovered a variety of precedents for their inquiry. Books, articles in scholarly journals, essays in popular magazines, novels, poems and plays, films and television scenarios, discussion groups at national and international conferences, and courses in universities, junior colleges, and high schools throughout the country all attest to the dramatic reversal of the silence Rich deplores. It is the purpose of this essay first to account for this reversal and the subsequent centrality of the mother-daughter relationship at this particular point in feminist scholarship and then to delineate the range and direction of the work done in this area. Although I shall concentrate primarily on major psychoanalytic and literary studies that have appeared since Rich, I shall by necessity go back to some of their conceptual and theoretical sources.[2]

I

It seems appropriate to begin with Rich's extraordinary and controversial book itself, *Of Woman Born: Motherhood as Experience and Institution,* the first systematic study of the fact that "all human life on the planet is born of woman. The one unifying, incontrovertible experience shared by all women and men is that months-long period we spent unfolding inside a woman's body. . . . Most of us first knew love and disappointment, power and tenderness, in the person of a woman" (p. 11). Rich's analysis of motherhood as an institution in patriarchy—a female experience that is shaped by male expectations and structures, and virtually unrecorded by women themselves to date—is revolutionary not only in its content but also in its methodology: "It seemed to me impossible from the first to write a book of this kind without being often autobiographical, without often saying 'I' " (p. 15). Rich's voice, both personal and scholarly, resting on research in various academic fields, as well as on her own experience as a mother and a daughter, has helped create a novel form of feminist discourse which, I would like to argue, has freed scholars to consider extremely personal experiences as valid objects of scholarly inquiry.

1. Adrienne Rich, *Of Woman Born: Motherhood as Experience and Institution* (New York: W. W. Norton & Co., 1976), p. 225.
2. For an earlier review of some of this literature, see Judith Kegan Gardiner, "The New Motherhood," *North American Review* 263, no. 2 (Fall 1978): 72–76.

Rich's chapter on "Motherhood and Daughterhood" is, as she says, "the core of my book" (p. 218). It contains, in fact, the germs of many of the other studies I shall mention in this essay. It is both an evocation of the desire that connects mother and daughter, of the knowledge they share, "a knowledge that is subliminal, subversive, pre-verbal: the knowledge flowing between two alike bodies, one of which has spent nine months inside the other" (p. 220), and an account of what Lynn Sukenick has called "matrophobia," the "desire to become purged once and for all of our mother's bondage, to become individuated and free" (p. 236). It traces a relationship "minimized and trivialized in the annals of patriarchy" (p. 236), as well as the close female bonds that seem nevertheless to have persisted. It deplores the silences surrounding this relationship: "The loss of the daughter to the mother, the mother to the daughter, is the essential female tragedy. We acknowledge Lear (father-daughter split), Hamlet (son and mother), and Oedipus (son and mother) as great embodiments of the human tragedy; but there is no presently enduring recognition of mother-daughter passion and rapture" (p. 237). And it reminds us of the Eleusinian mysteries that celebrated the reunion of mother and daughter, the assertion of a maternal power that could "undo rape and bring her [daughter] back from the dead" (p. 240). Most important, Rich reminds us forcefully and persuasively of every woman's participation in the experience and institution of motherhood: "The 'childless woman' and the 'mother' are a false polarity, which has served the institutions both of motherhood and heterosexuality. . . . We are, none of us, 'either' mothers or daughters; to our amazement, confusion, and greater complexity, we are both" (pp. 250, 253).

In drawing on literature, theology, psychology, anthropology, myth, and history, Rich's book announces in both content and form the work that has followed on mother-daughter relationships. Its emergence at this particular moment can be explained by a glance at prevalent trends in feminist scholarship. There can be no systematic and theoretical study of women in patriarchal culture, there can be no theory of women's oppression, that does not take into account woman's role as a mother of daughters and as a daughter of mothers, that does not study female identity in relation to previous and subsequent generations of women, and that does not study that relationship in the wider context in which it takes place: the emotional, political, economic, and symbolic structures of family and society. Any full study of mother-daughter relationships, in whatever field, is by definition both feminist and interdisciplinary.

The study of mother-daughter relationships situates itself at the point where various disciplines become feminist studies, as well as at the point where the feminist areas of a number of disciplines intersect: sociology, where it concentrates on sex-role differentiation, where it attempts to distinguish between the individual and the roles she has to assume, and where those roles are studied in relation to their social determinants; anthropology, where it examines theories of matriarchy and their validity, matrilineal social organizations, matrilocal residence, and the effects of these different kinship structures on gender configurations and power distributions; religious studies, where it seeks evidence for a mother-goddess and attempts to develop a female-centered spirituality; history, where it examines the private stories of women's lives in journals, letters, and autobiographies that document family relationships; philosophy, where it challenges the dominant Western dualistic thought that banishes woman into the position of nature to man's culture, matter to man's spirit, emotion to man's reason, object to man's subject;[3] and psychology and literary criticism, where the focus is so specific and where the points of intersection are so numerous that they demand detailed analysis.

The most complete and complex work on mother-daughter relationships to date has been undertaken in the area of feminist psychoanalysis. As Juliet Mitchell has demonstrated, psychoanalysis is particularly useful to feminist scholarship in that it shows us "how we acquire our heritage of the ideas and laws of human society within the unconscious mind."[4] In spite of certain limitations to which I shall return, it helps us to understand how the laws underlying and underwrit-

---

3. Jessie Bernard's important book *The Future of Motherhood* (New York: Dial Press, 1974) studies motherhood as a social institution, not as a fact of nature. It is a role that women learn, a role subject to certain cultural imperatives, and, at this point, a role that is being changed profoundly by factors such as women's increased participation in the labor force, an ever-decreasing birthrate, and the isolation of the nuclear family. Bernard studies, as well, the effects of all-female mothering on our society where it fosters a polarization of nurturance and power. On matriarchy, see J. J. Bachofen, *Myth, Religion and Mother-Right: Selected Writings*, trans. Ralph Manheim (Princeton, N.J.: Princeton University Press, 1967); and Robert Briffault, *The Mothers* (New York: Johnson Reprint Corp., 1969). See also Joan Bamberger, "The Myth of Matriarchy: Why Men Rule in Primitive Society," in *Woman, Culture, and Society*, ed. Michelle Zimbalist Rosaldo and Louise Lamphere (Stanford, Calif.: Stanford University Press, 1974), pp. 263–80; and Gayle Rubin, "The Traffic in Women: Notes on the Political Economy of Sex," in *Toward an Anthropology of Women*, ed. Rayna Rapp Reiter (New York: Monthly Review Press, 1975). In religious studies, see, e.g., Carol Christ and Judith Plaskow, eds., *Womanspirit Rising: A Feminist Reader in Religion* (New York: Harper & Row, 1979); Carol Christ, *Diving Deep and Surfacing: Women Writers on Spiritual Quest* (Boston: Beacon Press, 1980); and the critique by Rosemary Ruether, "A Religion for Women: Sources and Strategies," *Christianity and Crisis* 39, no. 19 (1979): 307–11. In history, see, e.g., Carroll Smith-Rosenberg, "The Female World of Love and Ritual: Relations between Women in Nineteenth-Century America," *Signs: Journal of Women in Culture and Society* 1, no. 1 (Autumn 1975): 1–29; Gerda Lerner, ed., *The Female Experience: An American Documentary* (Indianapolis: Bobbs-Merrill Co., 1977); and Mary Kelley, "Peculiar Circumstances: Literary Domesticity in Nineteenth-Century America" (Hanover, N.H.: Department of History, Dartmouth College). On woman as the "other," see Dorothy Dinnerstein, *The Mermaid and the Minotaur: Sexual Arrangements and the Human Malaise* (New York: Harper & Row, 1976); and Simone de Beauvoir, *The Second Sex*, trans. and ed. H. M. Parshley (New York: Alfred Knopf & Sons, 1953).

4. Juliet Mitchell, *Psychoanalysis and Feminism* (New York: Random House, 1975), p. xiv.

ing patriarchy function within each of us, whether male or female, and how they affect our most intimate relationships. Moreover, feminist revisions of psychoanalytic texts allow us to appreciate the specificity of female, as distinguished from male, development and the effect of those differences on relationships among women.

Female writers' accounts of the mother-daughter bond are the most articulate and detailed expressions of its intimacy and distance, passion and violence, that we can find; they are the most personal and at the same time the most universal. Recent critical studies of works written by women have answered Rich's charge: the story of mother and daughter has indeed been written, although it is not often found on the surface but in the submerged depths of literary texts. The question now becomes the analysis of its intricacies and complexities, and especially of its influence on literary forms and structures. For as Mary Carruthers wrote in "Imagining Women: Notes toward a Feminist Poetic," "Language is the medium in which we carry our past, determine our present, and condition our future."[5]

II

Three trends have emerged in recent feminist psychoanalytic works about mothers and daughters. Dorothy Dinnerstein's *The Mermaid and the Minotaur: Sexual Arrangements and the Human Malaise,* Nancy Chodorow's *The Reproduction of Mothering: Psychoanalysis and the Sociology of Gender,* Jane Flax's "The Conflict between Nurturance and Autonomy in Mother/Daughter Relationships and within Feminism," and Jean Baker Miller's *Toward a New Psychology of Women* all draw, more or less directly, on the Freudian oedipal paradigm and on neo-Freudian theory, especially object-relations psychology.[6] A second trend is represented by

5. Mary Carruthers, "Imagining Women: Notes toward a Feminist Poetic," *Massachusetts Review* 20 (1979): 281–307. Carruthers analyzes three main themes in women's poetry in the 1960s and 1970s: the mother-daughter relationship, the tradition of romantic love, and the nature of the powerful woman.

6. Nancy Chodorow, *The Reproduction of Mothering: Psychoanalysis and the Sociology of Gender* (Berkeley and Los Angeles: University of California Press, 1978). See also Chodorow's earlier essay, "Family Structure and Feminine Personality," in Rosaldo and Lamphere, eds., pp. 43–66, which includes a cross-cultural comparison of mother-daughter relationships that she unfortunately does not pursue in her book. Other essays by Chodorow include "Mothering, Object-Relations and the Female Oedipal Configuration," *Feminist Studies* 4, no. 1 (February 1978): 137–58, and "Feminism and Difference: Gender, Relation and Difference in Psychoanalytic Perspective," *Socialist Review* 46 (July–August 1979): 51–69, also reprinted in Hester Eisenstein and Alice Jardine, eds., *The Future of Difference* (Boston: G. K. Hall, 1980). See too Jane Flax, "The Conflict between Nurturance and Autonomy in Mother/Daughter Relationships and within Feminism," *Feminist Studies* 4, no. 1 (February 1978): 171–89. (This special issue of *Feminist Studies* is devoted to delineating "a feminist theory of motherhood." I shall mention some of the essays included

Jungian studies; Nor Hall's *The Moon and the Virgin: Reflections on the Archetypal Feminine*—as well as a number of literary studies—draw on Jung, on Erich Neumann's *The Great Mother: An Analysis of the Archetype*, and on Carl Kerényi's *Eleusis: Archetypal Image of Mother and Daughter.*[7] A third trend emerges in the work of French feminist theory, in particular Luce Irigaray's *Et l'une ne bouge pas sans l'autre*, but also at crucial points in the writings of Julia Kristeva and Hélène Cixous; all are based in Jacques Lacan.[8]

This brief and sketchy introduction already reveals the problem I perceive to be inherent in these analyses: at the source of each of these important and useful feminist theoretical studies we find not only a male theorist but a developed androcentric system, which, even if deconstructed and redefined, still remains a determining and limiting point of departure. I shall return to this criticism; first, however, it is useful to summarize these three trends and their points of intersection.

In his three late essays on female sexuality, Freud revises his equilateral theory of early individual development, and he stresses, for both boys and girls, the importance of the pre-oedipal attachment to the mother.[9] The significance for women of this pre-oedipal phase and of the resultant bond to the mother had for Freud the surprise that archaeologists experienced when they discovered the Minoan-Mycenaean civilizations behind the Greek. All three of his essays revolve around the central mystery of female development—the source of a girl's transfer of attachment to her father. Freud himself admits that his numerous theoretical explanations (mostly based in the girl's supposed hostility for having been deprived of a penis) are not ultimately satisfying. His admission clearly disproves the perceived notion that Freud outlines the Electra complex; in fact, he rejects the term, even while insisting, as best he can, on the idea of natural heterosexuality. Boys experience only rivalry with the same-sex parent; threatened with castration, they resolve

---

in it.) See also Jane Flax, "Mother-Daughter Relationships: Psychodynamics, Politics and Philosophy," in Eisenstein and Jardine, eds.; Jean Baker Miller, *Toward a New Psychology of Women* (Boston: Beacon Press, 1976).

7. Nor Hall, *The Moon and the Virgin: Reflections on the Archetypal Feminine* (New York: Harper & Row, 1980); Erich Neumann, *The Great Mother: An Analysis of the Archetype*, trans. Ralph Manheim (Princeton, N.J.: Princeton University Press, 1955); and Carl Kerényi, *Eleusis: Archetypal Image of Mother and Daughter*, trans. Ralph Manheim (New York: Schocken Books, 1976).

8. Luce Irigaray's work, translated by Hélène Vivienne Wenzel and entitled "And the One Doesn't Stir without the Other," appears in *Signs: Journal of Women in Culture and Society* 7, no. 1 (Autumn 1981): 60–67. The original French version, *Et l'une ne bouge pas sans l'autre*, was published in Paris by Editions de Minuit in 1979.

9. These three essays—"Some Psychical Consequences of the Anatomical Distinction between the Sexes" (1924), "Female Sexuality" (1931), and "Femininity" (1931)—are conveniently reprinted in Jean Strouse, ed., *Women and Analysis* (New York: Dell Publishing Co., 1974).

the oedipal conflict very rapidly. Girls, in contrast, feel ambivalent toward the mother who is both rival and object of desire. In fact, Freud emphasizes that the pre-oedipal attachment to the mother is never totally superseded by the desire for the father; neither is the oedipal rejection of the mother ever overcome. This ambivalent relationship dominates a woman's entire life, especially her relationship with her husband or lover.

Dinnerstein, Chodorow, and Flax take as their starting points the formative importance of the pre-oedipal period and the female parent's domination of that period for both sons and daughters. In studying the consequences of exclusive parenting by women for adult personality and for the gender configurations of our culture generally, Chodorow and Flax rely not so much directly on Freud but on the work of object-relations psychologists, in whose theory the pre-oedipal period is seen not as a stage through which infants progress instinctually (drive or *Trieb* theory), but as an interpersonal field of relationships internalized by the infant and therefore configurative in the adult personality.[10] The mother thus remains an important inner object throughout adult life. Chodorow and Flax find that this interpersonal field functions differently for male and female infants: mothers identify more strongly with female infants, seeing them more as extensions of themselves, whereas they encourage boys to become separate and autonomous. Ego boundaries between mothers and daughters are more fluid, more undefined. The girl is less encouraged to be autonomous, but she is also less nurtured, since the mother projects upon her daughter her own ambivalence about being female in patriarchal culture. Chodorow finds in these dissatisfactions the source of the "reproduction of mothering"—a woman becomes a mother in order to regain a sense of being mothered and in order to compensate for a heterosexual relationship with a man who values separation while she values connection and continuity. In her relationship with her daughter, a mother works out her unresolved relationship to her own mother. Differences in adult male and female personality are based, according to Chodorow, Flax, and Dinnerstein, on the different interpersonal configuration that occurs in the pre-oedipal phase:

> Feminine personality comes to be based less on repression of inner objects, and fixed and firm splits in the ego, and more on retention and continuity of external relationships. From the retention of pre-Oedipal attachments to their mother, growing girls come to define themselves as continuous with others; their experience of self

10. See esp. D. W. Winnicott, "Mirror-Role of Mother and Family in Child Development," in *Playing and Reality* (New York: Basic Books, 1971); Margaret Mahler, Fred Pine, and Anni Bergman, *The Psychological Birth of the Human Infant* (New York: Basic Books, 1975); and W. R. D. Fairbairn, *An Object-Relations Theory of Personality* (New York: Basic Books, 1952).

contains more flexible and permeable ego boundaries. Boys come to define themselves as more separate and distinct, with a greater sense of rigid ego boundaries and differentiations. The basic feminine sense of self is connected to the world, the basic masculine sense of self is separate.[11]

Chodorow's and Flax's conclusions about the continuity and the lack of separation or differentiation between mother and daughter has tremendous implications for anyone studying female identity. In *Toward a New Psychology of Women,* Jean Baker Miller concurs: "Women's sense of self becomes very much organized around being able to make and then to maintain affiliations and relationships"; her term "affiliation," of course, points to the connections between the relation to mother and all subsequent interpersonal relationships in a woman's life.[12] Dinnerstein's view of these pre-oedipal differences and of exclusive female parenting provides us with the most far-reaching analysis to date of the sources of woman's exclusion from history, of her own collusion in the perpetuation of patriarchy. She convincingly argues that woman is the "other" only because she is the "mother," that patriarchy itself is a reaction against female dominion in infancy. Maternal omnipotence is so great a threat that we are willing to acquiesce to male rule in adulthood; even to women, paternal authority looks like a reasonable refuge.

In a recent article, "The Bonds of Love: Rational Violence and Erotic Domination," Jessica Benjamin interprets the same fundamental asymmetry we all experience in early infancy differently; yet her conclusions are, in fact, quite similar to Dinnerstein's.[13] According to Benjamin, "Selfhood is defined negatively as separateness from others" (p. 148). Because of the ways boys and girls relate to and differentiate from their mothers, they grow up to play different roles in the relationships of submission and domination, object and subject. We all seem to need these oppositions in order to perpetuate a "false" sense of differentiation. As a result of the "false" differentiation we all choose instead of equality, "a whole, in tension between negation and recognition, affirming singularity and connectedness, continuity and discontinuity at once" (p. 161), our culture is dominated by a form of rational violence that is the basis of sadomasochism. "The male posture . . . prepares for the role of master. . . . The female posture disposes the woman to accept objectification and control. . . . He asserts individual selfhood, while she

11. Chodorow, *Reproduction of Mothering,* p. 169.
12. Miller, p. 83.
13. Jessica Benjamin, "The Bonds of Love: Rational Violence and Erotic Domination," *Feminist Studies* 6, no. 1 (Spring 1980): 144–74, also reprinted in Eisenstein and Jardine, eds. See also Benjamin, "The Oedipal Riddle: Authority, Autonomy, and the New Narcissism," in Kahn and Diggins, eds., *Authority in America: The Crisis of Legitimacy* (Philadelphia: Temple University Press, in press).

relinquishes it" (p. 167). Benjamin and Dinnerstein both demonstrate the disastrous, the lethal effects of the asymmetry of the pre-oedipal period.

Chodorow and Dinnerstein perceive shared parenting in early infancy as the most important challenge to patriarchal rule, as the only way to balance the severely skewed "sexual arrangements" in which we live now, the only way to make us "fully human" (Dinnerstein's term). Shared child rearing, in Dinnerstein's rather global vision, will lead us to conquer the ambivalence we now feel toward carnal mortality, toward self-creation and autonomy, toward treating others as sentient beings, toward growing up and becoming adults. As all these writers point out so convincingly, women, like men, need the nurturance that will allow them to become creative, productive adults, and as long as mothers carry the burden of child rearing alone, they will not be able to nurture and support their daughters in their struggle for self-realization: the maternal role creates too much ambivalence about their own and their daughters' female identity. Although these writers disagree about the details of the interaction between mother and child (where Dinnerstein talks of the mother's power, for example, Benjamin perceives her weakness and frailty), the bases of their arguments as well as their conclusions are quite similar.

Since the publication of their books, Chodorow and Dinnerstein have received criticism from many sides, much of it in the pages of this journal, most of it centering on the limitations of the psychoanalytic paradigm on which their theory rests.[14] Yet it is important to perceive the far-reaching implications of their work, as well as that of Flax and Benjamin; it is important to recognize the significance of a theory that links the most private family structures to social, economic, and political structures, a theory that treats women's mothering as a "social structure which affects all other structures."[15] Because of its wide scope, this psychoanalytic work is as pertinent to scholars in the humanities as to social scientists; it is interdisciplinary in the fullest sense. Even though I have reservations about aspects of this work, my training as a literary critic makes me particularly sensitive to a usefulness in it that I shall shortly demonstrate.

The points of intersection between the Chodorow-Flax-Dinnerstein

14. In an early essay, "Mothers and Daughters in the World of the Father," *Frontiers* 3, no. 2 (1978): 16–21, Marcia Westkott criticizes the "fatalism that informs the psychoanalytic mode Chodorow uses in her essays." This special issue of *Frontiers* is devoted to *Mothers and Daughters* and contains a number of informative essays, as well as poems, stories, and a play. See also Judith Lorber et al., "On *The Reproduction of Mothering:* A Methodological Debate," *Signs: Journal of Women in Culture and Society* 6, no. 3 (Spring 1981): 482–514; and Adrienne Rich, "Compulsory Heterosexuality and Lesbian Existence," *Signs: Journal of Women in Culture and Society* 5, no. 4 (Summer 1980): 631–60.

15. Chodorow, "On *The Reproduction of Mothering*," p. 501.

model of mother-daughter relationships and the model created by
Jung-Kerényi-Neumann in their studies of the archetype of the Great
Mother, Eleusinian archaeological evidence, and other maternal or
female symbolism are most illuminating. All stress the continuity between mother and daughter. Demeter and Kore are merely two sides of
woman, the mother and the maiden. As Jung says, "Every mother contains her daughter within herself, and every daughter her mother. . . .
Every woman extends backwards into her mother and forwards into her
daughter. This participation and intermingling gives rise to that peculiar
uncertainty as regards *time:* a woman lives earlier as a mother, later as a
daughter. The conscious experience of these ties produces the feeling
that her life is spread out over generations."[16] Nor Hall's recent book *The
Moon and the Virgin*, a "quest for origins" that begins with the Mother,
with the preconscious matriarchal phase in order to "remember . . . the
mother-daughter body," proposes thereby to "cure the void felt these
days by women—and men—who feel that their feminine nature, like
Persephone, has gone to hell."[17] Again it is a question of reaching a
balance or of correcting an asymmetry. However, because the Jungian
approach to mother-daughter relationships is highly individualistic,
particularly in its analysis of symbols and archetypes, it seems at this
point to have more resonance in literary analysis than in critiques of
social structures.

Even more illuminating are new points of intersection between
French and American psychoanalysis, two traditions that have come
more and more to be seen as divergent. In Luce Irigaray's "And the One
Doesn't Stir without the Other" (*Et l'une ne bouge pas sans l'autre*), we find a
similar insistence on the ultimate lack of separation between daughter
and mother and an emphasis on multiplicity, plurality, and continuity
of being. It is important to situate this short, lyrical address in the context of Irigaray's work, until recently a dense, heavily abstract deconstruction of Western philosophy from Plato to Freud and Lacan. As
Carolyn Burke shows, it is only in the last section of *This Sex Which Is
Not One*, entitled "When Our Lips Speak Together," that Irigaray begins to explore a different discourse, a "parler-femme," a "female-centered signification" that could express women's speech to each other.[18]
Relationships between women are neither relationships of sameness

16. "The Psychological Aspects of the Kore," in Carl G. Jung and Carl Kerényi, *Essays
on a Science of Mythology: The Myths of the Divine Child and the Mysteries of Eleusis* (Princeton,
N.J.: Princeton University Press, 1969), p. 162.

17. Hall, pp. xvi, 68.

18. Luce Irigaray, "When Our Lips Speak Together," trans. Carolyn Burke, *Signs:
Journal of Women in Culture and Society* 6, no. 1 (Autumn 1980): 69–79. This essay, "Quand
nos lèvres se parlent," first appeared in *Ce sexe qui n'en est pas un* (Paris: Editions de Minuit,
1977).

nor of difference, but of in-difference.[19] This new language and syntax must reflect the mutuality and interdependence of female being(s): therefore Irigaray insists on using the double pronoun "You/I" ("toi/moi"). "And the One Doesn't Stir without the Other" is Irigaray's first full work in this new, exploratory, and experimental mode. Desperately trying to untangle herself from within her mother and her mother from within herself, Irigaray comes to acknowledge and to accept the interpenetration that characterizes female identity.

Although this short text is the only French theoretical work directly concerned with the mother-daughter relationship, this relationship surfaces at crucial points in much current French feminist writing. Irigaray's project, based in part on Lacan and Jacques Derrida, is an attack on phallogocentrism and aims, like the work of Julia Kristeva and Hélène Cixous, to deconstruct what she so aptly calls "that sameness in which for centuries we have been the other," and to define the specificity of the female experience, which is to be found in the silences and absences, in all that our culture has repressed and suppressed.[20] The mother-daughter relationship is crucial in this process of exploration and definition. For Julia Kristeva, the repressed space—not exclusively female, but also to be found in the breaks that occur in avant-garde writing—is called "the semiotic" (*le sémiotique*) and is opposed to the symbolic—logic, logos, Name-of-the-Father. The semiotic is pre-oedipal, chronologically anterior to syntax, a cry, the gesture of a child. In adult discourse it is rhythm, prosody, pun, non-sense, laugh.[21] It is a break in the paternal order and woman, in large part because of her pre-oedipal relationship with her mother, has special access to it, at once privileged and dangerous. According to Kristeva, woman's access to the symbolic paternal order depends on her repression of her connection to her mother, her censoring of the woman within herself, her denial especially of maternal sexuality, or, as she calls it, maternal "jouissance." Woman in the symbolic order is the Virgin, impregnated by the Word. Woman has

19. Irigaray's use of *indifférence* and *indifférente* is a good example of her word play, as she shifts its meaning from "detached" to "nondifferent" or "undifferentiated"; see "When Our Lips Speak Together," p. 71n.

20. Ibid., p. 71. For an overview of this work, see Elaine Marks, "Women and Literature in France," *Signs: Journal of Women in Culture and Society* 3, no. 4 (Summer 1978): 832–42; Carolyn Burke, "Report from Paris: Women's Writing and the Women's Movement," *Signs: Journal of Women in Culture and Society* 3, no. 4 (Summer 1978): 843–55; Elaine Marks and Isabelle de Courtivron, eds., *New French Feminisms: An Anthology* (Amherst: University of Massachusetts Press, 1980), an anthology of these and other French theorists and writers; and Julia Kristeva, *Desire in Language: A Semiotic Approach to Literature and Art*, ed. Léon Roudiez (New York: Columbia University Press, 1981). See also Domna Stanton, "Language and Revolution: The Franco-American Disconnection," and Jane Gallop and Carolyn Burke, "Psychoanalysis and Feminism in France," both in Eisenstein and Jardine, eds. My own sketchy summary cannot do justice to these extremely complex concepts.

21. Julia Kristeva, *Polylogue* (Paris: Seuil, 1977), p. 14. See also "L'Herétique de l'amour," *Tel Quel* 74 (Winter 1977): 30–49.

access to the semiotic through the functions of her body, pregnancy and childbirth.[22] Yet that access is dangerous, and Kristeva recalls the suicide of so many female writers: "For a woman, the call of the mother is not only a call beyond time, beyond the socio-political battle. . . . This call troubles the Word. It generates voices, madness, hallucinations. After the superego, the ego, that fragile envelope, founders and sinks. It is helpless to stave off the eruption of this conflict, this love which has bound the little girl to her mother and then lain in wait for her—black lava—all along the path of her desperate attempt to identify with the symbolic paternal order."[23] Kristeva reminds us of Electra, her "father's daughter" whose hatred of her mother, and especially of her mother's "jouissance," is the basis of a larger order of the city and politics. The deconstruction of that larger symbolic order depends on the reunification of mother and daughter.

Cixous's excursus in "feminine" writing also emphasizes the mother-daughter bond. Her medium is white ink, or mother's milk, and in every woman, Cixous insists, "there is always more or less of 'the mother' who repairs and sustains and resists separation, a force that won't be severed."[24]

The project in which all three of these writers are engaged, that of dismantling the sameness and unity of the symbolic order that has excluded woman, of creating a discourse of plurality, depends on a redefinition of the individual subject: it must be seen not as unified, integrated, whole, and autonomous, but as multiple, continuous, fluid, or, as Kristeva calls it, "in-process." It is interesting that although American psychoanalysis is essentially based on ego psychology and French psychoanalysis insists on the explosion of the unified ego, they intersect where female identity is concerned; for woman the delimited, the autonomous, separated, individuated self does not exist (although much of our discourse still functions as if it did). In their analysis of female identity, Chodorow, Flax, Dinnerstein, and Miller, in spite of their radically different methodology and discourse, find themselves in surprising agreement with Irigaray, Kristeva, and Cixous. Woman's being, because of the quality of the pre-oedipal mother-daughter relationship, is, according to both traditions, continuous, plural, in-process: "And what I love in you, in myself, no longer takes place for us: the birth that is never completed, the body never created once for all time, the face and form never definitely finished, always still to be molded. The lips never open or closed upon one single truth."[25]

22. Kristeva, *Polylogue*, p. 412.

23. Julia Kristeva, *About Chinese Women*, trans. Anita Barrows (New York: Urizen Books, 1977), p. 39.

24. Hélène Cixous, "Sorties," in *La Jeune Née*, by Catherine Clément and Hélène Cixous (Paris: Union Générale d'Editions, 1975), p. 172.

25. Irigaray, "When Our Lips Speak Together," p. 78.

III

The usefulness of theoretical paradigms lies in their outline of general trends, which help us to locate individual experiences and to relate them to each other. In the last few years, several interview studies have appeared that enable us to test just how well the analyses of mother-daughter relationships put forward by psychoanalytic theorists apply to individual women's experiences. On the whole, these studies based on the plural voices of a great number of women—rich, moving, illuminating in their diversity—do corroborate feminist theory. But these individual accounts are difficult to untangle from the biases and assumptions of the interviewers.

Nancy Friday's *My Mother/My Self: A Daughter's Search for Identity* deserves attention because it has struck an extremely responsive chord in the female readership of several countries.[26] More than any other work, it is responsible for the popularity of this subject, if not for the rigor with which it is studied or the seriousness with which it is regarded. In spite of its intrusively familiar tone, in spite of its profound antifeminism,[27] and in spite of Friday's highly questionable and embarrassingly simplified use of theoretical and interview sources, *My Mother/My Self* is instructive in several ways. First, it demonstrates the dangers of simplifying complicated and theoretical issues. For Friday the importance of pre-oedipal symbiosis is exaggerated to the point where absolutely everything in a woman's life rests on her mother. Friday certainly does not heed her own warning: "Blaming mother is just a negative way of clinging to her still" (p. 61). Next, it shows us the psychological determinism that results from an argument that disregards social, political, and ideological contexts. Friday's perspective, despite her own observations, is static and resistant to change. Finally, it demonstrates the impossibility of envisioning change if one subscribes, as does Friday, to all the damaging, self-hating stereotypes of our culture, expressed, for example, in her statement, "We are the loving sex. . . . We feel incomplete alone, inadequate without a man."[28]

---

26. Nancy Friday, *My Mother/My Self: A Daughter's Search for Identity* (New York: Delacorte Press, 1977).

27. For example, Friday's familiar voice—"We are so embarrassed about menstruation that we cannot abide to hear it spoken about"—and her antifeminism—"They are the revolutionaries, we are still our mother's daughters" (ibid., pp. 123, 210).

28. Ibid., p. 33. More examples abound: "But females are so cunningly made it is as if mother had a hand in the design of the vagina." "What human relationship contains as much ambiguity and ambivalence as women with women?" "To the degree that on any given day that I can believe in what my husband feels for me, and in my work, that is the degree to which I have surmounted that day's residual anxiety about being my mother's daughter. . . . But if I had a daughter . . . I would be my mother's daughter all over again" (ibid., pp. 107, 175, 382–83).

Still, it is not difficult to find in Friday's book reasons for its popularity. It contains much that rings true even to those who find her assumptions unacceptable—and peculiarly and embarrassingly so. It echoes much of the ambivalence, pain, desire, and fear we as feminists need to examine, and that is precisely the goal of much of the work reviewed in this essay. Luckily, most of this scholarship is more responsible and rigorous than *My Mother/My Self*.

Signe Hammer's *Daughters and Mothers: Mothers and Daughters* and Judith Arcana's *Our Mother's Daughters* make much more extensive use of the accounts gathered in interviews.[29] Hammer's study again is limited by its preconceptions: her bias in favor of full-time mothering, her minimization of the father's role as "helper," her unquestioning acceptance of Erikson's notion of "inner space" and of woman as biologically programmed to nurture. Although Hammer's approach is sociological—she speaks of the roles we are taught to play—the book suffers from her failure to criticize the limited social possibilities open to women even in today's changing culture. She fails, for example, to question the need to choose between motherhood and career: "Mothers of all classes are still primarily concerned about their daughters' future as wives and mothers."[30] Arcana's book is by far the most intelligent and satisfying of the three, perhaps because of its successful blend of personal confession, interview, and analysis. More important, it examines and questions a social context in which women, whether mothers or daughters or both, are oppressed: "All our mothers teach us is what they have learned in the crucible of sexism. They cannot give us a sense of self-esteem which they do not possess. We must learn to interpret anew the experience our mothers have passed on to us, to see these lives in terms of struggle, often unconscious, to find and maintain some peace, beauty and respect for themselves as women."[31] In addition to extremely illuminating insights about subtle aspects of mother-daughter interaction—the daughter's inability to see her mother as a separate person, for example, or many daughters' resentment at having to mother their mothers—Arcana's book leaves us with a sense of her own sympathy for all those who struggle within a complex relationship and of her willingness to explore the intense pain, longing, nostalgia, and joy of that struggle. All the interview studies, however, leave us hungry for more, especially for studies that cross ethnic, as well as racial and economic, lines.

29. Signe Hammer, *Daughters and Mothers: Mothers and Daughters* (New York: Signet Books, 1976); Judith Arcana, *Our Mother's Daughters* (Berkeley, Calif.: Shameless Hussy Press, 1979).

30. Hammer, p. 74.

31. Arcana, p. 70.

IV

A different kind of confrontation between theory and individual experience can be found in textual analyses of literary representations of mothers and daughters. As moving as we find the accounts gathered by Hammer and Arcana, they cannot carry for us the weight and power of Demeter's reunion with Persephone in the Homeric hymn "To Demeter"; of the mother's crippling deathbed speech in *La Princesse de Clèves;* the appearance in *Jane Eyre* of the moon who guides, "My daughter, flee temptation!"; Mrs. Tulliver's instinctive though ignorant and uncomprehending loyalty to her daughter who has been disgraced; the plea of the middle-aged Colette for approval from the dead mother she conjures up in her imagination; Lily Briscoe's epiphanic vision of Mrs. Ramsay who, by appearing, approves; the mother's regrets in Tillie Olsen's "I Stand Here Ironing"; the mother's generous protection of the ugly and needy daughter in Alice Walker's "Everyday Use."[32] These and other portrayals of mother-daughter relationships subtly challenge traditional literary structures, and feminist criticism of recent years has begun to pay them a great deal of attention. The fictions by which women have imagined and represented their bonds with their mothers and daughters form the subject of books and articles already too numerous and varied to discuss in full in this essay. I shall concentrate primarily on the book-length critical studies, paying particular attention to the methodology that defines these analyses.

Like so much of the work already discussed, these studies respond to Adrienne Rich's statement of absence: they are attempts to prove that the story of mother-daughter relationships has been written even if it has not been read, that it constitutes the hidden subtext of many texts. The project to uncover these hidden or disguised plots—much like the discovery of the Minoan-Mycenaean civilizations behind the Greek, to use Freud's metaphor—is an archaeological search for prehistory. The critic's work consists not so much in analyzing as in searching for texts to analyze. Those studies that do analyze the texts, rather than just name and retell them, often use Jung and Neumann to reach, through the images and symbols of the text, powerful mythic motifs.[33] Jung's sus-

32. There are two anthologies devoted to mother-daughter relationships and motherhood. Lyn Lifshin, ed., *Tangled Vines* (Boston: Beacon Press, 1978), collects eighty-five contemporary mother-daughter poems, a number of them written specifically for this collection; Stephanie Spinner, ed., *Motherlove: Stories by Women about Motherhood* (New York: Dell Publishing Co., 1978) is an excellent collection of short stories from Colette to Tillie Olsen.

33. The best of these is Jane Lilienfeld's " 'The Deceptiveness of Beauty': Mother Love and Mother Hate in *To the Lighthouse," Twentieth-Century Literature* 23 (October 1977): 345–76. See also Myra Glazer Schotz, "The Great Unwritten Story: Mothers and Daughters in Shakespeare," and Karen Elias-Button, "The Muse as Medusa," both in Cathy Davidson and Esther Broner, eds., *The Lost Tradition* (New York: Frederick Ungar Publishing Co., 1980).

tained explorations of the links between our individual and our cultural prehistory make his work particularly resonant for these analyses. Three additional approaches seem to prevail: psychobiographical analysis, also an attempt to find the (pre)historic sources of literary motifs, this time in a writer's life, and often an attempt to read her work as a response to real-life pressures and conflicts;[34] sociological analysis, an attempt to interpret private family relationships in the context of social possibilities that shape women's lives;[35] and analysis of alternative literary forms (oral literature, autobiography, ethnic literature) which, because they are more flexible than many other genres, are perhaps better suited to the expression of women's relationships to other women.[36]

As its title indicates, *The Lost Tradition,* edited by Cathy Davidson and Esther Broner, combines all of these methodological trends. Its historical framework, its breadth and scope, as well as its excellent and extensive bibliography make it a valuable teaching and research tool. However, the inclusiveness to which the volume aspires weakens many of its individual essays: short, sketchy, and often sweeping, many rely on narrative paraphrase rather than analysis. All participate in the same project of tracing "a lineage not found in any genealogy": "We who make history, who retrace history, must erect new stones and inscribe them with lost names."[37] The collection begins with accounts of absence and suppression: the essays point out that the only fully explored mother-daughter relationship in the Bible is that between Ruth and her mother-in-law Naomi; that Kriemhild and Clytemnestra are punished for their independence and separated from other female family members by patriarchal ideology; that Shakespeare virtually condemns his heroines to motherlessness, except in *The Winter's Tale* where the reconciliation of Hermione and Perdita has the mythic force of renewal similar to the reunion between Demeter and Persephone.

The theme of absence is intensified in the two very useful sections

34. See, e.g., Sara Ruddick, "Learning to Live with the Angel in the House," *Women's Studies* 4 (1977): 181–200; and Bonnie Zimmerman, " 'The Mother's History' in George Eliot's Life, Literature and Political Ideology"; Barbara Ann Clarke Mossberg, "Reconstruction in the House of Art: Emily Dickinson's 'I Never Had a Mother' "; and Mary Lynn Broe, "A Subtle Psychic Bond: The Mother Figure in Sylvia Plath's Poetry"; all in Davidson and Broner, eds. See also Elaine Showalter, "Florence Nightingale's Feminist Complaint: Women, Religion, and *Suggestions for Thought,*" *Signs: Journal of Women in Culture and Society* 6, no. 3 (Spring 1981): 395–412.

35. See Nan Bauer Maglin, " 'Don't ever forget the bridge that you crossed over on': The Literature of Matrilineage"; Helen M. Bannan, "Spider Woman's Web: Mothers and Daughters in Southwestern Native American Literature"; and Natalie M. Rosinski, "Mothers and Daughters: Another Minority Group"; all in Davidson and Broner, eds.

36. See Germaine Brée, "George Sand: The Fictions of Autobiography," *Nineteenth-Century French Studies* 4 (1976): 438–49; and Lynn Z. Bloom, "Heritages: Dimensions of Mother-Daughter Relationships in Women's Autobiographies," in Davidson and Broner, eds.

37. Davidson and Broner, eds., p. 2.

that describe the British and American nineteenth-century traditions: the powerful and celebrated nineteenth-century mother is so inhibiting a force for her daughter's development that she needs to be removed from the fiction. Hence the absence or inconsequentiality of the mother in Jane Austen's novels, which makes possible the daughter's development; hence the lack of a healthy vision of motherhood in George Eliot's novels, even while her life, according to Bonnie Zimmerman, is devoted to a search for the Mother. Cathy Davidson sees the motherless daughter in American literature as a symbol of America's uncertainty as a nation. According to Barbara Mossberg, Dickinson can be an artist only because she has been dispossessed of the mother whose destiny as the servant of her family she will not repeat. Emancipation and changing roles for women in the early twentieth century do not ease the strains of the relationship, according to Adeline Tintner's "Mothers, Daughters and Incest in the Late Novels of Edith Wharton," but increase the competition, ambivalence, and ambiguity.

The early twentieth century witnesses a reversal of the absence and silence that has prevailed since biblical times, bringing us several writers who are able to celebrate strong maternal figures, often traditional wives and mothers, yet ultimately enabling rather than inhibiting to their artist-daughters. Jane Lilienfeld's essay, "Reentering Paradise: Cather, Colette, Woolf and Their Mothers" takes up again the generation Ellen Moers analyzes in *Literary Women*.[38] These three writers along with Gertrude Stein, according to Moers, move away from courtship to the theme of "maternal seduction," celebrating their mothers, "mature, calm women of still sculptural beauty . . . great queens, who impose order on the world."[39]

In *The Female Imagination*, Patricia Meyer Spacks also corroborates the historical picture that emerges in *The Lost Tradition*, when she says, "In nineteenth-century novels women express hostility toward their mothers by eliminating them from the narrative; twentieth-century fiction dramatizes the conflict."[40] This conflict is explored in the last two sections of *The Lost Tradition*. In "The Muse as Medusa," Karen Elias-Button explains that even in contemporary literature studying mother-daughter relationships is an archaeological process: "The process of reclaiming the mother involves, in part, an historical reaching-back to the lives women have lived before us, to find there the sense that our experience is rooted in a strength that has managed to survive the centuries."[41] The identification of that strength, however, requires an act of revision,

38. Ellen Moers, *Literary Women* (New York: Anchor Books, 1977). See esp. pp. 352–68.

39. Ibid., pp. 353, 359.

40. Patricia Meyer Spacks, *The Female Imagination* (New York: Avon Books, 1972), p. 191.

41. Elias-Button, p. 201.

and Elias-Button reverses Neumann's dichotomy of the Good/Terrible Mother as well as the mythic image of the Medusa, finding in the encounter with the Medusa a source of renewal: "We are turning toward the Terrible Mother to claim her as our own, . . . as a metaphor for sources of our own creative powers."[42] Conflict, imprisoning bondage, the fear of being devoured marks the writings of Lessing, Plath, the Jewish writers analyzed in Erika Duncan's "The Hungry Jewish Mother," and the authors examined in Lorna Irvine's "A Psychological Journey: Mothers and Daughters in English-Canadian Fiction." The minority fiction of "Matrilineage" which forms the subject of the last section of *The Lost Tradition* stresses for the most part a greater sympathy between mother and daughter, fellow victims in cultures where social conventions are more rigid and acceptable options for women are more limited.

One essay from *The Lost Tradition* has since been expanded into a book-length study of mother-daughter relationships in the medieval literary tradition: Nikki Stiller's *Eve's Orphans: Mothers and Daughters in Medieval English Literature.* The Middle Ages, as Stiller documents, were not only dominated by male authorship but also marked by an almost total separation between male and female spheres, to the point where most female experience was outside the domain of man's knowledge. It is therefore not surprising that "mothers are conspicuously absent" from medieval texts; all children legally belonged to their fathers and strong women identified with their fathers. Common sense, however, leads Stiller to look beyond this first impression: "Through all the barriers of class, male authorship and paternal domination, we begin to glimpse our mothers at last in an occasional reference, a fleeting portrait, or in a whole series of substitutes and surrogates: a hidden gallery in a closed-off wing." Stiller's search reveals natural mothers who are powerless, able to inculcate no more than passivity and subordination in their daughters. However, surrogate mothers appear to nurture and teach the heroines; supportive female communities emerge, mostly in religious contexts, to foster female autonomy; and women find in witches, hags, and crones "the powerful sympathetic mother whose amulets and charms give both the young woman and the old some control over the real world." The old hag/young girl opposition attests to the male writer's fear of the mother-daughter dyad, of female knowledge passed on from one generation to the next. Stiller's book asserts the strength of the mother-daughter bond that permeates a literature written by men who are "subconsciously opposed to it and afraid of it."[43]

42. Ibid., pp. 204, 205. See also Margaret Honton, "The Double Image and the Division of Parts: A Study of Mother/Daughter Relationships in the Poetry of Anne Sexton," *Journal of Women's Studies in Literature* 1, no. 1 (Winter 1979): 16–22.

43. Nikki Stiller, *Eve's Orphans: Mothers and Daughters in Medieval Literature* (Westport, Conn.: Greenwood Press, 1980), pp. 6, 7, 64.

More recent literary studies go beyond the "archaeological" approach represented by most of the essays in *The Lost Tradition* and by *Eve's Orphans*, beyond, as well, the purely thematic description of a number of other early essays, to analyze the effect of the mother-daughter relationship, in all its intricacy and complexity, on literary forms and structures. Psychological theory still offers the most useful and pervasive approach, although more and more literary critics are using Chodorow, Flax, Dinnerstein, and Miller instead of Jung and Neumann. Female identity in fiction can no longer be studied in the context of traditional ego psychology that fails to take into account women's fluid ego boundaries. As Jean Baker Miller states, "The ego, the 'I' of psychoanalysis may not be at all appropriate when talking about women. Women have different organizing principles around which their psyches are structured."[44] Literary critics are discovering these differences in women's literature and are beginning to study not separate and autonomous female characters but relationships between characters. Relationships between women emerge as important alternate, often submerged, plots, displacing the romantic love plot from the center of the text. Other themes are being studied: sister relationships, female friendship, female communities, women's work relationships, all related to, some based on mother-daughter affiliation. There are more general thematic studies about motherhood, such as maternal death and childbirth.[45]

More needs yet to be done. We need to look, for example, at the stylistic and linguistic characteristics of this literature: Is the sense of merging and fusion, of repetition and affiliation, of reflection and doubling, enacted in the texts' structure and style?[46] How is the author-character interaction affected by this network of relationships; how is the text's relationship to the female reader modified?[47] We need to speculate

44. Miller, p. 61.

45. For a study of submerged plots from a psychoanalytic perspective, see Marianne Hirsch, "A Mother's Discourse: Incorporation and Repetition in *La Princesse de Clèves*," *Yale French Studies*, vol. 62 (1981). On female friendship see especially Elizabeth Abel's excellent essay "(E)Merging Identities: The Dynamics of Female Friendship in Contemporary Fiction by Women," *Signs: Journal of Women in Culture and Society* 6, no. 3 (Spring 1981): 413–35; Janet Todd, *Women's Friendship in Literature* (New York: Columbia University Press, 1980); Louise Bernikow, *Among Women* (New York: Crown Publishers, 1980); and Nina Auerbach, *Communities of Women* (Cambridge, Mass.: Harvard University Press, 1978). For an excellent study of "matrophobia" and its effects, see Judith Kegan Gardiner, "A Wake for Mother: The Maternal Deathbed in Women's Fiction," *Feminist Studies* 4, no. 1 (February 1978): 146–65. See also Carol Poston, "Childbirth in Literature," ibid., pp. 18–31.

46. See Joan Lidoff, "Another Sleeping Beauty: Narcissism in *The House of Mirth*," *American Quarterly* 32, no. 5 (Winter 1980): 519–39. She is at work on an expanded study, "Fluid Boundaries: The Origins of a Distinctive Women's Voice in Literature" (Austin: Department of English, University of Texas at Austin).

47. Nancy Miller, in an illuminating essay, "Emphasis Added: Plots and Plausibilities in Women's Fiction," *PMLA* 96, no. 1 (January 1981): 36–48, speculates on ways in which

further about a female literary tradition: Can the Bloomian father-son model be replaced by a mother-daughter one—as Virginia Woolf suggests when she says, in *A Room of One's Own,* "We think back through our mothers if we are women"—and what would the effect of such a replacement be?[48] More and more, the mother-daughter relationship is integrated into broader literary studies of female development and experience, both individual and communal. We have become convinced of its crucial role in women's literature.[49]

V

It is not only in literary criticism that the study of mother-daughter relationships is being integrated into broader perspectives on female experience. Two recent essays will permit me to conclude with a comment on some new methodological directions and on some of the methodological and ideological divisions that surround all of this scholarship about mothers and daughters. Sara Ruddick's "Maternal Think-

---

"implausible" plots of women's fiction reflect the authors' characteristically female daydreams. Judith Kegan Gardiner is at work on a book entitled "The Hero as Her Author's Daughter" (Chicago: Department of English, University of Illinois at Chicago Circle). See also Ronnie Scharfman's "Mirroring and Mothering in Simone Schwartz-Bart's *Plui et vent sur Télumée-Miracle* and Jean Rhys's *Wide Sargasso Sea,*" *Yale French Studies,* vol. 62 (1981).

48. Virginia Woolf, *A Room of One's Own* (New York: Harcourt, Brace, Jovanovich, 1957), p. 79. On a female literary tradition, see Moers; Elaine Showalter, *A Literature of Their Own* (Princeton, N.J.: Princeton University Press, 1977); Sandra Gilbert and Susan Gubar, *The Madwoman in the Attic: The Woman Writer and the Nineteenth-Century Imagination* (New Haven, Conn.: Yale University Press, 1979); Joanne Feit-Diehl, " 'Come Slowly Eden': An Exploration of Women Poets and Their Muse," *Signs: Journal of Women in Culture and Society* 3, no. 3 (Spring 1978): 572–87; and Annette Kolodny, "A Map of Rereading: Or, Gender and the Interpretation of Literary Texts," *New Literary History* 11, no. 3 (Spring 1980): 451–67. In her recent book, *Women Writers and Poetic Identity* (Princeton, N.J.: Princeton University Press, 1980), Margaret Homans explores the effect of the mother-daughter relationship on women's ability to assume a poetic voice.

49. I am aware of several other works in progress that reflect some of these trends. Two works deal specifically with mother-daughter relationships: Jane Lilienfeld's "The Possibility of Sisterhood: Women, Mothers, and Their Texts from Mary Wollstonecraft to the Present" (Boston: Department of English, Boston University; and Marianne Hirsch's "The Double Image: Mothers and Daughters in Literature" (Hanover, N.H.: Department of French and Italian, Dartmouth College). One section of Elizabeth Abel's "Psyche's Semblances: Literary and Psychoanalytic Representations of Female Identity" (Chicago: Department of English, University of Chicago) is devoted to mother-daughter relationships. Many of the essays in the anthology "Formation/Deformation/Transformation: The Female Novel of Development," ed. Elizabeth Abel, Marianne Hirsch, and Elizabeth Langland (Nashville, Tenn.: Department of English, Vanderbilt University), touch on the mother-daughter relationship, some considering it the key factor in female development as it is represented in the novel. Many of the essays in *New Feminist Essays on Virginia Woolf,* ed. Jane Marcus (London: Macmillan Co.; Lincoln: University of Nebraska Press, 1981) focus on the mother-daughter relationship and other forms of female bonding in Woolf's life and work.

ing" is an attempt to identify a "coherent and benign account of maternal power and influence."[50] "Maternal," for Ruddick, is a social and not a biological category: she concentrates on what mothers do rather than on what they are; thereby her essay enables us more fully than any other study to break out of biological necessities. Ruddick insists on a privileged identification between maternal and female; thus, even those of us who are not mothers think "maternally" because we are daughters. The aim of Ruddick's essay, based in the terminology of Habermas and other philosophical relativists, is to identify how mothers think and to bring that form of thought (thought which responds to the demands of preservation, growth, and acceptability) into the public eye and the public world. To do so is to insist that the characteristically "womanly" be valued, thus freeing women from the "ideology of womanhood [which] has been invented by men."[51] Ruddick's clear and straightforward exposition of the conceptual and emotional ways in which mothers approach their work frees motherhood and consequently mother-child relationships from mythic and psychoanalytic visions of maternal power and powerlessness that tend to obscure the more practical realities of the work involved in mothering. Ruddick looks forward to a world where children will be raised not by "parents" but by "mothers of both sexes who live out a transformed maternal thought in communities that share parental care."[52] Ruddick's extension of the term "mother" is a valuable breakthrough.

The second essay I want to mention here, Adrienne Rich's "Compulsory Heterosexuality and Lesbian Existence," is more explicit in criticizing recent feminist scholarship, which, she says, confirms and participates in the mystification it aims at attacking. Feminist psychoanalysis in particular, Rich maintains, fails to deal with lesbian existence as a reality and as a source of power and knowledge available to women. According to Rich, Miller writes "a new psychology of women" as if lesbians did not exist, and Dinnerstein emphasizes so strongly women's collusion in their own oppression that she is led to ignore all those women who have resisted and refused to internalize the "values of the colonizer." Rich's critique of Chodorow is more qualified because, she says, Chodorow "does come close to the edge of an acknowledgement of lesbian existence" by implying that women find heterosexual relationships "impoverishing and painful." Yet Rich insists that "mothering-by-women is [not] a sufficient cause of lesbian existence."[53]

Rich's own vision of compulsory heterosexuality as an institution

50. Sara Ruddick, "Maternal Thinking," *Feminist Studies* 6, no. 2 (Summer 1980): 342–67.

51. Ibid., p. 345.

52. Ibid., p. 362.

53. Rich, "Compulsory Heterosexuality," pp. 634, 635, 636, 638.

enforced by physical violence and false consciousness calls many of our assumptions into question; she demonstrates rather convincingly that much of feminist scholarship is a part of that institution. Her accusation points out dissatisfactions and limitations fundamental to the research on mother-daughter relationships. Rooted so strongly in Freudian psychoanalysis, Chodorow's and Dinnerstein's theoretical framework makes it difficult for us to envision relationships between women outside of the context of patriarchal oppression, of competition between women for men, of male identification. Firmly based in the nuclear family, their framework makes it difficult for us to see and analyze the varieties of "families" in which children are raised today: adoptive families, single-parent families, lesbian and communal households, or multiple families in the case of shared custody. Despite their far-reaching and incisive analysis, despite their usefulness for literary critics, these works suffer from these limitations.

This debate within the feminist scholarly community is a serious one. It is important for us to be able to see and recognize ourselves and each other without the blinders imposed by the traditional paternal order. At the same time, it is important to foster whole and healthy relationships between women, between women and men, between men. As Nancy Chodorow says, "I think that children who live exclusively with women or men, gay or straight, need to be given every opportunity for developing ongoing close relationships with people of the opposite gender from that of their primary caretakers."[54] Although none of us can predict what a generation raised by "mothers of both sexes" will be like, Chodorow's and Dinnerstein's confidence that they will be "whole human beings," that changes in family structure will produce fundamental social changes, is our only hope.

I have found the work of Chodorow and Dinnerstein, Flax, Benjamin, and Ruddick, Irigaray and Kristeva useful in the most generous sense; I hope to have shown that I have also found it frustrating. The last five years have revolutionized our thinking but have also convinced me of the need to transform more radically the paradigms within which we think, to invent new theoretical frameworks that allow us, in our study of relationships between women, truly to go beyond patriarchal myths and perceptions. Rich suggests one such direction when she outlines the notion of a "lesbian continuum": "If we consider the possibility that all women—from the infant suckling her mother's breast, to the grown woman experiencing orgasmic sensations while suckling her own child, perhaps recalling her mother's milk-smell in her own; to two women like Virginia Woolf's Chloe and Olivia, who share a laboratory; to the woman dying at ninety touched and handled by women—exist on a lesbian

54. Chodorow, "On *The Reproduction of Mothering*," p. 512.

continuum, we can see ourselves as moving in and out of this continuum, whether we identify ourselves as lesbian or not."[55] This is one way to envision and to study the relationships between women outside of patriarchal conceptions, to approach perhaps the power and value they hold in themselves. There are other ways. Again Adrienne Rich has cut out our work for us.

Department of French and Italian
Dartmouth College

55. Rich, "Compulsory Heterosexuality," p. 651.

THE BORDERS OF ETHICAL, EROTIC, AND ARTISTIC POSSIBILITIES IN *LITTLE WOMEN*

ANN B. MURPHY

Twenty years of scholarship about Louisa May Alcott's most famous and enduring work, *Little Women*, testifies to the complicated process of reexamining a novel widely recognized as a classic in American children's literature.[1] This critical reevaluation of Alcott has been complicated by the publication of her previously uncol-

[1] The range of recent writing on Alcott is impressive, and the following is by no means an exhaustive bibliography: Nina Auerbach, *"Little Women,"* in *Communities of Women: An Idea in Fiction*, ed. Nina Auerbach (Cambridge, Mass.: Harvard University Press, 1978), 55–75; Jeanne Bedell, "A Necessary Mask: The Sensation Fiction of Louisa May Alcott," *Publications of the Missouri Philological Association, Warrensbury, Mo.*, no. 5 (1980), 8–14; Madelon Bedell, "Beneath the Surface: Power and Passion in *Little Women,"* in *Critical Essays on Louisa May Alcott*, ed. Madeleine Stern (Boston: G. K. Hall, 1984), 145–50; Brigid Brophy, "Sentimentality and Louisa May Alcott," in Stern, ed., *Critical Essays*, 93–96; Mary Cadogan, " 'Sweet, If Somewhat Tomboyish': The British Response to Louisa May Alcott," in Stern, ed., *Critical Essays*, 275–79; Ann Douglas, "Mysteries of Louisa May Alcott," *New York Review of Books* 25 (September 28, 1978): 60–63; Sarah Elbert, *A Hunger for Home: Louisa May Alcott and Little Women* (Philadelphia: Temple University Press, 1984); Judith Fetterley, "Impersonating *Little Women*: The Radicalism of Alcott's *Behind a Mask*," *Women's Studies* 10, no. 1 (1983): 1–14, and *"Little Women*: Alcott's Civil War," in Stern, ed., *Critical Essays*, 140–43; Carol Gay, "The Philosopher and His Daughter: Amos Bronson Alcott and Louisa," *Essays in Literature* 2, no. 2 (Fall 1975): 181–91; Sandra Gilbert and Susan Gubar, *The Madwoman in the Attic: The Woman Writer and the Nineteenth-Century Literary Imagination* (New Haven, Conn.: Yale University Press, 1979); Alfred Habegger, "Precious Incest: First Novels by Louisa May Alcott and Henry James," *Massachusetts Review* 26, nos. 2–3 (Summer–Autumn 1985): 232–62; Karen Halttunen, "The Domestic Drama of Louisa May Alcott," *Feminist Studies* 10, no. 2 (Summer 1984):

This essay originally appeared in *Signs*, vol. 15, no. 3, Spring 1990.

lected and largely unavailable gothic thrillers,[2] which reveal a new dimension to the familiar author, both enriching our reactions to *Little Women* (especially to the silencing of Jo March's own anxious authorship of pseudonymous thrillers) and confirming our sense of the subversion in that sentimental text.

Biographies exploring the darker side of Alcott and reinterpreting her complicated family, as well as ongoing feminist work retrieving, recuperating, and reenvisioning American literature and cultural history, have all contributed to the scholarship on Alcott during the past two decades.[3] Yet the text of *Little Women* remains something of a tarbaby, a sticky, sentimental, entrapping experience

---

233–54; Stephanie Harrington, "Does *Little Women* Belittle Women?" in Stern, ed., *Critical Essays*, 110–12; Carolyn Heilbrun, "Louisa May Alcott: The Influence of *Little Women*," in *Women, the Arts, and the 1920s in Paris and New York*, ed. Kenneth Wheeler and Virginia Lussier (New Brunswick, N.J.: Transaction, 1982), 20–26; Anne Hollander, "Reflections on *Little Women*," *Children's Literature* 9 (1981): 28–39; Elizabeth Janeway, "Meg, Jo, Beth, Amy, and Louisa," in Stern, ed., *Critical Essays*, 97–98; Eugenia Kaledin, "Louisa May Alcott: Success and the Sorrow of Self-Denial," *Women's Studies* 5, no. 3 (1978): 251–63; Linda Kerber, "Can a Woman Be an Individual? The Limits of Puritan Tradition in the Early Republic," *Texas Studies in Literature and Language* 25, no. 1 (Spring 1983): 165–78; Elizabeth Keyser, "Alcott's Portraits of the Artist as Little Women," *International Journal of Women's Studies* 5, no. 5 (November/December 1982): 445–59; Elizabeth Langland, "Female Stories of Experience: Alcott's *Little Women* in Light of *Work*," in *The Voyage In: Fictions of Female Development*, ed. Elizabeth Abel, Marianne Hirsch, and Elizabeth Langland (Hanover, N.H.: University Press of New England, 1983), 112–27; Ruth MacDonald, *Louisa May Alcott* (Boston: Twayne, 1983); Anne Scott MacLeod, "The Caddie Woodlawn Syndrome: American Girlhood in the Nineteenth Century," in *A Century of Childhood, 1820–1920*, ed. Mary Heininger, Karin Calvert, Barbara Finkelstein, and Kathy Vandell (Rochester, N.Y.: Margaret Woodbury Strong Museum, 1984), 97–119; Joy Marsella, *The Promise of Destiny: Children and Women in the Short Stories of Louisa May Alcott* (Westport, Conn.: Greenwood, 1983); Alma Payne, "Louisa May Alcott (1832–1888)," *American Literary Realism* 6, no. 1 (Winter 1973): 27–43; Lavinia Russ, "Not to Be Read on Sunday," in Stern, ed., *Critical Essays*, 99–102; Martha Saxton, *Louisa May: A Modern Biography of Louisa May Alcott* (Boston: Houghton Mifflin, 1977); Patricia Spacks, *The Female Imagination* (New York: Avon, 1972); Madeleine Stern, "Louisa May Alcott's Self-Criticism," in *Studies in the American Renaissance*, ed. Joel Myerson (Charlottesville: University Press of Virginia, 1985), 333–43; Charles Strickland, *Victorian Domesticity: Families in the Life and Art of Louisa May Alcott* (University: University of Alabama Press, 1985).

[2] Madeleine Stern, ed., *Behind a Mask: The Unknown Thrillers of Louisa May Alcott* (New York: Quill, 1984).

[3] Biographies include the controversial one by Saxton, as well as the ones by Elbert and McDonald, and another by Madelon Bedell, *The Alcotts: A Biography of a Family* (New York: Potter, Crown, 1986). Numerous articles have focused on the influence of Bronson and Abba Alcott and the role of such Concord luminaries as Emerson and Thoreau in shaping Alcott's life and work. A major, ongoing task of feminist scholarship in America has been to reinterpret and define the American experience—of which Alcott is so central a part—in light of women's lives.

or place rather than a knowable object—and thus a fitting emblem of its own subversive content, which resists women's objectification and seeks a new vision of women's subjectivity and space. Some critics begin by directly recognizing the extraordinary power this work had for them and others in childhood.[4] Others approach the novel with more apparent detachment, focusing on its repressive domesticity. For most of us, however, *Little Women* is a troubling text, a childhood icon that still resonates with images of positive female community, ideal and loving motherhood, and girlhood dreams of artistic achievement. Our reactions to the incarceration of Meg in claustrophobic domesticity, the mysterious, sacrificial death of good little Beth, the trivialization of Amy in objectifying narcissism, and the foreclosure of Jo's erotic and literary expression, are inextricably connected to our memories of our own struggles against these fates.

Not surprisingly, then, there is remarkable disunity in the contemporary reappraisals of the meaning and significance of Alcott's novel. Indeed, the disagreement is so pervasive and individual opinions so frequently contradictory, within and between essays, as to suggest both the abiding and seductive power of this text for many female readers, and the rich plenitude of its still unexplored critical possibilities. Is *Little Women* adolescent, sentimental, and repressive, an instrument for teaching girls how to become "little," domesticated, and silent?[5] Is the novel subversive, matriarchal, and implicitly revolutionary, fostering discontent with the very model of female domesticity it purports to admire?[6]

---

[4] For example, Carolyn Heilbrun claims that, "for youngsters, reading in search of legends they need not even consciously acknowledge or remember, it is Jo who is immortal" (Heilbrun, 25). According to Anne Hollander, the novel "has been a justly famous children's classic for a century . . . a pattern and a model, a mold for goals and aspirations" (Hollander, 28). Elizabeth Janeway calls the Marches "the most read about and cried over young women of their years" (Janeway, 97). Lavinia Russ claims, "I loved it too much when I was young to evaluate it dispassionately, loved it so much when I was a girl that Jo was the second most important person in my life" (Russ, 99).

[5] Martha Saxton, e.g., sees *Little Women* as "a regression for Louisa as an artist and a woman" (Saxton, 9), and Judith Fetterley, reading *Little Women* in light of Alcott's thriller, *Behind a Mask*, concludes that the famous children's novel was "an act of impersonation designed to save her psychological skin and ensure her economic survival" (Fetterley, "Impersonating *Little Women*," 13). Eugenia Kaledin believes that Alcott's "acceptance of the creed of womanly self-denial as much as her willingness to buy success by catering to middle class ideals aborted the promise of her art and led her to betray her most deeply felt values" (Kaledin, 251).

[6] Sarah Elbert claims that "Jo's journey is the only fully complete one in *Little Women* and it involves her learning to tell true love from romantic fancy. She must do so in order to reproduce her lost sisterhood in a new, feminist domestic union" (Elbert, 161). Elizabeth Keyser claims that the novel, "if read aright, can help us avoid the stumbling blocks of self-denial which, no less than those of self, obstruct a woman's path to creativity" (Keyser, 445).

The novel does not permit rigid answers to these questions. To account for its enduring power, *Little Women* must instead be seen as a multifaceted novel, a children's book regarded (or at least defined) as "moral pap" by its author.[7] It preaches domestic containment and Bunyanesque self-denial while it explores the infinity of inward female space and suggests unending rage against the cultural limitations imposed on female development. Like the patchwork quilts of her predecessors and contemporaries, Alcott's novel assembles "fragments into an intricate and ingenious design" containing both messages of "female patience, perseverance, good nature and industry" and "an alternative model of female power and creativity."[8] Its power derives from its contradictions rather than prevailing despite them.

At the same time, the terms of critical debate over *Little Women* are themselves instructive because they point obsessively to crucial episodes and characters, and to the book's uneasy closure. Thus Carolyn Heilbrun finds in Jo March "the single female model continuously available after 1868 to girls dreaming beyond the confines of a constricted family destiny to the possibility of autonomy and experience initiated by one's self," but she concludes that "Alcott betrayed Jo" and suggests that Jo is a positive model only if we overlook her marriage.[9] Patricia Spacks places the emphasis differently, finding that *Little Women* enforces repressive lessons in female docility, passivity, and silence, while its "glorification of altruism as feminine activity . . . reaches extraordinary heights." For Spacks, Jo's marriage is not ambiguous but punitive, not a betrayal but the logical culmination of the novel's didactic and regressive intent.[10]

By contrast, Nina Auerbach concludes that the novel's portrayal of female materiality and self-sufficiency subverts ideals of domesticated womanhood, and that the matriarch, Mrs. March, allows her daughters "the freedom to remain children and, for a woman, the more precious freedom *not* to fall in love." Including the entire March trilogy in her appraisal, rather than the single novel, Auerbach claims that by the end Jo "has attained the position of Marmee, but her title is more formidable than that comfortable, clinging name."[11] Rather than a betrayal or punishment, then, Alcott's treatment of Jo, and the implications of her marriage, are eventually affirmative, even triumphant.

[7] Quoted by Saxton, 16.

[8] Elaine Showalter, "Piecing and Writing," in *The Poetics of Gender*, ed. Nancy K. Miller (New York: Columbia University Press, 1986), 222–47, esp. 227, 232.

[9] Heilbrun (n. 1 above), 21, 23.

[10] Spacks (n. 1 above), 124, 127.

[11] Auerbach (n. 1 above), 62, 69.

Elizabeth Langland and Madelon Bedell both incorporate these tensions within their analyses, positing a multilayered text with ambivalent, even contradictory messages. "The narrative surface of *Little Women* asserts that marriage is woman's fulfillment. Underneath this principal narrative, however, lies a possibility closer to Alcott's experience," Langland claims, finding that covert text primarily embodied in Jo, who resists the book's lessons in "disengagement from the active world and its strife and a retreat from self-assertion into marriage."[12] Similarly, Bedell finds that beneath the surface narrative lies "the legend, which the story masks. The theme of the legend is also concerned with the sisters' struggles . . . against the inevitability of growing up, of leaving the delightful state of childhood for the restricted, narrow, and burdened condition of womanhood."[13]

Again and again, as this brief review suggests, feminist critics collide against the sticky, protean implications of this ostensibly childish text: the absent, passive, feminized father who yet ruthlessly diminishes his "little" women; the radically present, loving, self-sacrificing—and perpetually angry—mother who makes girlhood so literally seductive and adulthood so utterly deadly; the erotic, rich, musical, half-Italian brother-lover, Laurie, whom Jo eventually rejects for the elderly, patriarchal German professor; and above all Jo March, with whom we all so passionately identified: gawky, loving, intense, funny, furious, creative, and incredibly active. It is through Jo that we are compelled to question the painfully limited choices available to women artists. It is through Jo that we are forced to acknowledge acute discontent with Bunyan's model of Pilgrim's Progress—and the nineteenth-century model of active girls dwindling into docile little women. It is through Jo that we experience the complicated intersections and overlappings of eroticism, anger, and creativity—and mourn the apparent effacing of all three by the novel's end, without truly believing they are indeed gone.

Whether we see *Little Women* as "a perfectly disgusting, banal, and craven service to male supremacy"[14] or "a gratifying taste of [Alcott's] simple, stable vision of feminine completeness,"[15] we cannot evade the textured ambiguity and quiltlike complexity of its image of female development, the deep uncertainty with which Alcott struggles to portray female loss of freedom through acculturation and adolescence as somehow enhancing and morally sustain-

[12] Langland (n. 1 above), 118, 120.
[13] M. Bedell (n. 1 above), 146.
[14] Harrington (n. 1 above), 111.
[15] Hollander (n. 1 above), 28.

ing. In fact, these tensions and ambivalences contribute to the power of *Little Women*, focusing attention on the insidious as well as sustaining elements of the myth of female moral superiority and on the disjunctions between male and female stories of maturation.

* * *

> [The characteristic girls' stories of nineteenth-century America] were, typically, intensely domestic and interior. Where the boys' books increasingly revolved around a young man's encounter with the outside world—in the army, in the West, in the city—and around active, extroverted adventure, girls' novels focused on character and relationships, as, of course, girls' lives did as they approached womanhood.[16]

Little Women is often compared to another nineteenth-century American story of a young rebel whose moral development sets him at odds with his society—*Huckleberry Finn*. According to Eugenia Kaledin, for example, "the conclusion of *Little Women* seems to sound as false a note as the ending of *Huckleberry Finn*."[17] Linda Kerber regrets that "we have inherited no nineteenth-century fictional female image which can stand as a metaphor for America" and says that "Jo March cannot serve as Huck Finn's counterpart."[18] Yet Jo may very well stand as a metaphor for (white, middle-class) female America, and the contrasts between her narrative and Huck's are enormously instructive, especially as they illuminate those troubling, resistant closures to each novel.

In many ways, Huck Finn is as mired in romantic fictions which define and deny him as Jo March is. Although his journey of self-discovery is explicit, mythical, and outward, while Jo's is implicit, Christian, and domestic, both do reach a moment of truth within themselves in the course of their pilgrimages. Huck's occurs when he resolves to help Jim escape slavery, thus putting his personal loyalty to Jim above both social pressures to conform and the religious certainty that such an action damns him. By the end of his magical journey downriver, however, his commitment seems erased and trivialized when Huck is reenmeshed in Tom's silly, pernicious romantic fictions, texts wholly inappropriate to Huck's—and more compellingly, Jim's—needs.

[16] MacLeod (n. 1 above), 106.

[17] Kaledin (n. 1 above), 258.

[18] Kerber (n. 1 above), 175–76. Of course, it is an open question whether Huck is a "metaphor" for America any more than Jo March is. He may very well be a metaphor for white, middle-class male America, but his absolute universality, even while on the raft with Jim, is questionable.

Twain himself is equally trapped at this point in the constraints of representative fiction, doomed by the logic of his river/freedom versus land/captivity structure. Within these terms he cannot depict Huck finding a constructive, fulfilling adult life on shore, for life on shore is, at best, Tom's maddening, self-defeating narratives of imprisonment, and at worst the ugliness, violence, and horror of the Grangerfords, Sheperdsons, Duke, Dauphin, and slavery. So Twain abandons the genre, and Huck escapes civilization entirely, lighting out for "the Territory" at the penultimate sentence of the text, to an undepicted, unimaginable freedom beyond the confines of culture and fiction.[19]

Alcott and Jo March are not so fortunate. Jo's pilgrimage of moral development takes place almost wholly in interior spaces—both literal and symbolic. She meets and does battle with Apollyon within herself, not as embodied by evil people and others' actions. Furthermore, her life does not offer any periodic escape from her trials to an idyll on the river. Instead she must stay on land, so to speak, finding her haven in the same domestic experience and space that constitute the terrain of her pilgrimage. Indeed, Jo's culture defines female maturation as the process of acceding to—believing in—precisely those romantic fictions which entrapped Huck, and Alcott's efforts to resist such romanticizing are even more troubled, unsettling, and inconclusive than Twain's.

When, in her own moment of truth, Jo rejects the most obvious option available to her—marriage to the rich, handsome, and loving boy next door—her refusal is as much a violation of the standards of her world as is Huck's self-damning decision to help Jim. Yet Huck's rejection of his society is clearly a wise, moral choice which puts him outside and above Tom's romances, while Jo's rejection is a self-defeating, pointless decision that denies her heterosexual erotic fulfillment. Further, it does not even win her freedom from the fictions of romantic love Laurie represents, since it leads to her entrapment in even more primal fictions when she later marries her blatantly nonerotic father-figure and tutor, Professor Bhaer.

Yet the fact remains: Jo does assert herself, and Alcott does devise an ending that, however uneasily, depicts a reconciliation between the coercions of her culture and needs of her character. In

[19] For more on the way the American frontier appears gendered and defined as accessible only to male exploration (and exploitation), see, e.g., Nina Baym, "Melodramas of Beset Manhood," in *The New Feminist Criticism: Essays on Women, Literature, and Theory,* ed. Elaine Showalter (New York: Pantheon, 1985), 63–80; and Annette Kolodny, *The Lay of the Land: Metaphor as Experience and History in American Life and Letters* (Chapel Hill: University of North Carolina Press, 1975).

rejecting Laurie, Jo breaks as sharply with her society as Huck does in resolving to free Jim from slavery. In marrying Professor Bhaer, and hence committing herself to her work rather than to romantic love, Jo creates new possibilities for herself as a member of a community and as a professional in her own right—possibilities that are at least as subversive as Huck's rejection of civilization. Thus Jo March achieves full professional existence—at the apparent cost of literary expression and sexual intimacy—through her marriage to her father-professor. The novel's closure does not deny the freedoms of Alcott's much-affirmed spinsterhood but, rather, offers a fictional rendering of female choice that demands that we question its trade-offs and protest its price. The unsettling ambiguity and uncertainty of the ending are precisely its point.

Both Twain and Alcott lacked the necessary fictional images and structures to depict full adult satisfaction for their heroes within their genre and society. Yet Twain could allow Huck to escape the struggle between river and shore entirely. For Alcott, however, no symbol of female freedom existed. "In the context of the book . . . no other ending except this flawed one would be appropriate. What other future is possible for Jo? Can one really imagine her as an independent artist living an adventurous life in some sort of Bohemian quarter of Boston, *supposing such a place to have existed?*"[20]

Instead, Alcott had to devise a solution that (like Twain's) accommodated the demands of representational fiction, and (unlike Twain's) acknowledged the coercions of female domesticity—a solution, further, that was also appropriate to the constraints of children's fiction. Yet, while Jo's marriage accommodates the genre, the sexless but profoundly incestuous nature of that marriage—its oedipal inevitability, perhaps—is disturbingly coercive.

* * *

An initial focus on caring for the self in order to ensure survival is followed by a transitional phase in which this judgment is criticized as selfish. The criticism signals a new understanding of the connection between self and others . . . the concept of responsibility. . . . This concept . . . and its fusion with a maternal morality . . . characterizes the second perspective. . . . However . . . the exclusion of herself gives rise to problems in relationships, creating a disequilibrium that initiates the second transition . . . a reconsideration of relationships . . . to sort out the confusion between self-

[20] M. Bedell, "Beneath the Surface" (n. 1 above), 147–48; my emphasis.

sacrifice and care. . . . The third perspective focuses on the dynamics of relationships and dissipates the tension between selfishness and responsibility through a new understanding of the interconnection between other and self.[21]

While the surface narrative or pattern of *Little Women* may well be the standard sentimental "moral pap" produced in the nineteenth century to show girls their proper sphere, at least one of its many subtexts or pieces follows quite closely the outline of female ethical development suggested by Carol Gilligan. It does so, too, with the clearly subversive suggestion that such an alternative model of maturation is morally superior to (warring, money-hungry) male development. The novel opens on Christmas Eve, and the first words we hear are complaints about a lack of presents—of material presence. Quickly, however, the March sisters come to see their complaints as selfish: "I *am* a selfish girl!" Amy exclaims, "but I'll truly try to be better."[22] During the course of book 1, the sisters struggle heroically against such selfishness, moving toward understanding themselves in relation to others.

During these pilgrimages, Meg learns about the venality of high society, and by implication American capitalism, accepting in its place the alternate model of female adulthood Marmee offers: "I want my daughters to be beautiful, accomplished, and good; to be admired, loved, and respected; to have a happy youth, to be well and wisely married, and to lead useful, pleasant lives" (92). Amy, the least likeable and most narcissistic and ambitious of the four, learns—with Marmee's help—that "there is not much danger that real talent or goodness will be overlooked long; even if it is, the consciousness of possessing and using it well should satisfy one" (67). Beth, whose selfishness is less immediately obvious, learns—without help from Marmee—that her debilitating shyness may in fact be an unkindness to others. Jo, of course, battles the ferocity of her selfish anger. In the process of her arduous journey, Jo learns "not only the bitterness of remorse and despair, but the sweetness of self-denial and self-control" (77)—again instructed by Marmee.

By the end of book 1, these struggles produce significant changes that are named and approved by their father upon his return. The initial sacrifice of material goods—Christmas breakfast—has been so internalized that Meg abandons her vanity and materialism and becomes submissive to her comparatively

[21] Carol Gilligan, *In a Different Voice: Psychological Theory and Women's Development* (Cambridge, Mass.: Harvard University Press, 1982), 74.

[22] Louisa May Alcott, *Little Women* (New York: Signet, 1983), 10. All subsequent references to the novel will be noted parenthetically in the text.

impoverished future husband. Amy makes a will renouncing all her worldly goods. Beth nearly dies in sacrificial service to others, and Jo renounces not only her beautiful hair but her beloved sister, Meg, and the illusions of safety and childhood as well.

Book 2 marks their more painful attempts to negotiate a reconciliation between a notion of goodness equated with extreme self-sacrifice and the needs of their own authentic characters. Meg struggles to be both a nurturing mother and a fully sexual adult woman in her marriage, and she seems to achieve some kind of balance, moving beyond her initial self-immersion in the nursery and learning to share child care responsibilities with her husband. Amy devises a socially appropriate balance between narcissism and selfishness, becoming her own most triumphant art object: "Everything about her mutely suggested love and sorrow—the blotted letters in her lap, the black ribbon that tied up her hair, the womanly pain and patience in her face; even the little ebony cross at her throat seemed pathetic to Laurie" (390).

Beth, of course, dies from a mysterious disease arising from terminal goodness—from her inability to distinguish between nurturing others and the radical self-denial expected of femininity. Jo, after rejecting erotic love and renouncing a literary career, acknowledges her own vulnerability and need: "A sudden sense of loneliness came over her so strongly that she looked about her with dim eyes, as if to find something to lean upon" (411). Her marriage to Professor Bhaer offers her a way to balance personal need and cultural expectations: "I may be strong-minded, but no one can say I'm out of my sphere now," she tells her fiance, "for woman's special mission is supposed to be drying tears and bearing burdens. I'm to carry my share, Friedrich, and help to earn the home. Make up your mind to that" (438).

Yet while this heroic pattern certainly exists and provides some of the book's insidious power—a message of consolation to young girls for the loss of childhood freedom—it is mitigated and contradicted by its own terms, as well as by other, seriously conflicting, messages. Most notably, the journeys toward selflessness in book 1 and interconnection in book 2 are undercut both by an obsessive diminution of their context and by the incessant imagery of patriarchal observation that renders nearly every ethical achievement artificial, theatrical—an objectivized scene. Meg's domestic battles in book 2, for example, take place in a home so minuscule it is hard to imagine adult human beings living in it: "The little brown house . . . was a tiny house, with a little garden behind and a lawn about as big as a pocket handkerchief" (224). The last vision we have of Meg, before she disappears completely from sight in the text,

describes her as "on the shelf": "Safe from the restless fret and
fever of the world . . . learning . . . that a woman's happiest
kingdom is her home, her highest honor the art of ruling it not as a
queen, but as a wise wife and mother" (365).

More ambiguously, Amy's artistic efforts are consistently described as comical or insignificant, their only permanent memorial
being a suggestively oedipal gouged foot. Her work is either trivial
(mudpies) or dangerous (burning, cutting, immobilizing). Although
she apparently continues her lethal artistic activity after her
marriage—turning her frail daughter into yet another aesthetic
object—she decides after only one trip to Rome that "talent isn't
genius" and gives up all her "foolish hopes" (370), as if possessing
the genius of Michelangelo were a woman's only excuse for
pursuing artistic activity, as if she had no responsibility to nurture
mere talent. Beth, of course, is rendered literally angelic and
eventually nonexistent rather than simply tiny: like Meg she is
safely removed from the trials of life, and her death is the clearest
message in the novel about the ominous dangers of selflessness.

Still, it is Jo's struggle that most directly reveals Alcott's ambivalence about female morality and betrays the rage beneath the
obsessive diminution. When Amy burns Jo's much-cherished
manuscript, Jo is quite naturally furious—and thus guilty of being
quick-tempered. Yet even Jo refers to the manuscript as her "little
book" (71), while the narrator explains that "it was only half a dozen
little fairy tales . . . [and] it seemed a small loss to others" (72).
Later, Meg advises Amy on how to make up with Jo, telling her
"You *were* very naughty, and it *is* hard to forgive the loss of her
precious little book" (73), suggesting by her emphasis that Amy was
not very naughty and that the little book was not so precious. While
the cause of Jo's impermissable anger is ruthlessly minimized, the
consequences are nonetheless enormous—and deadly: Amy falls
through the ice and nearly drowns.

The narrative emphasis on the triviality of these tribulations
(especially in bk. 1), so ominously shadowed by images of death,
suggests Alcott's own ambivalence about the cult of feminine
altruism and its domestic context. Furthermore, she portrays the
entire pilgrimage itself as an act, a game; the progression of the
girls' roles is objectivized, viewed, and judged by a benevolent,
absent patriarch. The sisters are learning not simply to be selfless,
but to be objects, viewed by patriarchal subjects. Amy's original
sense of selfishness, for example, originates in a desire to be seen
differently by her father, while Marmee's image of ideal womanhood is explicitly of an Other, a third-person object: "beautiful,
accomplished, good, admired, loved, respected" (92). Her sermon

on anger reinforces this objectification, for she conveys her own laborious process of learning to control her anger specifically as an experience of being watched, observed, and judged by her passionless husband.

Alcott's penchant for the theatrical is well known, and numerous critics have noticed the degree to which the role of the little woman is a (painfully) learned one: "Indeed, discovering the real self of the woman playing the little woman is an impossible task, in part because the essence of the role is that it appears to be the 'real' self."[23] The March sisters' pilgrimage is a game in a way that Huck's river voyage most emphatically is not. Yet the game is as life-threatening and dangerous as anything Huck experiences, precisely because it excludes as hostile the entire outside world (defined by distant, deadly warfare, diseased and demanding poor families, and venal, trivial society) while imposing an ostensibly empowering role of female altruism which offers moral superiority as compensation for domestic bondage, gouged artistic aspirations, deadly self-sacrifice, and the immolation of voice.

The terms in which Alcott depicts this voyage of female ethical development suggest the impossibility of either freely choosing or fully rendering in fiction a new understanding of the woman-self in relation to others, if that understanding must be achieved within a culture that defines women as powerless and marginal, and confines all new understandings to the old, safe, and imprisoning domestic sphere. Yet the female pilgrimage Alcott traces is strikingly close to the shape of female ethical development Gilligan has described, and however impossible Alcott found it to move this pilgrimage fully beyond the confines of her own culture, the radically assertive image of female self-worth, struggle, and heroism she portrays in *Little Women* surely accounts for some of the book's insidious hold over its readers.

* * *

Carol Gilligan's theories of female ethical development begin to explain the power of *Little Women* by suggesting an underlying shape and direction for a reading of its characters' pilgrimage and an interpretation of its narrative failure, as located in its collapse against the borders of patriarchal culture. The feminist psychoanalytical theories of Nancy Chodorow, Jessica Benjamin, and Jane Flax—among many others—offer insights in their explorations of

---

[23] Fetterley, "Impersonating *Little Women*" (n. 1 above), 13. For a thorough examination of Alcott's theatrical interests and experiences, see also Halttunen (n. 1 above).

the site of collapse, the precise place where female narrative collides against patriarchal boundaries—the problem of desire.[24] Indeed, the pattern of the female infant's differentiation, as traced by these theorists, strikingly prefigures the pattern of conflict, and apparent impossibility of resolution, that the adult female experiences and that Alcott's novel so vividly demonstrates in Jo's struggle for love and voice.

Feminist theorists have begun to deconstruct and problematize the classical Freudian model of infant development, with its patriarchal assumptions about the nature of individuality, eroticism, and female otherness, and to reveal its implicit contradictions, while suggesting an alternative, less oppressive model of subjectivity, according to which "differentiation happens *in relation to* the mother. . . . Separateness is defined relationally; . . . adequate separation, or differentiation, involves not merely perceiving the separateness, or otherness, of the other. It involves perceiving the person's subjectivity and selfhood as well."[25] Central to much feminist theory is the return of the mother, not as scapegoat or savior, but as the primary, if inadvertent, enforcer of patriarchal values as well as their victim, and thus as fulcrum of the private and public. Such a perspective leads to a radically new understanding of the way a child's development is culturally determined, especially by the effect on the individuation of female—and male—infants. The institution of motherhood in a patriarchal culture achieves not only the reproduction of mothering but the perpetuation of patriarchy.

[24] Work done over the past decades in reexamining and reconstructing the narrative of infantile development and explicating the social and cultural forces shaping that narrative is enormous. Among the most significant are Jessica Benjamin, *The Bonds of Love: Psychoanalysis, Feminism, and the Problem of Domination* (New York: Pantheon, 1988); Nancy Chodorow, *The Reproduction of Mothering: Psychoanalysis and the Sociology of Gender* (Berkeley: University of California Press, 1978); and Nancy Chodorow and Susan Contratto, "The Fantasy of the Perfect Mother," in *Rethinking the Family: Some Feminist Questions*, ed. Barrie Thorne and Marilyn Yalom (New York: Longman, 1982), 54–75; Jane Flax, "The Conflict between Nurturance and Autonomy in Mother-Daughter Relationships and within Feminism," *Feminist Studies* 4 (June 1978): 171–89; Dorothy Dinnerstein, *The Mermaid and the Minotaur: Sexual Arrangements and Human Malaise* (New York: Harper, 1977); Marianne Hirsch, "Review Essay: Mothers and Daughters," *Signs: Journal of Women in Culture and Society* 7, no. 1 (Autumn 1981): 200–222; Adrienne Rich, *Of Woman Born: Motherhood as Experience and Institution* (New York: Norton, 1976).

[25] Nancy Chodorow, "Gender, Relation, and Difference in Psychoanalytic Perspective," in *The Future of Difference*, ed. Hester Eisenstein and Alice Jardine (New Brunswick, N.J.: Rutgers University Press, 1985), 3–19, esp. 6.

More than almost any other novel in the nineteenth century in England or the United States, *Little Women* restores the previously absent, repressed mother to her powerful place in the female child's development. While other fictional women—Emma Wood-house, Maggie Tulliver, Dorothea Brooke, Jane Eyre—are cursed with absent or unloving mothers, the March girls are blessed (and cursed) with the most powerfully present mother in literature. Their subsequent adventures reveal the enormous difficulty they face in individuating fully in both social and erotic terms while enmeshed in Marmee's loving, coercive, socializing, maternal bonds. Their pilgrimage, then, is not merely a quest for ethical development, thwarted by the limitations of their culture, but a narrative of subjectivity that must accommodate both the active seduction of maternal oneness and the compelling desire for separation. Yet Alcott attempts to move beyond such futile polari-ties by depicting a dream of reconciliation between autonomy and community, a dream made possible by the radical female presence of an active mother in this text.

Much of *Little Women*'s power derives from its exploration of the previously repressed, complex mother-daughter relationship, without portraying that bond as either idealized perfection or pernicious destruction. Marmee loves and socializes, nurtures and stifles her daughters, offering them a vision of perfect love and oneness that heterosexuality cannot hope to duplicate, and an alternate model of identity through community, domesticity, and altruism that their culture can only tolerate by subsuming it in the archetype of female goodness that kills Beth. Thus the dream of reconciliation—of expressing subjectivity in/through community—is, like the quest for ethical development, subverted by the limita-tions of a patriarchal culture that consistently trivializes the fe-male's narrative and objectivizes her subjectivity. The vision of community, altruism, and caring for others that Marmee expresses is either ambiguous (as in her request that they give their Christmas breakfast for the poor), or destructive (as in the painful, diseased effect of Beth's extreme selflessness), or trivialized (as in the girls' foolish, domesticated experiences spending one week pleasing only themselves).

Even more profoundly, however, Marmee's active presence in this text raises the dangerous possibility of nonphallic eroticism, a different focus of desire. Once again, the contrast with Huck Finn is instructive. Huck's journey downriver, away from the Widow Brown and civilization, conforms with remarkable precision to the young boy's patriarchally enforced and approved development:

"The salient feature of male individuality is that it grows out of the repudiation of the primary identification with and dependency on the mother . . . [leading] to an individuality that stresses . . . difference as denial of commonality, separation as denial of connection; . . . where independence seems to exclude all dependency rather than be characterized by a balance of separation and connection."[26] In moving downriver, Huck moves consistently away from dependency and connection, separating completely from the trappings of civilization in his quest for absolute independence. Jo March, of course, neither seeks nor achieves such a selfhood. Rather, her intensely loving connection with her mother has fostered "a balance of separation and connectedness, of the capacities for agency and relatedness."[27] Her crisis occurs not so much from a need to resist dependency or assert autonomy as from a need to express desire. However, this quest is deeply complicated by the same powerful maternal figure who offers hope of a more balanced vision of identity.

For Marmee's seductive, loving presence, which creates a profound and inescapable homoerotic undercurrent throughout the novel, eventually subverts the appeal of heterosexual eroticism entirely, while the text utterly refuses to imagine or tolerate any other kind of desire. Thus while homoeroticism is never permitted direct expression, it dominates the actions and feelings of the female characters. Even Meg's first thought, after being married, is of her mother: "The minute she was fairly married, Meg cried, 'The first kiss for Marmee!' and turning, gave it with her heart on her lips" (234). More significantly, when Jo confesses her loneliness and desire for love after Beth's death, she rejects her mother's characterization of heterosexual love as "the best love of all," claiming "Mothers are the *best* lovers in the world, but I don't mind whispering to Marmee that I'd like to try all kinds" (400).

Yet the distorting compromises enforced by patriarchal culture require that a girl repress her primal, homoerotic love for her mother, shifting instead to a learned, differentiating heteroerotic love for her father. Just as the patriarchal context of their pilgrimage prevents the sisters from fully exploring the potential of a new understanding of the self in relation to others, or a new vision of separateness defined relationally, the imperatives of phallocentric culture demand that women resist "our earliest carnal interaction"

[26] Jessica Benjamin, "A Desire of One's Own: Psychoanalytic Feminism and Intersubjective Space," in *Feminist Studies: Critical Studies*, ed. Teresa de Lauretis (Bloomington: Indiana University Press, 1986), 78–101, esp. 80.
[27] Ibid., 82.

with mothers, thus producing "women [who] are encouraged to behave narcissistically as sex objects or masochistically as mothers, either position being a defense against the female body's resonance with primitive fears and needs."[28] Both reactions are distinctly evident in *Little Women*, from Amy's narcissistic objectification of herself to Meg's domestic retreat into invisibility and Beth's deadly masochism.

Jo most vividly acts out the painful implications of this culturally distorted psychic and erotic development. Jo is the most passionate in her resistance to adulthood, and especially to heterosexuality, wanting to marry Meg herself to keep the childhood family intact (187) and wishing that "wearing flat-irons on our heads would keep us from growing up" (189). Jo is also the most tormented about her own gender, presenting herself constantly in masculine images. Her cross-dressing language and behavior reflect very real conflict: as a boy, Jo would be socially independent, able to go off to war with her father, or to "run away [with Laurie] and have a capital time" (196). More importantly, she would also be compensated for the price of that independence—the loss of her pre-oedipal oneness with Marmee—by the "promise of another mommy as a reward for the renunciation" of her maternally directed desires.[29] Thus her desire to be a boy reveals her erotic attachment toward her mother, while her culture denies Jo both the possibility of independence and the promise of sexual gratification that patriarchy offers boys. At the same time, the nurturing female community of her family, rather than providing an alternative world, is eroded by death and marriage and shadowed by suggestions of triviality and patriarchal observation and objectification.

Jo's terror of heterosexuality is the most obvious result of her passionate attachment to Marmee, while her sense of her own "sexuality is muted by the fact that the woman she must identify with, her mother, is so profoundly desexualized."[30] Numerous critics have noted, for example, how foolish and unconvincing are the stated terms of her rejection of Laurie.[31] "Our quick tempers and

---

[28] Copelia Kahn, "The Hand That Rocks the Cradle: Recent Gender Theories and Their Implications," in *The (M)other Tongue: Essays in Feminist Psychoanalytic Interpretation*, ed. Shirley Nelson Garner, Claire Kahane, and Madelon Sprengnether (Ithaca, N.Y.: Cornell University Press, 1985), 72–88, esp. 77.

[29] Flax, 179.

[30] Benjamin, "A Desire of One's Own," 83.

[31] Nina Auerbach (n. 1 above), e.g., claims that the "reasons given in *Little Women* [for Jo's rejection of Laurie] seem more rationalization than explanation" (69). Anne Hollander (n. 1 above) notes that "Laurie cannot marry Jo because he is

strong wills would probably make us very miserable. . . . I'm homely and awkward and odd and old, and you'd be ashamed of me . . . and I shouldn't like elegant society and you would, and you'd hate my scribbling" (333–34). Jo and Laurie get along so well precisely because of their passions (quick tempers and strong wills), while Laurie has always been the most devoted advocate of Jo's literary endeavors (unlike her eventual husband, Professor Bhaer, who oversees the burning of all her writing). Furthermore, our initial image of Laurie is of a moody, passionate Italian musician, and hence of someone equally bored by the triviality of elegant society, the Romantic ideal brother-lover, not the wealthy Indian tea merchant he somewhat implausibly becomes.

Beneath the superficial absurdity of these claims is Jo's bitterly negative self-image, a wounded self-esteem entirely consistent with her vehement maternal identification in a patriarchal culture. However, Jo's refusal of Laurie is essentially and explicitly an absolute rejection of heterosexual passion: "I don't see why I can't love you as you want me to. I've tried, but I can't change the feeling, and it would be a lie to say I do when I don't" (331). Her most intense attachment is to Marmee; she wants to mother Laurie, not marry him. The ambiguity of Jo's rejection of him derives not from her repudiation of romantic love and the conventional "happy ending" but from the fact that she cannot, within the confines of this text and of heterosexuality, find any way to act out her own desires.

When Jo does finally marry, she turns to the elderly and impoverished scholar, Professor Bhaer, and she does so not in passion but in need, companionability, and loss. Moreover, she turns finally to a man identical to her own father, a weak yet punitive figure who reinforces that cruelly negative self-image which Laurie so consistently challenged. Jo's husband is both suggestively feminine (poor, alien, and powerless) and explicitly patriarchal (scholarly, repressive, and authoritarian). Her marriage suggests a capitulation to the conventional Freudian narrative of female development in which a woman marries her father. If she cannot marry Marmee, or love another woman erotically, she can follow the dictates of her culture by becoming her mother and marrying her father. In doing so, she confirms the elusive authority

---

immutably erotic and she refuses to learn that lesson" (36). According to Elizabeth Keyser (n. 1 above), in rejecting Laurie "Jo has not only betrayed a friend but a crucial part of herself which she cannot hope to recover" (449). For Martha Saxton (n. 1 above), Jo "refuses, thinking they are too much alike, too male. The fact that they enjoy each other and share interests and honesty argues against Jo's decision. But Louisa declares inexorably that Jo must not have fun" (11).

of Mr. March, who, despite his physical absence from the text, is the primary agent of trivialization and objectification. Moreover, Jo confirms the inadvertent authority of her mother as a socializing force, a woman who produces daughters adept in sacrifice and suffering but unequipped to express desire of any kind.

In portraying the maternal figure as radically present and vocal, Alcott reveals the enormous difficulties daughters experience in finding their own identity under such a powerful shadow—especially in a patriarchal context that refuses to tolerate a vision of active, communal subjectivity and that cannot tolerate any challenge to phallocentric eroticism. Yet Marmee's subversive presence also violates the usual narrative of female development. Jo remains inescapably the subject of her own story, and her eventual marriage is enormously complicated, rejecting conventional heterosexual romantic models of erotic love, while reconciling her with her father (or with patriarchy) and offering her a place of her own. As comrade, teacher, and mother in the school she inherits from her aunt and manages with her husband, she creates a life that combines intimacy and community with agency and independence.[32] The conclusion of her oedipal narrative moves tentatively, ambiguously, toward a new statement of desire, "a relationship to desire in the *freedom to:* freedom to be both with and distinct from the other."[33]

* * *

The woman's unconscious is "the noise" in the system, the defect. It is a surplus which patriarchal society has always wanted to get rid of by denying it any specificity, thus positing that same society's right to talk about it in terms of identity with and resemblance to the male model. This unconscious had to be tamed, silenced out of fear that, were it unexpectedly to return in the midst of the existing order, it would bring the machine to a deadly halt.[34]

[32] Jo's married life contains as many puzzles and contradictions as her choice of a husband. She inherits her property from the ferocious paternal aunt who deprived her of a visit to the Continent because of her independence and inability to speak French, and she succeeds in running a school with far greater financial and educational skill than did Bronson Alcott himself. Further, she becomes a far more powerful maternal figure than Marmee, but her new community is determinedly male. Indeed, she herself has only sons and does not achieve a professionalized version of female intimacy and domestic community.

[33] Benjamin, "A Desire of One's Own" (n. 26 above), 98.

[34] Josette Feral, "The Powers of Difference," in Eisenstein and Jardine, eds. (n. 25 above), 90.

Desire and anger, creativity and independence, remain problematic in *Little Women*. Yet the thrillers Alcott wrote before turning to children's fiction—and the thrillers Jo writes in *Little Women*—are filled with precisely the active female power the text itself denies. The women in Alcott's *Pauline's Passion and Punishment* and *Behind a Mask; Or, A Woman's Power* are as sensual and powerful as the March girls are sexless and sacrificial. Our new access to these thrillers gives greater edge to our understanding of Alcott's characterization of Jo March as a writer struggling with the patriarchal silencing enforced by Professor Bhaer. What Jo renounces when she burns her texts is the imaginative rendering of erotic, assertive women who impose their private fictions on the public world.

In contrast to the silenced, self-denying girls of *Little Women*, Jean Muir in *Behind a Mask* so successfully acts the role of a sweet woman that she marries the aristocratic patriarch of the household she originally enters as a despised and powerless governess. More significantly, she prevails despite the fact that the rest of the family has learned the truth about her sordid past, and she even manages to burn the letters that inscribe her sins. In *Pauline's Passion*, the angry, jilted governess marries a young heir who worships her, and together they act out her carefully crafted script of revenge. While the conclusion is more ambiguous than that of *Behind a Mask*, the story never permits an easy splitting of good woman/bad woman, affirming Pauline Valary's full, flawed humanity in an enormously intelligent, angry, and seductive woman.

This gothic model of female assertion is, of course, deeply problematic in its duplication of precisely the exploitive, manipulative male model of power it seeks to evade. The pattern of these thrillers makes clear that Alcott had difficulty visualizing a new form of power, that she remained trapped by a seemingly endless process of either/or choices in which "two complementary elements that should be held in tension are instead set up as opposites, with one side idealized and the other devalued."[35]

In the thrillers, however, Jean Muir and Pauline Valary do act out their fantasies and desires—however ambiguous or male-identified their image of assertion may be. In *Little Woman*, Jo March's literary depiction of those same desires is absolutely effaced and domesticated by Professor Bhaer. In the thrillers, female duplicity and manipulation win power, wealth, and love; in *Little Women*, Marmee's suppression of her own anger is held up as a model of virtue: "I am angry nearly every day of my life . . . but

---

[35] Benjamin, "A Desire of One's Own," 91.

I have learned not to show it; and I still hope to learn not to feel it, though it may take me another forty years to do so" (75). The extremes of each text suggest the dilemma Alcott faced in devising images of female power and subjectivity beyond the irreconcilable dialectic of Marmee versus Jean Muir.

As generations of young readers immediately realize, however, Jo March seems at first to offer precisely such an alternative. Her voice is the first one we hear in the novel, naming the truth we all secretly recognize: that Christmas is about presents, and affirming "I like good strong words that mean something" (34). Yet, as we have seen, the text itself resists Jo's linguistic power, trivializing her early writing efforts and stressing the dangers of her anger rather than the authenticity of her voice. Thus the manuscript she hopes will be "good enough to print" (72) is ruthlessly diminutized, while the private, domestic writing of "The Pickwick Portfolio" is affirmed as "filled with original tales, poetry, local news, funny advertisements, *and hints, in which they good-naturedly reminded each other of their faults and shortcomings*" (95; emphasis mine).

The novel consistently devalues Jo's public voice, while her private writing, especially when it contains self-correction and criticism, is permitted. So when Jo creeps from the garret—where, as subversive as any madwoman in nineteenth-century fiction, she has converted the domesticity of "an old tin kitchen" (137) into a writer's desk—and takes her work to a publisher, her triumph is immediately undercut. Publication of her story leads to dreams that she may eventually "be independent and earn the praise of those she loved" (145).[36] Yet immediately after this, Meg is complaining that "nothing pleasant ever does happen in this family" (146), and within moments a telegram arrives with news of Mr. March's illness. Thus Jo's triumphant authorship is effaced by textual proximity to the catastrophe that deranges the household. Rather than supporting her family with her skills as a professional writer, Jo is forced into the self-destructive sacrifice of selling her hair to raise money for her father.

We do not hear of her writing again until book 2, when we learn that Jo, supplanted by Amy as companion to their disagreeable aunt, now earns "a dollar a column for her 'rubbish' as she called it" (223) writing for a local newspaper. Beyond its subversive function in offering her financial independence and freedom from domestic servitude, writing also provides the distinctly erotic lure of a plunge

[36] As Elizabeth Keyser (n. 1 above), notes, however, "the two wishes are incompatible: to achieve independence she will have to assert herself in such a way as to incur blame; and to win the praise of those she loves best, she will have to curtail her striving for independence" (450–51).

"into a vortex" which "she gave herself up to . . . with entire abandon, and [during which she] led a blissful life, unconscious of want,
care, or bad weather, while she sat safe and happy in an imaginary
world" (246). When she moves beyond the utility of her dollar-a-
column rubbish, however, to try her hand at thrillers, Marmee in-
tuitively feels "disquiet" and, indeed, we learn that Mrs. March
always looks a bit anxious when "genius [takes] to burning" (248).

This maternal disapproval is mild, however, when compared to
Mr. March's chilling response when Jo's thriller wins $100: "You
can do better than this, Jo. Aim at the highest, and never mind the
money" (249). Chastened, Jo retreats from the erotics of authorship
to a communal vision of literary expression only on behalf of others:
"I never get on when I think of myself alone, so it will help me to
work for you, don't you see?" (249). Again the power of Jo's
imagination is diminutized—even disparaged—by paternal authority, while her financial independence is domesticated, her stories
transformed into payments for the butcher, a new carpet, groceries,
and gowns (249).

Furthermore, even the potentially radical vision of communal
imagination and expression for the sake of others is subverted
during Jo's attempt to write something grander than thrillers.
Following everyone's (contradictory) advice, she predictably
pleases no one, and her first book produces such vehement criticism and ignorant praise that she is "thrown into a state of
bewilderment from which it took her some time to recover" (251).
Thus a potential synthesis of the erotics of voice with the altruism
of community responsibility fails; public self-expression remains at
best conflicting and at worst bitterly painful.

Jo's growing mistrust of her own voice is reinforced by her next
experience in speaking her mind, which deprives her of "several
years of pleasure, and [provides] a timely lesson in the art of
holding her tongue" (275). As punishment for her assertion of
independence—"I don't like favors, they oppress and make me feel
like a slave" (275)—and her difficulty speaking the erotic, romantic
French language, Jo loses the chance to visit Europe. The terms of
this loss explicitly blame her "blunt manners and too independent
spirit," leaving Jo wishing she could "learn to keep . . . quiet" (285).

Indeed, keeping quiet is her final lesson. Returning to her
thrillers in order to earn money to help care for the sickly Beth, Jo
is troubled by the dissonance between these tales of "banditti,
counts, gypsies, nuns, and dutchesses" (320) and her increasingly
internalized sense of female goodness, at once reinforced and
undercut by the vision of Beth's saintly, lingering death. The
narrator confirms the pernicious effect of these money-earning

tales: "Unconsciously she was beginning to desecrate some of the womanliest attributes of a woman's character . . . she was feeding heart and fancy on dangerous and unsubstantial food" (321). If Jo's thrillers are anything like Alcott's, then she is indeed violating those attributes of the woman's role she has been so painfully taught, exploring alternate images of female power. A steady diet of this Keatsian food might well whet her appetite for a new kind of fiction, in which independence is rewarded, and women are active, erotic, and assertive without being exploitive, manipulative, and destructive.

However, the forces of patriarchy that so consistently limit the choices in the novel once again rescue her from this dangerous and seductive vortex. Professor Bhaer is "moved to help her with an impulse as quick and natural as that which would prompt him to put out his hand to save a baby from a puddle" (325). Diminutized once more by this image of herself as an infant (while her imaginative world becomes a mere puddle), Jo endures a lecture on the evils of thrillers that conclusively inscribes her into the patriarchal order. When she rereads her own fictions, she sees them through the "Professor's mental or moral spectacles . . . the faults of these poor stories glared at her dreadfully and filled her with dismay" (326).

Powerless to resist the vision of selfless goodness with which Bhaer demolishes her efforts at financial freedom and literary expression, Jo abandons her own vision, stuffing "the whole bundle into her stove, nearly setting the chimney afire with the blaze" (327). Yet her subversive inner voice is still not silenced; Jo internalizes the professor's vision of her writing (and hence of herself as object) but still wishes she "didn't feel uncomfortable when doing wrong" (327). In reproving Jo for her seditious desires, the narrator confirms their legitimacy, claiming that "principles . . . may seem like prison walls to impatient youth, but . . . prove sure foundations to build character upon in womanhood" (327).

Little womanhood, then, is built upon an imprisoning set of values, and Jo's silence can be seen as voluntary incarceration in the only role she knows—the self-denying goodness of Marmee. Once again, Jo is both diminutized and objectified by a father figure: her reluctant conflagration of her life's work is observed by Professor Bhaer, who is "watching to see if she would accept and profit by his reproof . . . and he [is] satisfied" (328).

Later this bitter renunciation of voice is reinforced by another vision of goodness, when Jo promises the dying Beth to take her place "and be everything to Father and Mother . . . Jo renounced her old ambition, pledged herself to a new and better one, acknowledging the poverty of other desires, and feeling the blessed solace of a belief in the immortality of love" (382). Thus while the pilgrimage of ethical development allows ambiguous success and the narrative of female subjectivity explores subversive resolutions, the quest for artistic voice appears conclusively doomed, with Jo pledging to replace her deathly sister and remain permanently infantilized, married to her own father, duplicating her own mother's loving socialization and coercion.

* * *

The power of *Little Women* derives in large measure from the contradictions and tensions it exposes and from the pattern it establishes of subversive, feminist exploration colliding repeatedly against patriarchal repression. Like the log cabin quilt pattern Elaine Showalter uses to explore the underlying structure of *Uncle Tom's Cabin, Little Women,* too, is constructed on a "compositional principle . . . [of] contrast between light and dark,"[37] between exploration and entrapment, desire and denial, expression and repression. What Showalter terms the "symbolic relationship to boundaries"[38] in the quilting pattern perfectly expresses the narrative pattern in *Little Women,* which consistently moves us to the outer boundaries of representational fiction in its effort to depict a resolution beyond the either/or constraints of the author's culture.

The text is constructed of contrasting pieces that depict both the female narrative of ethical development and its dark, insidious alternative of static female saintliness; both the passionate quest for a reconciliation of desire with separation and its darker suggestions about maternal eroticism, coercion, and socialization, both the artist's search for authentic female voice and its painful shadowing image of the failure of existing forms to express that voice. In each voyage or pilgrimage—each pattern of female quest—Alcott moves the narrative simultaneously to the borders of possibility in patriarchal culture and to the deep core of yearning for maternal oneness. This book is passionately memorable for young girls because it warns of the dangers that lie ahead—domestic incarceration, narcissistic objectification, sacrificial goodness, and the enforced silencing of voice, eroticism, and anger—and partly because it offers an alternative vision of adulthood-in-community, of female subjectivity, and above all of female oedipal narrative, restoring the lost, maternal presence in our lives.

The sites where Alcott's narrative flounders, where the shape of her textual pattern crashes against the absolute nature of her

[37] Showalter (n. 8 above), 235.
[38] Ibid.

culture's borders, are the sites we are still exploring today. If her novel fails fully to sustain an image of resolution that transcends either/or choices, her failure suggests much that remains real and enduring in our own experience.

Department of English
Tufts University

LAURA INGALLS WILDER AND ROSE WILDER LANE: THE POLITICS OF A MOTHER-DAUGHTER RELATIONSHIP

ANITA CLAIR FELLMAN

In her diary entry for April 10, 1933, Rose Wilder Lane wrote:

> It is amazing how my mother can make me suffer. Yesterday
> . . . she was here. . . . She has it all planned. Cut off the
> electric bill and she can manage indefinitely. She's doing it
> to "let me go." Well, after all she didn't have electricity
> before; I've given her six "wonderfully easy years." How she
> hates it, that I'm her "sole source of support." Implicit in
> every syllable and tone, the fact that I've failed, fallen down
> on the job, been the broken reed. But never mind (brightly)
> she's able to manage nicely, thank you! . . . Perhaps an hour
> of simply hellish misery.[1]

Lane—divorced, childless, forty-six years old, widely traveled—had
come to live on her parents' Missouri farm voluntarily. She attributed her inability to leave to an only child's feelings of obligation

Research for this study was aided by grants from the Social Sciences and
Humanities Research Council of Canada and from the Herbert Hoover Presidential
Library Association. I am very grateful to Vivien Clair for her invaluable help on the
manuscript.
[1] Rose Wilder Lane, April 10, 1933, Diaries and Notes Series, no. 47, Rose Wilder
Lane Papers (hereafter Lane Papers), Herbert Hoover Presidential Library, West
Branch, Iowa. Both women's works are quoted with the permission of Roger Lea
MacBride.

This essay originally appeared in *Signs*, vol. 15, no. 3, Spring 1990.

toward her aging parents and to financial difficulties exacerbated by the Depression. Nonetheless, she also recognized that other forces may have caused her and her mother, Laura Ingalls Wilder, to live in uncomfortable proximity: "The curious thing is that she's sincerely reaching for some kind of companionship with me. She's trying to be friends. . . . She wants genuine warmth, sympathy. She has not the faintest notion what she's doing to me. But underneath, there's not a trace of generosity in her. (Anymore than there is, really, in me.)"[2]

Each woman needed but could not satisfy the other. Their desires and offerings failed to coincide. Wilder had come to depend upon her daughter to provide the means, and sometimes the money, to alleviate her profound anxiety about economic insecurity. Her offer to let Lane go may have bespoken a sincere intention to break her dependence on her daughter; it may also have been a gesture that she knew would be refused. Lane, on the other hand, wanting affirmation from Wilder but priding herself on the sacrifices she was making to help her mother, was angry and hurt at the intimation that this help was expendable. Resentful, she acknowledged Wilder's lifelong power over her: "She made me so miserable when I was a child that I've never got over it. I'm morbid: I'm all raw nerves. I know I should be more robust."[3]

The attempts by Lane and Wilder to meet their own needs for both nurturance and individuation dominated their relationship and informed the way they looked at the world. This common struggle between a mother and a daughter was remarkable in their case, for their demands on each other played a central role in their adult lives and their struggle did not remain private as it does for most. Wilder and Lane not only recorded it in their personal papers, they transformed it into literature. Because of the nature of the literary forms they chose, the political and mythic implications of their drama are apparent.

Laura Ingalls Wilder (1867–1957) is known as the author of the popular *Little House* books. *The Little House in the Big Woods*, the first book in the seven-volume chronicle of American pioneer life, sets the tone for the rest of the series in celebrating the virtues of individual effort and family self-sufficiency.[4] Paralleling the psy-

---

[2] Ibid.

[3] Ibid.

[4] It is the seven books dealing with her own family and published during her lifetime that I will be referring to as the *Little House* books. *Farmer Boy* (New York: Harper & Bros., 1933), the second book that she wrote, describes the New York state childhood of her husband, Almanzo Wilder. *The First Four Years* (New York: Harper & Row, 1971) is an unrevised account, published after the deaths of both Wilder and Lane, of the early years of Wilder's marriage.

chological isolation of the modern nuclear family, the Ingalls family lives alone, without daily access to neighbors or kin. Artfully, the author links their emotional self-sufficiency with a gratifying material self-reliance. The family's westward trek begins when new settlers invade their solitude, driving the game away. Much of what millions of children all over the world—and their parents—know about the pioneers and early farmers of the American Middle West comes from these children's books. The values and relationships described in Wilder's stories have served as benchmarks against which Americans have measured their own families.[5]

Wilder's daughter, Rose Wilder Lane (1886–1968), was a prolific journalist, best-selling novelist, and short-story writer whose work on a wide variety of subjects appeared from the 1910s through the 1930s in such major popular magazines as *Harper's Monthly, Country Gentleman, Saturday Evening Post,* and *Ladies' Home Journal.* During the years that she lived near her parents, her writings gradually became a paean to individualism and an explicitly political critique of the emerging welfare state. Lane is not as widely remembered today as her mother (although in the 1920s and 1930s Lane was by far the more famous figure), yet she retains a secure reputation among libertarians as one of the pioneers of the antistatist philosophy and politics that have been reemerging in the United States since the 1940s.

I began with an interest in the political philosophies of Wilder and Lane, but after reading through their papers, I became convinced that the intense and troubled relationship between the mother and daughter documented there (largely from Lane's perspective) was not irrelevant to my original focus but central to it. Their accumulated frustrations with each other predisposed each to be critical of a political system they saw as increasingly premised on interdependency. To understand the genesis and shape of their political ideas, one has to understand the dynamics of the relations between the two of them.

Keeping in mind the risks in applying twentieth-century social and psychological theories to a relationship that had its origins in the nineteenth century, I suggest that contemporary feminist writings about mothers and daughters, when used cautiously, illuminate the Wilder-Lane relationship. Furthermore, the well-documented evidence of that relationship can actually help qualify

[5] Charles Elliott, review of *The First Four Years* by Laura Ingalls Wilder, *Time* (March 15, 1971), 92; Elizabeth Segel, "Laura Ingalls Wilder's America: An Unflinching Assessment," *Children's Literature in Education* 8, no. 2 (Summer 1977): 64; Frances Flanagan, "A Tribute to Laura Ingalls Wilder," *Elementary English* 34, no. 4 (April 1957): 203; Emily Hanke van Zee, "A Letter to the National Broadcasting Corporation," *Horn Book Magazine* 51, no. 1 (February 1975): 94.

and refine some of the recent theories. Focusing on one mother and daughter in a specific historical setting enables us more clearly to identify the relationship as a social, economic, psychological, even intellectual creation.[6]

Good mothering is an ideological construct. Referring to white, middle-class America, Nancy Chodorow and Susan Contratto have warned us that "blame and idealization of mothers have become our cultural ideology," and that even feminists share in the widely held "fantasy of the perfect mother."[7] There is a tendency for many of us to feel cheated, possibly irreparably damaged, if we have had less than an unambivalently loving parent who has achieved toward us a perfect balance of nurturance, acceptance, and encouragement of autonomy. If we think ourselves entitled to such a mother, we may attribute all or many of our problems to that lack.

The cultural sentimentalization of motherhood and the ideal of maternal sacrifice in the nineteenth century did not imply that mothers were actively responsible for the psychological well-being of their children. By the end of the nineteenth century, however, as Nancy Theriot points out, female advice authors began writing about the rights of the child in this regard. "A child . . . must in every way, be made happy," wrote one such advisor, directing mothers to "make a child understand that you love him; prove it in your actions."[8] Unlike her mother, who came from a generation less preoccupied with either happiness or parental obligation, Rose Wilder Lane appears to have accepted this conception of the importance of love from an openly affectionate mother. Her reactions to her mother imply the expectation, and late in life she made explicit her assumption of its significance when she wrote to a friend that newborn children need love that they often do not get, "and they keep on wanting it for a long time after they no longer need it actually, sometimes all their lives. . . . When a shallow,

---

[6] Nancy Chodorow, "Gender, Relation, and Difference in Psychoanalytic Perspective," in *The Future of Difference*, ed. Hester Eisenstein and Alice Jardine (Boston: G. K. Hall, 1980), 3–19, esp. 16.

[7] Nancy Chodorow and Susan Contratto, "The Fantasy of the Perfect Mother," in *Rethinking the Family: Some Feminist Questions*, ed. Barrie Thorne and Marilyn Yalom (New York: Longman, 1982), 54–75, esp. 65. Even in American society, not all groups equally share this tendency. For instance, many African-American women appear to be able to put their mothers' efforts on their behalf into a context and consequently have more realistic expectations of them. See Gloria I. Joseph and Jill Lewis, *Common Differences: Conflicts in Black and White Feminist Perspectives* (Boston: South End Press, 1981), 75–76, 94–103.

[8] Prudence Saur, *Maternity: A Book for Every Wife and Mother* (Chicago: L. P. Miller, 1891), 376, quoted in Nancy Theriot, *The Biosocial Construction of Femininity: Mothers and Daughters in Nineteenth-Century America* (Westport, Conn.: Greenwood, 1988), 145.

frivolous Claire Booth Luce joins the Catholic Church, she wants Mama to love her, as Mama didn't when she was born."[9]

It seems appropriate, then, to look at the particular difficulties between mothers and daughters in that dominant American middle-class society of the last one hundred years to which Wilder and Lane belonged, so as to identify the dynamics that Lane may have interpreted as contributing to her unhappiness. Given a cultural ideal that suggests that a good mother loves her child unambivalently, there is much in the complex interactions between mothers and daughters that might contribute to a daughter's sense of grievance and to her efforts to compensate for the deficiencies of mothering.

Much feminist scholarship has indicated the difficulties for women in serving as the primary caretakers in societies that devalue them as individuals and deny them both resources to do their job properly and support for them apart from their mothering role.[10] A mother in such a society, plagued by problems of autonomy and self-worth, may have trouble asserting her own subjectivity to her child, may be so ambivalent about the requirements of her gender role as to undermine her ability to nurture, or may require complete identification with her child in order to feel whole.

When a mother cannot permit her children to differentiate from her, a son has his sexual difference and his anticipated place among men to compel a modicum of disengagement. However, a mother and daughter are left with the more subtle task of recognizing and accepting the other's subjectivity, of being like the other, yet not like her. The need of each to differentiate herself from the other, combined with an equally urgent hunger for connection as an affirmation of self, makes a potent mixture.[11] The daughter may not be able to become the person the mother wanted to be, compelling the mother to distance herself so as to avoid the pain of experiencing again her own impudence or timidity, gawkiness or flirtatiousness. Her task as a primary enforcer of the feminization of a female child may cause the mother (intending to prepare the daughter for life) to be anxious on the daughter's behalf and hypercritical of her

[9] Rose Wilder Lane to Garet Garrett, July 8, 1953, Lane Papers.

[10] Adrienne Rich, *Of Woman Born: Motherhood as Experience and Institution* (New York: Norton, 1976); Judith Arcana, *Our Mother's Daughters* (Berkeley, Calif.: Shameless Hussy Press, 1979); Jane Flax, "The Conflict between Nurturance and Autonomy in Mother/Daughter Relationships and within Feminism," *Feminist Studies* 4, no. 1 (February 1978): 171–89, are but a few of the feminist writings that deal with the impediments to good mothering in American society.

[11] Jessica Benjamin, *The Bonds of Love: Psychoanalysis, Feminism, and the Problem of Domination* (New York: Pantheon, 1988), 133–81.

child, which may well leave the daughter, expecting more, with a sense of impoverished partisanship.

In consequence, the daughter, even as an adult, may well impose on others, especially her own daughter, her need for affirmation and approval. Chodorow argues that women become mothers in part to regain a sense of being mothered, and Paula Caplan suggests that the mother's efforts to prepare the daughter for the nurturant role demanded of women in our society starts with the efforts to teach her "to take care of her closest companion, her mother."[12] By socializing her daughter in the approved manner, she benefits by being the first object of her daughter's apprentice nurturing. The daughter may collaborate in the mother's hunger for mothering, or she may resist, seeking mothering from other women, from men, or from her daughters. Possibly she may move between these two modes at various stages of her life.[13]

For some women the needs or patterns established by the mother-daughter relationship extend outward, beyond family relationships, into the shaping of work environments that allow for the kind of mutual nurturing with which they feel most comfortable. Carol Gilligan has argued that a sense of embeddedness, based on the daughter's connectedness to her mother, characterizes women's ethical views: they are preoccupied with context and responsibility, rather than with abstract rights, as is presumably more common with males.[14]

On the other hand, there are some daughters who, possibly for reasons of survival, come to repudiate attachment as a form of dangerous dependence. After all, there are female loners and women who are emotionally distant from their mothers. This process of separation may occur early in childhood when these girls' necessarily "more emphatic individuation" may have certain, but not all, elements in common with the process Chodorow describes for boys.[15] Alternatively, it may be an adult's attempt to protect herself from years of pain. This individual may also be drawn, more than the women Gilligan describes, to an ethic of

[12] Nancy Chodorow, *The Reproduction of Mothering: Psychoanalysis and the Sociology of Gender* (Berkeley: University of California Press, 1978), 90; Paula J. Caplan, *Between Women: Lowering the Barriers* (Toronto: Personal Liberty, 1981), 56.

[13] While males may also receive inadequate mothering, their chances of compensating for this lack through their marriages or other relationships is greater than women's likelihood of being well nurtured by male partners whose socialization and sense of gender identity make them less likely to take on such a role.

[14] Carol Gilligan, *In a Different Voice: Psychological Theory and Women's Development* (Cambridge, Mass.: Harvard University Press, 1982).

[15] See Chodorow, *Reproduction of Mothering*, 166–67.

rights, to a morality of noninterference. Such women may be more common than we suppose, and we need to know about their emotional life histories and about the values they espouse in order to have a richer and more varied picture of women's personalities and of their impact on a host of institutions.

In this regard, the intertwined histories of Laura Ingalls Wilder and Rose Wilder Lane are very informative, both as to the nature of the dynamics between them and as to their interpretation of their own life histories. Their fruitless quests for affirmation by the other, and their preoccupation with autonomy ultimately colored their views on the desirability of self-sufficiency and on the appropriate roles for family and state. These views permeate their writings, and as popular writers their deliberations on these subjects have contributed to the transmission of political individualism from one generation to the next.

Although Wilder and Lane drew heavily on a tradition of family stories for their own writing, they were also the inheritors of several generations of unchronicled experiences that may well have shaped their relations as mother and daughter. Generation after generation the women in Laura's family had raised their daughters in difficult conditions. Her maternal grandmother, Charlotte Quiner, who before her marriage had attended a female seminary in Boston, was widowed in 1846 on the Wisconsin frontier with a large family when Laura's mother, Caroline, was only seven.[16] Although Quiner eventually remarried, her children had to buckle down early to the grueling adult tasks on a new homestead. The experience gave Caroline a deep hunger for stability and for "a mother's watchful care and a sister's tender love."[17]

Marriage to Charles Ingalls in 1860 may have provided Caroline with many pleasures, but stability and proximity to her mother's and sister's company were not among them. The Ingalls family's frequent moves from one unsettled frontier area to the next, prompted both by economic difficulties and by Charles Ingalls' restlessness, made life lonely, and housekeeping, even with four daughters to help, an endless round of demanding responsibilities. Mary and Laura, as the two older girls, were pressed early into taking on their share of housework. Caroline tried valiantly to make sure that, despite their rambles, her girls would be both educated and ladylike. Mary took to this regimen more easily than Laura who, as she later told Rose, had a temper that "didn't grow any less

---

[16] William T. Anderson, "The Literary Apprenticeship of Laura Ingalls Wilder," *South Dakota History* 13, no. 4 (Winter 1983): 301.

[17] Caroline Quiner's school composition is quoted in Donald Zochert, *Laura: The Life of Laura Ingalls Wilder* (New York: Avon, 1976), 10.

as she grew larger" and who was called a "wildcat" by her big boy cousins because "she bit and scratched and put up a good fight on occasion."[18] Mary's report of eleven-year-old Laura's snowball throwing activities at school brought a warning from their mother that she was no longer to play with the boys in this manner.[19] This must have been hard for Laura, who recalled years later that the only way she had been able to endure what she had perceived as her homeliness as a girl had been through her ability to outdo the boys at their games.[20]

When a childhood illness caused Mary to be blind, Laura, at age twelve, was left with a greater share of housekeeping tasks and a mass of contradictory feelings about her own rebelliousness. Her high school teacher in De Smet, Dakota Territory, urged Laura's family to keep her in school as long as possible, but she relinquished her own wishes for a college education to begin teaching school, while not yet sixteen, to aid her parents in sending Mary to a college for the blind.[21] When, at eighteen, she married Almanzo (Manly) Wilder, Laura seems to have escaped from her family's pressing responsibilities into a reprise of childhood with an easygoing husband who gratified her material wants and who indulged her desire for frequent, unladylike horseback rides across the prairie.

The arrival of their daughter, Rose, in 1886, along with successive natural and economic disasters that threatened the Wilder farm outside of De Smet, put an abrupt end to their brief carefree period. Dust storms, hailstorms, and drought gave them one bad year after the next. Diptheria, followed by some mysterious ailment, left Manly weakened and with a permanent limp. An infant son born in 1889 lived only a few weeks. Laura's anxiety about their economic situation, which had begun to resemble the decades-long marginal existence of her own family, was compounded because Manly's optimism often overrode his realism.

Laura's anxieties, communicated to her young daughter through her frequent irritability, induced a kind of guilt in Rose. Already possessed of a sense that she might be a burden to her mother, Rose as a young child erroneously believed herself responsible for one of the more serious debacles of those years, the destruction of their house by fire. Although in *The First Four Years*, Laura recorded

[18] Laura Ingalls Wilder to Lane, January 25, 1938, Laura Ingalls Wilder Series (hereafter LIW Series), Lane Papers.

[19] Zochert, 125.

[20] Wilder to Lane, December 1937, LIW Series, Lane Papers.

[21] Laura Ingalls Wilder, "Pioneer Girl," 170, manuscript, Notes and Resource Materials, LIW Series, Lane Papers. This is the earlier of two typed versions.

leaving the stove unwatched herself, Rose had earlier maintained that she, trying to be helpful to a sick mother, had put more wood into the stove and set fire to the house. "I quite well remember," she wrote when an adult, "watching the house burn, with everything we owned in the world, and knowing that I had done it."[22]

Later, the family, in debt, moved to De Smet, and the Wilders did wage labor to maintain themselves and to save money for a migration from South Dakota to the Missouri Ozarks. While her parents worked, Rose spent her days with Grandma Caroline Ingalls. Lane's semi-autobiographical story about this period stresses the young mother's concern that her little daughter was failing to live up to the standards for goodness and industry set by a hard-to-please grandmother: "[Mama] never failed to ask Grandma a little anxiously, 'Has she been a good girl, Ma?'" Sometimes the relentlessly honest answer would be, "I don't want to tell you . . . but I've got to. She has not been very diligent." Then, the narrator of the story recalled, "A little sigh, no more than a sad breath, would come from Mama's chest."[23] If this is a faithful recapitulation of the dynamics in Rose's own family, Rose's inadequate behavior may have reminded Laura of her own childhood difficulties in meeting her mother's exacting standards.

The Wilders' years in South Dakota were capped by the Panic of 1893 and followed by the uphill struggle from 1894 on to establish a farm in the rocky soil of the Ozarks. The hard times sobered the family. Poverty in a cliquey, established Missouri town carried a meaning different from the shared poverty of the frontier settlement in Dakota Territory. Given their shaky economic and social position, Wilder, at least in Lane's gloomier recollections, seems to have been too busy and too anxious to provide the kind of support and acceptance that her young daughter craved. Manly Wilder, although better natured, became increasingly taciturn—his wife occasionally referred to him as "the oyster"—and he somehow lacked authority within the family to act as a dependable buffer between mother and daughter.[24]

[22] Rose Wilder Lane, "I Discovered the Secret of Happiness on the Day I Tried to Kill Myself," *Cosmopolitan* 80, no. 6 (June 1926): 42; Wilder, *The First Four Years* (n. 4 above), 128. For other indications that Lane believed herself to have been a burden, see Rose Wilder Lane, "Setting," in Laura Ingalls Wilder, *On the Way Home, The Diary of a Trip from South Dakota to Mansfield, Missouri in 1894* (New York: Harper & Row, 1962), 4.

[23] Rose Wilder Lane, "Grandpa's Fiddle" (n.d.), Manuscript Series, Lane Papers.

[24] "Mama Bess" (the family name for Laura Ingalls Wilder) is the person to whom Lane addressed her letters over the years, even though the letters were meant for both parents; "my mother" is the subject of many entries in Lane's diary. Lane owed money to Laura Ingalls Wilder, not Manly Wilder. The tension between mothers and

Prepared though she was to market nostalgia for the past in her later writings, Lane rarely was romantic about her own early years. She characterized the childhood of both her mother's and her own generation as "a hard, narrow, relentless life. It was not comfortable. Nothing was made easy for us. We did not like work and we were not supposed to like it; we were supposed to work and we did. We did not like discipline, so we suffered until we disciplined ourselves. . . . And we did not like that way of life. We rebelled against it because we did not like it."[25]

Although Lane left home in her mid-teens, sampling a variety of careers and places to live before becoming a globe-trotting journalist in 1915, she did not cast off her parents either emotionally or financially. Deeply scarred by their precarious financial situation during her childhood, Lane exhibited for much of her life an exceptionally strong sense of obligation to help her family. Before making what she thought would be a permanent move to Albania, Lane, who by this point had long been divorced, from 1924 to 1926 returned for long stretches to her parents' farm to help them put their social lives on a more solid footing.[26] Until the 1940s she sought to ease the family's economic situation as well. Her assumption, one commonly held in farm families, was that her mother's labor could subsidize the uncertain earning power of the family farm. From 1910 onward, she urged her mother, who was already publishing articles on poultry and on farm life, to devote more energy to writing for pay. From 1911 to 1926, when Wilder served as contributor, home editor, and columnist of the *Missouri Ruralist*, Lane often helped her prepare articles. Once Lane broke into the national periodical market in the late 1910s, she was ambitious for her mother to do so as well.

---

daughters forms the basis of most of the stories in *Old Home Town* (New York: Longmans, Green, 1935), Lane's fictional recreation of growing up in a small town at the turn of the century. For a rare glimpse of Manly Wilder's personality and place in the family, see William T. Anderson, "Laura Ingalls Wilder and Rose Wilder Lane: The Continuing Collaboration," *South Dakota History* 16, no. 2 (Summer 1986): 89–143, esp. 119; hereafter cited as "The Continuing Collaboration."

[25] Lane, *Old Home Town*, 23.

[26] Helen Boylston, who was Lane's housemate during these years, characterized that sojourn as "Mama says come, so she came." See Anderson, "The Continuing Collaboration," 92. Wilder described herself in a letter to her aunt, Martha Carpenter, as having had "a serious sickness, very near to nervous prostration" and as not yet very strong (Wilder to Carpenter, June 22, 1925, LIW Series, Lane Papers). The relation, if any, between Lane's plans to move to Albania and Wilder's sickness are not known.

Their careers as writers would be the arena in which their demands on each other were most fully articulated. Initially Lane relished her unusual role as journeywoman to her mother's apprentice, while Wilder was ambivalent about her dependence upon her daughter's editing. For a long time Wilder did not take seriously the skill involved in applying her talent for language and storytelling to the creation of polished compositions.[27] She expressed her resistance to Lane's thorough reshaping of her pieces by concluding that the articles were no longer hers because her daughter was doing all the work. "Don't be absurd about my doing the work on your article," Lane responded to one such complaint made by Wilder in 1919 in regard to her first article published in a national magazine. "I didn't rewrite it a bit more than I rewrite [the work of other authors]. . . . And not so much, for at least your copy was the meat of the article."[28]

While it is true that Wilder needed to learn some of the writing skills that Lane had already picked up, it is also the case that Lane needed to assume a position of seniority, even authority, over her mother so that Wilder's good fortune would be clearly dependent upon her. In the same letter in which she downplayed her role as rewriter, Lane also commented: "Well, I don't suppose [the editor] would have apologized for the size of the check, which is really a fairly decent price . . . considering that your name has as yet no commercial value, except that she knew I would think it very small if I had done the article myself, and she did not want to give me cause for selling my copy anywhere else."[29]

In 1924, Wilder's similar complaint that an article sold to *Country Gentleman* really had been her daughter's work rather than her own led to Lane's complex bid for acceptance, not just as an adult, but as an adult with authority over her mother: "[As] long as you live, you never will believe anything I tell you is the truth. . . . Above all, you must *listen* to me. . . . If you don't do what I tell you to, you must at least have good hard reasons for not doing it . . . and be able to show how and where and why your work is better because you didn't do as I said. . . . Just because I was once three years old, you honestly oughtn't to think that I'm never going to know anything more than a three-year-old. Sometime you ought to let me grow up."[30]

[27] For a detailed description and insightful analysis of the literary collaboration of the two women, see the two articles by Anderson (nn. 16, 24 above).

[28] Lane to Wilder, April 11, 1919, LIW Series, Lane Papers.

[29] Ibid.

[30] Lane to Wilder, November 23, 1924, LIW Series, Lane Papers.

The two women set up an elaborate dance in which Wilder both sought Lane's help with her writing and resisted it, and Lane helped with increasing ambivalence, trying to induce gratitude and guilt for the time and effort she expended. While Wilder never gave up either her expression of anxiety over the work she was causing her daughter or her hopes that she could do the writing wholly on her own, by the early 1930s she came reluctantly to accept her dependence upon Lane's editing: "I am glad you like my use of words and my descriptions, but without your fine touch, it would be a flop."[31] By the mid-1930s, however, Lane came to realize that her own involvement in her mother's career as a writer was not the straightforward effort to make her parents financially independent that she had long pretended.

Although Wilder continued her association with the *Missouri Ruralist* until the mid-1920s, she did not pursue writing for national magazines very assiduously. In 1925, perhaps roused by her own mother's death and by her daughter's suggestion that there might be a market for historical fiction, Wilder started researching an autobiographical work, a project with which she had been flirting for years. The eventual result of her labors was "Pioneer Girl," a first person, adult-level narrative, rather undetailed except for particulars as to dress and the retelling of her father's stories. It covers much the same ground as would the *Little House* books later. Notations on the manuscript suggest that Wilder expected Lane to edit and embellish the work. If writing was the arena in which much of the Wilder-Lane drama took place, then the fate of the stories from "Pioneer Girl" eventually filled the spotlight.

In 1928, Lane returned to her parents' Rocky Ridge Farm from Albania and once again helped her mother with her writing. She did not return, however, for that purpose. Albania, with which she initially had become infatuated during her postwar work as publicist for the Red Cross, had ceased to be a pleasant backwater in which to live. Even half-way around the world, she could not get away from the usual problems of being Rose Wilder Lane: the need

---

[31] Wilder to Lane, December 1937, LIW Series, Lane Papers. Also see Wilder to Lane, June 13, 1936, microfilm, roll 2, Laura Ingalls Wilder Papers (hereafter Wilder Papers), Joint Collection, University of Missouri Western Historical Manuscript Collection and State Historical Society of Missouri, Columbia, Missouri. Anderson maintains that it was the rejection by Harper's of the first version of *Farmer Boy* in September 1932 that compelled Wilder to recognize how dependent she was on Lane's help. See Anderson, "The Continuing Collaboration" (n. 24 above), 139. For Lane's perception of her mother's resentment of her help, see January 25, 1933, Diaries and Notes Series, no. 47, Lane Papers. For a sample of Lane's many efforts to induce gratitude and guilt, see Lane to Wilder, November 23, 1924, and February 16, 1931, LIW Series, Lane Papers.

to churn out story after story to make a living, the frictions and betrayals of friendships, the wearying "everydayness" of life. She had used up her youth without having resolved any of the conflicts and problems that limited her personally and professionally. Lane felt herself to be without convictions of her own, without a clear sense of self.[32] She concluded that she was driven from one residence, writing project, and relationship to the next without forethought or satisfaction, and without a sense of what suited her.[33]

It was to this inner hollowness that she attributed her increasing difficulty in finding ideas for new stories. Paring away most adult relationships, including love affairs, she seems to have wanted to start over again at the farm, to be re-formed in some more satisfactory way that would grant her greater reserves of self-confidence, energy, and will: "If I can only make it a fresh, sunny, open-air life—without all this smothered smoldering—a busy life, active and energetic. At the same time, a *learning* life, studious. So that when I'm free to go again, I shall be ready."[34] So too, did she wish to build up her financial reserves—"a safe and solid $50,000 properly invested"—allowing her future decisions to be based on carefully determined goals and desires, rather than merely on financial exigencies.[35] Lane intended her rejuvenating stay near her parents to be less than three years; she remained for more than eight years and left broke and dispirited.

Possibly she thought at first that her parents would play a role in the creation of the new Rose. Certainly she recognized that staying at Rocky Ridge Farm, which had always made her feel claustrophobic and resentful of old patterns with her mother, would require "delicate personal adjustments with the family."[36] By the time of her return Lane was forty-one years old, her mother sixty-one years old, and her father seventy-one years old; changing their relationships would not be easy. In the past Lane had always hated small-town life in Missouri and had loved her parents in direct proportion to her geographic distance from them.[37]

Apparently uncertain as to what she wanted from her parents in the way of nurturing, Lane responded to her reunion with them in

---

[32] Lane, October 1927, Diaries and Notes Series, no. 12, Lane Papers.

[33] Ibid., undated entries throughout 1928.

[34] Ibid., February 6, 1928.

[35] Ibid.

[36] Ibid.

[37] Over the years when they were apart, Wilder and Lane were able to express their affection for one another. Wilder was also able to express in letters her gratitude for all that Lane did for them, although sometimes she did this in ways that evoked Lane's need to keep giving (see Wilder to Lane, January 28, 1938; February 19, 1938; January 27, 1939; April 2, 1939; LIW Series, Lane Papers).

a manner that had become characteristic with her: she took care of them instead. She waited on them when they were sick and moderated their quarrels over the farm. She continued with her customary $500 annual subsidy of the farm. Most significantly, using the excuse that she was building her parents the house of their dreams, Lane went into debt to have a new cottage built for them on the other side of the property. She remodeled and moved into the farmhouse that her parents had built with their own hands.[38] Such activities cut into her time for writing, and residence so far from any publishing center seemed to undermine further her ability to generate story ideas. Maintaining that she needed the stimulation of periodic excursions away from the farm, Lane claimed that her mother did not think that she should leave her.[39]

Despite all the sacrifices she felt herself to be making, Lane never had the sense that she had done enough for her mother. "Rose was very much her mama's slave," recalled her female housemate of those days. "[Wilder] expected Rose to do everything, including mind what she was told on the instant."[40] Beyond Wilder's general bossiness, Lane felt herself to be the victim of what she described as her mother's "agonizing finger-tip hold on economic safety."[41] Assurance of financial security and help with her writing were the forms in which Wilder's need to be cared for by Lane were most clearly expressed. Acutely vulnerable to these signals on her mother's part, Lane both wanted to be her mother's provider and resented what sometimes seemed to be insatiable demands.[42] Every time that Wilder complained about lack of money, Lane took such remarks as an indictment of *her,* a declaration of *her* failure. Because Lane often suffered dry periods with her writing, her anxiety and guilt deepened; not only had she nothing of her own to say, but her failure to earn a steady income adequate to support the two expensive Rocky Ridge households both prevented her from leaving and let her mother down.[43]

[38] Lane to Merwin Hart, January 1, 1962, Lane Papers. Given Lane's lifelong fixation with houses, it is hard not to see her preemption and remodeling of her parents' house as another one of her efforts to usurp her parents' role as nurturers and to perform the role more to her satisfaction.

[39] Lane to Freemont Older, October 7, 1929, Lane Papers.

[40] Anderson, "The Continuing Collaboration" (n. 24 above), 99.

[41] Lane, January 5, 1933, Diaries and Notes Series, no. 45, Lane Papers.

[42] As Lane put it after an exchange with Wilder in which Lane found herself writing a check for her mother that would leave her without money for her own bills, "something in her knows exactly how to put the screws on me" (see April 10, 1933 [n. 1 above]).

[43] For an example of this mix of feelings, see Lane to Mary Margaret McBride, April 1930, Lane Papers.

Despite her resolutions to lead a "fresh, sunny, open-air life," Lane's diaries, journals, and correspondence show her to have been brooding and distraught again soon after her return to the farm. Lacking a diary or probing letters from Wilder, we cannot know for certain her response to her daughter's moodiness. It does appear, however, that there was a generational split in regard to the expression of deep feelings. Wilder's own family had encouraged stoicism in the face of all disappointments and many pleasures as well. "I know we all hated a fuss, as I still do," Wilder once recalled.[44] In contrast, Lane was accustomed to exploring and expressing her emotions, both negative and positive. No doubt her mother's attitude squelched any impulse she might have had to talk freely of her feelings to her parents and turned her unspeakable needs into feelings of resentment. After having been back at Rocky Ridge Farm for a year and a half, she concluded glumly: "I would change places with any young woman—about 20—with intelligent, simple, harmonious parents, good health, and a cultured background."[45]

Lane's plans to travel, already thwarted by her sense of obligation to her mother, were dealt a further blow in November 1931 by the failure of the investment company in which mother and daughter had placed their hopes of easy financial security. At that point neither one of them saw Wilder's writing as a way out of their plight. "She says she wants prestige rather than money," Lane's diary for July 1930 recorded of her mother, as she reworked "Pioneer Girl."[46] Lane had difficulty finding a publisher for her mother's story, but one finally took an interest in part of the manuscript as a story for eight-to-ten-year-old children. In the summer of 1931 the two women expanded and revised the relevant section, which Harper and Brothers published the following spring as *The Little House in the Big Woods*. "I'm feeling grand," Lane recorded.[47] Reviews and sales were immediately favorable.

Lane's exuberance at the publisher's acceptance of this first book was genuine but short-lived. Her health was poor, she owed money to several people, including her mother, and she failed in

[44] Wilder to Lane, February 1938, LIW Series, Lane Papers.

[45] Lane, July 13, 1929, Diaries and Notes Series, no. 12, Lane Papers.

[46] Lane, July 31, 1930, Diaries and Notes Series, no. 25, Lane Papers.

[47] Lane, September 19, 1931, Diaries and Note Series, no. 37, Lane Papers. Following a suggestion of Zochert's (n. 17 above), Rosa Ann Moore first examined the papers of the two women and established their collaboration on the *Little House* books. See Rosa Ann Moore, "The Little House Books: Rose-colored Classics," *Children's Literature* 7 (1978): 7–16, and "Laura Ingalls Wilder and Rose Wilder Lane: The Chemistry of Collaboration," *Children's Literature in Education* 11, no. 3 (Autumn 1980): 101–9.

attempts to continue her own work. Lane had provided the means by which Wilder could achieve public recognition at a time when Lane was feeling frighteningly empty and forgotten by her friends. Her mother was enjoying favorable publicity for the beauty and charm of a story that Lane had helped to create but for which she could take no credit outside her family. "All my trouble is still my old trouble of almost twenty years ago," Lane concluded in despair. "I am not leading my own life, because any life must coalesce around a central purpose, and I have none."[48]

In contrast, Wilder, aided by her daughter in shaping and refining her stories, suffered no writer's block. All she had to do was to reach into her storehouse of memories and experiences to have a theme she felt was uniquely hers yet was identified by others as nationally significant. By October 1931 she was planning at least two more juvenile books similar to *The Little House in the Big Woods*.[49] In addition to all its other benefits, this writing gave Wilder the opportunity to recast her past. Through the books, ostensibly realistic because she was carefully precise about physical details, she settled old scores and came to terms with a childhood in which she had played second fiddle to a smart, good, beautiful sister who was much like her mother and in whom her parents had placed many of their hopes. In this reconstruction of the past, Wilder elaborated her father's role at the expense of her mother's role, claimed his admiration and approval, and celebrated her childhood rebelliousness without ever denouncing—or acknowledging—the power of her mother's gentle repressiveness. A golden glow was cast over the Ingalls family unit and the sting taken out of the family's inability to establish itself successfully anywhere. The stories even enabled Wilder to reclaim her first name, which marriage had altered to "Bessie" and "Mama Bess" to distinguish her from Manly's sister, Laura.[50]

In contrast, nothing that Lane had ever written under her own name had proved satisfying on so many levels. Her compulsive giving to her mother was exacting a price: she was now giving away an essential part of her identity, that of writer. She had achieved the role reversal she had sought. Through her efforts and nurturance, Wilder's abilities had been stimulated and rewarded outside the family. Like many people who subordinate their own needs to those of others, however, Lane experienced profound depression with the sacrifice. She had aided her mother, who, rather than

[48] Lane, May 29, 1932, Diaries and Notes Series, no. 45, Lane Papers.

[49] Lane to George Bye, October 1931, Author File, James Oliver Brown Papers (hereafter Brown Papers), Butler Library, Columbia University, New York.

[50] William T. Anderson, *Laura's Rose: The Story of Rose Wilder Lane* (De Smet, S. Dak.: Laura Ingalls Wilder Memorial Society, 1976), 11.

affirming Lane in the way she needed as her part of the unstated exchange, demanded further help.[51] This may explain why Lane's preparation of Wilder's second juvenile story—"an inconsequential little job"—proved difficult for her to complete.[52]

As she did whenever she was depressed, Lane read obsessively. The book that lifted her spirits temporarily and energized her was Ludwig Lewisohn's *Expression in America*.[53] Americans, Lewisohn argued, hungered for beauty and idealism; the critical realists offered them cynicism and depicted life as arid. Foreseeing a creative rebirth, Lewisohn predicted the emergence, from the Middle West, of a genuine folk idiom expressing the collective life of the American people through their tradition of libertarianism. Artists would have a part to play in this rebirth, for "salvation comes from the individual who . . . re-envisages ultimate reality, creates first his autonomy, then freedom and flexibility for his fellows. It is that individual . . . [who is] needed . . . as a revolutionary, in American letters."[54]

Thus inspired, in July 1932, Lane, who had always claimed little interest in pioneer America as a source of stories, acted on her own to correct the balance of giving: she took from her mother material to sustain her as a writer. She too drew upon some of her mother's middle western memories as contained in the "Pioneer Girl" manuscript and used them in a two-part story which she published in the *Saturday Evening Post*. "Let the Hurricane Roar" covers much of the same ground that the third *Little House* book, *By the Banks of Plum Creek*, would later, but with crucial differences that show Lane's feelings of isolation and her emerging perception that individuals are essentially on their own. In *Plum Creek*, when Pa goes back East to find work, Ma (Caroline) is left in a tight frame house with three children, two of whom are old enough to do chores, and with a friendly neighbor. In contrast, "Hurricane" features a very young woman in a dugout with an infant and no neighbors whose husband goes East to work during a winter of brutal storms. Lane's heroine, also named Caroline, manages with no help from anyone and is saved only by her will to survive. Viewing the terrible stillness and blankness of the prairie after the first blizzard, Caroline realizes how "infinitely small and weak was

---

[51] Jean Baker Miller suggests that women frequently devote themselves to serving the needs of others, assuming that their own, often unidentified, needs "will somehow be fulfilled in return" (*Toward a New Psychology of Women* [Boston: Beacon, 1976], 64).

[52] Lane, May 23, 1932, Diaries and Notes Series, no. 21, Lane Papers.

[53] Ludwig Lewisohn, *Expression in America* (New York: Harper & Bros., 1932). Lewisohn scorned critical realism, the literary vogue that had peaked with the granting of the 1930 Nobel Prize for Literature to Sinclair Lewis.

[54] Ibid., 124, 195, 392, 590.

the spark of warmth in a living heart. Yet valiantly the tiny heart continued to beat. Tired, weak, burdened by its own fears and sorrows, still it persisted, indomitably it continued to exist."[55]

"Let the Hurricane Roar" was enthusiastically received as the lead story in the *Saturday Evening Post* and then as a well-publicized book.[56] With the exception of *Old Home Town* (1935), which deals with the era of her own girlhood and adolescence, the few triumphs that Lane achieved in the late 1930s as a fiction writer were all inspired by family stories, many of them found in the "Pioneer Girl" manuscript.[57] Wilder, however, resented Lane's appropriation of material that she was planning to use, and she was made uncomfortable by the degree to which her daughter took liberties with the facts of the Ingalls' lives.[58] She seems to have regarded this raw material as hers alone, not to be shared even with the daughter who had contributed importantly to the shaping and refining of her stories.[59]

The publication of "Let the Hurricane Roar" in book form prompted an editorial in the *Saturday Evening Post* reminding its readers that surely the dominant American national trait was self-reliance and warning them that the growth of government was undermining their self-reliance.[60] The only letter from a reader that Lane ever copied into her diary expressed appreciation that the serial could help "lead the world back from the defeatist thinking of the socialist militarist" European patterns, toward a vindication of the individual's ability under stress to endure and flourish.[61] Her book publishers, in the midst of the economic depression, used the political dimensions of this theme in their advertisements for the

[55] Rose Wilder Lane, *Let the Hurricane Roar* (New York: Longmans, Green, 1933), 128. Lane's working title for this novella was "Courage."

[56] Lane's diary indicates that ten thousand copies of the book sold within the first four months of its publication (see June 23, 1933, Diaries and Notes Series, no. 37, Lane Papers).

[57] Some examples of her successful borrowing are Rose Wilder Lane, *Free Land* (New York: Longmans, Green, 1938), "Object, Matrimony," *Saturday Evening Post* 207, no. 9 (September 1, 1934): 5–7, 57–58, and "Home over Saturday," *Saturday Evening Post* 210, no. 11 (September 11, 1937): 5–7, 53–54, 57–58, 60.

[58] Anderson indicates that, almost twenty years later, Wilder complained to a librarian that the existence of *Let the Hurricane Roar* created confusion with her own books. He also reports that rumors persist to the present in the Wilders' Missouri town about the mother-daughter tension over Lane's story. See Anderson, "The Continuing Collaboration" (n. 24 above), 109–10.

[59] For other evidence of their competition for material, see Wilder to Lane, March 20, 1937 and December 1937; Lane to Wilder, December 20, 1937, LIW Series, Lane Papers.

[60] "Let the Hurricane Roar" (editorial), *Saturday Evening Post* 205, no. 35 (March 4, 1933): 22.

[61] Lane, December 23, 1932, Diaries and Notes Series, no. 45, Lane Papers.

book: "What these two heroic young pioneers went through dwarfs your present hardships and makes you ashamed to complain."[62]

Critical and popular responses such as these and similar, although less overtly political, responses to the *Little House* books heightened Lane's and Wilder's sense that their own family's experiences had ideological implications. Watchful and at first neutral, Wilder and Lane became increasingly alarmed by President Roosevelt's efforts to combat the Depression. Thinking back over their own struggles, the Wilders and Lane became angered by government farm-relief programs that implied that individuals were incapable of coping with setbacks on their own.[63] Wilder left the Democratic Party and firmly opposed Roosevelt. Lane's vague liberalism and internationalism yielded to an increasingly firm conviction that anything more than minimal government was an unnecessary evil.

Although agreement between the two women on the political issues of the day created a strong bond, it failed to eliminate the tensions between them as mother and daughter. Their papers from this period reveal instances when Wilder and Lane slighted each other's achievements both privately and to other people.[64] The documents do not record the effect that this mutual dependency and competitiveness had on Wilder. They do show that Lane suffered. "Blue as hell, old, ugly, tired and useless and broke," she wrote of herself, and again and again: "must get away."[65] Despite Lane's attempts to redirect her need to mother onto a homeless teen-age boy who showed up on her doorstep (one of several surrogate sons in her lifetime), she continued to feel miserable and to be without energy. She was caught: seeking to prove herself a better parent than her mother, she could neither take what support Wilder could offer nor cease giving to her compulsively. She dreaded any identification with her mother—"I went to visit my

[62] "Let the Hurricane Roar," Reviews and Notices, 1933, Manuscript Series, Lane Papers.

[63] Wilder to Lane, 1936, Microfilm, Roll 2, Wilder Papers. The Wilders had spent fifty years trying to wrest crops from recalcitrant soils; they and Lane were aghast at the prospect of plowing crops under to lessen so-called surpluses.

[64] Anderson, "The Continuing Collaboration" (n. 24 above), 110; Lane to George Bye, February 15, 1933, April 27, 1933, Author File, Brown Papers.

[65] Lane did note bitterly once that her mother confirmed a palm reader's interpretation of herself as someone who always got what she wanted (September 24, 1934, May 4, 1933, February 26, 1935, March 1935, May 20, 1935, Diaries and Notes Series, no. 37, Lane Papers). Lane's feelings of emotional abandonment by her mother were reflected in her year-end dramatic contemplation of suicide: "I want to keep on going but do not quite see how, and there is no alternative—rather than justify my mother's 25-year dread of my 'coming back on her, sick' I must kill myself" (December 1933, Diaries and Notes Series, no. 47, Lane Papers).

mother and saw what awaits me in twice ten years"—yet she had difficulty achieving the separation and autonomy she required.[66] She could not give herself permission to loosen the ties.

Finally, it took decisive action by Wilder—or at least what Lane interpreted as an ultimatum from her mother—to compel her to leave Rocky Ridge Farm for good in July 1936.[67] Lane was bitter; this was not the supportive release that she was seeking. Nonetheless, even after she had moved East and was still too angry to return for a visit, Lane was unable to cease acting as the beneficent parent. She continued to assist her mother in her writing, to send her carefully chosen presents, and to offer advice on the maintenance of the farm.

However, long before Lane made her ungraceful exit, she had begun to prepare herself ideologically for a separation. Gradually in the mid-1930s, she had grasped at last that there would be no magic moment when, nourished and blessed by a mother made whole by her ministrations, she would step forth energized and ready to conquer the world; such support was not to be expected; the continuation of her life could not depend on its existence.[68] Recognizing her complicity in the debilitating relationship with her mother but unable to establish an equilibrium between independence and connection, Lane finally renounced personal attachment in favor of an exaggerated form of psychological individuation.[69] Not only was it useless to try to derive the satisfaction she needed from another individual through subordinating her needs to that person's, but even attempting to do so was destroying her. Politicizing her insights, she concluded that what was true for her was true for all people. In a 1936 essay, she declared: "My freedom is my

[66] Lane, October 7, 1931, Diaries and Notes Series, no. 37, Lane Papers.

[67] Lane's 1936 tour of the Midwest with anti–New Deal journalist Garet Garrett may in part have been a challenge to her mother, who was anxious about appearances when unconventional activities, such as an unmarried man and woman traveling together, took place close to home. Lane later maintained that Wilder ordered her either to come back from the Columbia, Missouri, hotel where she was living, to stay on the farm without her current female houseguest, or to get out altogether (see August 10, 1940, Diaries and Notes Series, no. 47, Lane Papers).

[68] Lane's financial records provide evidence of her distancing herself from her mother. Money is owed to "Mama Bess" in 1929, to "Mother" in 1933, and to "Mrs. A.J.W." in 1936 (Diaries and Notes Series, no. 12, Lane Papers). Her disillusionment with an emotional life dependent upon other women rather than upon a male found expression also in an extraordinary article she wrote that year, essentially denouncing the way she had led her own life. "My life has been arid and sterile at the core because I have been a human being instead of a woman, a wife" (Rose Wilder Lane, "Woman's Place Is in the Home," *Ladies' Home Journal* 53, no. 10 [October 1936]: 96).

[69] "Even if I am released from the obvious bondage, I shall probably never get away" (Lane, May 29, 1932, Diaries and Notes Series, no. 45, Lane Papers).

control of my own life-energy, for the uses of which, I, alone, am therefore responsible. . . . Individual liberty is individual responsibility. Whoever makes decisions is responsible for results. . . . The question is whether personal freedom is worth the terrible effort, the never-lifted burden and the risks of individual self-reliance."[70]

In the midst of the Great Depression, despite her bouts of personal despair, Lane committed herself to a philosophy of determined optimism. Yes, personal freedom was worth the "terrible effort"; it was responsible for the phenomenon of achievement that was America. Through a combination of lucky coincidences, settlers in British colonial America had come to disbelieve in any natural authority. Their denial of the inherent right of any person or institution to rule them had unleashed furious, chaotic, and fruitful energies that had transformed much of the world for the better in just one hundred and fifty years.

But under the New Deal Americans were lapsing into old, discredited patterns: belief in the abstraction called society or humanity, and empowerment of the state to infantilize its citizens by the removal of individual responsibility. Lane's sense of how autonomy was ceded by the individual informed her perception of how a nation might permit itself to be overgoverned. "The threat to republican government (lack of government), comes really from its own citizens. We let political power entrench itself and expand."[71]

However, Lane's painful acknowledgment of the essential isolation of each individual was not complete in the late 1930s. Her mother had more to teach her about emotional self-sufficiency. The two women struggled over the issue of emotional distance as they worked on the middle books in the *Little House* series, in which the characters face difficulties and isolation with equanimity, having learned to expect life to be a struggle and little to be their due. Throughout the writing of the books, Wilder stressed to her daughter the pioneers' stoicism, their refusal to give in to emotion when they faced disasters or partings from friends and relatives. Lane thought that her mother confused "showing some emotion" with being "excitable."[72] On this matter, however, Wilder's views

[70] Lane, "Credo," *Saturday Evening Post* 208, no. 36 (March 7, 1936): 30. An expanded version had a long life as a pamphlet entitled *Give Me Liberty*. In 1935 she had described herself in the *Saturday Evening Post* as a "fundamentalist American." "Give me time," she said, and "I will tell you why individualism, laissez-faire and the slightly restrained anarchy of capitalism offer the best opportunities for the development of the human spirit" ("Who's Who—and Why: Rose Wilder Lane," *Saturday Evening Post* 206, no. 1 [July 6, 1935]: 30).

[71] Lane to Dorothy Thompson, October 15, 1938, Lane Papers.

[72] Lane to Wilder, February 1938, LIW Series, Lane Papers.

prevailed over her daughter's. Indeed, Lane's capitulation on whether to depict sorrow among departing kin may have signaled Wilder's final victory on the issue of emotional self-sufficiency. "You know," she reminded her daughter, "a person can not live at a high pitch of emotion. The feelings become dulled by a natural unconscious effort of self-preservation."[73]

A chief distinction from the past, as Wilder saw it, was that people in the old days bore up to their troubles without grumbling. "There was no whining in those days, no yelling for help. A man did what he could with what he had."[74] The ability to make do without complaint seems to have been associated for Wilder with self-esteem and happiness. She then proceeded to turn this into an ethical principle. As she wrote to Lane in 1937: "I find my heart is getting harder. I can have no least sympathy for people any more who can do and will only holler that there is no chance any more. I wish they *all* might have had the opportunities we had when I was young *and no more*. Wouldn't it be fun to watch 'em?"[75] By this time, royalties from three *Little House* books were enabling Wilder to live with some financial security for the first time in her life. Lane, on the other hand, was between homes and between writing successes; her response to her mother's statement was not recorded.

Despite Wilder's praise of stoicism, the *Little House* books do not paint a picture of cold people. Wilder evokes, through cumulative portraits of Ingalls family life, a sense of well-being that gives vicarious pleasure to the reader. The family often has to depend on their own resources for companionship, but the time spent together is almost always peaceful or fun, rather than tension-filled. Ma and Pa love Laura even though she is naughty sometimes. The Ingalls children are both eager and able to please their parents. Whatever the situation, Ma and Pa can find ways to provide for their four girls. In volume after volume, Wilder firmly associates these gratifying characteristics of Ingalls family life with other aspects of their experience: hardship and deprivation, gratitude for little rewards, family self-containment and isolation, individual self-sufficiency, parental ingenuity and skill. Conversely, whenever government appears in the books, it is associated with bungling and stress, as in the homesteading allocations and regulations. Also, whenever heightened emotion is introduced, it is connected with undesirable behavior.[76]

[73] Wilder to Lane, March 7, 1938, LIW Series, Lane Papers.
[74] Ibid., March 20, 1937.
[75] Ibid., March 12, 1937.
[76] Laura Ingalls Wilder, *By the Shores of Silver Lake* (New York: Harper & Row, 1971), 234–37, *The Long Winter* (New York: Harper & Row, 1971), 99–100, and *Little Town on the Prairie* (New York: Harper & Row, 1971), 161–63, 277–82.

These links are present throughout the *Little House* books, along with many other illustrations of the ethical and political principles to which Wilder and Lane had become increasingly devoted. They imbued all the meticulous details in the books, how to build a chimney or make sour-dough biscuits, with an ideology of self-sufficiency. Ma and Pa refuse to be beholden to anyone, even for a few nails, a slate for school, an invitation to a party, or a pail of wheat to ward off starvation. A comparison of the less adorned, more strictly autobiographical "Pioneer Girl" manuscript with the more developed *Little House* series reveals that over time Wilder and Lane further accentuated the family's ingenuity and its geographic and economic separateness from its community, while minimizing the degree to which Pa had been dependent upon wage work. For example, the surveyor's house in which the family spends a solitary winter in *By the Shores of Silver Lake* (book 4 of the series) in actuality had been shared with a boarder whom they accommodated in order to have another man present in case of trouble.[77] The portrayal of Laura in *Little Town on the Prairie* (book 6), caring for her two younger sisters and cleaning the house from top to bottom while Ma and Pa take Mary to the college for the blind, gives a satisfying impression of her self-reliance and desire to please her parents. The "Pioneer Girl" manuscript, however, indicates that a neighboring brother and sister stayed with the girls to take care of them and to do the chores.[78] In "Pioneer Girl," Laura inadvertently finds a book of Sir Walter Scott's poems that she realizes is to be a present for her. In *Little Town on the Prairie*, the book becomes Tennyson's poems. Wilder and Lane almost certainly made the alteration so that Laura could express disgust with the sailors in "The Lotus Eaters" who give themselves up to sloth when they reach the land where it always seems to be afternoon: "They seemed to think they were entitled to live in that magic land and lie around complaining."[79]

The Long Winter, volume 5 of the series, centering on the relentless blizzards of 1880–81, offered the authors ample opportunity to emphasize the need for ingenuity and self-reliance in adversity.[80] At the beginning of the story, Pa tells Laura that, as the

[77] Wilder, "Pioneer Girl" (n. 21 above), 82.
[78] Ibid., 114, and *Little Town*, 116–22.
[79] Wilder, "Pioneer Girl," 114, and *Little Town*, 235.
[80] The propaganda value of *The Long Winter* was immediately realized; soon after the Second World War, the book was translated into German and Japanese for the edification of those defeated peoples. In response to Lane's suggestion that previously described relatives should be reintroduced in this volume, Wilder replied, "I think it adds to the feeling of [the hard winter] that the Ingalls family

Declaration of Independence asserts, humans were created free by God and hence have to take care of themselves. The rest of the book includes numerous examples of Pa's and Ma's inventing ways to keep the family warm and fed. Unlike "Pioneer Girl," *The Long Winter* rarely notes that such practices were not unique to the Ingalls family or that the townspeople sometimes used communal techniques to survive the harsh conditions. When Laura bemoans the social isolation caused by a blizzard, her shocked mother replies, "I hope you don't expect to depend on anybody else, Laura. . . . A body can't do that." Throughout this volume, as in the others, the Ingalls girls are taught self-denial as well as self-sufficiency.[81] The linkage between political and personal behavior is made most explicitly in Laura's often-quoted realization in *The Little Town on the Prairie:* "Americans won't obey any king on earth. Americans are free. That means they have to obey their own consciences. No king bosses Pa; he has to boss himself. Why (she thought) when I'm a little older, Pa and Ma will stop telling me what to do, and there isn't anyone else who has a right to give me orders. I will have to make myself be good."[82]

Wilder's and Lane's reinterpretations of their personal and familial history in light of the political changes initiated by the New Deal caused the two women to reshape their goals as writers. Wilder came to believe that she had a larger purpose in her writing. She had written the "Pioneer Girl" memoir hoping to preserve her father's stories and to make money. Later, with the publication of the first books in what became the *Little House* series, she desired prestige and wished to please her appreciative audience. Nonetheless, by the late 1930s, she viewed the *Little House* books as an important seven-volume novel for children, capturing the essential aspects of the American frontier and agricultural experiences. Later, Lane claimed that her mother specifically intended the series to be a criticism of the New Deal.[83] In a speech in 1937, Wilder alluded to her efforts in the books to describe the pioneer ingenuity and self-sufficiency that had propelled America into the present day: "I realized that I had seen and lived . . . all the successive

should be more of a solitary unit than they would be with kinfolks around" (Wilder to Lane, March 20, 1937, LIW Series, Lane Papers).

[81] Wilder, *The Long Winter*, 13, 127, 171, 196–97, quote found on 127. Lane's description of the seventy-five-year-old Wilder suggests that the lessons took: "She is completely self-reliant, is never lonely, has no need of companionship" (quoted in Irene Smith, "Laura Ingalls Wilder and the Little House Books," *Horn Book Magazine* 19, no. 4 [September 1943]: 293–306, esp. 297–98).

[82] Wilder, *Little Town on the Prairie* (n. 76 above), 76.

[83] Lane to J. Howard Pew, October 8, 1963, Lane Papers.

phases of the frontier. . . . I understood that in my own life I represented a whole period of American history. That the frontier was gone and agricultural settlements had taken its place when I married a farmer. . . . I wanted the children now to understand more about the beginnings of things—to know what is behind the things they see—what it is that made America as they know it."[84] A dozen years of writing about America as she believed it had been, enabled her, the recipient of many loving, public tributes, to live in comfort until her death in 1957 on the Missouri farm that could never pay for itself.

For a period from the mid-1930s, Lane infused her fiction with her political convictions. "Free Land," her 1938 magazine serial which became a best-selling novel, while capturing some of her father's early farming experiences, was also an attack on the supposed benevolence of a government which offered settlers free land that, in reality, was far from free.[85] By 1940, when Lane had abandoned her efforts to achieve a more satisfying relationship with her mother and had given up her introspective diary, she lost her taste and imagination for writing fiction and turned instead to polemical writing and individualist causes. Lane's main political treatise, *The Discovery of Freedom: Man's Struggle against Authority* (1943), displays the same preoccupation with the individual's responsibility to combat those forces that would drain him or her of energy that marked her own efforts to free herself from trying to please her mother. "The planet is energy," she begins the book, "Life struggles to exist, among not-living energies that destroy it." The daughter who could never receive what she needed from her mother came to believe that "men cannot live, unless they use their energies to create their necessities from this earth which gives human beings nothing whatever."[86]

Her most popular post-1940 publication, *The Woman's Day Book of Needlework* (1963), reveals that even after her mother's death, she was still stressing the independence of each human being as the source of the success of America. In the tradition of the *Little House* books, Lane consciously used the craft book to instruct women about the political ideas that she considered basic to an understanding of American history.

[84] Wilder, Detroit Bookweek Speech, 1937, LIW Series, Lane Papers.

[85] Lane, *Free Land* (n. 57 above).

[86] Rose Wilder Lane, *The Discovery of Freedom: Man's Struggle against Authority* (New York: John Day, 1943), vii, 54. See also xii–xiii, in which Lane writes of the desperate necessity for humans "to combine their energies in order to live" although human wills are inevitably in conflict, each trying to control the other with which it is in conflict.

In typical Old World needlework, each detail is a particle of the whole; no part of the design can stand alone whole and complete in itself . . . American women . . . made the details create the whole, and they set each detail in boundless space, alone, independent, complete. . . . As Americans were the first to know and declare that a person is the unit of human life on earth, that each human being is a self-governing source of the life energy that creates, controls, and changes societies, institutions, governments, so American women were the first to reverse the old meaning in needle-work design.[87]

In 1963 Rose Wilder Lane denied that her mother's books were fictional in any way, "They are the truth and only the truth."[88] The truth as she and Laura Ingalls Wilder had come to see it was an America made prosperous and energetic by individuals from self-sufficient families, people dependent upon no one. It was of a society in which the only legitimate ties were not of blood nor friendship but of neighborliness, which was "not love, nor friend-ship. . . . may be less than liking . . . the mutual helpfulness of human beings to each other, an unforced, voluntary co-operation springing from a sense of equality in common humanity and human needs."[89]

Theirs was a vision nourished by their experiences as mother and daughter in a specific historical context that reinforced their austere view. Their childhoods on the American frontier and their adult experiences as self-employed people evoked the virtues of self-sufficiency to them. The transition that occurred in their lifetimes, to a more collectivist notion of society and a more interventionist role for government, violated their interpretations of their own histories. These women's final assessments, greatly influenced by their own family relationships, of what people could realistically expect from one another predisposed them to a percep-tion of the solitary individual as the true social unit and to a belief in political individualism. Of course this individualism is not inevitably the outcome of a strained mother-daughter relationship in a culture with exclusive mothering. Such a stance has other sources outside the dynamics of family life. Nonetheless, Wilder's and Lane's responses to their relationship contributed to a view of

[87] Rose Wilder Lane, *The Woman's Day Book of Needlework* (New York: Simon & Schuster, 1963), 12.

[88] Louise Hovde Mortensen, "Idea Inventory," *Elementary English* 41, no. 4 (April 1964): 428–29; Lane to Wilder, January 21, 1938, LIW Series, Lane Papers.

[89] Lane, *The Woman's Day Book of Needlework*, 98.

the world that was at once uniquely theirs and yet resonant with that of many other Americans.[90]

Each woman in her way turned her sense of deprivation into a moral principle by which to gauge the world. To both, the material world—mother earth—although for moments beautiful, was ultimately an unyielding place that granted nothing without a struggle. In parallel fashion, their beliefs about human society provided the individual with no sure allies. For Rose Wilder Lane, these beliefs led to an individualist libertarian philosophy that has gained in influence since 1940.[91] The warm and broad reception of Laura Ingalls Wilder's books shows that aspects of a more extreme vision of individualism are widely shared by Americans and, in fact, are so generally accepted as truthful as to not be deemed "political" in implication.

Department of History and Women's Studies Program
Old Dominion University

---

[90] They might have drawn other lessons from their sense of insufficient nurturing. For example, one hundred years before Wilder and Lane presented their views, English reformer Harriet Martineau, plagued by a relentlessly deflating mother, had fervently espoused the importance of education and human development and the necessity of justice for all. And just thirty-five years before, American feminist Charlotte Perkins Gilman drew conclusions opposite to theirs from her sense of being inadequately nurtured. She recommended a program of social mothering to compensate for the unreliability of individual mothers. See Mitzi Myers, "Unmothered Daughter and Radical Reformer: Harriet Martineau's Career," in *The Lost Tradition: Mothers and Daughters in Literature*, ed. C. N. Davidson and E. M. Broner (New York: Frederick Ungar, 1980), 70–80; Ann Lane, "Charlotte Perkins Gilman" (paper presented at the Sixth Berkshire Conference on the History of Women, Northampton, Massachusetts, 1984).

[91] One noteworthy example of Lane's influence is her adopted grandson and heir, Roger Lea MacBride, for whom she served as mentor from his teen years. MacBride ran for U.S. President on the Libertarian Party ticket in 1976, laying the groundwork that would result in almost a million votes for the Libertarian candidate in 1980. His *A New Dawn for America: The Libertarian Challenge* (Ottawa, Ill.: Green Hill, 1976), dedicated to the memory of Lane, shows clear evidence of her impact on him.

READING "SNOW WHITE":
THE MOTHER'S STORY

SHULI BARZILAI

It is no news, yet still interesting to consider, that myths and fairy tales are complex reflectors of the conscious and unconscious concerns of their readers. A case in point is the story of Snow White. In the familiar version collated and edited by Jakob and Wilhelm Grimm, a young girl flees from the murderous intentions of her wicked stepmother, finds shelter with the seven dwarfs, undergoes three trials or temptations, succumbs to the poison apple, and is rescued from her death-sleep by a charming prince. Two close readings of this version, one psychoanalytic and the other feminist, suggest that because "Snow White" is part of a literary as well as a folkloric tradition, it may be studied as a cultural artifact and text valid in itself.[1]

As part of a people's oral tradition, a folktale is a continually recreated narrative. Even when written and codified, the tale still

Special thanks to Gannit Ankori and Zephyra Porat for their many valuable suggestions and encouragement.

[1] From the standpoint of anthropological and folkloristic research, an analysis based on only one variant and, moreover, on a reading of two readings of that variant might be seen to exemplify what Steven Jones calls the "pitfalls of Snow White scholarship." Hundreds of versions of the story are cited by Antti Aarne and Stith Thompson. I have chosen to focus on the Grimms' version mainly because of its familiarity to most readers, but also because it is representative of the basic structure and themes that inform the tale (see Steven Jones, "The Pitfalls of Snow White Scholarship," *Journal of American Folklore* 92 [January–March 1979]: 69–73; and Antti Aarne and Stith Thompson, *The Types of the Folktale: A Classification and Bibliography* [Helsinki: Academia Scientiarum Fennica, 1961], esp. 245–46).

This essay originally appeared in *Signs*, vol. 15, no. 3, Spring 1990.

reflects the conflicts and concerns of earlier generations of tale-
tellers. An analysis of numerous versions will yield interesting and
valuable information about a variety of individual, national, and
cultural characteristics. However, as the typologies identified by
several folklore studies indicate, certain episodes associated with
the tale type of "Snow White" remain constant. Though details or
motifs might vary considerably, general patterns such as jealousy
and expulsion are invariant.[2] This constancy suggests that the fairy
tale draws on a communality of human experience that is not
contingent upon the time and place of the telling. Whether we
examine one version of "Snow White" or one hundred versions, we
will always find the persecutor—be it a cruel stepmother, treacher-
ous sister, or jealous mother—who resents and engages in hostili-
ties against a young girl.[3] Even details of a particular version can
exemplify the patterns underlying various oral and written versions. Such is the case with the version of "Snow White" collected
in the Grimms' *Kinder- und Hausmärchen.*[4] A study of the psychoanalytic and feminist contributions to an understanding of this
version is, then, a useful introduction to a third possible reading
that will present what happens in "Snow White" from the mother's
perspective.

The father's law: A psychoanalytic reading

Retold from the vantage of Freudian theory, the story of Snow
White is about "being in love with the one parent and hating the
other."[5] This retelling applies, of course, not only to "Snow White,"
or *Oedipus Rex,* or *Hamlet* but to countless other legends and lives
as well, for it identifies the core or nuclear complex which is the
source, in Freudian terms, of all intrafamilial conflict and deviant
(i.e., neurotic) behavior. Thus Bruno Bettelheim proposes that the

---

[2] For a discussion of the narrative patterns found in "Snow White" and a survey
of other typological descriptions of the tale, see Steven Swann Jones, "The
Structure of 'Snow White,' " in *Fairy Tales and Society: Illusion, Allusion, and
Paradigm,* ed. Ruth B. Bottigheimer (Philadelphia: University of Pennsylvania
Press, 1986), 165–86.

[3] Aarne and Thompson, 245.

[4] As N. J. Girardot writes, "an examination of available handbooks" suggests that
the Grimms' version, "at least with regard to the specific tale of Snow White, can be
taken as generally representative" (see "Response to Jones: 'Scholarship Is Never
Just the Sum of All Its Variants,' " *Journal of American Folklore* 92 [January–March
1979]: 73–76, esp. 75).

[5] Sigmund Freud, *The Interpretation of Dreams,* in *The Standard Edition of the
Complete Psychological Works of Sigmund Freud,* ed. and trans. James Strachey, 24
vols. (London: Hogarth, 1953–74), 4:260.

inimical relations between the two female protagonists in "Snow White" are generated by rivalry over the male, a father figure. "The story deals essentially," says Bettelheim, "with the oedipal conflicts between mother and daughter."[6]

Yet, in "Snow White" the oedipal rivalry is not evident in the narrative itself, and the object of contention—the father—is virtually absent from the story. Bettelheim's reading addresses this objection by invoking the psychoanalytic claim that the analyst is precisely equipped to reveal something concealed, to distinguish the latent desire from its manifest expression in a dream, or a story. "Fairy stories teach by indirection," Bettelheim contends. "In the well-known story of Snow White, the jealous older female is not her mother but her stepmother, and the person for whose love the two are in competition is not mentioned. So the oedipal problems— source of the story's conflict—are left to our imagination."[7]

The Freudian imagination, by contrast, leaves little to our own. Following the principles outlined in *The Interpretation of Dreams*, Bettelheim proceeds to unravel the story's tissue of disguises, distortions, and subterfuges. Indirections are turned into signposts: Bettelheim's reading provides a name (the Oedipal Father) for the source of conflict in "Snow White" and also specifies why the issue of beauty is central to the story. Because competition over the father is not an acceptable form of contestation for a queen or a king's daughter, it undergoes repression and reemerges through displacement onto beauty. Bettelheim writes: "Much as the child wants the father to love her more than her mother, she cannot accept that this may create jealousy of her in her mother. . . . When this jealousy— as is true for the queen in 'Snow White'—cannot be overlooked, then some other reason must be found to explain it, as in the story it is ascribed to the child's beauty."[8] The wish to be "fairest of them

---

[6] Bruno Bettelheim, *The Uses of Enchantment: The Meaning and Importance of Fairy Tales* (New York: Vintage, 1977), 202.

[7] Ibid., 201.

[8] Ibid., 203. On the question of "who's jealous of whom?" Bettelheim offers two different explanations. At times, he treats the queen's jealousy as a projection of Snow White's feelings: "I am jealous of all the advantages and prerogatives of Mother" turns into the wishful thought: "Mother is jealous of me" (204); and "Lasting hatred and jealousy of the mother . . . are projected onto the evil queen" (206). At other times, however, he considers the queen's rage and jealousy solely in terms of her rivalry with Snow White: "The stepmother begins to feel threatened by Snow White and becomes jealous" (202); and "this is not the first story of a mother's jealousy of her daughter's budding sexuality" (207). It is only toward the close of the "Snow White" chapter that Bettelheim briefly addresses the discrepancy his analysis generates: "Snow White and the queen's relations are symbolic of some severe difficulties which may occur between mother and daughter. But they are also projections onto separate figures of tendencies which are incompatible within one person" (210–11).

all" attributed here to the queen (though later Bettelheim assigns it to Snow White as well) is yet another one of the story's subterfuges. In addition to the alteration of mother to stepmother and the tell-tale absence of the father, beauty itself is a cover-up for the sexually motivated competition between two women. Nor is it an entirely gratuitous transposition on the part of a mother and daughter. The woman endowed with the greater portion of beauty has a better chance of seducing the king.

Bettelheim's revision of "Snow White" reflects the culture of patriarchy in two ways. First, through his tale of repression and displacement, Bettelheim finds a key to the story: the paternal phallus. As he says, "We are told nothing about [Snow White's] relation to her father, although it is reasonable to assume that it is competition for him which sets (step)mother against daughter."[9] Yet this same observation may also suggest an opposite conclusion. It would seem equally reasonable to assume that the relation has little or no significance for Snow White's story; but according to the psychoanalytic rules that order Bettelheim's discussion, denial is an admission, and absence a presence. There is nothing more incriminating than the patient's protest: "That lady in my dream was *not* my mother!" Further, a Freudian approach precludes the possibility of a conflictual relationship between women in which the male is only peripheral. "A year later the king took a second wife."[10] There is no further mention of the king in the story. Nevertheless, Bettelheim puts the father at stage center and keeps him there.

Second, a Freudian approach refuses the possibility that women value beauty, give and receive pleasure through beauty, for reasons unrelated to a paternal presence. The physical vanity of women, Sigmund Freud asserts in "Femininity," has its source in penis envy: "They are bound to value their charms more highly as a late compensation for their original sexual inferiority."[11] Therefore Bettelheim maintains that the queen, "who is fixated to a primitive narcissism," orders the huntsman to return with Snow White's lungs and liver; for the queen wants above all "to incorporate Snow White's attractiveness, as symbolized by her internal organs."[12] In

[9] Ibid., 203.

[10] Jakob Ludwig Karl Grimm and Wilhelm Karl Grimm, *Grimms' Tales for Young and Old: The Complete Stories,* trans. Ralph Manheim (New York: Doubleday, 1977), 184–91, esp. 184. All citations to "Snow White" refer to this version. The Doubleday edition is based on the Winkler-Verlag (Munich) edition of *Kinder- und Hausmärchen,* first published in 1819.

[11] Sigmund Freud, "Femininity," in Strachey, ed. and trans., 22:132.

[12] Bettelheim, 206–7.

other words, by means of beauty the queen tries to compensate for the defectiveness of her genital organs or deflect attention from her female wound. Snow White, according to Bettelheim, is likewise preoccupied. The development of her narcissistic investments, presumably a displacement or distortion of an underlying penis envy, is reflected in the magic mirror: "As the small girl thinks her mother is the most beautiful person in the world, this is what the mirror initially tells the queen. But as the older girl thinks she is much more beautiful than her mother, this is what the mirror says later."[13] As Bettelheim tells it, feminine preoccupation with physical appearance becomes the focus of the story; the vanity attributed by Freud to women as a compensation for their originary lack is once more underscored. The central interest of these women's lives reduces to the question of whether they look good or not.

The father's law: A feminist reading

Sandra M. Gilbert and Susan Gubar offer us an innovative, alternative reading of "Snow White." As a starting point, Gilbert and Gubar concede the psychoanalytic premise that "myths and fairy tales often both state and enforce culture's sentences with greater accuracy than more sophisticated literary texts."[14] Yet the deliberately ambiguous use of the word "sentence," in conjunction with "enforce," already points to the direction that their interpretation of the cultural consensus will take. Citing extensively from male literary sources, Gilbert and Gubar argue that "for every glowing portrait of submissive women enshrined in domesticity, there exists an equally important negative image that embodies the sacrilegious fiendishness of what William Blake called the 'Female Will' ''; moreover, "the monster may not only be concealed *behind* the angel, she may actually turn out to reside *within* (or in the lower half of) the angel."[15] Thus the conflict in "Snow White" arises between two oppositional images or arche(stereo)types imposed upon women by Western patriarchal society: the angel and the monster. Snow White epitomizes an image of femininity— "patriarchy's angelic daughter"—that the rebellious queen actively rejects.[16]

[13] Ibid., 207.
[14] Sandra M. Gilbert and Susan Gubar, *The Madwoman in the Attic: The Woman Writer and the Nineteenth-Century Literary Imagination* (New Haven, Conn.: Yale University Press, 1979), 36.
[15] Ibid., 28–29.
[16] Ibid., 39.

In this view, Snow White and the queen become representations in an intrapsychic drama; that is, rather than two people in a
nuclear family with its inevitable oedipal problems, for Gilbert and
Gubar the female protagonists are dissociated parts of one psyche.
In terms of the Jungian symbology suggested by their analysis,
Snow White and the queen constitute a house divided against
itself:[17] "Shadow fights shadow, image destroys image in the crystal
prison, as if the 'fiend' . . . should plot to destroy the 'angel' who is
another one of her selves. . . . The Queen, adult and demonic,
plainly wants a life of 'significant action.' . . . She wants to kill the
Snow White *in herself*, the angel who would keep deeds and
dramas out of her own house."[18]
    In thus describing the angel and the monster of "Snow White,"
Gilbert and Gubar reverse traditional valuations of these images of
women. Their "demonic" means dynamic; "fiend," a vital female
force: "For the Queen . . . is a plotter, a plot-maker, a schemer, a
witch, an artist, an impersonator, a woman of infinite creative
energy, witty, wily, and self-absorbed as all artists traditionally are."
In contrast to the queen, Snow White is an "angel in the house of
myth . . . not only a child but (as female angels always are)
childlike, docile, submissive."[19] The competition between Snow
White and the queen turns into a struggle for survival between two
halves of a single personality: passivity and tractability as opposed
to inventive and subversive activism. Were the best woman to win,
clearly victory would—that is to say, should—belong to the queen.
    Yet Gilbert and Gubar go beyond reversing our conventional
assessment of Snow White and her wicked stepmother. In their
revisionist reading, the story of the angel-monster woman holds out
no hope of a happy ending. Such a divided house cannot stand.
Thus the queen dances herself "to death in red-hot iron shoes,"
while Snow White merely exchanges "one glass coffin for another."
Although she is "delivered from the prison where the Queen put
her," Snow White ends up "imprisoned in the looking glass from

[17] In Freudian dream symbology, a house is typically a symbol of the body: "The
human body as a whole is pictured by the dream-imagination as a house and the
separate organs of the body by portions of a house" (Freud, *The Interpretation of
Dreams* [n. 5 above], 258–59). By contrast, for Carl Jung houses and parts of houses
are frequent symbols of the psyche. See, e.g., Jung's analysis of a dream he reported
to Freud: "I dreamed that I was in 'my home.' . . . The dream is in fact a short
summary of my life, more specifically of the development of my mind" (see Carl G.
Jung and M.-L. von Franz, eds., *Man and His Symbols* [1964; reprint, London:
Picador, 1978], 42–43; see also 175–76).
    [18] Gilbert and Gubar, 36–37, 39.
    [19] Ibid., 38–39.

which the King's voice speaks daily."[20] There is no living happily ever after with the prince. Domesticity as the fulfillment of every-woman's wish is a male myth of happiness. The lesson of Snow White is that the achievement of psychic integration, of balanced selfhood within the patriarchy is difficult, perhaps even impossible, for a woman.

Despite their evident differences, there are certain similarities between these two responses to "Snow White." For Bettelheim, the king is absent precisely because he is too completely present, because direct oedipal confrontation would be too painful. For Gilbert and Gubar, the king is absent or "need no longer appear" in the story because "the woman has internalized the King's rules: his voice now resides in her own mirror, her own mind."[21] It is not the daughter as Bettelheim contends: "The magic mirror seems to speak with the voice of a daughter."[22] Instead, according to Gilbert and Gubar, it is the father who speaks: "His, surely, is the voice of the looking glass, the patriarchal voice of judgment that rules the Queen's—and every woman's—self-evaluation."[23] It is noteworthy, however, that in either case the king's presence looms large in spite of his virtual absence in the story. In Gilbert and Gubar's account, as in Bettelheim's, the conflictual relationships in "Snow White" are determined by male rule and male influence. Gilbert and Gubar observe that, compounding the angel-monster dichotomy within every woman, discord and division between women are all too frequent: "Female bonding is extraordinarily difficult in patriarchy: women almost inevitably turn against women because the voice in the looking glass sets them against each other."[24] Although their emphasis is on the "sentence" of the collective rather than the personal father, Gilbert and Gubar's argument is not so far removed from the psychoanalytic insistence that oedipal rivalry is the source of contention between Snow White and her (step)mother.

Creative and compelling as either (or both) of these readings are, the issue for literary criticism is: How well do they account for

[20] Ibid., 42.

[21] Ibid., 38.

[22] Bettelheim (n. 6 above), 207. Bettelheim notes that the mirror might also express the fears of the queen: "A mother may be dismayed when looking into the mirror; she compares herself to her daughter and thinks to herself: 'My daughter is more beautiful than I am.' " However, because of the wording "she is a thousand times more beautiful," Bettelheim finds the mirror's voice "much more akin to an adolescent's exaggeration," and therefore attributes it to "the voice of a daughter rather than that of a mother" (207).

[23] Gilbert and Gubar (n. 14 above), 38.

[24] Ibid.

what actually happens in "Snow White"? Whereas Bettelheim must put something into the text in order to have it fit his psychoanalytic model, namely, the father as object-choice, Gilbert and Gubar leave something out. For their feminist poetics, the specificity of the familial relationship, the fact that the queen and Snow White are (step)mother and daughter, is largely irrelevant. They could just as well be neighbors, housemates, cousins, or no kin at all. Any two similarly contrasting women would serve the same interpretive function. In both instances, the critics arrive at a description, claim to find a meaning; however, these readings require ignoring basic elements of the text in order to sustain their arguments.

Bettelheim's and Gilbert and Gubar's revisions of "Snow White" thus are not only indicative of their specific theoretical commitments but suggest a paradigm of the projective processes that govern reader-text relations as well. In addition to the mirror within the fictional world of Snow White, the text itself becomes a mirror; or, as the narrator of *Jacob's Room* says, "Nobody sees anyone as he is. . . . They see a whole—they see all sorts of things—they see themselves."[25] Yet while these readings offer partial (in both senses of the word) psychoanalytic and feminist interpretations, they are not "wrong," nor is there a "right"—a one and only—approach to the text. It is a critical commonplace that folktales and literary fairy tales consist of multivalent symbols and communicate on many levels. The oedipal and the angel-monster theories may have relevance for different readers at different times. Hence the considerable explanatory powers of these competing theories. As Norman Holland has observed: "The unity we find in literary texts is impregnated with the identity that finds that unity"; and "all of us, as we read, use the literary work to symbolize and finally replicate ourselves."[26] The reading I now propose is not excluded from this observation. It is as convinced and convicted (or, rather, as reflected) by its interpretive commitment as those readings that have come before.

What the mother wants

The story of Snow White, then, is not just another variant of the myth of King Oedipus, nor a tale of any two women (psychic fragments) in conflict. Rather it is also a story about mothers and

[25] Virginia Woolf, *Jacob's Room* (1922; reprint, Harmondsworth: Penguin, 1965), 28.
[26] Norman Holland, "Unity Identity Text Self," in *Reader-Response Criticism: From Formalism to Post-Structuralism*, ed. Jane P. Tompkins (Baltimore: Johns Hopkins University Press, 1980), 118–33, esp. 123–24.

daughters. This is another source of its enduring appeal. It inscribes the difficulties inherent in the closest of female bonds. It portrays relations gone radically wrong, or what happens when mothers and daughters cannot work out the problems created by the special, intense bond between them.

"Snow White" is the daughter's story. Her perspective orients the narrative from beginning to end. As Bettelheim has noted: "Since the hearer identifies with Snow White, he sees all events through her eyes, and not through those of the queen."[27] The text is full of indications of Snow White's perspectival dominance. There is first and foremost the jealousy of the queen, repeatedly and graphically expressed: "The queen gasped, and turned yellow and green with envy."[28] An angry or hostile response is never explicitly attributed to Snow White. Whatever negative feelings she might have toward the queen are indirectly conveyed through the narrative structure (see, e.g., the episodes in which her persecutor's plans are repeatedly foiled) and language. The queen is characterized throughout in unremittingly negative terms: she is most often deemed "wicked," but she is also proud, overbearing, and envious. "Envy and pride [grow] like weeds in her heart" while at her behest the huntsman prepares to pierce Snow White's "innocent heart."[29]

Such one-sidedness of characterization typifies the fairy tale and indicates its governing perspective, but complete disregard of the variety of traits to be found in real human beings is, as Freud has observed, a typical feature of daydreams and phantasies as well. All of the characters are defined in relation to the hero, either as helpers or as enemies and rivals.[30] "Snow White" has this and other features in common with daydreams; both personal and cultural phantasies are elaborated in the daughter's story. Thus the description of Snow White's remarkable coffin, like the characterization of her (step)mother, also bears the unmistakable signature of her daydreaming consciousness: " 'We can't lower her into the black earth,' [the dwarfs] said, and they had a coffin made out of glass, so that she could be seen from all sides, and they put her into it and wrote her name in gold letters on the coffin, adding that she was a king's daughter."[31] We may easily recognize here what Freud calls "His Majesty the Ego, the hero alike of every day-dream and of

[27] Bettelheim, 203.

[28] Grimm and Grimm (n. 10 above), 185.

[29] Ibid.

[30] Sigmund Freud, "Creative Writers and Day-dreaming," in Strachey, ed. and trans. (n. 5 above), 9:150.

[31] Grimm and Grimm, 189–90.

every story." Similarly, the pattern of Snow White's close escapes
from the strange deaths plotted by the queen corresponds to the
Freudian scenario of the adventures that befall this invulnerable
("Nothing can happen to *me!*") hero: "If, at the end of one chapter
of my story, I leave the hero unconscious and bleeding from severe
wounds, I am sure to find him at the beginning of the next being
carefully nursed and on the way to recovery."[32]

That Snow White is the story's dreamer is born out by the fact
that all the male figures come under the spell of her incomparable
beauty. Thus, "because of her beauty the huntsman took pity on her
and said: 'All right, you poor child. Run away.' " Later, " 'Heavens
above!' [the dwarfs] cried. 'Heavens above! What a beautiful child!'
They were so delighted they didn't wake her but let her go on
sleeping in the little bed." The dwarfs obligingly provide a halfway
or transitional home, a place for Snow White to stop on the journey
from her father's house to the assumption of her husband's. In the
dwarfs' cottage, "everything was tiny, but wonderfully neat and
clean": a manageable and nonthreatening doll-like world (with
little cups and little plates) for a young princess to play
housekeeping.[33] The daughter's daydream resonates with the patriarchal culture that has shaped her individuality. Then one day
Snow White's erotic and ambitious wishes are fulfilled: a prince
comes along and falls in love with her at first sight.[34] The queen's
plans are foiled again: "The jolt shook the poisoned core, which
Snow White had bitten off, out of her throat, and soon she opened
her eyes . . . and was alive again. 'Oh!' she cried. 'Where am I?'
'With me!' the prince answered joyfully."[35] Then in a final flourish

---

[32] Freud, "Creative Writers and Day-dreaming," 9:150, 150, 149.

[33] Grimm and Grimm, 185, 186, 185.

[34] Compare Freud: "The motive forces of phantasies are unsatisfied wishes,
and every single phantasy is the fulfillment of a wish. . . . In young women the
erotic wishes predominate almost exclusively, for their ambition is as a rule
absorbed by erotic trends. In young men egoistic and ambitious wishes come to
the fore clearly enough alongside of erotic ones" ("Creative Writers and
Day-dreaming," 9:146–47).

[35] Grimm and Grimm, 190. In Donald Barthelme's imaginative revision of the
tale, the prince also gallantly saves Snow White—but with a difference: "Jane gave
Snow White a vodka Gibson on the rocks. 'Drink this,' she said. 'It will make you feel
better.' 'I don't feel bad physically,' Snow White said. 'Emotionally is another story
of course.' 'Go on,' Jane said. 'Go on drink it.' . . . 'This drink is vaguely exciting, like
a film by Leopoldo Torre Nilsson,' Paul said. 'It is a good thing I have taken it away
from you, Snow White. It is too exciting for you. If you had drunk it, something bad
would probably have happened to your stomach. But because I am a man, and
because men have strong stomachs for the business of life, and the pleasure of life
too, nothing will happen to me. . . .' 'Look how he has fallen to the ground Jane!'
Snow White observed. 'And look at all that green foam coming out of his face! And
look at those convulsions he is having! Why it resembles nothing else but a death

of wish-fulfillment, the (step)mother drops down dead at the wedding.

The narrative focus of "Snow White" would seem consistently to occlude the queen's experience. Whatever she sees and feels is filtered through an external, and implicitly hostile, perspective. Yet, the various plots the queen contrives against Snow White could be an expression of her unconscious wishes; the narrated events could be symbolizations (or symptoms) of her repressed desires. This is not an entirely wild or willful supposition; folkloric studies provide corroborating grounds for such a reading. As Ruth Bottigheimer observes, German *Märchen* are "assumed to have originated in or to have passed through . . . the *Spinnstube,* for it was there that women gathered in the evening and told tales to keep themselves and their company awake as they spun. And it was from informants privy to this oral tradition that Wilhelm and Jacob Grimm gathered many of their folk tales."[36] Karen Rowe also cautions: "To have the antiquarian Grimm brothers regarded as the fathers of modern folklore is perhaps to forget the maternal lineage, the 'mothers' who in the French *veillées* and English nurseries, in court salons and the German *Spinnstube* . . . passed on their wisdom."[37]

This emphasis on the mother as principle narrative agent is not intended to rule out the daughter. Rather, it suggests that the *same* dream/text may be attributed to or seen as woven by two different dreamers. A single dream component may be read from the perspective of either the mother or the daughter. The textual attribution, the perspective we choose to follow, necessarily alters our reading of the action, but the two perspectives coexist rather than supplant one another. Moreover, since every mother is also a daughter, different phases of her development may be represented simultaneously in the dream.

One character trait remains constant throughout the mother's story. Her artistry does not belatedly emerge with her transformation into a "wicked witch." In the opening scene the "good" queen is already an artist, inventing, designing, creating her child: "If only I had a child as white as snow and as red as blood and as black as the wood of my window frame." Being mad or bad is not, as Gilbert and Gubar contend, a necessary correlative of female

---

agony, the whole scene! I wonder if there was something wrong with that drink after all? Jane? Jane?' " (see Donald Barthelme, *Snow White* [1967; reprint, New York: Athenaeum, 1978], 174–75).

[36] Ruth B. Bottigheimer, "Tale Spinners: Submerged Voices in Grimms' Fairy Tales," *New German Critique* 27 (Fall 1982): 141–50, esp. 143.

[37] Karen E. Rowe, "To Spin a Yarn: The Female Voice in Folklore and Fairy Tale," in Bottigheimer, ed. (n. 2 above), 53–74, esp. 68.

creativity in this story. "A little while later," we are told (this is surely in dream time), "she gave birth to a daughter."[38] The child initially fulfills her maternal expectations. She answers exactly—as white as snow, as red as blood, and as black as ebony—to the queen's wishful description. What the beginning of "Snow White" represents is the imaginative or creative aspect of motherhood, the child as mother's work of art. If there is nothing overtly deviant or disturbing in this story as yet, it is not only because mothering (i.e., nurturing and socializing as well as bearing a child) is commonly women's labor, but also because women's creative impulses have few alternative outlets in the patriarchy. Mothers thus tend to regard their children as objets d'art, and with a complicity born of convenience, men encourage them to do so.

That the wicked queen is an artist has already been suggested by Gilbert and Gubar. That she is a surrogate for the real mother has been posited by Bettelheim, who brackets the references to her foster function: (step)mother. I would further suggest that the monster-mother develops out of the Madonna-mother, that the two queens may be seen as temporally successive aspects of the mother as artist.[39] Thus, after Snow White takes a bite out of the apple and falls down dead, the woman who once wished for this child laughs "a terrible laugh" and says: "White as snow, red as blood, black as ebony. The dwarfs won't revive you this time."[40] The second queen bitterly mocks the wishes of her former self. This radical division between self and self is represented in the fairy tale by the presence of a good mother and a bad mother; that is, the doubling of mothers need not invariably be read as an expression of the child's ambivalence, manifested by the splitting of the parental imago into two opposing characters. It may also be read as a symbolization, a casting out onto the external world, of the alterations that occur within a woman as a result of her own experiences in the maternal role.

Viewed thus, the initial "death" of the queen—"when [Snow White] was born, the queen died"—signals her first transformation or rebirth into motherhood. Significantly, her second transformation into "wicked witch" occurs when Snow White reaches the age of

[38] Grimm and Grimm (n. 10 above), 184.

[39] This relationship between mother and stepmother is reinforced by the many variants of "Snow White" in which the child's persecutor is her actual mother. Only with the nineteenth-century German reworking and editing of the tale was the mother definitively recast as a stepmother (see Jones, "The Structure of 'Snow White' " [n. 2 above], 168–70). Kurt Ranke points out that the Grimms' substitution of stepmother for mother served "to make the villainess an outsider in the family circle" (see Kurt Ranke, ed., *Folktales of Germany*, trans. Lotte Baumann [London: Routledge & Kegan Paul, 1966], xviii).

[40] Grimm and Grimm, 189.

seven and is presumably no longer as dependent or docile as she once was. One bright morning, for example, Snow White might have woken up and said: I want to dress all by myself. Then she might not have stood still while her mother tried to comb her hair. She might even have stamped her little foot and said: I don't want pigtails anymore! Or: Can't you do anything right? Be that as it may, at this juncture the queen's dream of maternity turns bad: "But as Snow White grew, she became more and more beautiful, and by the time she was seven years old she was . . . more beautiful than the queen herself." It is only then that the queen undergoes a change of heart ("her heart turned over in her bosom"), and she begins to rage against her growing (step)daughter.[41]

The king need not be imported into the argument in order to understand this. Corresponding to separation anxiety in children, to the fear of being cut off from parental love and protection, there is a comparable anxiety in adults: a fear of being cut off from the child's proximity and dependence, a fear of freedom from the thousand and one tasks that structure the life of a mother.[42] However, the rewards for overcoming separation anxiety in the child are increased independence, a sense of selfhood and progress. For the adult the implications are radically different: a passage from ascendancy to decline, from omnipotence or, at least, control to a dwindling of authority. This process is inseparable from aging.

Hence, beauty is at issue. Following Freud, Bettelheim says that the overevaluation of beauty is "an impulse inhibited in its aim," a displacement of the desire for the father.[43] Gilbert and Gubar argue

[41] Ibid., 185.

[42] Separation anxiety can occur, of course, in male and female parents but is more likely to be found in the culturally designated primary parent or caretaker, i.e., the mother. For an illuminating analysis of maternal separation anxiety, see Erna Furman, "Mothers Have to Be There to Be Left," *Psychoanalytic Study of the Child* 37 (1982): 15–28. In discussing the trauma of weaning, Furman observes: "It is often the first time when a mother is called upon to be there to be left. Since she is then still so utterly close with her baby . . . , she is especially likely to experience his turning away from her and reaching out for more advanced and independent satisfactions as a narcissistically hurtful rejection, abandonment or attack" (20). The infant's subsequent conflicted and stressful behavior is largely a reaction to "his mother's upset at his leaving of her," rather than to "the loss of his earlier state and satisfactions" (20). On the consequences of women's monopoly of child rearing and the ambivalent responses it promotes, see esp. Nancy Chodorow, *The Reproduction of Mothering: Psychoanalysis and the Sociology of Gender* (Berkeley and Los Angeles: University of California Press, 1978); Dorothy Dinnerstein, *The Mermaid and the Minotaur* (New York: Harper & Row, 1977); and Jane Flax, "Mother-Daughter Relationships: Psychodynamics, Politics, and Philosophy," in *The Future of Difference*, ed. Hester Eisenstein and Alice Jardine (New Brunswick, N.J.: Rutgers University Press, 1987), 20–40.

[43] Sigmund Freud, *Civilization and Its Discontents*, in Strachey, ed. and trans. (n. 5 above), 21:30. See Bettelheim, 203.

that beauty is an imposition of the patriarchy that dictates the terms of conflict and inhibits female bonding. Man, in either case, is the measure of all things. Yet the mother's story suggests that, quite apart from the oedipal complex or patriarchal constraints, beauty may have an intrinsic aesthetic value for women. Further, the issue of beauty is inseparable in "Snow White" from the generational conflict, from youth and ascent as opposed to aging and descent. Ann Sexton, in her *Transformations,* renders with precision the core of this conflict: "Once there was a lovely virgin / called Snow White. / Say she was thirteen. / Her stepmother, / a beauty in her own right, / though eaten, of course, by age, / would hear of no beauty surpassing her own." In Sexton's poem, the issue of aging is directly linked to the queen's change of attitude toward her (step)daughter. There is no reference at all to the father: "Suddenly one day the mirror replied, / Queen, you are full fair, 'tis true, / but Snow White is fairer than you. / . . . now the queen saw brown spots on her hand / and four whiskers over her lip / so she condemned Snow White to be hacked to death." Then immediately after: "Bring me her heart, she said to the hunter."[44] Eating Snow White (and I will return to this later) is one way of not letting go.

If the wished for child had been a boy instead of a girl, this story of separation would probably have required an entirely different development. Nancy Chodorow speaks of mothers' differential treatment and experiencing of their sons and daughters. Drawing on clinical and cultural evidence, Chodorow points out that ego boundaries (a sense of personal psychological division) between mothers and daughters are less easily formed, less clearly defined than those between mothers and sons. Mothers normally identify more or have "a greater sense of sameness" with daughters than sons.

> Because they are the same gender as their daughters and have been girls, mothers of daughters tend not to experience these infant daughters as separate from them in the same way as do mothers of infant sons. In both cases, a mother is likely to experience a sense of oneness and continuity with her infant. However, this sense is stronger, and lasts longer, vis-à-vis daughters. Primary identification and symbiosis with daughters tend to be stronger and cathexis of daughters is more likely to retain and emphasize narcissistic elements, that is, to be based on experiencing a daughter as an extension or double of a mother herself.[45]

[44] Ann Sexton, "Snow White and the Seven Dwarfs," in her *Transformations* (Boston: Houghton Mifflin, 1971), 3–9.
[45] Chodorow, 122, 109.

The conflict in "Snow White" thus reflects an exaggerated form of an otherwise normal relationship in everyday life. This is not to say that all mother-daughter relations display this type of conflict. Since a mother regards herself and is regarded by others as responsible for the growth of her child, she typically takes pride in "the production of a young adult acceptable to her group"; yet, since pain as well as pleasure may be part of the maternal experience of a child's growing autonomy, "mothers engage in practices other than and often conflicting with mothering."[46] It is the queen's radical attempt to perpetuate primary intimacy and identification with her (step)daughter that marks the specific pathology of her story.

Jacques Lacan's analysis of the mirror phase or stage (*Le stade du miroir*) suggests that the magic mirror is central to the queen's experience of identification with—as well as alienation from—her daughter. According to Lacan, this phase takes place between the ages of six to eighteen months, when the child first perceives "the total form of the body," that is, its complete reflection in a mirror, instead of the incomplete or fragmented image previously seen without a mirror.[47] The child's specular experience of its bodily unity inaugurates the formation of the *"moi,"* or what is to become the ego. The mirror phase is thus a turning point, a "coming-into-being (*le devenir*)," which, says Lacan, "manufactures for the subject . . . the succession of phantasies that extends from a fragmented body-image (*une image morcelée du corps*) to a form of its totality."[48] Although the ego is a construct of successive imaginary identifications, and hence for Lacan a "mirage," the mirror phase is vital for the maturation of the subject.

The queen's confrontations with her magic mirror set and keep the plot of "Snow White" in motion. However, these confrontations dramatize a reversal or regressive form of the mirror phase. The queen who once upon a time saw a whole in the mirror—ratified by the assurance, "You are the fairest in the land"—no longer sees that image. She repeatedly turns to the mirror in an attempt to recapture

[46] Sara Ruddick, "Maternal Thinking," *Feminist Studies* 6 (Summer 1980): 342–67, esp. 348–49.

[47] Jacques Lacan, "The Mirror Stage as Formative of the Function of the I as Revealed in Psychoanalytic Experience," in his *Ecrits: A Selection*, trans. Alan Sheridan (New York: Norton, 1977), 1–7, esp. 2. In addition to J. Laplanche and J.-B. Pontalis's discussion of the mirror phase in *The Language of Psycho-Analysis*, trans. Donald Nicholson-Smith (London: Hogarth, 1983), I have found Malcolm Bowie, "Jacques Lacan," in *Structuralism and Since: From Levi-Strauss to Derrida*, ed. John Sturrock (Oxford: University Press, 1979), 116–153; and Jane Gallop, "Where to Begin?" in her *Reading Lacan* (Ithaca, N.Y., and London: Cornell University Press, 1985), 74–92, particularly helpful.

[48] Lacan, 4.

the sense of totality, albeit of an imaginary order, which the birth of her daughter had extended and enriched. Suddenly, the daughter's otherness is asserted. The mirror refuses to sustain any illusion of identification with the daughter; in its truth function, the specular image shows the mother that her daughter is discordant with her own identity. The mother loses control over the beauty, the creation that seemed an extension of herself. Something is taken from her, a vital part of her is cut off. Symbolically, what she perceives in the mirror is a body-in-pieces.[49] The mirror reflects disintegration without possibility of regeneration. All the king's horses and all the king's men cannot put this queen together again.

The voice in the mirror thus belongs to neither the king nor the queen's daughter. The voice she hears is her own. To put it in another way, the mirror images the mother's wound. This is not that general "genital deficiency" Freud finds in all women; rather, this is the wound inflicted by the mother's experience of separation. The child of her own making finds completion without her. For the mirror not only says that Snow White is "a thousand times more fair"; it also repeatedly reminds the queen that Snow White "has gone to stay / With the seven dwarfs far, far away."[50] This distancing is a symbol of maternal loss. It signals the disruption of a dream of exclusive and everlasting attachment.

Hence the desperate queen attempts to regain control over her "far, far away" daughter. First, she orders the hunter to kill Snow White and return with her lungs and liver: "The cook was ordered to salt and stew them, and the godless woman ate them, thinking she was eating Snow White's lungs and liver."[51] This shares, but reverses, one of Freud's strangest and most powerful insights. In *Totem and Taboo* Freud speculates that the sons of the patriarchal horde assumed the father's authority by murdering him and consuming him, literally: "The violent primal father had doubtless been the feared and envied model of each one of the company of brothers: and in the act of devouring him they accomplished their identification with him, and each one of them acquired a portion of his strength."[52] By contrast, in "Snow White" the consumer is the all too powerful and jealous mother.

[49] According to Laplanche and Pontalis, in Lacanian theory the mirror phase is also seen as retroactively responsible for "the emergence of the phantasy of the body-in-pieces . . . where anxiety about fragmentation can at times be seen to arise as a consequence of loss of narcissistic identification" (Laplanche and Pontalis, 251–52).

[50] Grimm and Grimm (n. 10 above), 187–88.

[51] Ibid., 185.

[52] Sigmund Freud, *Totem and Taboo: Some Points of Agreement between the Mental Lives of Savages and Neurotics*, in Strachey, ed. and trans. (n. 5 above), 13:1–161, esp. 142.

On the daughter's part, this reversal may be constituted by projection. Her wish to incorporate the authority of the parent, who presents a formidable obstacle to her demand for independence and power, is projected onto that parent. The unnatural mother is therefore seen as desiring to eat rather than to feed her child.[53] On the queen's part, this same episode is the expression of an entirely different wish. It represents a preemptive strike: she wants to eat (leave) me; I will eat (make her leave me) first. Conversely, the attempt to incorporate or consume Snow White may also represent a refusal to relinquish the daughter. Julia Kristeva speaks of and from the mother's position in "Stabat Mater": "What connection is there between myself, or even more unassumingly between my body and this internal graft and fold, which, once the umbilical cord has been severed, is an inaccessible other? . . . No identity holds up. A mother's identity is maintained only through the well-known closure of consciousness within the indolence of habit, when a woman protects herself from the borderline that severs her body and expatriates it from her child."[54] In "Snow White," however, the mother denies the fact of expatriation. Too much was perhaps invested in her artistic vision of a child "as white as snow, as red as blood, and as black as ebony." It is the queen's wish to take the daughter back into herself, to recreate the condition in which her creation was the very flesh of her own flesh. There was no clash of wills in those edenic days when mother and daughter were still an intermingled and undifferentiated unit.

When the queen fails to eat Snow White, she tries to alter the course of their relationship three more times with laces, a comb,

[53] Interestingly, whereas in *Totem and Taboo* Freud envisions this conflict only in terms of fathers and sons, the fairy tale—with greater insight perhaps—attributes totemism to mothers and daughters as well. See Kenneth Burke's discussion of totemism as an instance of Freud's overemphasis on patriarchal patterns: "I submit that this emphasis will conceal from us, to a large degree, what is going on in art. . . . Totemism, as Freud himself reminds us, was a magical device whereby the members of a group were identified with one another by the sharing of the same substance. . . . And it is to the mother that the basic informative experiences of eating are related." For these reasons Burke suggests that there is "a tendency for rebirth rituals to be completed by symbolizations of matricide," and therefore "the phenomena of identity revealed in totemism might require the introduction of matricidal ingredients also" (Kenneth Burke, "Freud—and the Analysis of Poetry," in his *The Philosophy of Literary Form: Studies in Symbolic Action*, 3d ed. [Berkeley and Los Angeles: University of California Press, 1973], 258–92, esp. 273–74). A harrowing dramatization of this argument is to be found in the "rebirth" of a group of schoolboys as savage hunters and their slaughter of a nursing sow in William Golding's *Lord of the Flies* (London: Faber & Faber, 1954), 146–51.

[54] Julia Kristeva, "Stabat Mater," trans. Léon S. Roudiez, in *The Kristeva Reader: Julia Kristeva*, ed. Toril Moi (New York: Columbia University Press, 1986), 160–86, esp. 178–79.

and an apple. Her continuing obsession with issues of intimacy and separation is evident in the repetitive nature of her plots. For Bettelheim, whose emphasis is on the child's experience of sexuality, the similarity of these episodes consists in "the readiness with which Snow White repeatedly permits herself to be tempted by the stepmother." This readiness symbolizes the adolescent girl's "unconscious wish to be sexually attractive"; her deathlike sleep after eating the apple is evidence that "she became overwhelmed by the conflict between her sexual desires and her anxiety about them."[55] Gilbert and Gubar stress the creativity and ingenuity of the queen's schemes, pointing out that each of her plots "depends on a poisonous or parodic use of a distinctively female device as a murder weapon. . . . The girl finally falls, killed, so it seems, by the female arts of cosmetology and cookery."[56] Though these readings recognize the importance of recurrent aspects of the plot, they do not take into account that the queen invariably chooses to "get at" Snow White by doing what a mother does for a very young child: dressing, combing, and feeding. The immediate outcome in every instance is to render Snow White helpless and passive, as if an unsatisfying reality could be corrected by returning to the time when Snow White was still, literally, a baby.

What the queen wants, therefore, is not so much to destroy Snow White (which is borne out by the fact that the daughter does not die) but, rather, to set back the clock and then stop it. For the other aspect of keeping Snow White in a state of infantile passivity is keeping herself perpetually young. To eat or to infantalize Snow White is thus not merely to hold onto her. It is to recapture youth and vitality. It is to distance the death that lurks behind the mirror. The phantasy underlying the mother's story is twofold: the desire, always unappeasable in reality, to remain one with the child of her body; and the painful and equally impossible desire to ward off age and aging, to remain forever "fairest in the land."

The failure of the queen's plots does not defeat or transform her, however. (Only her relationship with Snow White brings about transformations in the queen, as her death at the wedding shows once more.) She continues to try. Her last plot is the most ingenious, desperate, and regressive one of all. The queen offers Snow White the object of their first relationship: her breast. As Linda Nochlin points out, "apples and breasts have been associated from the time of Theocritus' pastoral verse down to Zola's eroticized

---

[55] Bettelheim (n. 6 above), 211–12.
[56] Gilbert and Gubar (n. 14 above), 39–40.

paean to fruit in *Le Ventre de Paris*."[57] In attempting to explain the universality of the breast-apple metaphor, Nochlin argues that it derives from "man's erotic association of inviting fruit and a succulent, inviting area of the female body." I suggest that the association is not confined to male tropes or, as Nochlin puts it, "the apple-female sexuality syndrome."[58] In the following account Marguerit Sechehaye describes a twenty-one year old psychotic patient who can only eat green vegetables and unripe apples, still attached to the tree, which she must pick for herself:

> I persist in trying to understand the symbolism of the apples. To the remark that I gave her as many apples as she wanted, Renée cries: "Yes, but those are store apples, apples for big people, but I want apples from Mummy, like that," pointing to my breasts. "Those apples there, Mummy gives them only when one is hungry."
>
> I understand at last what must be done! Since the apples represent maternal milk, I must give them to her like a mother feeding her baby. . . . To verify my hypothesis I carry it out at once. Taking an apple, and cutting it in two, I offer Renée a piece, saying, "It is time to drink the good milk from Mummy's apples, Mummy is going to give it to you." Renée then leans up against my shoulder, presses the apple upon my breast, and very solemnly, with intense happiness, eats it.[59]

For the very young child, the mother's breast is, normatively, a good object, representing comfort, connection, and security; for the oedipal child and adolescent, the breast represents a bad object, symbol of transgression and loss ("forbidden fruit"). The apple in "Snow White" conjoins these two trends; that is, it has its good side and its bad. In the fairy tale: "Snow White longed for the lovely apple, and when she saw the peasant woman [i.e., the queen] taking a bite out of it she couldn't resist."[60] The scene has a certain resemblance to the analytic situation in Sechehaye's account: the queen offers her apple to Snow White, but, in contradistinction to the analyst, she shares it with her as well. Partaking of the apple

[57] Linda Nochlin, "Eroticism and Female Imagery in Nineteenth-Century Art," in *Woman as Sex Object*, ed. Thomas B. Hess and Linda Nochlin (New York: Newsweek, 1972), 9–15, esp. 11.

[58] Ibid., 11.

[59] Marguerit A. Sechehaye, *Symbolic Realization: A New Method of Psychotherapy Applied to a Case of Schizophrenia*, trans. Barbrö Würsten and Helmut Würsten (New York: International Universities, 1951), 50–51.

[60] Grimm and Grimm (n. 10 above), 189.

together symbolizes a reciprocal regression to the oral stage when the child is most completely dependent and the mother most needed in every way. This is, therefore, "a very poisonous apple" for the developing child.[61] The queen extends to her daughter the possibility of a return to infancy or early childhood, and Snow White is unable to resist the temptation. For together with the desire to break away from the mother, Snow White experiences a yearning for the carefree days of childhood, for a symbiotic and nonconflictual relationship with her mother.

"Snow White," then, is the story of two women, a mother and a daughter: a mother who cannot grow up and a daughter who must. Hate rather than love becomes the keynote of their story. The conclusion of this tale, like the narrative in its entirety, could be read as the product of two perspectives. From the mother's perspective, the wish she held most dear has turned into a tale of loss and fragmentation. There is no resolution in sight for the relationship, only hostility and conflict. In the end, the queen dies of grief. From the daughter's perspective, the old nurturing gestures—be it grooming or feeding—are threatening. Mother always smothers, as when "[she] pulled the lace so tight that Snow White's breath was cut off and she fell down as though dead."[62] Snow White would like, therefore, nothing better than to get this interfering older woman, this deadly dragon-mother, out of her life. The conflict is finally resolved, and the daughter's wish fulfilled. In the end, the queen dies of spite.

Yet once more from the mother's perspective: Snow White is going to be ever so sorry when the babies start coming, and the king goes out hunting, and no woman really close and caring is around to help her.

At this point I return you to the opening statement.

Department of English
Hebrew University of Jerusalem

[61] Ibid.
[62] Ibid., 187.

REASSESSING MOTHER BLAME
IN INCEST

JANET LIEBMAN JACOBS

Over the last decade there has been a growing body of literature on the causes, effects, and therapeutic approaches to dealing with the problem of family violence as it is manifested in increasingly high numbers of reported cases of incest.[1] Within this field of research, feminist analysis has treated sexual abuse within the family as a source of female victimization that results from patriarchal family arrangements that create and foster female dependence and powerlessness through male control over women and children. While this analysis provides a compelling social and political explanation for female victimization in the family, it focuses primarily on the power of the father and thus fails to address the nature of mother-daughter relationships within incest families and the conflicts that characterize maternal bonding under conditions of sexual abuse.

The most important studies of incest to date reveal the extent to which the mother becomes the focus for feelings of anger, hatred, and betrayal on the part of daughters who were abused by their

I would like to thank the anonymous reviewers at *Signs* for their helpful suggestions and critical insights throughout the revision process.

[1] David Finkelhor reports that 20 percent of the women in the United States report experiences of sexual abuse *(Sexually Victimized Children* [New York: Free Press, 1979]). Diane Russell's research indicates a much higher proportion of cases, suggesting that the number of victimized women is closer to 40 percent. In 85 to 90 percent of reported cases, the perpetrators are male (see Diane Russell, "The Incidence and Prevalence of Intrafamilial and Extrafamilial Sexual Abuse of Female Children," *Child Abuse and Neglect* 7, no. 2 [1983]: 133–46).

This essay originally appeared in *Signs*, vol. 15, no. 3, Spring 1990.

fathers.[2] In this regard, Judith Herman reports that "whatever anger these women did feel was most commonly directed at women rather than men. With the exception of those who had become conscious feminists, most of the incest victims seemed to regard all women, including themselves, with contempt. . . . They identified with the mothers they despised and included themselves among the ranks of fallen and worthless women."[3] Similarly, Karen Meiselman found in her study of incest victims that 40 percent of the women expressed strong negative feelings toward their fathers while 60 percent were forgiving, with the reverse percentages being true for their attitudes toward their mothers. Thus, she concludes, as does Herman, that negative relationships with the mother prevail.[4]

These findings are supported by clinical data from an incest support group project that treated twelve girls, ages thirteen to nineteen, who had been victims of sexual abuse.[5] Treatment of these young women through support group therapy reveals that they, too, possess deep feelings of rage toward their mothers. For instance, Janie had been sexually abused by her father since the age of ten. She repeatedly spoke to the group about her hatred for her mother: "I hate my mother. I have no use for her. The social worker wanted me to see her but I said, no way. Fuck you and fuck her. I never want to see her again for the rest of my life." As Janie's attitude clearly expresses, the apparent effect of sexual abuse on the child-victim is to destroy the mother-daughter bond in such a way that it is the mother who is thought culpable and responsible for the violation and betrayal that are experienced as a result of the incest.

Theories of mother blame and the dysfunctional family

The prevalence of mother blame among incest survivors is a troubling phenomenon, particularly as existing theories of sexual abuse and family pathology incorporate both subtly and explicitly a

[2] Judith Herman, Father-Daughter Incest (Cambridge, Mass.: Harvard University Press, 1981); Judith Herman and Lisa Hirschman, "Father-Daughter Incest," in The Signs Reader, ed. Elizabeth Abel and Emily K. Abel (Chicago: University of Chicago Press, 1983), 257–78; Karen Meiselman, Incest: A Psychological Study of Causes and Effects with Treatment Recommendations (San Francisco: Jossey-Bass, 1978).

[3] Herman, 103.

[4] Meiselman.

[5] The clinical data reported here and throughout the essay are derived from an incest support group project that took place in Boulder, Colorado, between 1985 and 1986 at a group home for adolescent girls.

strong bias toward mother blame. A review of the literature on incest reveals a family dysfunction approach that casts the mother in the role of the parent who is somehow impaired: she is unable or unwilling to carry out her functions as caretaker for her children and sexual provider for her husband, and so becomes a collaborator in the incestuous relationship.[6] The family dysfunction approach thus supports the notion that the mother is in some way responsible for the acts of the father, a view that is consistent with cultural norms that justify male violence by blaming the female victim for the actions of the aggressor.

Theories about the role of the mother in the incestuous family can be classified into the following categories: the mother as colluder; the mother as helpless dependent; and the mother as victim herself. As collusionary participant in the incest relationship, the mother is the parent who, either intentionally or inadvertently, sacrifices her daughter in the service of her own needs. This interpretation informs two points of view about the mother's behavior.

The first view portrays the mother as "the family member who 'sets up' the father and daughter for the incest relationship, usually by withdrawing from her sexual role in the marriage and ignoring the special relationship that may then develop between husband and daughter."[7] The second view attributes a deeper and more selfish motive on the part of the mother, maintaining that the mother actually derives unconscious pleasure from the sexual interaction through the voyeuristic role she assumes in the parent-child triangle.[8] The effect of both of these views has been to treat and explain incest as a family problem that is the result of the selfish and irresponsible behavior of a dysfunctional mother.

Other analyses, some of which are more feminist in orientation, focus on the mother as a helpless dependent who is powerless to protect her child.[9] This role, however, is not perceived in collusionary terms but in terms of the power relations of patriarchal family arrangements. Aaron Hoorwitz explains the mother's ineffectuality in this way: "In one variant of the classic [incest] situation, the father is a dominant powerful man, keeping his wife in a dependent

[6] Meiselman; Alvin A. Rosenfeld, "The Clinical Management of Incest and Sexual Abuse of Children," *Journal of the American Medical Association* 242, no. 16 (October 19, 1979): 1761–64.

[7] Meiselman, 112.

[8] Kevin McIntyre, "Role of Mothers in Father-Daughter Incest: A Feminist Analysis," *Social Work* 26, no. 6 (November 1981): 462–66.

[9] See, e.g., Meiselman; and McIntyre.

helpless role. She may suffer from a disabling condition such as depression or physical infirmity. Although this may have been a reciprocal role relationship which satisfied both partners in the first years of marriage, the strain on the husband of his wife's dependency tends to anger the husband, who eventually distances his wife. He turns to a daughter, thereby obtaining emotional gratification."[10] Thus, the wife's dependency is the source of marital strain that leads the husband to engage in a sexual relationship with his daughter. A variation of this perspective is found in the personality approach to family dysfunction. According to this view, women who are the subjects of oppression come to exhibit characteristics of passivity, dependency, and masochism. Meiselman describes the clinical data on this personality type as follows:

> In many incestuous families the husband is overcontrolling, emotionally cold, and even physically abusive in a manner that verges on overt sadism. We then assume that the woman must be extremely dependent on her husband and tend to attribute immaturity to her since her dependency needs exceed the adult norm, even for women. In extreme cases, especially when physical abuse is involved, the concept of masochism is invoked, evidently because it seems as if the woman must positively enjoy physical and emotional pain in order to remain in the marital situation. The term masochism is not generally used in its narrow meaning of deriving sexual pleasure from pain or humiliation; in this context, it denotes a kind of satisfaction gained from being a virtuous victim who suffers endlessly for her family and actively seeks to perpetuate her victim role in the face of well-meaning attempts by others to help her to escape from her miserable situation. . . . The three characteristics that we have been discussing—passivity, dependency, and masochism—appear repetitively in descriptions of the wives of incestuous fathers.[11]

Within the context of female personality disorders as described above, the mother contributes to incest through a role reversal wherein she becomes the dependent and her daughter must assume the responsibilities of her mother in all areas of family life including the sexual realm. In one study, for example, 45 percent of

[10] Aaron Hoorwitz, "Guidelines for Treating Father-Daughter Incest," *Social Casework* 64, no. 9 (November 1983): 515–24, esp. 515.

[11] Meiselman (n. 2 above), 120.

the victims reported major responsibility for housework and child care in addition to their sexual relationship with their fathers.[12]

Another variation on the theme of helplessness and dependency in the incest family describes the mother as the more independent parent on whom the father, in spite of his apparent dominance, is heavily dependent for emotional support.[13] Mothers in this type of family are reported to be emotionally distant from both their daughters and their husbands, thus creating conditions under which the daughter becomes the surrogate wife and sexual partner.

The third category of mother blame—mother as victim—takes a longitudinal view of incestuous families, maintaining that many mothers in incest families had themselves been abused as children. Their failure to intervene in the father/daughter relationship is, in part, a form of denial of their own childhood victimization. Meiselman labels this cross-generational pattern the "transmissable quality of incest."[14] Margot Zuelzer and Richard Reposa maintain that for women, "denial and repression of the realities of their family dysfunction and of their emotional pain is in the service of their own fragile self-esteem, and in the way they have typically learned to deal with unresolvable conflict in their early life."[15] Thus, the mother as victim both of a male-dominated family structure and of her own abusive history offers perhaps the most compelling understanding of the nonprotective parent: the mother who is prone to ignore or deny her daughter's victimization in order to maintain a thinly constructed sense of self-worth and the pretense of a tolerable reality.

The prevailing theories of mother blame have been discussed briefly here in order to provide a background for presenting an alternative explanation for the phenomenon. In the analysis that follows, the emphasis will be on mother blame from the perspective of the victimized child. Although this analysis also treats the family as dysfunctional, the source of this dysfunction is not found in the inadequacy of the mother but in structural arrangements that separate sources of emotional and social power into feminine and masculine realms of control within the nuclear family.

Power in the nuclear family

Feminist analyses of family power relations approach the study of male dominance primarily from one of two perspectives, materialist

---

[12] Herman (n. 2 above).

[13] See the Ciba Foundation report, *Child Sexual Abuse within the Family* (New York: Tavistock, 1984).

[14] Meiselman, 115.

[15] Margot Zuelzer and Richard Reposa, "Mothers in Incestous Families," *International Journal of Family Therapy* 5 (Summer 1983): 99–108, esp. 104.

or sociopsychoanalytic.[16] The materialist view assumes the centrality of the economic mode of production in determining the structure of the family, socialization, and reproduction.[17] The sociopsychoanalytic perspective assumes the centrality of patriarchy in
personality development and gender identification.[18] While the
materialist school emphasizes the significance of the instrumental
role of the father in economic production, the sociopsychoanalytic
school stresses the importance of the affective role of the mother
within the male-dominated family.

The nature and impact of maternal power in the family is a much
debated issue in the study of mothering in industrial societies.
Theorists such as Diane Ehrensaft discuss female power in terms of
the woman's domain:

> While men hold fast to the domination of the "public
> sphere," it has been the world of home and family that is
> woman's domain. Particularly in the rearing of children, it is
> often her primary (or only) sphere of power. For all the
> oppressive and debilitating effects of the institution of moth-
> erhood, a woman does get social credit for being a "good"
> mother. She also accrues for herself some sense of control
> and authority in the growth and development of her children.
> As a mother she is afforded the opportunity for genuine
> human interaction, in contrast to the alienation and deper-
> sonalization of the workplace.[19]

In contrast, theorists such as Juliet Mitchell reject the notion that
women are powerful because of their central socializing role within
the family, arguing that this approach mistakes isolation for

---

[16] The term "sociopsychoanalytic" is used here to reflect the development of
feminist scholarship that integrates a social-structural analysis of the family and
society with the analysis of personality formation within the family. This approach is
found in the work of Juliet Mitchell and Nancy Chodorow (see Juliet Mitchell,
Woman's Estate [New York: Pantheon, 1971], and *Psychoanalysis and Feminism*
[London: Allen Lane, 1974]; Nancy Chodorow, "Family Structure and Feminine
Personality," in *Woman, Culture and Society*, ed. Michelle Rosaldo and Louise
Lamphere [Stanford, Calif.: Stanford University Press, 1974], 43–66, and *The
Reproduction of Mothering: Psychoanalysis and the Sociology of Gender* [Berkeley
and Los Angeles: University of California Press, 1978]).

[17] The materialist perspective is represented in the work of theorists such as
Angela Davis and Ann Ferguson (see Angela Davis, *Woman, Race and Class* [New
York: Random House, 1981]; Ann Ferguson, "On Conceiving Motherhood and
Sexuality: A Feminist Materialist Approach," in *Mothering: Essays in Feminist
Theory*, ed. Joyce Trebilcot [Totowa, N.J.: Rowman & Allanheld, 1984], 153–67).

[18] See n. 16 above.

[19] Diane Ehrensaft, "When Women and Men Mother," in Trebilcot, ed., 41–61,
esp. 49.

freedom.[20] Despite their differences, however, these theorists share the common goal of establishing objective measures of power and, as a consequence, they overlook the importance of subjective accounts of familial power relations. In order to understand the impact that incest has on a child's relationship to her mother, the child's interpretation of her experience must be examined in relation to the dominant role that the mother assumes in primary child care. The concept of power within the family can thus be divided into the affective (emotional) domain of maternal control and the social (structural) domain of paternal control.

In this model, a theory of mother blame in incest draws on a feminist reinterpretation of the object relations approach to psychoanalytic development, a theoretical approach that focuses on the significance of mothering in the formation of personality. Although object relations theory has contributed to the misogynistic development of traditional psychoanalytic thought, it is nonetheless useful to a discussion of mother blame in incest. The field of object relations, as it emerged through the work of Ronald Fairbairn, Michael Balint, and particularly D. W. Winnicott, provided the basis on which the phenomenon of mother blame came to be associated with explanations of family pathology that focused on the mother's personality dysfunction and poor emotional adjustment.[21]

In *An Object Relations Theory of the Personality,* Fairbairn maintains that the first social relationship experienced by an infant is that between the child and the mother and that the "nature of the relationship so established exercises a profound influence upon the subsequent relationships of the individual and upon his (or her) social attitude in general."[22] Having thus established the developmental primacy of the mother-child bond, he then elaborates on the stages of dependency through which the child passes as he or she experiences the mother love-object as a source first of physical gratification (sucking and feeding) and then emotional gratification (attention and affection).[23] Michael Balint argues that the social-

---

[20] Mitchell.

[21] Ronald Fairbairn, *An Object Relations Theory of the Personality* (New York: Basic, 1952); D. W. Winnicott, *Collected Papers* (London: Tavistock, 1958); and Michael Balint, *Primary Love and Psycho-Analytic Technique* (London: Tavistock, 1965). See also Janet Sayers, *Sexual Contradictions: Psychology, Psychoanalysis, and Feminism* (London: Tavistock, 1986), for a feminist critique of traditional object relations theory.

[22] Fairbairn, 11.

[23] Ibid., 38–48.

relational needs of love and attention are as significant to the primary maternal relationship as are the more physical needs identified first by Freud then elaborated by Fairbairn.[24]

These theorists maintain that the primary source of gratification, the mother, is perceived by the child as omnipotent, a powerful figure on whom the child is totally dependent from the first moments of life. The mother is both the object of love who offers total and immediate gratification and the object of frustration and anger when such gratification is not provided instantly or is withheld. The relationship that develops is therefore one defined by dependency, helplessness, and ambivalence.

Winnicott, like Fairbairn, focuses on the merging of infant with mother, explaining the relationship of connectedness not only in terms of the child but in terms of the mother as well. The adequate mother, according to Winnicott, fulfills and gratifies her child's needs through a process of "primary maternal occupation" in which she perceives herself to be merged physically with the child, a psychic state of relatedness that lays the foundation for the development of the child's ego.[25] Thus, Winnicott theorizes that splits in the ego, rather than an inevitable consequence of infantile frustration and anger, develop as a result of inadequate mothering. When the mother fails to merge with the child, fails to meet the infant's needs to the exclusion of all other concerns, the child is likely to develop a false self characterized by a splintering of the ego that interferes with emotional and interpersonal development.[26]

This analysis of infant-mother dependency, as Janet Sayers suggests, "hardly seems promising stuff out of which to forge a feminist perspective on psychology."[27] In this regard, Gayle Rubin has noted the danger inherent in borrowing from sexist ideologies in the construction of feminist theory.[28] Still, as Rubin points out in defending her own use of psychoanalysis, the work of the Freudians "enables us to isolate sex and gender from 'mode of production' and to counter a certain tendency to explain sex oppression as a reflex of economic forces."[29] In identifying the relationship of

[24] Sigmund Freud, "On Narcissism: An Introduction," in *Standard Edition of the Complete Psychological Works*, ed. James Strachey (London: Hogarth, 1914), vol. 14; Balint, 74–90.

[25] Winnicott, 50–53.

[26] Ibid., 302–6.

[27] Sayers, 67.

[28] Gayle Rubin, "The Traffic in Women," in *Toward an Anthropology of Women*, ed. Rayna R. Reiter (New York: Monthly Press, 1975), 157–210.

[29] Ibid., 202.

structural forces to family dynamics and psychological development, feminist analysis of object relations theory counters the
tendency toward reflexivity without undervaluing the role that
economic forces play in forming and maintaining gender relations.
In particular, the work of Nancy Chodorow has provided a basis for
reframing an understanding of the context of mothering and child
development in patriarchy by linking the structural characteristics
of child-rearing patterns to the role of the father in economic
production.[30]

In Chodorow's application of object relations theory to an
analysis of family structure, she, like Fairbairn and Winnicott, seeks
to explain personality and ego development in relation to the
primary bonding of mother and child. In her analysis, the father
becomes a secondary and less important figure in the emotional life
of the child because his instrumental role within the family places
him outside the sphere of emotional development and attachment.
Thus, the patriarchal family, because it embodies a rigid sex-role
structure and division of labor that allocates sole responsibility for
child care and nurturing to mothers, contributes to the creation of a
separate sphere of female responsibility on the basis of which
mothers are judged to be either good or bad, successes or failures,
both by society and by the child. In cases of incest, the child's
identification and acknowledgment of the existence and importance of the affective maternal domain plays a crucial role in mother
blame. That the child sees the mother as the most significant source
of power within the family, irrespective of the social reality of the
situation, is a result of the expressive role allocated to women as the
providers of emotional needs and protection within the family.

Child development, as it is understood within a feminist framework of object relations theory, is not based on the adequacies or
inadequacies of the mother but on a structural arrangement of
family relations that locates the mother in a central position with
regard to the affective realm of personality formation. At issue here,
then, is not the quality of bonding per se but the structural
conditions that define emotional development as exclusively the
mother's province—conditions that legitimize mother blaming.
Such structural arrangements, according to Chodorow and Susan
Contratto, create conditions through which "blame and idealization
of mothers have become our cultural ideology. This ideology,
however, gains meaning from and is partially produced by infantile
fantasies that are themselves the outcome of being mothered
exclusively by one woman. If mothers have exclusive responsibility

[30] Chodorow (n. 16 above).

for infants who are totally dependent, then to the infant they are the source of all good and evil."[31]

Chodorow and Contratto are particularly critical of contemporary writers who confuse infantile fantasy with the reality of maternal actions and, thereby, contribute to the notion that mothers are in actuality all-powerful ominous caretakers whose control is real and absolute.[32] In the case of incest victims, however, what Chodorow and Contratto term infantile fantasy is in fact the subjective reality through which the child experiences her relationship to her mother. As a result, victimized daughters often confuse the true role that their mothers played in the sexual abuse with their idealized expectations. The following interchange, which took place during group therapy, is indicative of Janie's subjective assessment of her mother's involvement:

GROUP LEADER: Why do you think your mother knew about the abuse?

JANIE: She just knew. I know she knew. How could she not know? We were doing it right outside the trailer and she was right inside.

GROUP LEADER: Did you ever try to talk to your mom about what was happening?

JANIE: No, I was afraid to tell her, I guess.

Janie, like many other young women in the support group, was convinced that her mother was aware of the incest, although she never explicitly told her, nor had she witnessed her mother observing the abuse. A similar case is that of Fran, who was fourteen years old when she became involved in the support group. Early in treatment Fran reported that she told her mother about her father's sexual advances but that her mother had done nothing to prevent the abuse. When asked how she explained the incest to her mother, the young girl said, "I asked her not to go to work at night. I said I didn't like being home alone with Daddy." When probed further, Fran indicated that although her mother asked why she was uncomfortable with her father, she said she didn't know exactly but

---

[31] Nancy Chodorow and Susan Contratto, "The Fantasy of the Perfect Mother," in *Rethinking the Family: Some Feminist Questions,* ed. Barrie Thorne with Marilyn Yalom (New York: Longman, 1982), 54–75, esp. 65.

[32] In particular, Chodorow and Contratto discuss the work of Nancy Friday, *My Mother, My Self* (New York: Delacorte, 1977); Judith Arcana, *Our Mothers' Daughters* (Berkeley: Shameless Hussy, 1979); and Dorothy Dinnerstein, *The Mermaid and the Minotaur* (New York: Harper & Row, 1976).

just liked it better when her mother was at home. Both Fran and Janie expressed a deep and unrelenting conviction that their mothers knew about the incest and had therefore committed an unforgivable act of betrayal. Implicit in this notion of betrayal is the belief in the all-powerful and all-knowing mother who is capable of protecting the child from any and all harm, regardless of the reality of power relations within the family.

The issue of maternal protection is particularly germane in considering the role that fathers assume in patriarchy vis-à-vis the sexualization of daughters. According to Miriam Johnson, the primacy of the mother in the child's emotional life is accompanied by the father's enforcement of sex roles.[33] "Because of the initial identification of children of both sexes with the mother and because it is in connection with the mother that both sexes are inducted into 'socialized' behavior, the maternal aspect of the feminine principle is seen as generic and symbolizing the common humanity of both sexes. The sex differentiating principle is introduced by the father. The woman's status as a sex object is related symbolically and ultimately to the father."[34] The father accomplishes his socializing role by conditioning his daughter's sexuality, interacting with her as the prospective husband for whom she is ultimately preparing herself.

In Johnson's analysis of the father's sexualization of the daughter, she is describing normative family structures in which the incest taboo is respected. Thus, a daughter's relationship with her father can act as a model, within safe bounds, of an adult heterosexual relationship. The incestuous family, however, places the father-daughter dynamic in an entirely different context. Where incest is present, the daughter's sexualization violates the boundaries of her physical safety and well being. Issues of control and power in the family become more focused and intensified as the child's right to her own person is undermined by the father's sexual invasion. Such violations conflict with the child's assumptions about maternal protectiveness. The incest victim therefore experiences the powerlessness of women in the most personal and painful of ways, first through her own victimization and then through the knowledge of her mother's ineffectuality. The rage that comes to dominate her relationship with her mother is the anger of betrayal as well as the anger of deception, as the illusion of maternal omnipotence is destroyed in the face of the real power relations of paternal control and dominance.

[33] Miriam M. Johnson, "Fathers, Mothers, and Sex Typing," *Sociological Inquiry* 45, no. 1 (1975): 15–26, and "Heterosexuality, Male Dominance, and the Father Image," *Sociological Inquiry* 51, no. 2 (1981): 129–39.

[34] Johnson, "Fathers, Mothers, and Sex Typing," 24.

Ann Ferguson thus characterizes incest as a form of male domination that destroys the mother-daughter bond by forcing the daughter's affective involvement away from the mother.[35] The effect on the mother-daughter relationship is twofold since the child turns against her mother even while her mother is powerless "to escape the oppressive economic, political, and psychological structures" of the patriarchal family.[36] Both Johnson and Ferguson conclude that any assessment of incest and the role that the mother plays *must* be considered in relation to the structural constraints of male dominance. Furthermore, Ferguson maintains that "such constraints, such as economic dependence, legal restrictions on reproductive control, lack of strong female bonding networks that support sexual freedom for women or parental responsibilities for men, and physical violence by one's partner are all empirical factors that make women less free in parenting and sexuality than men."[37] These objective measures of control, however, are realities of which the victimized child is as yet unaware. Therefore, the phenomenon of mother blame grows out of the anger and helplessness that both mother and child experience in the victimized household.

Anger, powerlessness, separation, and individuation

Clinical findings with respect to mother blame among incest victims can be explained, at least in part, within the perspective of an object relations understanding of mother-child bonding in the patriarchal family. This perspective argues for a reevaluation of the notion of women's power within the family, using a conceptual framework in which the child's understanding of her social world is based on how she experiences herself first and primarily through her connection to the mother. The process of ego development thus takes place within a psychic arena whose parameters are defined by the child's struggle to separate from her mother, the first object of love, in order to attain a separate and distinct sense of self.

Johnson supports the notion that it is the father who "promotes independence and autonomy (from the mother) in both sexes while at the same time he reinforces sex differentiated behavior."[38] Growing into adulthood thus involves separating from the primal relationship with the mother. Although the process of individuation seems to be difficult and problematic for both boys and girls, it

[35] Ferguson (n. 17 above).
[36] Ibid., 164.
[37] Ibid., 160–61.
[38] Johnson, "Heterosexuality, Male Dominance, and the Father Image," 15.

appears to be more difficult for female children in that the ego boundaries between mother and daughter are more easily blurred and confused than the boundaries between mother and son. According to Chodorow: "As long as women mother, we can expect that a girl's preoedipal period will be longer than that of a boy and that women, more than men, will be more open to and preoccupied with those very relational issues that go into mothering—feelings of primary identification, lack of separateness or differentiation, ego and ego boundary issues, and primary love not under the sway of the reality principle."[39]

In the case of incest victims, the need for separation becomes crucial because the daughter has internalized her mother's sense of powerlessness. Typically, female victims of abuse internalize anger, directing hatred and aggression against themselves.[40] Anger at the mother provides a means through which separation and individuation can be facilitated, with rage and rejection acting as a source of empowerment for the victimized child. The mother blaming that becomes associated with victimization is therefore a response to the disaffection created by the incest experience and thus should be validated within the therapeutic setting.

Focusing anger on the mother allows the daughter to externalize her feelings. Once this anger has been expressed and validated, a feminist perspective on the incest can be introduced in order to help the victim arrive at a less distorted perception of the mother's role in her victimization. The mother-directed rage represents a first stage in coping with the intense feelings engendered by the abuse. A later stage, in which anger is appropriately focused on the perpetrator, is more likely to occur once the daughter acknowledges and understands her initial reaction to the mother's perceived role.

In addition to the therapeutic value associated with the externalization of anger, mother-directed rage also provides the psychological separation necessary for the daughter to assert her independence and autonomy. In the circumstances of sexual abuse, the striving for autonomy that Sayers recognizes as essential in the creation of an independent self may be manifested in a severe rejection of the powerless (the mother), accompanied by an intensive identification with the powerful (the father).[41] Since the father represents male power in patriarchal culture, the daughter's perceptions of him emerge through the child's developing awareness of power relations both inside of and outside of the

[39] Chodorow, *The Reproduction of Mothering* (n. 16 above), 110.

[40] Patricia Perri Rieker and Elaine (Hilberman) Carmen, "The Victim-to-Patient Process: The Disconfirmation and Transformation of Abuse," *American Journal of Orthopsychiatry* 56, no. 3 (July 1986): 360–69.

[41] Sayers (n. 21 above).

family. For the victim the father is both a perpetrator of violence and the symbol of power and independence; in contrast, the mother represents helplessness and ineffectuality. Thus, a victimized daughter might identify with the abuser, expressing sympathy and forgiveness for his actions. In this psychological transformation, the object of identification shifts in part to the father as the manifestation of real power through which the victimized child imagines her own reflection and thus empowers herself.

While this shift in identification offers a strategy for psychological survival, it also forces the victimized child into a conflictual relationship with her mother and her gender identity. Though the child rejects a self-image of helplessness and powerlessness, at the same time, the sexual violence perpetrated by the father has reinforced the victim's identification with her mother as sexual object. In order to separate from this association with the devalued feminine image, the victim must reject the first object choice and in so doing denies her own gender identification by rejecting her mother.

For incest victims, then, a significant aspect of their response is separation from the failures that come to be associated with maternal power. The result is the hatred and denigration directed at the mother. It is a painful consequence of mothering in patriarchal society that daughters in abusive families need to devalue mothers, and women in general, in order to achieve a sense of self.[42]

Indeed, separation from the mother underlies the process of individuation for all children who are raised in a sociopolitical system wherein emotional bonding is the primary responsibility of mothers. Thus, the phenomenon of adolescent rejection and anger typically experienced by female children in Western industrial society captures the painful moments in a young girl's life when she is torn between maintaining the primal connection to the mother and rejecting the maternal identification that prevents her from becoming her own person. In the incestuous family this dilemma is magnified and intensified as separation from the mother is invested with issues of powerlessness and betrayal as well as the desire for autonomy. The tension characteristic of mother-daughter relationships in general thus becomes manifested in its most extreme form under conditions of sexual abuse.

The notion that incest destroys the mother-daughter bond presupposes that a bond of some kind existed prior to the family violence. In the climate of postincest family relations, however, it is

[42] According to Chodorow, it is also a consequence of mothering in patriarchal society that sons in contemporary nuclear families must devalue the mother and that which is feminine in order to achieve a sense of their masculine identity. For a further discussion of this point, see "Family Structure and Feminine Personality" (n. 16 above).

difficult to ascertain the qualities of that bond since all subsequent family relations are influenced and to some extent determined by the occurrence of incest. The retrospective information provided by the young women in the support group presented a profusion of feelings that were sometimes contradictory but for the most part tended to idealize the family prior to victimization. This idealization was evident in accounts of loving and caring home environments that were remembered with nostalgia during support group therapy. In checking the case histories of these children, it became evident that few of the families offered the security or safety that was both imagined and desired by the abused girls. Yet at least six of the group members said that they wished they could go back in time to a childhood in which they felt sheltered and protected by the presence and love of a caring mother. As one young woman, seventeen years old, poignantly reported: "It wasn't always the way it is now. We used to go to picnics and to the zoo. I thought my mother loved me and I loved her. Now I feel like I hate her. Why didn't she stop him? Why did she let him do it?"

The subjective reality of the child, as it is constructed through the process of primary maternal bonding and perpetuated through cultural ideology, includes an idealized and omnipotent mother figure around which the child's expectations of safety and security develop. Feminist interpretations of patriarchal power need to take full account of the reality of the child's subjective experience of her mother as the most powerful figure in the child's emotional life if we are to understand fully the processes by which patriarchy is sustained. In turn, analysis of family violence and its effect on the child must take into account the significance of maternal control and influence if we are to offer effective therapeutic support. It must be pointed out, however, that in stressing the significance of the mother in the emotional life of the daughter who has experienced incest, the intent is not to perpetuate the misogynistic tradition of mother blame. Rather, in recognizing and addressing the child's perspective on power relations within the family, it becomes painfully clear that as long as children are exclusively nurtured by women, the victimizers will not be held accountable for their actions.

Women's Studies Program
University of Colorado, Boulder

ABOUT THE CONTRIBUTORS

ANN TAYLOR ALLEN   is professor of history at the University of Louisville. Her published works include *Satire and Society in Wilhelmine Germany: Kladderadatsch and Simplicissimus, 1890–1914* (Lexington: University Press of Kentucky, 1984); "German Radical Feminism and Eugenics, 1900–1918," *German Studies Review* 9 (February 1988): 31–56. Her *Feminism and Motherhood in Germany, 1800–1914* is forthcoming (New Brunswick, N.J.: Rutgers University Press, 1991).

JUDITH L. ALPERT   is a professor in the doctoral programs of the school of psychology and child/school psychology at New York University; she is also a psychoanalyst in private practice. Her research interests focus on the intersection of psychoanalytic theory with women's issues. She is editor of *Psychoanalysis and Women: Contemporary Reappraisals* (Hillsdale, N.J.: Analytic Press, 1986); and author of "Contemporary Psychoanalytic Developmental Theory," in *Views from the Sciences*, vol. 1, *The Women's Studies Encyclolpedia*, ed. H. Tierney (Westport, Conn.: Greenwood Press, 1990), 299–301.

SHULI BARZILAI   is lecturer in the department of English at the Hebrew University of Jerusalem. Her research interests include literary theory, feminist theory and criticism, and psychoanalytic approaches to literature. Her publications include "New Criticism and Deconstructive Criticism; or, What's New?" *New Literary History* 18 (Autumn 1986): 151–69, coauthored with Morton Bloomfield; "Unmaking the Words That Make Us: Doris Lessing's 'How I Finally Lost My Heart,'" *Style* 22 (Winter 1988): 595–611; and "Lacan on Hamlet: The Man Who Lost the Way of His Desire," *Psychoanalysis and Contemporary Thought* 12, no. 2 (Autumn 1989): 313–40.

ANITA CLAIR FELLMAN   is director of women's studies and associate professor of history at Old Dominion University. Her publications include the forthcoming *Rethinking Canada: The Promise of Women's History*, 2d ed. (Toronto: Copp, Clark, Pitman, 1991), coedited with Veronica Strong-Boag. Her research interests include the exploration of unconventional sources for the transmission of women's ideas, and she is currently writing on the place of the *Little House* series in American culture (Urbana: University of Illinois Press, forthcoming).

MARY-JOAN GERSON   is associate clinical professor in the postdoctoral program in psychotherapy and psychoanalysis at New York University. She has studied the desire for a child as a reflection of gender differences, feminist identifications, and couple dynamics, and she is particularly interested in how children synthesize the shared conflicts and identity issues of their parents. Her publications include "The Prospect of Parenthood for Women and Men," *Psychology of Women Quarterly* 10, no. 1 (1986): 49–62; and "The Prospect of Fatherhood for Young Men: Emergent Conflicts, Fantasies and Identifications" in *Fathers and Their Families*, ed. S. H. Cath, A. Gurwitt, and L. Gunsberg (Hillsdale, N.J.: Analytic Press, 1989), 127–44.

MARIANNE HIRSCH   is professor of French and chair of the comparative literature program at Dartmouth College. Her publications include *The Mother/ Daughter Plot: Narrative, Psychoanalysis, Feminism* (Bloomington: Indiana University Press, 1989); *The Voyage In: Fictions of Female Development* (Hanover, N.H.: University Press of New England, 1982), coedited with Elizabeth Abel and Elizabeth Langland; and *Conflicts in Feminism* (New York: Routledge, 1990), with Evelyn Fox Keller.

NANCY ROSE HUNT   is a doctoral candidate in history at the University of Wisconsin—Madison; she is presently studying at the Université Catholique de Louvain in Brussels. Her dissertation will explore changes in colonial representations and Africans' experiences of birthing and motherhood in a markedly pronatalist regime, the Belgian Congo. Her most recent publications are "'Le Bébé en brousse': European Women, African Birth Spacing and Colonial Intervention in Breast Feeding in the Belgian Congo," *International Journal of African Historical Studies* 21, no. 3 (1988): 401–32; and "Placing African Women's History and Locating Gender," *Social History* 14, no. 3 (October 1989): 359–79.

JANET LIEBMAN JACOBS   is an assistant professor adjunct in women's studies at the University of Colorado, Boulder. She is currently studying family dynamics and violence stemming from teen pregnancy and focusing on the teen mother's family of origin. She is the author of *Divine Disenchantment: Deconverting from New Religions* (Bloomington: Indiana University Press, 1989); and "The Effects of Ritual Healing among Female Victims of Abuse," *Sociological Analyses* 50, no. 3 (Fall 1989): 265–79.

SANDRA R. JOSHEL   teaches in the department of liberal arts at the New England Conservatory of Music. Her research interests center on women and gender roles in antiquity. She is author of *Work, Identity, and Legal Status at Rome* (Norman: University of Oklahoma Press, in press), and she is currently researching a book on the construction of gendered subjects in imperial narratives.

ANN B. MURPHY   is an instructor in the department of English at Tufts University. Her research interests include composition theory and feminist criticism of eighteenth- and nineteenth-century novels. Her most recent publication is "Transference and Resistance in the Basic Writing Classroom," *College Composition and Communication* 40, no. 2 (May 1989): 175–87. She is currently studying the depiction of female narratives in Gothic novels.

MARGARET K. NELSON   is professor of sociology and director of the women's studies program at Middlebury College. Her publications include *Circles of Care: Work and Identity in Women's Lives* (Albany: State University of New York Press, 1990), coedited with Emily K. Abel; and *Negotiated Care: The Experience of Family Day-Care Providers* (Philadelphia: Temple University Press, 1990).

ANN OAKLEY   is deputy director of and a reader in education at the Thomas Coram Research Unit in the Institute of Education at the University of London. Her current projects focus on the social support of pregnancy as well as adolescent health and parenting issues. Her works include *The Captured Womb: A History of Medical Care of the Pregnant Woman* (New York: Basil Blackwell, 1984); *Taking It Like a Woman* (New York: Random House, 1984); and *The Men's Room* (New York: Atheneum, 1988).

MARY SUE RICHARDSON   is professor in the department of applied psychology in the school of education, health, nursing, and arts professions at New York University. In addition, she is the director of a counseling psychology program, and she has been raising two children. Her current interests include psychoanalytic investigations of incest and male gender identity within the context of feminist theory and relational perspectives in psychoanalysis, as well as an integration of life-span developmental theory and career developmental theory for both women and men. She is currently coediting, with Michael Patton, a special section of *Counseling Psychology Quarterly*, which will appear in issues published between October 1991 and October 1992.

MARGARETE J. SANDELOWSKI   is associate professor in the department of women's and children's health at the University of North Carolina at Chapel Hill. Her research interests include women's health, infertility, and reproductive technology, and she is author of *Pain, Pleasure, and American Childbirth* (Westport, Conn.: Greenwood Press, 1984). She is currently conducting a longitudinal study of infertile couples seeking parenthood through pregnancy and adoption.